The Story Of Oriental Philosophy

L. Adams Beck
(E. Barrington)

SANAGE
PUBLISHING HOUSE

Paperback: 978-939-0896-93-6

Any references to historical events, real people, or real places are used fictitiously. Names, characters, and places are products of the author's imagination.

Printed by: Manipal Technologies Limited, Manipal

Designed by:
allpublishingsolution.com

CONTENTS

PREFACE

In writing this book upon the thought and thinkers of Asia my aim has been to convey what I have to tell in as clear and simple a manner as possible to readers unaccustomed to oriental modes of expression. This has meant more than translation from original languages, for beyond that lies the necessity for familiar English terms, which sometimes do not express the full implication of the original. I can hope only that I have not been wholly unsuccessful and that as little as possible has been lost on the way.

The value of the thought of Asia is daily more realized by western thinkers. The demand for knowledge of its riches grows more and more insistent. The caravans still journey from the heart of Asia, carrying merchandise more to be desired than gold or jewels.

The attainment of the West has been mainly on the intellectual-practical side. In the Orient it has been in the development of human consciousness, with the interesting exception of Japan, which appears to aim at the combination of both and to partake alike of eastern and western mentality. Iranian thought is necessarily included in any survey of Asiatic attainment.

The values of East and West do not clash. They are supplementary and interchangeable; and it will be well for the world when this is fully realized, and there is free circulation of thought. The faith of a nation is her soul. Her literature is her intellect. Nations who do not meet on these grounds cannot understand one another, and understanding is the most vital need of the present day. In this book, readers will at least find the Asiatic thought systems set forth with the deep sympathy I feel for what I regard as the highest reach of human thought in such matters as they deal with.

In addition to my personal knowledge of the countries, peoples, faiths, and philosophies of which I write, I must acknowledge my sincere gratitude to the writers of the many books that I have consulted and to the many oriental friends with whom I have discussed these subjects.

A detailed list of authorities would form a volume in itself and would be impossible. I can say only that in one sense such a book as this can never be original. The bibliography does not attempt to cover my debt in quotation, paraphrase and spirit, or to name a tenth part of the books to which I owe so much. It gives a few books (under the headings of different countries), intended to be useful to students, advanced or otherwise, who wish to know more of the subjects treated. If any scholars should look into this book I ask them to remember the enormous difficulty of clarifying Asiatic thought for the general reader. They will realize obstacles which none can know who have not faced them.

L. Adams Beck,
(E. Barrington.)
Ceylon,

CHAPTER 1

THE ARYAN PEOPLE OF INDIA

If the average man were approached on the subject of Asia and asked to state his impressions they would probably be to the effect: that Asia is a continent with high possibilities for romance, and film stories, and for commercial intercourse to be conducted strictly under the tutelage of the West; that it is inhabited by races of semi- civilized or wholly uncivilized peoples much in need of Christianization and civilization before they can be dealt with at all on equal terms; that Japan, with the imitative, talent of a highly specialized monkey, has unexpectedly and dangerously broken loose into western allotments and has thereby inspired the rest of Asia with the unfortunate notion that she is capable of managing her own affairs instead of having them managed for her by western nations.

Such a man would add a few emphatic sentences on the menace of Asiatic cheap labor and of any Asiatic foothold among western peoples; and if he had intellectual aspirations might ask with some warmth what Asia's contribution to social philosophy, urban architecture, thought, and the religions of the world had been. He might concede that the Chinese make good servants and balance that concession with the remark that Japanese methods in trade are what you might expect—wholly untrustworthy. And he would go off without waiting for a rejoinder, secure in his conviction of the vast superiorities of the West.

Such a man will soon be extinct as the dodo, but because under every one of these so common assertions and implications lies the question of what philosophies have guided Asiatic nations on their way, and because Asia becomes every day a more vital and urgent problem for America and Europe as the narrowing of the world's confines draws them closer together, it is well worth while to study their philosophic thought with its national outcome, and the men who have been its creators, and thus to arrive at some definite conclusion of its and their worth. And my hope is to achieve this in words so simple that anyone who cares for the information may have it for use when he is obliged to consider Asia and his own relation and reaction to its life. There is no question but that these considerations will be thrust upon us even violently by the force of events, and it will then be vital that we shall understand. The interest also seems to me and to many others profound, but that is naturally a matter of opinion.

Lately there have been put before us in a striking way certain ignorances and social failures of India: the bloody sacrifices, infant marriages, shames and weaknesses of her dark places. It cannot be denied that these exist; but the other side was not dealt with, nor the causes given which would have invited understanding. I wish sincerely that equal courage and candor with a little more knowledge could be brought to bear on our own dark places by a qualified Asiatic and an equal shock administered. But in either case persons of philosophic mind would know that the whole story had not been told and that after such fashion no true appraisal of a nation's value to the world can be reached. And they would desire in either case to examine sources, before any final judgment could be passed. Examination of sources is what I attempt now.

In a book which professes to set forth the philosophies of Asia one is not concerned, however, with their practical results. Philosophy does not ask what use is made of the truths it sets forth, nor shall I. The quest of truth has no earthly goal, and when philosophy becomes consciously utilitarian it half renounces its own name. Nor shall I detail all the smaller philosophies or faiths that have occupied the ground marked out by the great men who were the sources. That would take libraries. My hope is to show the determinants; and I begin with India, for in a very real sense she has been the determinant of the highest thought of Asia. An exception must be made here and there, as in China, but China later so wholeheartedly accepted Indian influence and thought that too much stress should not be laid on that exception.

With India accordingly I begin.

It is difficult at all times to draw any hard and fast line between philosophy and religion. This has always been the case, even in modern times, and it was especially difficult in India, where religion was so deep a preoccupation that it still molds the whole outer form of life even more imperiously than among the Jews. Therefore in writing of Indian philosophy it can never be dissevered from religion.

The people who first shaped Indian philosophy were a branch of that mighty race from which the Indo-European races including the Anglo-Saxon have sprung. In their own language they called themselves the *Arya*— that is to say the "Noble People" (a word which still survives in the German *ehre,* or "honor"); and with the tradition of exclusiveness on the point of color, which is still so strong a mark of the race in America and England, they held themselves proudly apart for as long as possible from the dark-skinned natives of the country they had invaded and conquered.

Where was the cradle of the race that, dividing into the Indo-European and Aryan branches, was to rule the destiny of so great a part of the world? This is not certainly known; but it is known that though the time of separation is hidden in the mists of years we and the Aryan settlers of India had common ancestors; and it is now agreed by scholars that this still undivided people were to be found *circa* sixty thousand years ago as nomads or wandering shepherds on or about the lands now known as the plateau of the Pamirs and the northern grasslands. There or thereabouts came upon this people the two great urges: pressure of population and that adventurous spirit which today sends the descendants of one branch flying across the Atlantic or climbing Himalayan peaks and long ago committed the other to spiritual adventures higher and more daring still. And so, probably never in one great exodus, but in errant bands here and there like the princes of a fairy-tale setting out to seek their fortune, this ancient people parted and went out east and west. Many and strange events were to happen before they met again—with the clash of arms.

A part, let us call it the western division, went down into Europe, probably through Southern Russia into the (now-named) Polish and Austrian countries. Another, deflecting eastward, pressed through the mountain passes to India along many tracks which invaders were to follow later, and coming down upon the glorious river Indus, which gives its name to Hindustan, realized that here was a fair home for a haughty and courageous people.

Thus, they left their friends and kinsmen, little guessing what vast seas of custom, language, philosophy, and even of color, were to divide them; though indeed both sections carried indelible marks of identity, which would in coming ages reveal the history of their parting.

There were deep grooves of thought traced by the original language, in which the thought of both Indian and European philosophers must move henceforth, however far apart their lives. A family likeness can still be traced between the thoughts of Indo-European philosophers, such as the Greeks, and those of the great Aryans of India. Their mythology is unmistakably alike in earlier stages. There are identities of language. They had the verbal copula that existed before the separation—in Sanskrit *asti,* in Greek *esti,* in Latin *est,* in English *is.* They kept (like ourselves) the relative pronoun and the article, definite and indefinite. Those who have studied such alien languages as Hebrew, Chinese, and Japanese know all this implies, but there is much more. Both branches kept the indicative and subjunctive in the verb, the comparative and superlative in the adjective; both use the genitive case. It would be tedious to elaborate these points; but they are extremely interesting, and expose the rudimentary structure of thought, as the identical bones and teeth of animals may prove them to be of the same species.

Philologists assert that this ancestral language common to ourselves and the Aryans of India dates from at least ten thousand years B.C. and must then have been in a high state of development. We find it a strong and beautiful variant when we catch our first glimpse of it in Indian sacred and philosophic literature. It was for a long time unwritten, but was handed down in the marvelously cultivated memories of the East, and afterwards written and codified by their learned men. It was the opinion of Max Müller, the famous oriental scholar, that writing for literary purposes does not appear in any nation much before the seventh century B.C. in alphabetic writing.

It is a curious fact that many root-words employed in philosophic terms still connect us. In Sanskrit there is *manas,* the mind, which is *mens* in Latin and which we use as *mentality,* and so many more that it is impossible to recapitulate them. In short, there is between the separated Indo-European and Aryan peoples a now deeply submerged stratum of thought—like a reef covered with sea-water which forms a submarine bridge between islands, and accounts for identities of animals and plants otherwise inexplicable.

Yet we must not overrate the degree of philosophic thought at which our common ancestors had arrived. We know from what we see in India that it must have been rudimentary, though marvelous, in that it held the materials for the mighty palaces of thought which Greece and India were to rear on the racial foundations.

It is a very much debated question whether after the long separation Greece was indebted for some of her highest flights of thought to India; and here there will aways be differences of opinion as there were among the Greeks themselves. The Persians, also Aryans or Noble People, and closely allied in faith with their Indian cousins, entered Greece freely, and brought with them Indian teachings. The name of their prophet Zoroaster or Zarathustra was familiar to both Plato and Aristotle. In the third century B.C. there existed in Greece an analysis of his teaching.

I cannot enter into the proofs of Indian influence, but a story of the visit of an Indian philosopher to Socrates cannot be passed over. Aristoxenus asserts that Socrates told the stranger that his work consisted in inquiries about the life of men, and that the Indian smiled, replying that none could understand things human who did not understand things divine—a note of thought so deeply and peculiarly Indian that Max Müller says this alone impresses him with the probability of the truth of the story.

There is no reason why it should not be true. The caravans came and went down the passes to India, as I have seen them myself in the Khaibar Pass, and others traveled down the ancient Asiatic trade-route through Kashmir from Ladakh and Turkestan, or from China down the mighty Burmese river, the Irawadi. Standing in these places I have realized that it was not only the merchandise of food, garments, and jewels which went to and fro. Men's thoughts have journeyed along these ways from time immemorial, far more abundantly, I believe, than has been allowed.

Wise men took their wisdom with them, lovers their ardors of verse and story; and that India should havecommunicated to Plato her teaching of reincarnation, which he held so strongly, is as possible as that it sprang up in his own mind, or in the minds of both from some dim forgotten heritage of their once united peoples. Who can say? It matters little. For choice I prefer to think that the ancestral intelligence working in both countries independently produced the greatest philosophers the world has known.

Certain other points of resemblance are at first notable also : a deep and reverent devotion to the unseen, destined to fade in Europe later under the glare of unrivaled warlike and commercial genius; a high respect for their women as mothers and wives, to fade later in India under the torment of foreign invaders and alien races whose practice was very different from that of the Arya. Destiny had decreed that the two branches were to draw farther and farther apart, receding from the common home and kinship until a modern poet of their blood could write:

> Oh, East is East and West is West, and never the twain
> shall meet.

Yet in a fine outburst he ends:

> But there is neither East nor West, Border or Breed
> or Birth,
> When two strong men stand face to face, tho' they
> come from the ends of the earth.

The strong men were to meet often in the clash of thought and sword. In the former they are now meeting more fruitfully every day.

So the eastern-traveling Aryans settled in India, and still in their traditions and most ancient writings are embedded hints of the fact that they came to their home originally as strangers and pilgrims. This is not a common racial trait. The Hebrews recorded the entry into the Promised Land, but the Briton, the Teuton, and the Greek, as nations hold apparently no racial memory of a time when they were not settled in their countries, though there were aborigines about them who might have served as reminders. In Indian folk-lore are many hints and reminiscences of a dark-skinned people, often beautiful and dangerous, who opposed the advance of the Arya and tempted them with the beauty of their women from the Aryan tradition of race, insinuating their own lower formulas of life into the code of the new rulers.

Still, the Indo-Aryans carried with them the sense of an aristocracy qualified and resolute to dominate all opposing races, and while ruling them justly to teach them that submission was their role and obedience their only concern with law and custom. This racial trait is repeated in the history of America and Canada and all the far-flung dominions of the Indo-European races.

When we first come upon India it is a comparatively civilized country, aiming at and attaining a deep and true sense of its relation to the Unseen and to social order as it conceived it. These people might have quoted Schleiermacher's definition of religion and philosophy as one which they frankly accepted: "Religion is the knowledge of our absolute dependence, something which determines us and which we cannot determine in return." And this presupposes great teachers, mighty minds, who gathered together the hopes and aspirations of a race and summed them up into the eternal question of humanity.

But in India the figures of these ancient teachers are legendary at first. Before the days of the Buddha they move, almost mythical and semidivine, caring profoundly for the thoughts they loosed among the people, but nothing for their own personalities and renown. How could it be otherwise in a land where personality tends always to merge in the Universal? All this is so alien to the Indo-European mind that—if one might dream—it might be said that possibly the great eastern and western branches fell apart because the westerners concerned themselves little with metaphysics and the things of the spirit, whereas every instinct of the easterners drew them with passion to the solution of the eternal problem of man's relation to the Unseen.

This is pure imagination; but it is true that the westerners have never evolved a faith of their own and have been compelled to import religions from the East as they did tea and spices. They got no further than a ritual of human or bestial sacrifice to fearful or lustful gods. They could rise later into the great philosophies of Greece, relegating the old stories into the inane. But for the spiritual inspiration which rules the daily life of a nation they have been compelled to look to the East. The gods of Greece, Rome, early Gallia and Britannia exist no longer. "Great Pan is dead" was the cry which rang down the AEgean Sea as a conquering eastern faith prepared to rule the West with scepter and sword. The East in the form of the Galilean had conquered.

To many it seems that eastern thought as developed in Asia is to come again to rescue the western world from materialism, and that so the Indo-European and Aryan races may meet once more. This innermost difference has been a hitherto unbridgable gulf between them. The East, haughty, aristocratic, spiritual and other-worldly, leisured, tolerant of all faiths and philosophies, moving on vast spiritual orbits about the central sun; the West eager, hurried, worldly, absorbed in practical and temporary affairs, opinionated, contemptuous of other peoples and faiths, money-loving less for money's sake than its pursuit, younger, infinitely younger in tastes and psychic development than the East—what point of fusion can there be between the philosophies of these two divergent branches of the same great root? That, the thoughts recorded in this book may shadow forth.

For the growth of true philosophy such as walks hand in hand with religion, peace is needed and the absence of extremes of wealth and poverty. And when the Aryans had settled themselves they found a land that philosophy might have created for her own. Great mountain walls rose about them, and the safeguards of hill-passes dangerous and difficult even today. Before them rolled mighty rivers to unknown seas. Vast forests provided natural sanctuaries where men might meditate on the cosmic riddle. The climate induced repose and reflection. Commercial competition was unknown, for the land produced all they needed, and they were a pastoral and agricultural people content for many centuries with very simple luxuries.

Before them lay the task of welding together a just and prosperous social organization of themselves and their subject races. It was necessary therefore that they should evolve a high philosophy, for that is the foundation stone of all social effort. They said: "Philosophy is the lamp of all the sciences, the means of performing all works, the support of all the duties."

So their philosophy was not confined to the study or lecture hall. It became a part of daily life and experience because it was never divorced from religious experience; it was never the possession of the rich educated classes only. The "common people" snatched at it with avidity for what they could understand, and where its deeps were beyond them, what they had absorbed was enough to color their thoughts and lives as it does today. Why was this never the case with Europe? Why, with all its instinct to democracy now realizing itself along such painful roads, were the "working classes" of the West never uplifted into a sphere of spiritual passion at even the comparatively low level reached by their educated classes? The answer will appear as the study of Asiatic philosophy develops.

India has had a spiritual freedom never known until lately to the West.

Christianity when it came offering its spiritual philosophy of life imposed an iron dogma upon the European peoples. Those who could not accept this dogma, whatever it happened to be at the moment, paid so heavy a penalty that the legend of the Car of Juggernaut (Jaganath) is far truer of Europe than of Asia. And the natural result of the fetter upon European passion for freedom was the casting off of dogma and with it the consequent loss of much that was valuable. Whereas in India the soul was free from the beginning to choose what it would, ranging from the dry bread of atheism to the banquets offered by many-colored passionate gods and goddesses, each shadowing forth some different aspect of the One whom in the inmost chambers of her heart India has always adored. Therefore the spiritual outlook was universal. Each took unrebuked what he needed. The children were at home in the house of their father, while Europe crouched under the lash of a capricious Deity whose ways were beyond all understanding.

But while India fixed her eyes on the Ultimate she did not forget that objective science is the beginning of wisdom. There the foundations of mathematical and mechanical knowledge were well and truly laid by the Noble Race. Professor Radhakrishnan writes: "They measured the land, divided the year, mapped out the heaven, traced the course of sun and planets through the zodiacal belt, analyzed the constitution of matter, and studied the nature of birds and beasts, plants and seeds."

Here, written two thousand years before the birth of Copernicus, is an interesting passage from the Aitareya Brahmana:

"The sun never sets or rises. When people think the sun is setting he only changes about after reaching the end of the day and makes night below and day to what is on the other side. Then, when people think he rises in the morning, he only shifts himself about after reaching the end of the night, and makes day below and night to what is on the other side. In truth, he does not set at all."

Monier Williams says that whatever conclusions we form as to the source of the first astronomical ideas in the world it is probable that we owe to the Hindus the invention of algebra and its application to astronomy and geometry. And that from them the Arabs received the numerical symbols and decimal notation, which now used everywhere in Europe have rendered untold service to the cause of science.

And again: "The motions of the sun and moon were carefully observed by the Hindus and with such success that their determination of the moon's synodical revolution is a much more correct one than the Greeks ever achieved. They introduced the period of Jupiter with those of the sun and moon into the regulation of their calendar in the form of sixty years common to them and the Chaldeans. They were keenly interested in logic and grammar, and in medicine and surgery they once kept pace with the most enlightened people of the world."

As to art, I must entirely disagree with Dr. Breasted's opinion that either Chinese or Indian art was "transformed," if by transformed he means improved, as a result of the importation of Greek civilization to India by Alexander the Great in the fourth century B.C. Critics who have studied the work of the Greco-Buddhist School, as I have done in Peshawur and the neighborhood (its center), must agree that it lacks the spiritual beauty and nobility of primitive Buddhist art. When the smirking Buddhas of the Greco-Buddhist School are contrasted with the dignified and exquisite work to be seen at Amara- vati, Sanchi, and Ajanta, it is not difficult to discriminate between a great national art and imported prettiness, which may amuse the multitude but never deceives those who can recognize and feel the expression of the faith of a people.

It is the philosophies of this great race that I propose to examine. It is interesting to wonder along what lines it might have developed later if its ancestral heritage had been less diffused and intermingled with other such different stocks as it found in India on arrival, or were forced by many invasions and conquests to accept later.

CHAPTER 2

THE BEGINNINGS OF INDIAN PHILOSOPHY AND SOCIAL ORGANIZATION

Indian philosophy may be said to begin with the "Vedanta" (or end of the Veda), which includes the famous books known as the Upanishads and the great commentaries upon them, and for this reason my account of the Vedas shall be slight, though the seeds of the philosophies are in them.

The Vedas are not only the earliest records of Aryan thought but also among the earliest that survive of the human mind. The Rig and Yajur Vedas long precede the earliest beginnings of Greek civilization. They are posterior only to the Egyptian dynasties, of which we know little but records interesting chiefly to the student of dead empires. The Vedas are human and living. There are four: the Rig, Yajur, Sama, and Atharva. Some Indian scholars assign the Rig-Veda to 6,000 B.C. Others to the fifteenth century B.C. But it should be remembered that a very long period must have elapsed between the time when the hymns were composed and that when they were collected. The literary age is entered when collections are compiled.

The Rig-Veda is a collection of more than one thousand hymns which the Aryans brought with them to India. They were used during the sacrifices, of which the Yajur-Veda gives the ritual. They are partly in prose, partly in verse. The Sama-Veda contains liturgies. The Atharva-Veda is the latest of the four and interesting for its relation to magic, spells, and charms. It shows a gradual tincturing of the Aryan mind by the worships of the subject peoples. For this reason it had not at first the high position of the other Vedas.

Each Veda has three parts—the mantras, or hymns; the Brahmanas, or precepts and religious duties; the Upanishads, which discuss philosophy. The Upanishads contain the background or foundation of the whole subsequent thought of India, and their value to the world is inestimable. It will be seen that the hymns represent the poets, or aspiration of the race; the Brahmanas the priests, and questions of conduct; the Upanishads the philosophers, or intellect touched with spirituality; and thus we have religion and philosophy as closely and naturally wedded as, for the welfare of mankind, they should always be.

The Rig-Veda is incomplete and much is lost. The hymns are addressed to nature-gods. The poets spoke of rain and it was considered that this implied a Rainer. Thus *indu* (rain) became Indra the Rainer. They spoke of fire and light, and these became a god Agni, whose name we (the far-off cousins of the Aryans) take in vain when we "ignite" anything. They spoke of a Heavenly Father, Dyaus-pitar, whose name we repeat when we say "Jupiter," its latter half being preserved in our own word "father." Though in this way there arose many divine agents to be propitiated, the Aryan people perceived them at times as facets of the one truth and manifestations in different activities of one divine spirit. Thus some of the Vedic poets openly stated the belief that enthroned above these many names is One. They said:

> The sages called that One in many ways. They called
> it Agni, Yama, Matarishvan.
> That One breathed breathlessly by Itself. Other than
> It there has been nothing since.

Here we have the germ of a monotheistic religion and a unifying philosophy. Among bygone mythological details, we find in these hymns passages which catch the mind with a quick sense of human interest and presuppose deep reflection.

> I do not know what kind of thing I am.
> Mysterious, bound, my mind wanders.

In that one sentence may be found the germ of philosophy. For all philosophy begins with wonder.

Thus wondering, they conceived the gods as those who *give* to men. Their collective name of *Deva* implies a giver. The sun god is a giver of light and warmth. Its secondary meaning is the Shining One. Allied with this and springing from the same source is our own "divine."

So even in those early hymns they were feeling after a One Cause, and gradually as wonder increased and speculation strengthened, the higher thought of these Indian thinkers passed into a recognition of monotheism, which they were to transcend later.

"Priests and poets with words make into many the hidden reality which is One," they said in the Rig-Veda.

As Max Müller writes: "Whatever may be the age when the Rig-Veda collection of hymns was finished, before that age the conviction had been formed that there is but One Being, neither male nor female, raised high above all conditions and limitations of personality and of human nature. In fact the Vedic poets had arrived at a conception of the Godhead which was reached once more by some of the Christian philosophers at Alexandria, but which even yet is beyond the reach of many who call themselves Christians."

But because the masses cannot comprehend philosophical abstractions this Divine is sometimes called "He" as well as "It." It was recognized that the Divine can be worshiped in spirit and in truth even under the personal conception of one God, and though there were those who could breathe in a rarer air of wisdom they were the first to realize that the soul must seek the bread for her own nourishing and that what will nourish one will not nourish another who is on a different spiritual plane. An Inquisition has always been inconceivable in India.

Here is a hymn of questions, very marvelous considering its remote antiquity. The translation is Professor Max Müller's. It is a poem of creation.

There was then neither what is nor what is not.
There was no sky nor the heaven beyond.
What covered ?

Where was it and in Whose shelter?
Was the water the deep abyss?

There was no death, hence there was nothing immortal.
There was no distinction between night and day.
That One breathed by itself without breath.
Since then there has been nothing other than It.

Darkness there was in the beginning, a sea without light.
From the germ that lay covered by the husk that One was born by the power of heat.

Love overcame It in the beginning, the seed springing from mind. Poets having searched in their heart found by wisdom the seed of what is, in what is not.
Their ray was stretched across. Was It below or was It above? There were seed-bearers, there were Powers; self-power below and Will above.

Who then knows, who has declared from whence was born this creation ? The Gods came later.
Who then knows whence it arose?
He from whom this creation arose, whether He made or did not make it only the highest seer in the highest heaven knows. Or perhaps he does not know.

That is to say perhaps the gods themselves cannot read the riddle of the universe.

This poem conceives a period when there was no Personal God, or rather he was as yet unmanifested by the Absolute Reality which is beyond all finite reason or words. This Ancient is older than and beyond any state of life or death that we have power to conceive. The depth of this conception is astonishing, and it will be realized that a primitive people who could thus reflect and state their case would certainly go far in the field of metaphysics and philosophy.

Their thought indeed developed swiftly; but before following it I shall say something of the social order it developed and that in reaction developed it, because it is difficult to realize the stories in which, as in parables, much of the wisdom of the Upanishads is conveyed, without setting them in their own background of the life of the people. For this reason I now turn to "The Laws of Manu," that famous book which holds such a high position in India and gives so perfect a picture of the life of the ancient Aryan communities that it was granted a divine origin by the beliefs of the people.

"The Laws of Manu" is a compilation of most venerable laws and customs written in a style that insures popular understanding. It would be impossible to say to what antiquity they may be traced. The compilation is variously dated at from 1200 to 500 B.C. Few books will better repay study by those interested in social questions and especially in those concerning the western problems of democracy. Though named "The Laws of Manu" it should rather be "The Laws of the Manavas." The word "manu" has its root in the verb "to think"; and the collection is said to be "the quintessence of the Vedas" and therefore of all knowledge. It gives us the *dharma* of the Indian people to this day.

What is "dharma"—a word occurring so often in Indian philosophy and having no one equivalent in English? I should describe it as the national spirit, which consecrates social custom, tradition, conduct, and religion, and is a uniting force, which in greater or less degree conditions the life and thought of every person born in that nation. But though inside the national circle it is a unifying energy, outside it is a dividing one and the source of much misunderstanding; for every nation has its own dharma, nor is it possible that any should wholly understand that of another or that it should adopt it. One may perhaps call it the national spirit, though that does not give its origin.

What then are the laws and precepts which built up the Indian dharma—so difficult for the West to understand, so easy for it to misjudge through surface judgments?

"The Laws of Manu" saw life steadily and saw it whole, as it applied to young and old, to men and women. They are founded on the Four Orders and the Four Castes. *Varna,* the Indian word for caste, denotes originally color division. The Four Orders are those of the student, the householder, the forest-dweller, and the ascetic who has renounced the world. These are the *Ashramas,* and all these are founded upon the householder. Without him there is no cohesion. The Four Castes are the Brahmin or teacher, the warrior, the merchant, and the laborer. Of these the first three are the "twice-born" castes. "And outside these is no fifth class," say the Laws.

It is interesting to compare this statement with the jungle of castes that has since grown up in India with their bewildering cruelties and fetters. Manu states that all men naturally belong to one of these four divisions, and that all are rooted in the life of the householder because he nourishes and supports the others with food for the body and the mind. "Therefore the householder occupies the position of the eldest."

But this division means little in India today. Brahmins are now not only priests and teachers but are found in almost every calling, and this is the case also with caste artizans. Indian caste has nothing in common with western social divisions. A servant may be of much higher caste than his master. It is conceivable there that it would be a most terrible mesalliance for the man servant of a house to marry the wealthy daughter of its master.I have known a Brahmin official who would have died sooner than eat with his royal master, so much was his sovereign's caste lower than his own. Yet even in the present aberrations of caste may be seen the original germs of a dharma not only wise but inevitable where a ruling race had to make good its position among races of different color and lower racial types. The caste system was a vital necessity to the Aryan race and still has certain virtues.

To return to "The Laws of Manu"—the caste divisions made it possible for all to pass through the desirable experiences of all stages of life. In earliest Vedic times caste probably did not exist other than as a color line, but as society became complex, organizations developed which allotted different functions to different groups. At first the priest had no special concern with religious or sacrificial rites. The householder performed his own sacrifices and oblations and there it ended.

This could not last. The Aryans perceived the need of specialization. Therefore the Brahmin gradually assumed that care of education and of spiritual affairs which the people considered the most honorable in the social system. The next caste, the Kshatriya or warrior caste, was made responsible for war, political matters, government and public work. The third caste, the Vaishya, concerned itself with all affairs of trade and industry. The fourth, the Shudra, represented labor. The Shudras were "the feet and pedestal of all." Some scholars believe that the fourth caste—the Shudra—may have been formed from the aboriginal people; some that when the Aryans came to India they had already a laboring caste of their own. This is not certain.

The Brahmin was the servant of all on the higher planes of thought. The Shudra was the servant of the community on the physical plane because he was not developed into the higher forms of thought.

It will be seen that in the ancient caste-conception each caste is a school for the one above it, rising from lowly and yet preparative labor to the highest form of human consciousness.

Dharma was the constructive and binding force for all the castes. It constituted a brotherhood of differently apportioned but collective and cooperative work.

The Mahabharata states that "the order of wise men who dwell in forests and live on fruits, roots, and air, is prescribed for the three twiceborn classes, but the order of householders is prescribed for all."

Thus it was only when all duties to the family and state had been accomplished that any man of the three higher castes could betake himself to the life of contemplation. Unless indeed he had a high and special vocation and in that case even a Shudra was not shut out. "Harmlessness, truthfulness, honesty, cleanliness, self- control : these are declared by man to be the duty of all the four castes." Distinction between the secular and the religious was not drawn. That with its disastrous consequences was to be a much later development.

Naturally, because upon it all depends, the first concern of "The Laws of Manu" is education. This ideal involves a certain asceticism very foreign to western notions and therefore perhaps the better worth considering. I think there is much to be learned from it.

For different boy-types different ages were set for the beginning. Those who were to do the high work of the Brahmins as storers and dispensers of knowledge must begin early. They must not spend so much time in games. The next, the warrior and governing class, may begin later and for them very pronounced physical development is of more importance. The next caste the Vaishyas, or merchants, whose intelligence is slower for higher aims, may begin a little later than the caste above it.

"The Brahmin should be led up to the teacher and invested with the sacred thread in the eighth year; the Kshatriya boy [governing] in the eleventh, the Vaishya boy [merchant] in the twelfth. But if a boy shows exceptional promise and desire for the qualifications of his vocation, such as the light of wisdom if a Brahmin; physical vitality and might of body if a Kshatriya, commercial enterprise and initiative, if a Vaishya, then he should begin his studies in the fifth, sixth, and eighth years respectively."

Education must on no account be delayed beyond the sixteenth, twenty-second and twenty-fourth years for the three castes. After that the mind is no longer flexible.

Bhagavan Das (who has written a remarkable book on "The Laws of Manu") points out that the ancient teacher was spared one serious modern difficulty. He knew exactly to what end his pupil's faculties were to be directed. Not only so, but he was spared the greatest problem of the modern world. "By one of those paradoxes which Nature has invented to maintain her balance the modern man, while laying all stress on differentiation as the prime factor in human society, aims at making all men equal." With the Aryan teacher this question of equality did not exist.

The western teacher must treat each pupil as a separate and individual caste, for his place in social rank and work is never fixed. Therefore his main view-point must be the bread-education—the possibility of making as much money as lies within the boy's powers. The future profession of the pupil, still perhaps quite undecided, will further complicate the problem of education. What will be his choice? Where will he best fit into a crowded market?

These questions were answered in India by the caste system. It offered broad lines, within which there could be specialization to follow later as the boy's faculties developed into those of the man. And it followed naturally that much more time could be given to education, varying for the different castes but longest for the Brahmin. For him it was considered that the ideal demanded thirty-six years of dwelling with his teachers. Knowledge, which comprised the Vedas, the Trinity of Sciences, the Science of the Trinity, and all the subsidiary sciences, needed thirty-six years! If that were impossible it should be eighteen. The least was nine. But, it was added, it must in any case be until the necessary knowledge was; gained. That would vary with different pupils.

"Only after having spent the first quarter of life with the Teacher and undergone the discipline which produces real knowledge and consecrated his soul in the recognized way—only after this preparation should the twice-born man take a wife and become a householder."

It was held that a man so trained would be trained to cope with life at any point, spiritual, intellectual, and physical. He would understand the reaction of temperaments upon each other. He would have learned the uses of silence and reflection. He would know that the procreation of feeble and diseased thoughts is worse if possible than the procreation of a feeble and diseased family. He would become the mainstay of the wisdom of communities, the counselor of kings. Such men would combine knowledge with spiritual wisdom. They would be the racial patriarchs. In a lesser and differing degree the same system applied to the education of the two lower castes who were also twice-born.

The Kshatriya, greater in physical power, qualified for endurance and the outleap of valor, less concerned with the training of the supernormal powers yet severely trained in spiritual wisdom, was fitted for his great task of government and the leadership of men.

The Vaishya, trader and agriculturalist, trained also in spiritual insight, was fitted, so far as wisdom could fit him for his part in life. Education was, as it were, a fugue—the dominant was the Brahmin, but all harmonized, each constructing and supporting the other, each developing from the one into the full harmony.

But what was the position in education of the fourth caste—the Shudra? Was he wholly neglected as was his lot in Europe until comparatively late years? By no means.

The Shudra was considered the child of the social system. The belief in what may roughly be called reincarnation gave him the status of one who for reasons of a past life was reborn in a sphere where he could scarcely hope to understand the inner and higher wisdom to which I shall come in later chapters. For his lifetime his status would be that of the three twice-born castes before they had received education and discipline.

The Laws say: "Everyone is born a Shudra and remains such until he receives the sacrament of the Veda and is thereby born a second time."

The Shudra's education was therefore necessarily comprised in obedience to the higher castes and to the training of a householder's life. But there was one important exception. Special explanations of the Vedas had been prepared by the Rishis (sages) for the understanding of simple folk. These are known as the Puranas, and in them the truths of the Vedas are presented by tales and parables suited to less evolved mentalities. Their object was to interest the masses in the higher metaphysic, and this object was completely achieved though not without the consequence that the parable and analogy were often received as final truth. At these popular lectures men, women and children who escaped the net of the higher caste education assembled as eager hearers. All the necessary knowledge of the Vedas is in the Puranas and therefore none were compelled to go ignorant of what was then considered necessary education. The position of the Shudra in ancient India may be compared, judging from "The Laws of Manu," with that of a valued house- servant of the present day. And in case of exceptional development he could study further, though still under certain restrictions.

Now comes a very curious and very interesting point. Life was to impose its hardest burden upon the higher castes. *Noblesse oblige.* Where the Shudra could go scot-free was no escape for them.

"The Shudra cannot commit a sin which degrades in the same sense as can the twice-born person. This is his advantage. His disadvantage is that he cannot be given the secret mantras [the hymns and sacred formulas]. He has no compulsory religious duty to perform but if he does it there is no prohibition. Indeed the Shudras who wish to gather dharma and learn its ordinances, and follow the way of the good among the twice-born, and perform the five daily sacrifices, etc. (but without the secret mantras) do not infringe law but rather gain the approval of the good and receive honor."

But what of the education of women in such a society?

There was no question of the equality of the sexes, for in a society so divided into separated duties such a thought never could arise. Women were plainly differentiated by nature for different duties, and their training must follow those lines. It is true that all the sacraments were prescribed for the girls also. But they, like the Shudras, were debarred from use of the secret hymns and formulas, not because of inferiority but because of the differences which prevented right use of them. But the marriage ceremony which united man and woman was performed with the mantras, and the theory was that the girl, now a part of her husband and living with him, was in the position of the disciple with the master. Otherwise, generally speaking, the girl should be nurtured and educated in the same way and as diligently as the boy. No prohibition exists in "The Laws of Manu" against the education of girls on the same lines as their brothers, but their education must follow the general lines laid down for caste, though they were so differentiated for girls as to give more training in the fine arts.

The Brahmin girl must have a more intellectual education. The Kshatriya girl more physical activity, the Vaishya girl more training in economic matters. But it was never supposed that she could give the same time to these subjects. Nature called her imperatively and at a much earlier age to a quite distinct employment. Even there, however, the different trainings tended to blend. The wives of the Rishis (sages) are often represented as women of learning in the great knowledge to be described later in the philosophies. And the women of the Kshat- riyas could take part with their husbands in very different enjoyments. Here is a classical passage from the Maha- bharata, the ancient epic of India, describing the elopement of the Lady Subhadra with the all-beautiful, all- valorous Prince Arjuna. They fled in his chariot and were pursued.

"Then the sweet-voiced lady Subhadra was highly delighted to see that force of excited elephants, rushing cars, and horses. In great glee she said to Arjuna:

" 'For a long while I had a mind to drive your chariot in the midst of the battle with you fighting beside me . . . you who have a great soul and strength of limb! Let me now be your charioteer, O son of Pritha, for I have been well instructed in the art.' "

And so it was. He fought. She, like a well-taught girl of the warrior caste, hurled the chariot against the foe, and they were victorious. Great and powerful and wise are the women of the Mahabharata! I possess the monumental book and can truly say that, on the subject of her heroines of old, India can well afford to speak with her enemies in the gate. They are not surpassed in any literature or history.

CHAPTER 3

THE ANCIENT SYSTEM OF EDUCATION

What was the method of education for the three great castes? The first care was to form character. Intellectual education took a second place, but with certain knowledge of the caste and destination of the pupil intellectual education was a direct progress on a charted road, and it was unnecessary to fill the mind with wagonloads of indigestible knowledge shoveled in in case they might come in useful later. All effort could be directed to a clearly seen end.

"Having taken up the pupil that he may lead him to the Highest, the teacher shall impart the ways of cleanliness, purity and chastity of body, with good manners and morals. And he shall teach him how to tend the fires sacrificial and culinary and, more important than all, how to perform his daily devotions."

It was a part of character-building that the home of the teacher was the university. The pupil became part of the family—a family naturally of high standing because of the honor attached by caste and public feeling to the position of the Brahmin. A filial tenderness traditionally subsisted between pupil and tutor. All this was no small thing. It was the pupil's duty to earn his food and sometimes his teacher's by the mendicancy that from remote antiquity has been a sacred part of Indian life.

There was nothing humiliating in this, and the gift of food was the part that citizens took in the duties of education. To give was and is considered a boon; for that reason the mendicant monks in Burma (who all teach the boys) return no thanks for what is given. They have conferred an obligation. To the student, however rich his family, this was a training in the wealth of that Lady Poverty whom St. Francis of Assisi adored. There were rules, however:

"He should at first beg from his own mother or sister or his mother's sister, from whom he may not feel shame or shyness in taking. Later, he should not beg among the family and relations of his preceptor but from the houses in the neighboring town and the good householders in whose homes the sacrifices enjoined by the Vedas are kept alive. And having secured the needed food and no more, he should present it to his preceptor and then, with his permission, should eat, facing east, after the customary mouth-rinsing and purification."

Much stress was laid on manners, and who can sufficiently regret the cruel and disastrous loss of this education in modern life? Those taught in India had not the formalities of China and Japan, but seem to contain the root of the matter: the selflessness of the gentleman; the obedience which is the training for authority.

"Tell the truth, but pleasantly and gently. Do not tell it rudely, for truth-telling that hurts and repels does not carry conviction, but is only a display of aggressive egotism. Yet never tell a pleasing falsehood. Such is the ancient law."

"Affluence, good birth and breeding, high deeds with much experience, knowledge—these are the five titles to honor. Each succeeding one is higher than the preceding."

The code of manners included reverence to elders, tenderness to the young, and affection to equals. A good deal of friction, in both daily life and business was thus spared, and boys were fitted to hold every position with dignity. Health was also made an important branch of training. The science of Yoga was devised to control health and vitality. It included certain forms of asceticism—a training the modern world begins very slowly and painfully to recognize as necessary. Perfect continence was insisted upon during student life. And it is suggested that the total physical life will be four times as long as the period of continence observed before the duties of the householder as regards procreation and family life are taken up. Manu puts this point strongly: "Because of the neglect of Yeda-knowledge and permitting the right knowledge to decay, because of abandoning the right way, because of mistakes in food and because of careless failure in continence, does death prevail over the knowers."

Thus hunger and desire, two primal human motives, were to receive the strictest training, and knowledge on these points was to be a part of the education of the young. Full directions were given as to the quality of foods and for the disciplining of reproductive energy.

Here I must quote the interpretation by Bhagavan Das of the Laws of Manu (though I shall return to the subject in consideration of the system of Yoga), which gives a strong reason for continence during pupilage.

"If any subdivisional part or cell ceases to subdivide further and remains undivided [through continence] it may continue to do so for an indefinitely long time and become comparatively immortal. Such is the promise of teaching, walking in the path of Brahma, storing up and perfecting the germ and source of life and all vitality and power, the potency and principle of infinite reproduction and multiplication, and also storing up and perfecting the seed of knowledge, which again is power and has also the potency within it of infinite expansion."

It will be seen that it is not *this* teaching which has led to the early marriages of India and the resulting misery and deterioration. Neither the unwholesome and too early devoured fruit of the body nor that of the mind had any place in the system of Manu. The duties of the householder were enjoined when he was in his prime. not otherwise. For those who had another vocation a way of escape was provided to what was thought to be an even higher sphere of duty, and the ascetic became the power-station of the race; from him men would derive light and strength. He would be the master of supernormal powers. It was taught that after a certain stage of this knowledge the energy latent in food would function on a plane more subtle than the physical and be transmuted into finer, more intellectual and spiritual energies. I shall return to this most interesting subject later.

It is impossible to give details of study here. It included the classics of the race and education as to man's position in relation to the universe. Nearly all this was conveyed in the form of carefully planned aphorisms easily remembered. Much attention was given to acoustics and phonetics, and in teaching grammar, philology, and physiology in a condensed form much was necessarily included. Rhetoric, logic, and reasoning were important. Manu says, agreeing curiously with the views of Confucius:

"All meanings, ideas, intentions, desires, emotions, items of knowledge are embodied in speech, are rooted in it and branch out of it. He who misappropriates, misapplies, and mismanages speech, mismanages everything." A profound truth.

The study of the Vedic books was interspersed with these secular subjects, but separate days were given to each so that the pupil's mind might not be hurried from one subject to another. For posture, he must stand upright, hands folded on the chest. Since there were no books, memory and vocal power were highly developed and eyesight spared. The holidays were short and frequent, and many depended on atmospheric and magnetic conditions, which were closely studied and given special importance in connection with special studies."

We learn from the Puranas that martial exercises, wrestling, fencing, archery, mock fights, foot and horse races, the management of horses, camels, bulls, and elephants, were all part of the training according to the type of student. Manu taught that rhythmic and considered movement is good. "Let him not move his hands and feet and eyes restlessly and crookedly. Let him not think of always outracing others and injuring them."

It is strange to consider that all athletics were considered to be a part of the lower division of divine knowledge. And this belief is not wholly dead in Asia. The ju-juTsŭ of Japan, for instance, has a very singular occult side that is not known to all the Japanese who practice it. I have had interesting talks on this, in Japan.

But we must leave the schools for adult life. It will be easily realized what emphasis must be laid in such communities on the perfection of family life, and it is interesting to compare it with the later and lower Greek ideals.

"The whole duty of husband and wife to each other is that they do not anger each other nor wander apart in thought, word, or deed until death. And the promise is that those who righteously fulfil this duty are not parted by the death of the body, but shall be together beyond death."

"Let the widow follow the Brahmin teaching, improving soul

and body by study and the service of the elders. Let her triumph over her body and walk in the ways of purity. . . ."

"And if the wife be noble of soul and the husband ignoble, and still she wills to die a widow for his sake, then shall her giant love and sacrifice grip his soul and drag it from the depths of sin and darkness to the kingdoms of light. . . ."

"The mother exceeds a thousand fathers in the right to reverence and in the function of education. Good women should be honored and worshiped like the gods. By the favors and powers of true women are the three worlds upheld."

So must the husband and wife be souls like twin flames illumining all about them. It was not a question of equality between them but of identity. And here is the ideal marriage, from which noble children were to be expected. The description is drawn from the Vishnu Purana and the Vishnu Bhagavata. It is great poetry as well as great truth.

"She is Language; he is Thought. She is Prudence; he is Law. He is Reason; she is Sense. She is Duty; he is Right. He is Author; she is Work. He is Patience; she is Peace. He is Will; she is Wish. He is Pity; she is Gift. He is Song; she is the Note. She is Fuel; he is Fire. She is Glory; he is Sun. She is Motion; he is Wind. He is Owner; she is Wealth. He is Battle; she is Might. He is Lamp; she is Light. He is Day; she is Night. He is Justice; she is Pity. He is Channel; she is River. She is Beauty; he is Strength. She is Body; he is Soul."

This is a passage of extraordinary beauty and insight in its recognition of the primitive nature of women as contrasted, not to dishonor but to honor, with that of man.

In a singular passage the Law of the Manavas declares the right of primogeniture on the ground that the eldest son is the child of dharma, *i.e.* of duty and necessity. The children born after him are those of earthly desire. He is therefore, in the absence of his father, father of all the younger ones.

The elasticity of the caste system under the Laws of Manu as opposed to its modern rigidity is very noticeable. The three castes interchange food and fire, dwell in the house of the teacher together, beg food together and mostly from Vaishya homes, for to the

Vaishya (merchant) caste (the third) fell the special duty of providing food for guests and the community. The Brahmin vowed to poverty could exert himself thus for none but those in real distress. But a rule was compelled to be laid down as regards the Shudra, the lowest caste, and this naturally; for the Shudras were exempt from much of the strict discipline forced upon the three upper castes. Yet even here the liberality of the teaching will astonish those who know modern India.

"One's own plowman, an old friend of the family, one's own cowherd, one's own servant, one's own barber, and whosoever else may come for refuge and offer service; from the hands of all such Shudras may food be taken."

These could be trusted for good-will and cleanliness, therefore from them nourishment could be accepted. One is reminded of Ramakrishna, the saint of modern India who died some thirty or forty years since. He knew by instinct the spiritual purity or impurity of the hands from which his food had come, and rejected or accepted it accordingly.

"This comes from a good man. I can eat it," he would say.

"For after doubt and debate," say the Laws of Manu, "the gods decided that the food-gift of the money-lending Shudra who was generous of heart was equal in quality to the food-gift of a Brahmin who knows all the Vedas but is small of heart. The food-gift of that Shudra is purified by the generous heart, while that of the Brahmin is wholly befouled by the lack of good-will."

Much has been made, to the discredit of the ancient system, of the ritual impurity imposed upon households in cases of disease and death. The cause was that all diseases were regarded as infectious in the sense that they affected the health of those drawn into their atmosphere. All strong disturbing emotions were infections, whether for good or evil, and in case of fear and sorrow aloofness was judged best. Ten days of impurity were fixed for the Brahmin family, twelve for the Kshatriya, fifteen for the Vaishya, thirty for the Shudra, apportioned according to the trust the community placed in each caste.Another strange and significant circumstance in the Puranas is the admission that in earlier Yugas (cycles) it was possible for whole families and tribes to change into the higher castes; and this is followed by the confession that the confusion of castes is now so complete that many a gentle and noble soul born in the Shudra caste may in truth belong to a higher. In the great and ancient epic, the Mahabharata, the Pandava king Yudhisthira says: "Nor birth nor sacraments nor study nor ancestry can decide whether a person is twice-born. Character and conduct only can decide."

And the Laws of Mānu pronounce:

"By the power of self-denial, acting selectively on the potencies of the primal seed in all, persons born in one caste may change into a higher or by the contradiction of self-denial, by self-indulgence, and selfishness may descend into a lower. The pure, the upward-aspiring, the gentle-speaking, the free from pride, who live with and like the Brahmins and the other twice-born castes continually—even such Shudras shall attain those higher castes."

India has fallen far from this grace. What might happen in a man's lifetime under certain conditions has now become a matter of long evolution and rebirths.

For the learned there was a voluntary poverty which all could understand and honor. How should a man have time to seek wealth whose body and soul and strength were absorbed in the effort "to follow knowledge like a sinking star"? The Brahmin therefore was exempted from personal effort for livelihood. His living would come from the reverent offerings of food and clothing, from the community which owed him so much as the second father and educator of their children. Yet in the extraordinary honor, as of an earthly god, paid to the Brahmin it is easy to see the germ of what was to become the enslavement of India. It was not so easy then. The theory is noble. Life did not offer so many temptations.

Public opinion being small and local could concentrate in a ray of fire upon the Brahmin who misjudged or misused the grandeur of his position; but yet the end was sure where human power was so exalted. Under the Buddha India made one last despairing struggle to cast off the yoke of Brahminism, and failing, accepted her doom with the apathy which still dominates her.

The duty of the Kshatriya (warrior, ruler) is summed up in the description of Kalidasa:

"He who guards the weak from injury by the strong: how shall he be a king who does otherwise? What shall the man do with his life if it be blasted by ill-fame and the unanswered cry for help of the suffering?"

So it was inculcated in the Laws of Manu that the whole duty of the Kshatriya is protection, charity, sacrifices, study, and non-addiction to pleasure. Could such an ideal realize itself on earth? Only here and there, and then against an oncoming sea of temptation. Many instructions of the highest type are given as to the care of the people—their food, clothing, recreation, and the care of orphans, widows, and helpless persons. A tax on the industrial classes supported the king and the Kshatriya class, who represented the defense of the nation. It varied from one-fourth in times of stress to one-tenth in times of ease. Out of this all public servants and institutions were maintained, including the amusements of the people. Brahmins and ascetics not supported by public gifts received their share.

It is interesting to consider here what form of government the Laws of Manu inculcate. Certainly not a democratic one. Equally certainly not an autocratic one. The Kshatriya king did not rule autocratically. He may be described as being at the head of a council composed of the highly educated and experienced Brahmins. He must himself follow the teaching of the Vedas in his rule.

"But where it is not explicit or new legislation becomes necessary, then what the well-instructed and perfected Brahmins declare to be the law, that shall be the law. They are the well-instructed who have acquired knowledge and thus have the power to make visible the physical and superphysical truths of revelation. That which an assembly of ten such, or of three at least, may decide to be law shall be taken for law."

Later this number might be increased; there might be a number of each caste, and in an assembly of twenty-one one Shudra must be present. It is of great interest to consider these provisions and to contrast them with the modern conception of untrained legislators chosen by the votes of uneducated electors—uneducated in the truest and possibly only real sense of the word. Cooperation among the differentiated and disciplined is a very different conception from government by the majority.

We now come to the system of punishments laid down in this ancient social order, and here the view departs strangely from that of the modern world.

"The king who punishes the innocent and does not punish the guilty gathers infamy here and shall descend into the hells hereafter. The first degree of punishment he can inflict is warning by word of mouth. The second, public warning and degradation in status. The third, fine and forfeiture in addition to these. The last, corporal punishment (ranging from whipping to death and including imprisonment, infliction of wounds, branding, and mutilation)."

Where a common man guilty of wrong-doin'g might be fined a trifle, a ruler, a person in authority, should be awarded a sentence a thousand times more heavy. The punishment of the Vaishya (merchant) should be twice as heavy as that of the Shudra (laborer). The punishment of the Kshatriya (warrior, ruler) twice as heavy again. The punishment of the Brahmin should be twice as heavy as that of the Kshatriya or even four times as heavy, "for he knows the far-reaching consequences ofsin and merit." The king must restore to all four castes the property stolen from them by thieves. If he fails to do so the sin of the thief passes to the king. "By confession, repentance, by self-imposed penances, study, and gifts of charity, the sinner and the criminal wash away their crimes. The man who is held to punishment by the king becomes cleansed in truth from all stain of his offense when he has paid the penalty. He is restored to his original status and goes to heaven like the doers of good deeds."

In other words the criminal is not called upon to pay twice over in the original punishment and in all loss of public confidence. Paid is paid. The receipt is written, and the debtor to society goes out free from henceforth.

The system of warning to first offenders has only just been rediscovered in modern jurisprudence. The records of English law (which certainly hold no bad preeminence) reek with terrible punishments inflicted upon juvenile offenders, going even so far as capital punishment for trifling offenses, and this through the eighteenth century. The principle of severer punishment for an educated man also invites deep consideration. One may well smile in remembering certain well-known cases of recent "justice" and their result.

Even the sacred, the venerated Brahmin was not exempt from corporal punishment. The Laws of Manu authorize every man to kill a Brahmin in self-defense or when caught in the act in certain cases. After he had fallen and lost caste for repeated offenses he would hold the position of a Shudra with regard to punishment.

With regard to the honor of different employments it is interesting to see that after the two highest castes, those occupied with wisdom and government, agriculture is placed first among the employments of the Vaishya (merchant) class.

"Agriculture. Cow-keeping. Trade."

Thus it will be noticed that first in honor comes provision of the necessities of life and second its luxuries. And this leads us to the views held in the Laws of Manu on the subject of food. They are very well worth consideration today, when food is a question merely of liking and disliking and, in the long result, of the money which can be afforded.

"Do not give the messed leavings of food to any. Do not eat between the fixed and suitable meal-times. Do not eat while the last meal remains undigested. Do not go anywhere without ablution after a meal. Anxiously avoid overeating, for it wars against health, against the functioning of the higher mind, and therefore against the hope of heaven and the way of the virtuous; it breeds gross passions, and it is also against the rules of what is seemly and the equitable division of food amongst all who inhabit the world.

"As far as possible take the clean and bloodless foods. It is true that the mental inclination of the world on the path of pursuit is in the direction of flesh-foods and spirituous drinks, and physical loves and lusts; and it may be said there is not sin in these, especially in regulated forms (and for the Kshatriya and Shudra). But refraining from them brings high result. Flesh cannot be had without the slaughter of animals, and the slaughter of breathing beings does not lead to heaven. Therefore flesh-foods should be avoided. The man who has no will to bind and torture and slay innocent living beings, who wishes well to all, shall be blessed with enduring joy. And he who slays none shall achieve what he thinks, what he plans, what he desires, successfully and without pain."

It has long been clear to me that the perception involved in this law is reached only in a certain stage of evolution and psychic development. For this difference in status the Law of Manu appears to make allowance. To live by bloodshed is not a crime but an ignorance and an almost incalculable loss. Happy are those who attain the higher plane.So, as to the Brahmin fell the duty of providing the food of the spirit, to the Vaishya (merchant) fell that of providing the no less necessary food of the body, pure, uncontaminated, and infused by the spirit of good-will and recognition of deep responsibility to the community. Food itself had its aspect of divinity.

So also of the tiller of the soil:

"The dharma that any man performs, the merit of good works that anyone gathers—three parts of the merit belong to him who provides the food that is the support of the worker of merit, and one only to the doer himself."

This is high ground. Again, how far from the modern conception!

There are errors and follies in the Laws of Manu from many points of view. There are certain points unadaptable to the complexities of modern life. There is, however, much worth reflection from the point of view of the philosophy of social organization; in nothing more than in their conception of the right distribution of the four castes in a state. The bulk of the people must not be Brahmins, they must not be Kshatriyas. Least of all must they be Shudras. They must be Vaishyas (merchants and agriculturalists), for they represent the ultimate needs of the community—its relation to the earth, to concrete science and economics. They are the physical brain and system of the community. They represent the middle class of modern life. They, "twice-born" also, with a high practical training in psychological science, bound to the duties of sacrifice, charity, and study, were by far the larger part of the population.

The Shudra was the "little brother" of the community, and I think he compares favorably with the Greek slave, as regards duties and rights. The higher responsibilities were not expected from him, though he might assume them if he could. He was the substance out of which in other births great leaders might develop, but not yet.

But a warning not wholly inapplicable to the democratic ideal exists in the Laws of Manu:

"The kingdom in which Shudras preponderate over the twice-born and in which error and lack of the higher wisdom are therefore rampant—that kingdom shall surely perish before long, oppressed with the horrors of misgovernment."

A sharp contrast between the opinions of the Indo- Europeans and their cousins the Indo-Aryans must be noted here. The four castes of the community were divided by the measure of spiritual and intellectual attainment. The wisest must lead. The laws of Solon, wisest of the Greeks, the first codified laws of Europe, also recognized four classes, *but* they were graded according to income. The wealthy had the higher offices, the poorer the lower. It may be said that this striking contrast in aim marks the vast spiritual gulf still dividing Asia from Europe.

Why, with laws and aims higher than those of the Republic of Plato, is India what it is? Many reasons may be given. The inevitable deterioration of faith seen in all countries, repeated invasions and the thrust of the lower ideals of conquerors, division of races, conflicts of religion and national spirit, and, last but not least, a foreign ideal of education, wholly unsuited to the national genius, imposed upon them (as far as it has gone) in the sacred name of Lord Macaulay and others of the same limitation in knowledge and sympathy.

CHAPTER 4

THE STORIES AND PARABLES OF ANCIENT INDIA

We now take up the beginning of the age of philosophy. The priestly caste to evolve strength later (as is the case with all priestly castes) to the hurt and danger of India was now firm in the saddle of its rights and powers. The Brahmin had become almost a living god. Yet it must be remembered that he was the repository of wisdom and holiness and that his dignity was real. He was custodian of all the people most valued, and they valued it with all their souls and strength. So far as we know there has never been a people in all the world's history that in every class concerned itself so universally and profoundly with philosophy and the spiritual life.

They had now reached the stage where philosophy is seen to be latent in myth. This is the point at which the Upanishads developed from the Vedic hymns, and in them all the spiritual and intellectual life of India has its roots. The Upanishads are the end and logical development of the Vedas and are called the "Vedanta"—a name meaning the end or summing up of the Vedas. The word "upanishad" means "sitting near," and thus suggests the moments of teaching when the pupils surrounded the Rishis or sages who taught them.

Are these Upanishads of more worth than the early sacred books of other nations? I am so certain that they are, knowing what I owe them, that I must buttress my conviction with a few of those of great thinkers and scholars of the principal European nations.

Max Müller quotes the German philosopher Schopenhauer as saying: "In the whole world there is no study so beneficial and elevating as that of the Upanishads. It has been the solace of my life. It will be the solace of my death." Max Müller himself adds:

"If these words of Schopenhauer's require endorsement I shall willingly give it, as the result of my own experience during a long life devoted to the study of many philosophies and many religions. If philosophy is meant to be a preparation for a happy death, I know no better preparation for it than the Vedanta philosophy."

Sir William Jones, the distinguished oriental and classical scholar, writes: "It is impossible to read the Vedanta or the many fine compositions in illustration of it without believing that Pythagoras and Plato derived their sublime theories from the same foundation with the sages of India."

Victor Cousin, eminent philosophical historian of France, lecturing in Paris before a great audience of men said: "When we read with attention the poetical and philosophical monuments of the Orient, above all, those of India, we discover there many a truth so profound and making such a contrast with the meanness of the results at which the European genius has sometimes halted that we are constrained to bend the knee before the philosophy of the East and to see in this cradle of the human race the native land of the highest philosophy."

And to conclude with an august name, Schlegel, one of the greatest of German thinkers wrote: "Even the loftiest philosophy of the Europeans, the idealism of reason as set forth by the Greek philosophers, appears in comparison with the abundant life and vigor of oriental idealism like a feeble Promethean spark against the full flood of sunlight. It is faltering, weak, and ever ready to be extinguished. What distinguishes the Vedanta from all other philosophies is that it is at once religion and philosophy. In India the two are inseparable."

It will be owned that such books are worth study. Yet they need sifting for the average reader. There are many repetitions, necessary at a time when in the absence of books all knowledge had to be memorized. There are many Sanskrit words for which there are scarcely English equivalents, many primitive traces which have lost interest for the majority. These things must be pruned away before the great thought of the Upanishads can be presented to the West, but when this is done I think its majesty cannot fail to impress all to whom the mysteries of life and death are dear.

There are ten chief Upanishads. Their exact date cannot be given but the most widely held opinion assigns the earliest to a period from 800 B.C. to 3000 B.C. Certain of the most important follow after the life and teaching of the Buddha at about B.C. 500. There is silence when the names of the authors of these early Upanishads are asked. They cared nothing for personal renown—so little that they permitted their wisdom to be attributed to deities and mythical sages. Biography therefore must come later. Yet certain names will always be remembered as associated with them—such sages as Yajna- valkya, such kings as Janaka. From the Upanishads spring all the ten philosophies of India.

Max Müller, Professor Radhakrishnan, and other scholars have divided the great philosophies of India into six systems. Behind them lies a vast reservoir of national philosophy springing from the sacred Vedic books, upon which all are founded and from which each thinker drew what he would, sometimes with variants so slight to a foreign mind as only to confuse issues. For popular understanding it is best to follow the main currents of thought, considering rather their essentials than their differences, though naturally this would not be the scholastic method. Our object is to obtain a clear and simple view of what has been described by those qualified to judge as the highest form of thought in the world—that of ancient India; and it may be truly said that this includes the diverging philosophies of modern India, except in so far as they have been swept into the vortex of modern western speculation.

In one respect it is easier to write of Hindu philosophy than of any other; in another, far more difficult. The great Indian philosophers had a commendable system, unknown to the Greeks, of summing up their conclusions in a series of short aphorisms known as Sutras, which he who ran might read. Easy enough so far. But he who ran must have acquired the habit of thinking in high regions of the mind, more rarefied than the atmosphere of the peak of the mountain we call Everest, and the Indians Gaurishankar. There lies the difficulty.

And there is another profound difference between Indian philosophers and such a thinker as Aristotle. They will not for one moment admit that the life of man and therefore his consciousness can be bounded by logical reason. Man's consciousness of self is not to be the foot- rule of the universe. The animal is conscious but not conscious of self. The average man is conscious of self; but above him, as far as he stands above the animal, is the man who is superconscious, who perceives an order of the universe before which self-consciousness stands dumb and dazzled. This utmost reach of thought is the basis of the six divisions of the philosophy of India.

Let us begin with the essentials upon which the six systems are at one. All accept the vast universe-rhythm which consists of Creation, Maintenance, and Dissolution. They conceive a universe without beginning.

> The Books teach Darkness was at first of all,
> With Brahm sole meditating in that night.

From that Thought the universe proceeds. For untold periods it subsists. Finally it is resolved again into the primeval dark. Much later this conception is symbolized in the parable of the Trinity of Brahma the Cre-ator, Vishnu the Maintainer, and Shiva the Destroyer. Does this re-solution of the universe compel a return to primal chaos and wasted eons of progress? By no means. From each "Night of Brahm," as it is called when the rhythmic Breath is indrawn (if I may use such an illustration), the universe emerges remolded, but re- molded of the stuff fructified or blasted in its last emergence. The history of universal evolution thus proceeds as steadily and rhythmically as the second act of a well- conceived play unfolds from the necessities of the first. Rightly considered this is a part of the vast history of the ascension of man along the path of realization. Realization of what? Of whom? That explanation is the object of the philosophies.

The six philosophies unite in their object. In all six this is the education of man in the realization of his part in the universe. Not in his village or city or country. True, he has his dharma, but the whole thing is on a far vaster scale than that conceived in Greece or in China; though in China Taoism had a cloud-driven glimpse of this issue, which I shall relate in its place. Aristotle and Confucius lay down the moralities by which a man may duly and rightly fill his place in the world. So and more does Plato. But the Indians aim at his place in the universe, and the difference is as great as the universe is greater than the planet we inhabit.

There is another essential on which the six systems agree. All accept the teaching of rebirth and preexistence. Plato accepted this doctrine also, possibly deriving it from Indian sources; and certain other Greek philosophers earlier and later have done the same. It seems indeed to have been an instinct of the human heart, for it is found not only in Asia but among many other races civilized and uncivilized. It has been traced in Africa. Caesar in his history of the Gallic wars asserts that "the Druids inculcate this as one of their leading tenets that souls do not become extinct but pass after death from one body to another, and they think that men by this tenet are in a great degree spurred on to valor, laying aside the fear of death."

It was held in Wales and Ireland also. The famous Welsh bard Taliesin sings in the sixth century:

> "I was a speckled snake on the hill.
> I was a dragon in the lake.
> I was a herdsman.
> I have been in many shapes before I attained a congenial form."

And in Rome, we have Ovid declaring:

> "Death, so-called, is but old matter dressed In some newT form. And in a varied vest From tenement to tenement though tossed,
> The soul is still the same, the figure only lost."

Many of our modern poets and writers in the West could be quoted to the same effect—from Shakespeare (in his fifty-ninth sonnet) to the latest comers. It may be said that many of the greatest minds in the West have held it. To any Asiatic philosophic mind it was impossible to suppose that the soul of man began with conception or birth. Very early the Katha Upanishad declared:

Never the spirit was born; the spirit shall cease to be never.
Never was time it was not. End and beginning are dreams.
Deathless and birthless and changeless abideth the spirit forever.
Death cannot touch it at all, dead though the house of it seems.

In Radhakrishnan's fine phrase: "The development of the soul is a continuous progress, though it is broken into stages by the baptism of death."

But realization of the truth can never be, where the eyes of the intelligence and of the soul are blindfolded by ignorance. Therefore the aim of the six philosophies, as of all philosophy, is to tear away that bandage and to show to the man the universe as it is. Then he will perceive his relation to it and be at peace.

While all the systems aim at a philosophy of ethics, ethics can and must be transcended by realization. Thus ethics are no end in themselves but simply a condition of the road upon which a man must travel—to the point where roads are no longer needed or possible, for there he develops wings. Meanwhile love (the great prison-breaker of selfish individuality), altruism, and cleansing of the heart are makers of the Road. Upon this point all systems are at one. They are at one also upon the rules of caste, such as I have described them in the Laws of Manu, and the division then given of the different stages of life, as the student, the householder, and the qualified ascetic.

The Buddhist philosophy, in some respects the most interesting of all, from its world-wide influence, must be treated separately. So we begin with the Upanishads and in them with the earliest Vedantist parables. In these is all Indian philosophy, as the wine is contained in the unripe grape. Were all the philosophy based on them to perish it could be reconstructed from those marvelous books, though I do not deny their defects in stating their grandeur.

The Upanishads turn from the bright picture of the outer world as presented by the senses to explore the inner and unseen. They do not deny the many gods, but make them as it were manifestations of the One.

"The Self-Existent pierced the openings of the senses, so that they turn outward, therefore man looks outward, not inward into himself. Some wise man, however, with closed eyes and desiring immortality saw the Self hidden behind it."

It followed from this attitude that in the Upanishads formal and ritual religion does not hold a very high place. It must exist, for ritual worship is an end to many people, and in a certain sense is the scaffolding upon which divine philosophy must be built. But the thinkers of the Upanishads beheld these proceedings with the irony of those who have transcended ritual and for whom it has lost meaning. There were times when they permitted themselves to mock at the respectably established verities of the religion of the multitude and even of the Brahmins. As an example: the syllable A U M or O M was held in the highest veneration, for reasons to be given later, and magical properties were ascribed to it. At this and at what it represented the embryo philosophy of the Upan- ishads mocked when it was so minded, as in the following example:

"Next, the Aum of the dogs! Vaka had gone forth to study the Vedas. To him appeared a white dog. Other dogs approached it and said: 'O Lord, pray for abundance of food for us. We desire to eat it.'

"To them answered the white dog: 'Come here to me, tomorrow morning.'

"As those who wish to pray through the hymns assemble to set to their work, so did the little dogs come together and march like a procession of priests, each holding the tail of the one in front and barking out: "'Aum! let us eat. Aum! let us drink. Aum! may the resplendent Sun who showers rain and grants food to all mortals grant us food. O Lord of food, bestow food upon us. Deign to grant it.'"

There was little fear of the priests in such utterances.

The thinkers of the Upanishads had a very different food in view from that so satirized and on which the average Brahmin dwelt so tenderly; and while they could respect the Brahmin who manifested the ideal consecrated in him, they could also perceive that it was the ideal only which was the consecration, and that certain qualities transcend caste, whatever the Brahmins might teach. Hear the strange story of Jabala, relic of a primitive time when a wife might be offered to the honored guests of her husband:

"Satyakama Jabala asked of his mother Jabala:

"'I wish to dwell with a teacher as a pupil in Brahmalore. Of what caste am I?' (It was needful that should be known.)

"She answered:" '

My son, I do not know. During my youth when I conceived you I attended on many guests who frequented my husband's house and I had no way of asking. So I know not of what caste you are. Jabala is my name, and Satyakama yours. You must therefore call yourself "Satyakama, son of Jabala" when asked.'

"He went to Haridrumata of the Gautama clan and said:

" 'I approach your venerable person that I may abide with you as a pupil in Brahman lore.'

"The teacher asked.

" 'Of what caste are you?'

"He answered:

" 'I do not know this. My mother said, "In my youth when I conceived you I was attending upon many. You are Satyakama, son of Jabala!" '

"Then said the other:

" 'None but a Brahmin could answer thus, for you have not departed from the truth. I will invest you with the Brahminical rites. Do you, child, collect the necessary sacrificial wood.'"

So even caste, even the teaching of the Vedas, was not sacrosanct in the eyes of the teachers of the Upanishads. The Vedas were sacred, yes, but that sight which could look through the self of man to the Universal Self was more sacred still. They shared the feeling which was to be expressed later, that "the worshipers of the Absolute are the highest in rank; second to them are the worshipers of the personal God; then come the worshipers of the Incarnations like Rama, Krishna, Buddha; below them are these who worship ancestors, deities, and sages, and lowest of all are the worshipers of the petty forces and spirits." And again: "The wise man finds his God in himself." That is, in the realization of the Absolute, of which he is a part. This therefore was the highest form of knowledge. They said:

"Two kinds of knowledge are to be known, the higher and the lower. The lower knowledge is that given by certain Vedas. The higher knowledge is that by which the Absolute is apprehended."

The problem of the Upanishads is therefore the cause and the realities of life and death. Their thinkers strove to find the way of understanding to the infinite and central Truth which is infinite existence and pure bliss. A famous Upanishad prayer is:

> From the unreal lead us to the Real,
> From darkness lead us to Light.
> From death lead us to Immortality.

But even this high ideal fell a little below that of later Vedantic philosophy, in which any possible interpretation of immortality as "heaven" was felt to be a little vulgar and suited only to conceptions associated with that of a personal God. Philosophy looked higher and further.

Knowledge must begin by philosophical understanding of the self of man. It must pass from the objective, which all could see and about which all could reason, to the deep subjective self, felt as a dim stirring within, to be gained only by the love and intuitions of wisdom. Philosophy, not revelation, was the aspiration of the Upanishads.

"The soul within me; it is lighter than a corn, a barley, a mustard seed, or the substance within it. The soul within me is greater than this earth and the sky and the heaven and all these united. That which performs and wills all, to which belong all sweet juices and fragrant odors, which envelops the world and is silent and is no respecter of persons, *that* is the soul within me. It is BRAHM.

When this conception was rooted in belief it demanded definition. There is a most interesting story in the Chandogya Upanishad where Prajapati, Lord of Creation—being approached by Indra, representative of the Shining Ones, the Angels, and Virochana, representative of the Dark Ones, the Demons—is questioned by them as to what is the true, the real Self, which inhabits the body of man. Prajapati is a personal divinity. He begins by a statement:

"The Self free from sin, from age, and death, and grief, and hunger, and thirst, which desires nothing but the Desirable and imagines nothing but what it should imagine, *that* is the object of our search. He who has searched out that Self and comprehends it obtains complete beatitude."

So the two served Prajapati for thirty-two years (after the manner prescribed for pupils in the Laws of Manu) and then came to demand knowledge as their reward. I condense:

Testing the two he desires them to look in the eye. The image seen there, is not that the Self?

They took his meaning not as that of the person within who sees through the eye but as the image reflected in the pupil; and Prajapati, seeing this, commanded them both to dress and adorn themselves in their best and to look into a pail of water and report what they saw.

Both answered: "We see the Self, a picture even to the hair and nails."

Prajapati reflected within himself: "They both go away without having seen the Self, and whichever of the Shining Ones or Dark Ones follows this doctrine will perish."

And Virochana, his shallow mind satisfied, went away and preached to the Dark Ones that the self alone is to be worshiped and served, and that he who does this gains the best of both worlds—this and the next. But Indra, on his way to preach this doctrine to the Shining Ones, saw a difficulty and paused. He returned to Prajapati.

"Sir, as this self is well adorned when the body is finely adorned, clean when this body is cleaned, so it will be blind and lame if the body is blind and lame, and perish as the body perishes. I see no good in this teaching. This is not the Eternal Self."

[Note that the word Self (with a capital) applies in Indian philosophy to Brahm or Brahman— as distinguished from Brahma the Creator—the Universal Cause and only Self. Without a capital it refers to the so-called individual self of man.]

"So it is. Live with me for another thirty-two years," said Prajapati. And at the end of that time he said:

"He who moves about happy in dreams, he is the Self, the Immortal, the Fearless He is Brahman [or Brahm]."

And Indra was about to return to the Shining Ones with this doctrine when again he paused and returned.

"Sir, it is true that the dream-self is not blind or lame though the body may be both. Yet in dream also that self is pain-conscious and weeps. I see no good in that doctrine. Here is not the Eternal Self."

"So it is indeed, Maghavat [Indra]. Live with me for another thirty-two years."

And at the end of this time Prajapati said:

"When a man in perfect sleep sees no dream, that is the Self, the Immortal, the Fearless. That is Brahman."

But Indra was growing wiser.

"In that state a man does not know that he is 'I' nor anything that exists. It is utter annihilation. I see no good in this."

"Live with me another five years and you shall know."

Then at the end of five years Prajapati said to Indra: "This body is mortal, and death holds it. But it is the abode of that Self which is immortal and bodiless. When in the body, by thinking 'This body is I' the Self is fettered by pleasure and pain. But when a man knows himself apart from the body, then neither pleasure nor pain touches him more. The eye is but the instrument of seeing. The self who knows, 'Let me see this,' it is the Self. He who knows, 'Let me think this,' he is the Self; the mind is but the divine Eye. He who knows that Self and understands it, obtains all worlds and all desires."

Thus said Prajapati; yea, thus said Prajapati.

This is surely a wonderful passage for such an antiquity. As Max Müller points out it enters into the minds of few even of philosophers to ask *what* the ego is, what lies behind it and is its real substance. But here is the question asked and answered. The body is but a garment for the soul; age is a changing garment; the baby of eight weeks develops into the man of eighty and is yet the same. Nationality, all outer things, are garments to be discarded; and behind them abides the Eternal Self unchanged, traveling toward its inevitable goal.

The story faces life. Now let us take a story from the Upanishads which faces death.

There is a youth, Nachiketas, who through a sudden anger of his father is sent to the House of Yama—the god of death. Yama is away at the time of his arrival and on returning finds to his horror that a young Brahmin has waited for three days without receiving food or any of the rites of hospitality. The gods themselves are shamed by such an oversight.

He speaks with grave courtesy:

"O Brahmin, because you, a guest to be venerated, have waited in my house for three nights without food, therefore be salutation to you and welfare to me! Now choose three boons in return for those three nights you spent without hospitality."

What will Nachiketas choose?

"O Death, as the first of my three boons I choose that my father's anger toward me be appeased and that he may remember me as his son."

"Through my favor he will remember you with love as before. He will sleep happily at night, and free from anger he will see you when released from the jaws of death."

Nachiketas speaks again:

"In the place of heaven is no fear of any kind; beyond all grief all rejoice in the place of heaven. You, O Death, know the heavenly fire of the sacrifice by which heaven and immortality must be gained. Reveal it to me as my second boon."

"I know the heavenly fire, Nachiketas. Know that that fire is placed in the cavity of the heart."

He gives directions which Nachiketas repeats.

Satisfied, the magnanimous Lord of Death speaks to him:

"I grant another boon. That fire shall be called after your name. Take also this many-colored chain. Now choose the third boon, Nachiketas."

The youth considers:

"There is this question. Some say the soul exists after the death of man. Some that it does not. On this I desire knowledge from you. This is my third boon."

Then said Death, starting back in alarm:

"This question was inquired into even by the gods; hard is it to understand. Subtle is its nature. Choose another boon, Nachiketas. Do not compel me to this. Release me from this boon!"

Nachiketas replies:

"There is no other boon like this. There is no other speaker like to you."

Death protests passionately:

"Choose sons and grandsons living a hundred years. Choose herds of cattle, elephants, gold, and horses. Choose the wide-spread earth, and live what years you will. Be a king. Over the great earth I will make you enjoyer of all desires. Nay, even the beautiful maidens of heaven with their chariots and instruments of music—such as are not to be gained by mortal men—you shall be served by them. I will give them to you. Only ask me nothing of the state of the soul after death." Will Nachiketas be tempted by these great offers? He answers:

"These things are of yesterday. All the glory of the senses wears out, O End of Man! Short is the life of all. Keep for yourself your horses and the like, your dance and song! How should man rest satisfied with wealth? Having wealth and seeing Death, how can we live but at your pleasure? The boon I choose is what I asked. What man living in the world, knowing he decays and dies while beholding the changeless Immortals, can rejoice in beauty or love or care for long life? I ask no other boon but that which concerns the soul. I ask the hidden knowledge."

Then Death, seeing himself face to face with a man indeed, speaks at last; the truth shall be revealed.

"The good is one thing; the pleasant, another. Both chain man. It is well with him who chooses the good. He who chooses what is pleasant misses the object of man. But you, Nachiketas, considering the objects of desire, have abandoned them. You have not chosen the road of wealth, upon which so many perish. You desire knowledge. For *He,* the Soul, is inconceivably more subtle than the subtle. By no reasoning can this thought be reached. Only when a Teacher teaches can it be learned, dearest friend. But you are stedfast and persevering in the truth. May we have other seekers like to Nachiketas !

"You are the seeker of Him who is hard to see, who dwells in the mysteries, who is hidden in the caverns of the heart and the impenetrable thicket. When a man has heard and accepted this, and has stripped off all sense of right and wrong, when he has attained to That Subtle One, then he rejoices. I see in Nachiketas a dwelling whose door is open for Him."

Says Nachiketas:

"Then make known to me this thing you see which differs from virtue and vice, differs from the whole of effects and causes, differs from past and present and future."

Death answers:

"The soul is not born nor does it die. It is not produced from anyone nor does it produce. It is unborn, eternal, timeless, ancient. It is not slain when the body is slain. If the slayer thinks he slays or the slain that he is slain, both err. The soul is neither slain nor slays.

"The Self that lodges in the heart of each man is smaller than the small, greater than the great. The man whose will is at rest sees Him and is freed from sorrow; through the serenity of the senses he sees the glory of the Self. Who but I can know that divine Self is joyful—yet above joy. He is bodiless yet dwells in things incarnate. He is permanent yet dwells in things impermanent. He is the All-Pervading. Know the embodied soul is the rider, the body is the car, intellect is the charioteer, and mind is the reins. The senses, they say, are the horses, and the objects of sense the roads. If a man is without wisdom and uncontrolled, his senses are like the vicious horses of the charioteer.

"If a man is without wisdom and impure, he does not attain to his Home but goes on the road of birth and death. If a man has wisdom he attains that Home from which he does not return again to birth.

"Higher than the senses are their objects, higher than these objects is the mind, higher than the mind is Intelligence. Higher than Intelligence is the Great Self. Higher than the Great Self is the Unmanifested. Higher than the Unmanifested is the Soul. Higher than the Soul is nothing! That is the goal.

"Arise! Awake! Receive your boons. Understand! Hard is the

way, having the sharp edge of a razor. But he who has understood the Nature of Brahm [the Universal Self] is freed from death."

The wise who says and hears this eternal tale which Nachiketas received and Death related is honored in the world of Brahma.

Here ends this great and ancient story, wonderful in its knowledge and insight, set forth at a time when it seems little less than a marvel that such an analysis should be produced. Clear and beautiful it shines as the face of Nachiketas, the youth in the dark House of Death—to be the foundation of mighty thoughts and great philosophies. For what the teaching of Death conveys to Nachiketas is nothing less than that "when the sun has set, when the moon has set, and the fire is extinguished, the Self alone is Light." And why?

Because, as is told in another brief parable of the Upanishads with which I will end this chapter, the soul is itself the Universal. It is no child of the Divine but the Divine itself; imprisoned in flesh but divine—the changeless, the immortal.

> A father says to his son:
> "Fetch me a fruit of the *nyagrodha* tree."
> "Here is one, sir."
> "Break it."
> "It is broken, sir."
> "What do you see?"
> "Almost infinitesimal seeds."
> "Break one."
> "It is broken, sir."
> "What do you see?"
> "Nothing, sir."
> The father said:

"My son, that subtle essence there which you cannot perceive, of that very essence this great *nyagrodha* tree proceeds. Believe it, my son. In that which is the subtle essence every existent thing has its Self. It is the Self and you, O Shvetaketu, are T H A T."

How pale beside this eternal wisdom are the bloodless spectral worlds after death of Greece and Rome. In the words of a great

Indian thinker: "Coming and going is all pure illusion; the soul never comes and goes. Where is the place to which it shall go when all space is *within the soul?* When shall be the time for entering and departing when all time is *in the soul?"* It must be remembered that the story of Nachiketas not only conveys the highest teachings of the Vedanta, but is an early and most beautiful story of rebirth. He dies, dwells in the house of Yama, the god of death, and returns to earth to bless it with his wisdom in a new birth.

And it must never be forgotten that in the eastern philosophies there is an open meaning for the many and a hidden meaning for the few who are thus initiated and instructed. This is emphatically so with the Vedanta and certain teachings of the Buddha.

Moving about in India, Ceylon, Burma, and Japan, one is much struck with the fact that these esoteric meanings are most carefully guarded and seldom meet the observer except in the most favorable circumstances. Yet they are none the less there and known to those who are able to penetrate beneath the surface.

CHAPTER 5

SHANKARA, THE GREAT YOGIN AND PHILOSOPHER

We are but broken lights of Thee" may be taken as the central point of the philosophy of the Upan- ishads, which was to be developed by the great commentators. But what is the Eternal Unchanging Light, reflected as it were in broken light on the reflectors of man's experience? We must question what THAT is before we can decide what man is. This necessity is the reason of the already quoted Indian philosopher's reply to Socrates, when the greatest of the Greeks asserted that his philosophy consisted in inquiries about the life of man.

"No one can understand things human who does not first understand things divine." That understanding is the object of the Upanishads.

In the ancient Vedic stories of the passing of the soul, standing before the Throne of Brahman after death it makes the solemn and unshrinking assertion:

"Thou art the Self, and what THOU art that am I." There is but One.

Brahman is a neuter noun, neuter because the conception transcends all ideas of sex. But in India then and now, as in Europe at the present time, lower flights of thought could circle about the image of a personal God or gods having the attributes of humanity on a vaster scale. Such a God was and is conceived as possessing form or forms. Of such a God can be asserted the human emotions of love, pity, anger, jealousy, vengeance, and many more. He is comprehensive even in the most tangled flights of the theologians, because humanity could read humanity into what it worshiped. In the bewildering mazes of the Trinity of the Athanasian creed, for instance, the Father is felt as a dominant Sovereign, the Son as Love which reconciles and softens power, the Holy Spirit as an inspiration and consolation in the immensities.

So it is and was in India for those for whom the Vedantic philosophy was too high. There the most famous of the personal gods are Shiva, Brahma, and Vishnu, Three in One and One in Three. Brahma is the Creator, Vishnu the Maintainer, Shiva the Destroyer, expressing the inevitable process by which worlds are brought into being, are sustained, and finally pass through destruction to other forms. To humbler intellects each of these often expresses all they can contain of godhead, and each has his uses. None is or was condemned by those who could perceive higher or other aspects.

"Whosoever comes to Me, through whatsoever way I reach him, all men are struggling through the paths which lead to Me," says a Hindu scripture; and this truth the Upanishads fully realize. But they assert that eventually the flash of true realization destroys all doubts or lesser loves, fuses the plurality of Godhead into the One, and restores man instantly to knowledge of the truth that he himself is divine and that outside the circumference of the Divine nothing at all can have any existence.

But they teach also that the Absolute can never be defined. It eternally escapes the reason. They assert that when any quality, action or intelligence is suggested in relation to the Infinite the truth-seer will shake his head and say, "Not so. Not so." For the clouded and fettered divinity in man can never stretch to the comprehension of its source, excepting only in the state known in the West as that of the higher or cosmic consciousness. And those who have thus beheld can make no report when they return to the earthly plane, because earthly words cannot cover that perception. Thus St. Paul says:

"And I knew such a man, whether in the body, or out of the body, I cannot tell; God knoweth;

"How that he was caught up into paradise, and heard unspeakable words, which it is not lawful for a man to utter."

And in the same spirit a sage, asked by King Vashkali to explain the nature of Brahman, was silent, and when the question was repeated answered: "By my silence I answer but you cannot understand it. This Brahman is Peace. Quiet."

How did this great conception begin? Except to scholars does it matter very greatly how such an idea shaped itself in the growing consciousness of man? It is Brahman, the Absolute Reality which none can apprehend but those who know Brahman. In what spirit must such knowledge be approached? How is that which has hitherto only realized itself as a finite creature to draw near to the assurance that it is infinite, that it is a wave of the infinite ocean, only lifted for a moment by a wind of illusion into a belief in difference?

Here the Upanishads are very explicit.

Intellect fails before the conception of Reality partly because intellect concerns itself with the little thoughts, dogmas, and creeds which play about like bubbles upon the surface of thought. Intellect also is the finite creature of the working of the human brain. It is so to speak mechanical. It fails, as speech fails, in the presence of the Real. Both intellect and speech depend upon the Real, but they are in a different category. They cannot be adjusted to this work of unification. Their very essence is differentiation. It is not because of them or through them that we can say, "THAT art thou." With the finite universe about us, speech and intellect can deal, but not with the Truth which lies behind it.

At this point it is interesting to notice how true is this statement even of the utmost flights of modern science today. Would not its highest exponents admit that, "Veil after veil will rise, but there must be Veil after veil behind"?

Never for one instant have they touched the Ultimate Cause and it is probable they never can, along the road of the physical sciences, and that the only hope is where the Upanishads place it (together with the mystics of all the faiths) in the developed consciousness of man. For the Upanishads declare that there is within man a quality which, because it is in itself Reality, enables him to conceive it. It is a something divinely simple that entirely transcends reason. It does not use the words "true" or "false," "ignorance" and "knowledge." These are words made for and used by reason, and they can cover the ground reason is capable of covering. But no more. A man perceives Reality and can only say, "It is. I am."

The Upanishads precede the teaching of Christ on this point by stating that only by divesting oneself of the panoply of reason does intuition become possible.

"Let a Brahmin renounce learning and become as a child."

"Not by learning is the Self attained, nor by genius nor much knowledge of books."

"It is unknown to those who know and known to those who do not know."

Afterwards divine philosophy may perhaps base its conception of the world and life on what is perceived, as we see in the lives and teachings of the Buddha and the Christ, but neither the one nor the other attained his perception by learning. St. Paul was a learned man in his way, but his experience of the state of perception never came by that channel. It came in the blinding flash of light outside Damascus, toward which inward processes of simplification had doubtless long been tending.

But it may be said: "This is religion. What about philosophy?" I answer again in the words of the Indian philosopher. "He who does not understand the Divine— what can he know of human life?"

This knowledge does not contradict the highest human reason. It expands it in hitherto unknown directions by superadding another form of vision. It will enable us to reconcile opposites in philosophy, and see at what point light and darkness, ignorance and knowledge, good and evil, meet and are transcended by something including them all—in an identity the unilluminated consciousness is incapable of perceiving, or of admitting when others perceive it.

The true percipient will behold with perfect tolerance the worship of the personal God whether as Allah, Shiva, or Yahve. He knows these beliefs are all relatively true. They are not the whole truth, but they represent different stages or inns on the road of percipience, where the soul of man may put up for a night, and refreshed resume its upward way. Certainly the intellectual faculty finds its appointed place in this Identity as everything else does; but it is not the gate—far otherwise. Better the loving follies of the simplest belief than the iron ethics of dogmatic intellectualism.

Life, more life! is the cry. The Upanishads thirst for what will give the whole of life a new meaning, lifting it into the universal and making each thought and action of a man of the same vital import to the universe as the sweep of the mightiest planet upon its orbit And as the planet evolves into order and harmony from chaotic forces, so the soul of man evolves into harmony and unity through the psychic evolution of many lives.

Did then these mighty thinkers believe, as certain Buddhist sects were to teach later, that the world as the senses conceive it is only mirage to dissolve into mocking sand and nothingness? No.

What they perceived is that there is identity. Nothing stands alone. The thing seen is also the seer. Objective and subjective are one. And this final truth, on which the sciences depend as does philosophy, was realized in India before the Buddha, before Plato.

Deussen, the great German scholar, says, and his utterance is well worth reading:

"If we strip this thought of the various forms—figurative in the highest degree and not seldom extravagant— in which it appears in the Vedantic texts, and fix our attention on it solely in its philosophical simplicity as to the identity of the Divine and the soul, the SELF and the self, it will be found to possess a significance reaching far beyond the Upanishads, their time and country. Nay, we claim for it an inestimable value for the whole of mankind.

"We cannot look into the future; we do not know what revelations and discoveries await the restlessly inquiring human spirit, but one thing we may assert with confidence: Whatever new and unwonted paths the philosophy of the future may strike out, this principle will remain permanently unshaken, and no deviation can possibly take place from it.

"If ever a general solution is reached of the great riddle that presents itself to the philosopher in the nature of things, the further our knowledge extends, the key can be found only where the secret of nature lies open to us from within, that is to say in our innermost self. It was here that for the first time the original thinkers of the Upanishads found it to their immortal honor, when they recognized our self, our inmost individual being, as the SELF, the INMOST BEING of universal nature and of all her appearances."

This agrees with what I expressed above—that the advance of the sciences must in future rest not on the extended knowledge but the extended consciousness of man, and that this can be attained only by realization that man is himself one with the Inmost Being. The conceptions of all the gods are derived from instincts that lead to guesses at this Inmost Being, and it underlies all the phenomena which surround us. Therefore in the highest teaching of the Upanishads these appearances are not what has been called in Europe *maya* (wrongly attributing to that word the meaning of "illusion") but they are appearances uncompleted by full knowledge on our parts; and they are therefore wrongly seen and reported—which is a very different matter. To quote the New Testament instance of newly restored sight: "I see men as trees, walking."

From this point in the development of Vedantic thought it becomes most interesting to observe its contacts with the conceptions and inspired guesses of modern science, such as those of Einstein and of the mathematicians who are dimly conceiving a new spatial consciousness, where Riemann, Hinton, Oumoff, and Lobachevsky have laid a trail.

It is not my purpose here to enter into this but there are readers who will perceive the points, as they loom through the dark of the centuries separating Vedantic thought from our own day. That thought penetrated to the Inmost Being of nature, saw it as the dynamo of the universe and humanity as a part of the dynamo—not subject to it, except in so far as every part is subject to the whole, but changeless, deathless, eternal, dynamic as the Source itself. And this conception and the enormous conclusions to which it led the thinkers of India have not yet been grasped by the western world.

So they accepted Absolute Being, which functions on all planes, in every form of existence and is pure essence, bliss, beauty, wisdom, instantaneous and spontaneous and yet a Process. And having said this, thought fell lamed on the threshold of discovery, and they could only repeat, "Not so. Not so," knowing that all attempt at expression travestied the inexpressible.

Great indeed were these thinkers. They became, though human enough, half deified in the belief of India because of the wisdom with which they faced the conclusions implied in the stupendous recognition of the true place of man in the universe.

It will be interesting to give here the life-story of Shankara, the greatest commentator and elucidator of the thought of the Upanishads. I feel that in reading such a story it is unwise to smile at certain incidents; for it is easy to laugh at what one does not understand, and we have not followed the way these men trod. We believe such things to be impossible, but have not fulfilled the conditions which make them possible. Western mystics certainly have allied statements, and our accepted Scriptures corroborate them in some important points. At all events India has studied the science of the soul by practice and experiment in ways we have never tried.

Shankara's very date is uncertain, but scholars give their vote for his birth in a.d. 788 and at that we may perhaps leave it.

He was a Brahmin of Malabar and went early to a Vedic school where he was imbued with the Vedantic knowledge of the Universal Self. In the Hindu account of his life he is credited with miraculous feats of scholarship as a child and of vision as a saint. It is told that at the age of two he learned to read, at three he studied the Puranas and understood many portions of them by intuition. Here may be recalled the early wisdom of the Christ. His mother had practiced many austerities before his birth to gain the gift of a son from the favor of the gods, and Shankara's devotion to her was very great. His story must be considered as that of a great adept in Yoga, as a prophet destined to lead his people to truth, and as a most learned man, though according to his horoscope he was fated to die in boyhood.

At the age of seven he returned from the house of his teacher and not long after his mother was seized with a dangerous illness. It is told that she fainted from the heat and that the child, by his power of Yoga—which must have been intuitive rather than disciplined if he possessed it at that age—caused the river to rise and cool the burning heat from which she suffered.

The fame of the young saint and yogin went far and wide over

India, even as such would and does today, though there are none now who can lay claim to the towering genius of Shankara.

Messages came from the King of Kerala, offering gold and elephants if he would shed the light of his presence upon the court, and not content with sending these messages by a minister he came himself to pay reverence and plead his desire for a son, hoping that the Yoga of Shankara might open the way to his heart's longing. The king received instruction on the discipline to be followed; and I may note that a chapter of the Brihadaranyaka Upanishad is devoted to this subject, and for that reason is left either in Sanskrit or Latin. It gives directions as to food ceremonials and recitation of mantras, and prescribes the ritual to be followed before and after the birth of the child. These secrets are never publicly taught, but are verbally conveyed from master to disciple.

About this time a great Rishi (sage) foretold that the wonder boy would die at the early age of thirty-two, and it was perhaps this knowledge that determined him to renounce home-life and become a wandering sannyasin, or holy man who embraces the life of ascetic contemplation. This is a part of the discipline of a yogin. His mother wept bitterly desiring that he should marry and beget a son before resigning the world for the life of quiet. It is told that a miracle was needed to defeat her yearning and that it was forthcoming, for as he bathed, a crocodile caught his foot, and when her son and the bystanders assured her that the crocodile would not let him go until she herself released him, she consented though with bitter grief. Shankara gave her into the care of relations, and promising to return if she ever needed him melted into the wandering millions of India.

And now begins the interesting part of his short life. Wandering with his begging bowl through towns and forests, by lonely hills and wide rivers, he came at last as though drawn by one desire to a cave in a hill, on the banks of the holy Narbada River, where a saint named Govinda Yati had fixed his hermitage. With him Shankara became a pupil and received instruction concerning the Universal Self, which is named IT or Brahman. It was given in four great sentences:

"Knowledge is Brahman. The soul is Brahman. Thou art That. I am Brahman."

Here again he manifested a great Yoga. One day when his teacher was lost in the trance of the higher consciousness Shankara calmed a furious tempest of rain, thunder, and lightning; and his master, returning to earthly consciousness, was overjoyed, and bade him go instantly to the holy city of Benares and receive the divine benediction.

So the young Shankara set forth in the yellow garment of the sannyasin, his face illumined by the twin lights of peace and power, going toward the sacred city, which is the goal of the highest Hindu pilgrimage. There many strange events met him. There his beloved friend and pupil Padmapada came to his class—the friend for whom he reserved his deepest thoughts and teachings.

A strange story, not unfamiliar to western ears, is told of this friendship. Once Shankara, standing on the bank of the Ganges, called Padmapada to come to him from the opposite shore, and without fear Padmapada walked the shining surface, and wherever he set foot a lotus sprang from the depths, and from this grace came the name of Padmapada—or Lotus-Foot.

At Benares the young philosopher composed his masterpiece and one of the masterpieces of the world— his commentary on the Brahman Sutras—and not only this but his mighty commentary on the Upanishads and also on that Song of the Lord (the Bhagavad Gita) which is known and loved even in the West.

It yet remains for western thinkers to gage the mind of Shankara though these commentaries have been brought before scholars by the devoted work of Max Müller, Radhakrishnan and others, including some distinguished Germans. His learning was vast, but it was informed by the spirit of the higher consciousness and the power of the yogin; and it is this combination which sets him apart even in India from the great scholar or the great yogin. It was said of him that in himself he combined all knowledge, all wisdom.

It was his habit to hold disputations and debates with learned men, and it was believed in India that one of the ancient and legendary sages, Vyasa, returned to life in the appearance of an ascetic Brahmin, to sift his learning by contradicting the propositions of his glorious commentary on the Brahman Sutras.

But not even by unearthly wisdom could Shankara be conquered. Again like the young Christ in the Temple he answered and justified all, and for the prize of his victory received an addition of sixteen years to his life as ordained by his karma. This fulfilled the thirty-two years promised by the prophet.

Wandering on from Benares he came to the house of the learned Mandana Mishra, and there a hot argument took place between Shankara and his host, while the wife of Mandana Mishra stood by as umpire: a story which illustrates the higher position of women at the time. So wise was she that she was believed by many to be an incarnation of Saraswati, the Indian Athena. As she stood by, the fire kindled in her, and after the first debate was ended she invited him to dispute with her.

One may imagine the beautiful woman and the young scholar in stern debate; he, cold and calm; she, angry, baffled, casting about to find some rift in his shining armor. With a woman's wit she found it and her sword flashed! What could the young ascetic know of the nature and spirit of earthly love? Not the spiritual love which is a part of Vedantic teaching—there he could foil her easily—but the love of man and woman.

She drove her question at him, and he was dumb. He could not answer. He begged a month in which to consider her question and left the house a beaten man for the first time in his life. A rather humorous dilemma!

Very anxiously he considered what to do? How could such a question be answered by a yogin in whom the sexual forces had been transformed into high and incomprehensible energies? How could his disciplined body, clean as a cup to hold the wine of the gods, be soiled by an earthly experience common to man and the lower planes of consciousness? Yet how could any sphere of knowledge be left unexperienced and unanswerable? Now comes a solution very strange to western thought, but a declared stage in the highest India Yoga.

As he wandered through the forest meditating the problem of Saraswati he beheld a king named Amaraka lying dead at the foot of a great tree, surrounded by mourners, men and women. Instantly the solution, the way, flashed upon the mind of Shankara.

It is believed to be within the power of the highly trained yogin to cast his spirit into the body of another, as we shall see in my chapter on the Yoga of Patanjali. Shankara knew that he could enter the corpse of Amaraka and so doing taste without wrong the experiences of a king. He committed his own empty shell to the charge of his pupils, and the corpse of Amaraka, enlightened and inspired by one of the greatest spirits that ever lived on earth, renewed its life to the joy of the mourners. They could not know. Their king had awakened from a deathlike trance; but it was past, and this was all that concerned them. With song and shout they bore him back to the royal city.

It is told that the queen was bewildered by certain changes in the spirit and intellect of her husband. Yet the man was the same—who could doubt it? As a royal and loyal wife she met him, radiant with love and joy, and so on the highest earthly plane Shankara learned the lesson of earthly love—which is a stage also in the evolution of the soul. And he knew that he could answer the question of Saraswati. Not only so, but he wrote a treatise on that strange and fascinating subject which has been more studied in its delicacies and grossnesses in India than perhaps in any other country in the world.

But still the queen doubted, and the high ministers recognized the new greatness of the king. It is significant that an order was given, inspired by the queen, that every corpse to be found in the city should forthwith be burned to ashes and that the king should know nothing of this order. The heavenly bird they had caged for the glory and good of the kingdom must not be allowed to flit away again on his own ethereal errands. His body must be destroyed lest he should seize it and be gone.

Meanwhile his disciples, headed by the loyal Padma- pada, longed for him. How could they live without him? Had he forgotten them in the queen's arms? They set out to the city of King Amaraka in the guise of a group of singers who would perform before the king. Their petition was granted, and they were ushered into the hall hidden in gold garments and heavy head-dresses fringed and veiled with gold. And they sang of high things and noble until the courtiers were spellbound—believing the very music of the spheres was sounding in the palace. Had it become the dwelling of Indra, Lord of the Shining Ones? Were these the musicians who play for the rejoicing of the gods?

And the king heard, and the silver arrows found his heart. With great gifts and in silence he dismissed the musicians, and in doubt and dismay they retreated. But that night the sleep of King Amaraka deepened into the sleep that has no dawn, and that night Shankara opened his eyes among his rejoicing disciples—wiser, gladder than of old, as one to whom no page of human experience has been closed. And returning with his disciples he answered the question of Saraswati and went on his way.

It is told that a little later by the power of his yoga he knew that his beloved mother was dying, and traveling by that power as one who runs a race with death he came to her side. She implored him to share his light with her, and very patiently unbending to her ignorance he tried to instruct her in the great Brahman knowledge, over which death has no dominion. She could not understand more than that Love underlies Law. For her his experiences and knowledge were too high, but thus quieted and holding the hand of her son she entered the peace.

Then ensued a difficulty. Like the Greek gods the purity of the yogin or sannyasin must not be tarnished by contact with death. Yet in his great love for her he would not be shut out from the last observances, and confronted the angry disapproval of relatives and friends. Did he not know that he himself was a divine—a flaming fire in which all impurity could be burned up as her body would be? He raised his right hand, and a tongue of fire shot from it which consumed her body into ashes as it lay, and there was a great silence.

He passed from place to place doing deeds of power, debating, spreading the great Vedantic knowledge, composing treatise after treatise to make clear the revelations of the Upanishads. So at last he came to Kashmir and to a temple with four portals of which one, the southern, had never been opened. Could it have been that mysterious little temple of Pandranthan, which stands beyond the great curving bend of the Jhelam that has given the sweeping design for so many decorations? I have thought this should be, even when I knew it could not.

The priests would not suffer the entrance of the austere young scholar until they had examined him as to his life—in which indeed their scrutiny could find no flaw. But when he entered the temple, pacing quietly with downcast eyes, the voice of the goddess Saraswati was heard as a great cry.

"Omniscient you are. There is no knowledge which escapes you. But in this holy place more is required. The man who enters this sanctuary must never have lain in the arms of a woman. What then is your case?"

Shankara answered, still with downcast eyes:

"This body is pure. It has never lain in the arms of a woman. It is clean from brow to heel." And he passed into the sanctuary.

A very little more toil was left to him, and he had then entered his thirty-second year which he knew limited the time allowed to him in this incarnation. Anandagiri relates the end:

"In the city of Kanchi, the place of absolution, as he was seated he absorbed his gross body into the subtle one and became Existence, then destroying this subtle one he became pure reason; then, attaining to the world of *Ish- vara* [the personal God], with full happiness completed like a perfect circle, he passed on into the Intelligence which pervades the Universe, and in this he still exists. And the Brahmins of the place and his pupils and their pupils, reciting the Upanishads and the Song Celestial and the Brahman Sutras, then excavated a grave in a very clean place and making due offerings to his body raised a tomb."

They buried him but did not burn him; for so pure is the body of a yogin that it needs no purifying flame.

I have told this story as it is told in India and not after the manner of western scholars, who cautiously confine themselves to an account of his young asceticism and scholarship. It can be taken on that plane, and there also it will mean much. Perhaps to some it may mean more. But I prefer to take it as it is told in the love and worship of his own land; surely the strangest story of a philosopher that ever was told in any. I have given it, though it dates so long after the Vedas and earlier Vedanta, because it undoubtedly gives the type of man to whom we owe them. The lives of those men can never be recovered, except in so far as they may or may not be the originals of some of the wonderful stories of the oldest Upanishads such as I have quoted and reluctantly left unquoted. But in Shankara we see their living likeness.

One should not end this chapter without some words of his own which may help to send students to his books:

"Owing to the appearance of a rope in the twilight it seems to be a serpent. In the same way the unhappy condition of the individual soul is imposed upon it by want of realization. When the illusion of the serpent is dispelled by the admonition of a friend only the familiar rope remains. So, by the admonition of my own Master I am no longer the individual soul but the Immutable Self that is the Seer. I am the Supreme Bliss. Such a man lives in bliss because his mind is freed from all contrasts (of happiness and misery, gain and loss, etc.), ever pure, devoid of my-ness and I-ness, always contented, steady in thought, imperturbable, cleansed of all illusions."

His Century of Verses is a very beautiful little devotional book. His philosophy is an exercise for the highest intellect.

CHAPTER 6

CONCENTRATION AND ITS POWERS

We now come to a very remarkable development of the Vedanta—one which to many will seem incredible, but which must have a profound interest to those in the West who have made even a preliminary study of Indian philosophy and modern psychology.

The word "yogi" is well known in the West as connoting a roving imposter who will stand on his head for ten years or more with a watchful eye for gain, who will cheat and lie and juggle with the same end in view, who must be despised yet to a certain extent feared as the possessor of some possible power of black or white magic, by which he may rival the palmist in foretelling an amatory or wealthy future. He is vaguely confused with the juggler who charms serpents or produces the sleeve- hidden mango tree, which grows at your feet while you do your best to believe the growth is spontaneous.

The true yogin is really the exponent of a wonderful and ancient system of psychology, one far more highly developed than any known in the West. He is the representative of the occult sciences taught in the great Buddhist University of Nalanda in the ancient days of India. He is the man who in mastering the secrets of the phenomenal life of the senses prepares us for the approach through death to Reality. In India he survives for those who know how to find him. In Tibet he is thought to hold the key to the inmost meaning of the teachings of the Buddha and therefore it may almost be said of the Vedanta.

In this matter India took her straight and fearless flight to the inmost and outermost confines of thought and experience. You may or may not believe—that does not concern her thinkers. They unhesitatingly assert that they have made their experiments and *know.* You can do likewise if you are so minded. But if without doing this you condemn, if you say a thing is impossible because it is unexpected and highly incredible, if you deny the supremacy of the psychic over the physical, then India smiles and passes on.

What is Yoga? Who are its great exponents in India?

The word "Yoga," like words of our own, is differently used in different connections. Sometimes it means "a method"—which indeed it is: a method of freeing the intelligence to higher perception. Sometimes it means "yoking" in the sense of yoking-up or union with the Supreme Self set forth in the chapter on Shankara's philosophy. Sometimes it is a word used to express "effort"—hard, persistent, strenuous endeavor to restrain the senses and the mind ; so that the essential in man imprisoned behind them shall go free, to achieve that realization of its oneness with the Supreme, on which Shan- kara lays such stress in his teaching. Sometimes it may mean "division" in the sense of division from the imputed self.

The aims of the royal or Raja Yoga, as it is called, are high and noble even from the physical side; and they are wide as high. The body must be brought to heel as an obedient dog, the reasoning and logical mind the same. Therefore it becomes necessary to secure a great tranquillity in the nervous system, and to that end the body must be freed of any impurities which would clog the circulation and irritate the nerves. It follows that practices are enjoined to secure these ends, and the extraordinary health and longevity thus gained are to be used like a sort of compound interest in the furtherance of the quest for spiritual freedom.

There are other systems of Yoga: Mantra Yoga— healing by mantras or a kind of spells, likely to be very efficacious in nervous cases; Hatha Yoga, which is almost wholly medical and not wholly commendable. But none have the interest of the Raja Yoga of Pantanjali.

We need not fear that we are in bad company in considering this form of Yoga. It was founded on the Vedanta and closely allied to the famous Shankhya Vedantic philosophy, which differed from Shankara on points only those deeply skilled in Vedantic lore could think of vital consequence. The Buddha himself was a yogin in the fullest and deepest sense of the word. His famous teacher Alara was a master of the science, and Alara's pupil the Buddha practiced the ascetic austerities to an even terrible point. He completed these with the highest contemplation and possessed "the powers." The same may be said of other masters of Indian thought. Of Buddhist Yoga I shall speak in its own place.

How ancient the science of Yoga (or a disciplined search to attain perfection) may be, none can say. The Rig-Veda—the earliest poetic collection of documents of the Indo-Aryans—mentions its possibilities of ecstasy and the hypnotic trance, though in a crude form. The Upani- shads accept the Yoga practice in the sense of a conscious inward search for the true knowledge of Reality. One of the most famous Upanishads, the Katha, speaks of the highest condition of Yoga as a state where the senses together with the mind and intellect are fettered into immobility. These are the terms it uses:

"Immortal are those who know it. The state which ensues when the five organs of knowledge remain alone with the mind, and the intellect does not strive, is called the highest aim."

"This they call Yoga which is the firm keeping-down of the senses."

I will give as succinctly as possible the means whereby it can be practiced.

Patanjali is said to have codified the ancient systems and knowledge of Yoga in the second century B.C., though some scholars put the codification later. By some the codifier, who never laid claim to be the author, was believed to be the great grammarian Patanjali, author of a famous book knowm as the "Mahabhashya," but this is doubtful. In any case the collection represents no author—but an era.

It consists of four parts. First is treated the nature of the ecstasy to be attained. Second, the means of attaining it. Third, an account of the supernormal powers to be had through Yoga. Fourth, the nature of the liberation of the soul, which is of course the highest aim of Yoga. I shall speak of Patanjali throughout, since he is the recognized exponent of this Yoga; but it must always be remembered it is no system of his own. It is a codification.

The seventh aphorism in the first part should be carefully remembered because it indicates the spirit in which the task of understanding or practicing Yoga (this latter should never be done without a skilled teacher) must be approached. Its sound is strangely modern.

"Direct perception, inference, and competent evidence are proofs of right knowledge."

I mention this because in reading what is to follow it might be thought absurd that some of the statements should be classed under the title of philosophy. Here I must fortify myself with the support of Professor Max Müller who says:

"What we must guard against in those studies is rejecting as absurd what we cannot understand at once or what to us seems fanciful and irrational. I know from my own experience how what often seemed to me for a long time unmeaning, nay, absurd, disclosed after a time a far deeper meaning than I should ever have expected."

Professor Radhakrishnan also treats the Yoga system with respect.

I begin with the second aphorism of Patanjali and I shall condense the explanations given by Vivekananda with my own.

"Yoga is restraining the mind-stuff from taking different forms."

In other words it asserts the dominance of mind. The mind-stuff may be imagined as a calm, translucent lake with waves or ripples running over the surface when external thoughts or causes affect it. These ripples form our phenomenal universe—i.e., the universe as it is presented to us by our senses. If we can make these ripples cease, we can pass beyond thought or reason and attain the Absolute State.

Does it sound impossible to restrain or avert these ripples? No, for it may happen daily and by chance. If you are deeply engaged in work—or even in subjugating emotion—noises may roar down the street, and you will not consciously hear them, or if you do will receive no impression whatever from them. It is the You behind the mind, which is for the moment detached, and the mind-stuff being in itself unintelligent receives no impression, while the real

You is busy elsewhere. This proves that the possibility exists. As a rule, however, you are not fixed in any profound work or contemplation and are at the mercy of the outer breezes, which blow over your mind-stuff and obscure the surface with foolish, useless passing impressions and thoughts—if they deserve the name of thought at all.

Continuing the image of the mind-stuff as a lake, let us take the bottom of the lake to represent the true, the Absolute Self in man. We can never hope to see the bottom unless the water is clear and the surface perfectly calm. All living creatures possess mind-stuff in varying degree, but so far as we know it is only man who can inspire his mind-stuff with intellect, and so use it as an instrument by which he can pass through the various stages of Yoga to the liberation of the soul.

Third aphorism: "At the time of concentration the seer rests in his own (unmodified) state." In other words, when we begin to concentrate and the mind-stuff is calm and we no longer need to identify ourselves with it, it is as when the ripples on a lake cease. We can then see down through the quiet translucency to what is beneath it.

Fourth aphorism: "At other times he who sees identifies himself with the alterations of the mind-stuff."

For instance, a grief comes and sets up a ripple in the mind-stuff. You can then no longer see the bottom of the lake (the true Self), which is quite undisturbed by the ripples of grief on the surface. When one loses sight of the true and immobile Self and identifies oneself with disturbed mind-stuff, the result is grief.

Fifth aphorism: "There are five classes of modifications (ripples) of the mind-stuff, some painful, others painless."

Sixth aphorism: "These are right knowledge, indiscrimination, verbal delusion, sleep, and memory."

Seventh Aphorism: "Direct perception, inference, and competent evidence are proofs of right knowledge."

This is an important aphorism. When two of our perceptions do not contradict each other we call it proof. But there are three kinds of proof. Direct perception is the first, unless the senses have been misled. Inference is the second, which is to say you see an indication and from that deduce the thing indicated. Third, is the direct perception of the yogin, which is of quite a different order from the normal perception. The two first forms of proof demand reason. The yogin need not reason; he sees and knows. For him time in the ordinary sense does not exist. In other words it does not flow past him, he beholds it like a picture, like something in which past, present, and future can be read at a glance, and his sight becomes proof. No ripples in or on the mind-stuff disturb him. He sees to the bottom of the lake; i.e., to the true Self in which all knowledge abides in calm forever.

What proof have we of the declarations of a person who says he thus sees? It is necessary that he should be an entirely disinterested and saintly person, that he should have passed beyond the illusions of the senses, and that what he says does not contradict the past certain knowledge of mankind, for no new truth can contradict any old truth. It can only amplify it. It is also necessary that the truth he utters should be verifiable. The seer must be one who does not sell his knowledge, and he should offer only what it is possible for all men to attain if they will. In these ways we can have direct perception, inference, and competent evidence as regards the true yogin.

There follow several aphorisms on the various sorts of ripples; memory, sleep, dream, etc., which disturb the mind-stuff.

Twelfth aphorism: "Their control is by practice and non-attachment." Why should this practice be needed? Because when a large number of impressions of one kind are left on the mind-stuff they form habits. This is consolatory, for if a man is a bundle of habits made up by himself he can unmake and remake the bundle. Character is nothing but repeated habits.

Thirteenth aphorism: "Continuous struggle to keep the ripples perfectly restrained is practice."

Fifteenth aphorism: "The state of mind which comes as the effect of giving up sense-desires and in which one becomes conscious of power of control over these desires is called non-attachment."

Non-attachment (or renunciation) means that the mind-stuff may be kept in the tranquil state in spite of the breezes of outer circumstance, which tend to blow it into ripples. Renunciation is the only means of attaining this end. Example: A man snatches your watch in the street. A wave of anger instantly rises on the mind-stuff. With all your strength withstand the rising of that wave. Fling your impulse elsewhere. Difficult? Yes. But when it is done and no angry word is said and the mind- stuff remains unruffled—that is renunciation. So with the sensual enjoyments prized by the ignorant as happiness. To deny access to them, to forbid their ruffling the mind-stuff with their images—that is renunciation. If you do not govern the waves or ripples on the mind-stuff, they will govern you. Governing them you attain power.

Seventeenth aphorism: "The concentration called Perfect Knowledge is that which is still related to reasoning discrimination, bliss, and unqualified egoism."

This is a very interesting aphorism. It declares that two sorts of attainment, known as Samadhi or ecstasy, are attainable by the yogin. The one described in this aphorism is the lower and has dangers. This one offers perfect knowledge of the subject of meditation—let us say, if that were the chosen subject, of the categories or elements of nature—and when this point of concentration is reached the mind-stuff will take in the forces of nature and project them as thought. In other words as *power.*

But Patanjali warns us that to practice Yoga only for the purpose of attaining the powers gained by complete knowledge of the forces of nature is a very dangerous thing. None but the entirely freed soul is fitted to use the powers, and this first state of Samadhi does not free the soul. It is still allied with reasoning discrimination, and egoism. The effect is to gift a man with the powers of a god, and what may not happen!

Can it be possible that some of the great manifestations of uncontrolled and evil power in the world have sprung from this source? For no man of spiritual instinct would enter Yoga with this end in view, and he who attains it thus has reached the stage which is called "bereft of body," i.e., is freed from the limitations of the flesh and becomes pure intellect. The dangers of this are obvious if it is not joined to what in Europe we call perfect spirituality, and

India understands much more by this phrase than we. Thus this lower Samadhi may be called the ecstasy of intellect. The yogin may attain all powers yet fail as a spiritual entity.

Eighteenth aphorism: "There is another spiritual Samadhi, which is attained by the constant practice of cessation of all mental activity, the mind-stuff then retaining only the unmanifested impressions."

This is the highest state of all. This is the perfect superconsciousness, which gives all powers and perfect freedom, perfect union with the Absolute, as taught in the philosophy of the Vedanta. The man who has attained this can fall no more, can return to no more rebirths. He does not need them—has passed as completely beyond them as the Absolute itself of which he is a part. The means to this end is to hold the mind-stuff free of all impressions of thought thus making it a perfect vacuum. Why?

An English poet expresses the reason in words perhaps more comprehensible to the western mind:

> If thou couldst empty all thyself of self,
> Like to a shell dishabited,
> Then would He fill it with Himself instead.
> But thou art all fulfilled with very thou,
> And hast such shrewd activity
> That when He comes He says, "It is enow.
> The place is full. There is no room for Me."

All our own small activities and "busynesses" of mind must be banished. There must be motionless stillness, or banishment of thought and reason, before what is higher than either—higher, no, but the ONLY—can take their place. In lower forms of consciousness the waves or ripples in the mind-stuff still remain in the form of tendencies. In this highest are no tendencies, nothing remains out of which proceed the seeds of rebirth and death.

Do you ask what remains if consciousness and knowledge are transcended? They are low states compared to what lies beyond both. To the ignorant mind they may seem to be Nothing, because extremes most truly meet. In the very low vibrations of ether we get darkness; the very high are also called darkness, for there also we cannot see; but the one is darkness, the other perfect light.

"So"—to quote Vivekananda's words—"though ignorance is the lowest state and knowledge the highest, yet the state of ignorance and that beyond knowledge appear alike to us. . . . Then will the Soul know it had neither birth nor death, want of neither heaven nor earth. That it never went nor came, that it was only the phenomena of nature, apparently moving past it, which convinced it that in itself were change and movement. . . . Then the freed soul can command, not pray. What it wills will be fulfilled. What it wants it can do."

Twentieth aphorism: "To some [this Samadhi]

comes through faith, memory, energy, concentration." In other words, by perfect spirituality. Those who study the Christian scriptures carefully will in a measure understand this aphorism, for there one may see it exemplified in certain cases without the Yoga training.

Twenty-first aphorism: "Success is speedy for those who long to attain Samadhi [the highest form of consciousness]."

Passing over many aphorisms I will come now to the physical means of attainment.

The first physical step is changing the mental attitude. This in India would be considered a physical step because the mind belongs to the phenomenal world, the world as reported by the senses. There must be feelings of good-will to all—"peace on earth, good-will to men." We must react to no evil, to no ill-will, and that side of renunciation being active stores up good energy in our favor.

Next comes the government of the breath. The word used in the aphorisms belonging to this section is *prana*. *Prana* represents the sum total of energy in the Universe. Whatever has life—and what has not?—is a manifestation or *prana*. All is therefore according to Patanjali a combination of *prana* (energy) and *akasha* (omnipresent existence). But *prana* is not breath; it is that which causes the breath. Mind-stuff draws in the *prana* or vital energy, and manufactures from it the various mental forces which preserve the body. And by controlling the breathing processes the various motions in the body and the nerve-currents can be controlled. It is the earliest way in Yoga of getting in touch with vital processes.

Later yogins state that there are three main currents of this vital energy in the body. One, they teach, flows through the right side of the spinal column, another through the left, and the third through a channel in the middle of the spinal column. The right and left are vital currents in every man, and through them all the functions of life are performed. The third, that through the middle, is latent in all but is used only by the yogin.

As Yoga is practiced, the body and its powers change. It makes, as it were, new channels for its power, on the same principle that formed habits may be said to make such ruts in the brain that they become automatic. It is obvious then that great and stedfast practice is needed to form the new bodily and spiritual habits. I should point out here that the directions as to deep and rhythmic breathing and the utmost simplicity of eating and drinking are more and more endorsed by modern medical science. They endorse them empirically—that is from watching the effects—for they do not know all the reasons these things are needful; but that perhaps makes their agreement more impressive.

How is this breathing to be done? The change must be gradual at first, for we are accustomed only to surfacebreathing and this is a very different matter. We must remember that the center which controls the breathing system has a sort of controlling action over the nerve- currents, and that this center is placed in our body in the spinal column opposite to the thorax.

This is why breathing-practice is enjoined in Raja Yoga. From rhythmic breathing comes a tendency for all the molecules in the body to move in the same direction; and this is needed, for when the mind is focused into will the nerve-currents change into a motion resembling that of electricity. The nerves have been proved to show polarity under the action of electric currents. This indicates the fact that when the will is transformed into nerve- currents it has something of the force of electricity. So the rhythmic breathing helps to transform the body into a gigantic battery of will. When this is gained, the yogin speaks of rousing the coiled-up power latent at the lower end of the spinal cord.

Now the point of rousing that power into action is as follows:

We know there are two kinds of action of the nerve-currents; one sensory and one motor; one centripetal and the other centrifugal. One carries sensation inward to the brain; the other outward to the body; but all are connected with the brain. Electric motion is produced only when the molecules all move in the same direction. Now when the force at the base of the spinal column is roused it rises through the center of the spinal column, and reaching that end of the canal which opens on the brain it helps to bring about what is known in Yoga as the perception which has no object.

All the sensations and motions are sent to the brain through the network of nerve-fibers. The right and left sides of the spinal column are the main channels through which the efferent and afferent currents travel. But Yoga teaches that the mind can send nerve-currents without any network of nervous system, if you can break the bad habit of depending only on the right and left channels. Yoga states that if you can train yourself to use the central channel in the spinal column you will solve this problem and be rid of the problem of matter. It is taught that when men pray with passionate fervor they unconsciouslyloose a little of this coiled-up power and so receive the answer—from outside as they suppose, but in reality from the latent power within themselves.

When the released power travels upward to the brain the reaction is tremendous; and when it reaches the brain the centers of perception become as it were illuminated with a great light.

The exercises are as follows:

Posture is important, for the body must be aware and alert. Sit straight upright, the chest, neck, and head must be in a straight line. First breathe in and out in a rhythmic way. That brings harmony and tranquillity. Then join to this the inward repetition of some sacred word. Repetition is advised because the act of repetition sets up certain rhythms and vibrations. The sacred word AUM is chosen in India because of its mystic meanings. It is a great sound-symbol and sums up all world sounds. It is composed of three letters A, U, M. The first letter "A" (pronounce as in French) is a root sound pronounced without touching any part of the tongue or palate. The "U" sound rolls from the very root to the end of the sounding-board of the mouth. "M" concludes the series and closes the lips on sound. And, for this and other reasons relating to various trinities of thought and worship, religious discipline in India has centered about this word.

Rhythm, concentration, and skilled breathing all tend to banish the enemies of progress in the science of Yoga. These are disease, sluggishness, doubt, indifference, pursuit of sense-enjoyments, stupor, false perception, diffused will, and restlessness. Grief, mental distress, tremor of the body, and irregular breathing are hindrances also.

Concentration will bring perfect repose to body and mind where it is rightly practiced.

Now for the first lesson in breathing after simple rhythmic breathing has been attained.

Let the word AUM flow in and out with the breath rhythmically. This is instead of the system of counting to regulate the breath. Gradually you will perceive the restful effect. It is better than sleep.

The second lesson when the first is learned is to breathe rhythmically, using the nostrils alternately. Close the right nostril. Draw the air slowly in through the left. When the lungs are full, close the left nostril and exhale the air slowly by the right. Repeat this process with alternate nostrils. This must be practiced for a considerable time to fit the pupil for higher breathing exercises.

The effect of this process will appear in the disappearance of harsh lines from the face and mental calm. It improves the voice immensely.

Then comes the third lesson. Fill the lungs with breath through the left nostril and at the same time concentrate the mind on the nerve-current it produces. Believe—*know*—that you are sending this nerve-current down the spinal column until it strikes with strength on the last plexus at the base of the spine where is stored the coiled-up energy alluded to. Hold the current there for a while; then realize that you are slowly drawing out that nerve-current with the breath into the other side and slowly expel it through the right nostril. Since this is difficult stop the right nostril with the thumb, and draw in the breath through the left. Stop both nostrils with thumb and forefinger while you realize you are sending the current down the spinal column and striking the latent force at its base. Then take the thumb off the right nostril, still stopping the left, and thus exhale the air. And so alternately.

At first begin by retaining the breath for four seconds. Thus. Draw air in for four seconds, hold it for sixteen. Throw it out in eight. Let all this be lessened if it is a strain. This done three times and with alternate nostrils represents one *pranayama* as it is called. Remember to concentrate on the strength at the base of the spinal column. Let the whole process be extremely gradual.

The next lesson is to inhale slowly and immediately exhale slowly. Then do not inhale for the same number of repetitions of AUM as in the previous lesson. At first begin all these exercises with only four in the morning and four in the evening.

One day the knowledge will come that the stored force at the base of the spinal column is aroused and at work. Then the whole aspect of nature will be changed, and the book of knowledge will be opened. The highest force in the body is *ojas*. This form of energy is stored- up in the brain, and its quantity determines intellectuality and spirituality. All forces in the body when not frittered away go to form *ojas*. And especially the reproductive and sexual energies when controlled are easily transmuted into *ojas*. Thus chastity and continence are an integral part of Yoga.

I think it should be noticed how in all the faiths when it is desired to form spiritual experts this form of austerity is not only recommended but enjoined. I believe this to be instinct in the western developments of monasti- cism, but in India it is science, for Yoga is the science of religion. I have no space here to follow this thought further, but I have found it well repays consideration. Yoga insists upon the chastity of Hippolytus or Galahad and issues the warning that without it there is danger.

We now come to concentration—a process most difficult in the West yet necessary for achievement. I noted in Count Keyserling's "Travel Diary of a Philosopher" that he recommends that this particular practice should be taught in all our schools. If I may venture a personal experience I may say I have found it invaluable.

The mind springs about like a monkey in a tree. One thought slips over into another and dilutes it. You start a train of thought and unconsciously are in another in a moment. Impossible! Yet the thing can be controlled.

You first sit and let the mind run on. Watch the monkey jumping. Take note of its tricks. Thoughts terrible, even hideous, may flash past. Watch. But you must sit as a spectator and distinct from what you watch. It is the mind-stuff which is rippling, waving, wavering, presenting distorted reflections. It is not you. You will observe the distinction. Gradually the motion of the mind-stuff will become less violent. While you watch, it will tend to calm. It will slow down. Thought will be less confused, mixed, and rapid. At last, and under the influence also of stedfast resolution, it will calm gradually. Finally it will be controlled. Then it can be concentrated. This process, it will be noted, is to watch and analyze the mind by focusing the ray of its own light on itself and examining it by that illumination, a process extremely rare in the West, where the power of the mind is almost invariably directed to objective or outside objects.

I may say here that I believe one value of the almost universal practice of prayer is that, however poor and small, for however unworthy objects, it is a form of concentration. There may be—I firmly believe there *is*— truth in the statements of great spiritual experts as to its might when realized as a power.

Of course, as in all else, all depends upon practice— stedfast, unhindered. The prize is great, but again the warning of Patanjali should be repeated. Nothing can be done without a teacher and one of the highest spirituality.

CHAPTER 7

CONCENTRATION AND ITS ATTAINMENT

When the mind is controlled it must next be focused on certain chosen points. Let us say certain parts of the body to begin with. Say you concentrate on the nose; after a while wonderful perfumes are smelled. If on the tongue, strange and delicate flavors. On the ears or eyes, beautiful sounds or lights may be perceived. And since Yoga asks no one to take anything for granted it puts forward these experiences that they may form tests of truth. Concentration should later be on high and sacred objects. Everyone will know what is his highest and will choose that.

Indeed, in the whole of Yoga there is selection. Certain points of it will for deep inherent reasons appeal to some more than to others. Follow those. But certain broad rules of high morality are the gateway for all, and a very simple diet, avoiding flesh and alcohol is necessary. There again I can add personal testimony to the value of a food system which I have practiced for very many years.

This must be true. As the organism purifies itself you must the more avoid disturbance. As a wise doctor said to me, "You see mud best in a clean wineglass." And it is true that the finest organisms are most easily thrown out of gear if foreign matter is thrust into them. But here again, great is the reward, even on lower planes than the beginnings of Yoga. I would say, indeed, that to simplify the food with the right motive, and as far as possible to exclude cruelties from it, is in itself a form of Yoga and has fine results. I have set this forth in my novel "The House of Fulfilment," which is concerned with the whole subject of Yoga, and shall say no more on that special point here.

Now when concentration and meditation become systematic and instinctive a very high point indeed is reached. The three planes of meditation are, first, the body as I have said above; then the mind-stuff and the intellectual world; lastly the Absolute—at first in its various aspects then in its one and unchanging. And, in meditating, the yogin becomes a part of what he meditates upon, as a crystal with red or blue behind it becomes red or blue. Realizing that he shares its nature he absorbs its powers. Here I quote a fine passage from Tennyson which is pure Yoga and should be deeply considered as a remarkable western experience of an oriental scientific result:

> For more than once when I Sat all alone revolving in myself
> The word that is the symbol of myself, [i.e., "I."]
> The mortal limit of the self was loosed,
> And passed into the Nameless, as a cloud
> Melts into Heaven. I touched my limbs—the limbs
> Were strange, not mine—and yet no shade of doubt
> But utter clearness, and through loss of self
> The gain of such large life as matched with ours,
> Were Sun to spark—unshadowable in words,
> Themselves but shadows of a shadow world.

That indeed is the difficulty. One cannot relate one's experiences in words, for words belong to the world of reason, not indeed a shadow world—Tennyson would scarcely have used that image had he known his Vedanta better—but a world where things are most erringly perceived. We need a new dialectic for the knowledge of psychic consciousness and of physical science, which is pressing forward more eagerly every day to meet the first and so flow with it, two rivers in one, to the ocean.

Max Müller says that these thoughts occurrent in the great minds of the West show that the Indian leaven still works in us. It seems that so it is. That it may work more strongly and generally must be the hope of all who dread the growth of materialism in western thought and life.

I do not for one moment deny that in some cases these austerities of Yoga were carried too far and so defeated their own end. This will appear in the experience of the Buddha. We find the same exaggeration in the experiences of the western mystic, especially in medieval times where such men as Suso appear in their nail-studded shirts. With that side of the subject I have no space to deal, though it exists. True Yoga is in all things wise and calm. I regret indeed that I have not space to give a more detailed examination of the discipline. But the bibliography appended will help those who wish to study it further.

Now what are the powers inherent in Liberation of the Soul, in passing "into the Nameless" as Tennyson puts it? Here the belief of the western reader will be sorely tried. Max Müller speaks of "the feeling of wonderment" produced.

The technical name for these powers is the *siddhis,* but avoiding foreign terms as I do I shall call them the powers. I can mention only a few. But let it be remembered they belong to the first or lower degree of ecstasy. They are still concerned with the world-as-it-appears, and therefore, though they have been used by such masters as the Buddha and the Christ, it was always with specified purpose and with what I may almost call a certain element of constraint and distaste. The reason for this is easily understood by those who have studied preceding chapters.

Patanjali expresses the truth that even omniscience or omnipotence in earthly phenomena does not free the soul from the chain of birth and death or unite it with the source. Therefore let it be remembered that the powers, however interesting, are not the goal of Yoga, and still smell of earth.

A man on attainment of knowledge acquires a power named *samyama.* This is the power of identifying himself with any object. I must unwillingly use this Sanskrit word, for English translations are circumlocutions. It means, as it were, *indenting* upon any object to take possession of its own powers. I can express it no better at the moment.

Thus, "by making samyama on word, meaning, and knowledge, which are ordinarily confused, a yogin may understand all animal sounds," says Patanjali. He will understand the meaning of any sound whether expressed by man or animal. Here I should direct attention to that passage in the Acts of the Apostles, where every man heard the apostles speak in his own tongue, whatever it might be. To an Indian mind there would be nothing strange in that statement. He would say they had made samyama on their audience.

So in the same way a yogin can make samyama on any man's body, and enter into full knowledge of the nature of his mind. Later, he can make samyama on his mind and possess himself of its contents.

Again, by making samyama on his own body, he can cut off its power of appearing as a perceived form, and can thus appear to vanish. For, by the yogin who has attained, the form of an object can be separated from the object. Those who have read my chapters on the world as a phenomenal world will see exactly how this can be. The yogin does not really vanish, but the ideal of his body becomes for the time unphenomenal; and indeed he can also make samyama upon the power of sight in those present and obstruct their view in consonance with his act. Here I refer again to the Christian Scriptures, where such disappearances are recorded.

By this, the power of making words or any object disappear are explained. And by making samyama on the impressions of his mind, which are now working and about to work, a yogin knows exactly when his body will die. The Hindus think this knowledge important because the "Song Celestial" teaches that the thoughts at the moment of separation of the soul and the perishable body are of consequence in their impression on the intermediate state before reincarnation. In the very singular "Tibetan Book of the Dead," to which I devote a succeeding chapter, are allusions to this belief.

The Buddha, the greatest of yogins, has left clear specific (directions as to the attainment of the "one-pointed state of mind." They are of profound interest as coming from him. I condense his words to his disciples:

"If, brothers, the disciple is living a life of virtue and is possessed of mastery over the senses and filled with clear consciousness he seeks out a dwelling in a solitary place. He sits himself down with legs crossed, body erect, mind present and fixed. Far from impressions that allure the senses, but still reasoning and reflecting he enters into the First Ecstasy, which is full of the rapture and happiness born of concentration.

"And, after the suppression of reasoning and reflecting the

disciple attains the inward peace and *oneness* of mind that is born of concentration, he attains the Second Ecstasy.

"And, after the suppression of rapture, the disciple dwells in equanimity and thus he enters the Third Ecstasy.

"And, further, brothers, when the disciple has rejected pain and pleasure, then he enters into the neutral clear- minded state of the Fourth Ecstasy. This, brothers, is called right concentration.

"Develop your concentration, brothers, for the monk who has concentration understands things according to their Reality. And what are these things? The arising and passing away of form, feeling, subjective differentiation, and consciousness."

This is the highest opinion the world can offer on this subject.

But to return:

By making samyama (or an indent) on the strengths of friendship, mercy, and such qualities, a yogin may excel in them, and remarkable instances of this are recorded.

When a yogin needs supernormal strength he may have it in making a samyama upon (say) the strength of the elephant. Infinite energy is at the disposal of any man if he knows how to get it. And this is a part of the science of Yoga. Again I call attention to stories in the Old and New Testaments. Suppose for a moment that Samson with his supernormal strength were a yogin— and his unshorn hair oddly connects him with the Indian conception of such a figure—it would be obvious instantly to the Indian mind how Delilah deprived him of it. Not indeed by cutting his hair, in which the ignorant supposed the secret of his strength to lie, but by flinging him into the stream of sensuality, whence he could no longer make samyama on energy and thus returning him to lower levels of consciousness. By making samyama on the Effulgent One, knowledge of what is happening at a distance or in places cut off by mountains can be had. This is because the yogin whose soul is utterly freed is at one with Omniscience and can draw upon it. And this applies to all various forms of knowledge, which in reality are all united in the One.

When the yogin makes samyama on the throat, sensations of hunger and thirst cease. Respiration and the heart's action can also be made to cease. Here I refer again to our Scriptures and to authenticated events in India with regard to the power of the yogins in suspending and renewing life.

When the soul is freed the yogin can by his power; enter the body of another. In the Hindu story of the life of Shankara, the great philosopher of the Advaita Vedanta, I gave such a case, which is typical of many. The yogin can enter a dead body, but also a living one by holding its owner's mind and organs in check. If he needs to enter the body of another he makes samyama upon it, because not only his soul but his mind has the quality of universality. For each individual mind is part of the universal mind, and he who has realized this from experience has power to work upon each and all. Here I suggest that such a power misused by a yogin who had only attained the lower (or intellectual) form of Samadhi would in India certainly be thought to account for certain forms of what is termed "possession."

By conquering the nerve-current that governs the lungs and upper part of the body the yogin does not sink in water. He can walk on thorns and sword-blades and can leave this life when he will. Here I refer to many stories in all the faiths, and it may be allowable to allude to the ecstatic joy of the martyrs in what would have been agony to ordinary humanity.

By making samyama on the relations between the ear and *akasha* or etheric or universal force, the yogin can hear supernormally at any distance. By making samyama on the relation between *akasha* and the body the yogin can levitate himself and pass through the air. Again I allude to our Scriptures and the evidence given for such events elsewhere. Can it be possible that the undoubted answers to concentrated prayer are gained by an unconscious samyama on the universal force? The yogin would certainly answer yes.

With these powers may come the glorification of the body in beauty, strength, and endurance. "Breaking the rod of time the yogin may live in this universe with his body." For that man there is no more death or disease. He possesses the elemental secret for renewal of the body processes and of that from which they are renewed. This will of course mean that the yogin will perceive time with far other eyes than ours. He will not perceive it as a flux, passing from minute to minute and hour to hour, but in its static and eternal quality. Perhaps one has the right to say he will perceive and use it as another dimension in addition to those we know logically and through the reason as length, breadth, and height.

By his knowledge the yogin will perceive beings on, other planes of being than those commanded by our own normal perception.

It is almost needless to say that the yogin will have no desire for heaven, which is a limited state, in so far as it can be said to exist, and one offering no real enfranchisement to the soul from the round of birth and death.

There is a curious view of the means of obtaining immortality for the body which I must mention before I quit the subject. Yoga claims that this can be attained by chemical means. There was an Indian sect named the Rasayanas, who, believing in Yoga, deplored the interruptions that death made in a man's acquisition of perfected knowledge. Mind has manufactured the body— then why cannot mind keep it in existence and in the state in which it would have it? These people believed the secret lay in chemistry. It was sought for especially in certain combinations of such substances as mercury and sulphur. Vivekananda states that many remarkable medicines of today in India are owing to the Rasayanas, especially the use of metals in medicine.

Some lower types of yogins use opium and self-hypnotism.

There are many yogins who believe that certain of their principal teachers have not died, but still inhabit their old bodies.

In this connection I may tell a story related by Max Müller, who naturally approaches the subject with extreme caution. I have alluded to what he says of his feeling of wonderment. He also says (condensed) :

"The same writer who can enter into the most abstruse questions of philosophy will tell us with perfect good faith how he saw his master sitting in the air several feet above the ground. One instance of these miracles supposed to have been wrought by a yogin in India must suffice.

"A writer with whom I have been in correspondence, the author of a short life of his teacher Sabhapati Swami, who was born in

Madras in 1840, relates not only visions which the young student had, but miracles performed in the presence of many people. We are told that it was in the twenty-ninth year of his age that Sabhapati, thirsting for a knowledge of Brahman, had a vision of the Infinite Spirit, who said to him:

"'Know, O Sabhapati, that I, the Infinite Spirit, am in all creations and all creations in ME. You are not separate from ME, nor is any soul. I accept you as my disciple, and bid you rise and go to the Agastya Ashrama where you will find ME in the shape of sages and yogins.

"In the dead of the night, for it was one A.M. when he saw this vision, Sabhapati left his family and traveled all night until he reached the temple of Mahadeva (Shiva) seven miles from Madras. There he sat for three days and three nights in deep contemplation and was again commanded in a vision to proceed to the Agastya Ashrama. After many perils he reached it and found there in a cave a great yogin, two hundred years old, his face benign and smiling with divinity. He had been expecting him. Sabhapati became his pupil, acquired Brahman knowledge and practiced Samadhi (ecstasy) until he could sit several days without food. After seven years his teacher dismissed him with words which sound strange in the mouth of a miracle-monger.

" 'Go, my son, try to do good to the world by revealing the truths which you have learned from me. Be liberal in imparting the truths which should benefit the householders. But beware lest vanity or importunity should lead you to perform miracles and show wonders to the profane.'

"Sabhapati seems afterwards to have taught in some of the principal cities and to have published several books, declining, however, to perform any miracles. In 1880 he was still living at Lahore. But though he declined to perform miracles he has left us an account of one performed by one of the members of his own order.

"About 180 years ago a yogin passed through Mysore and visited the raja, who entertained him with great reverence and hospitality. Meanwhile the Nawab of Arcot paid a visit to Mysore, and they all went with the yogin to his colleagues.

"The nabob being a Mussulman asked: 'What power have you that you arrogate to yourselves divine honor? and what have you that you call yourselves divine persons?'

"A yogin answered: 'Yes, we possess the full divine power.'

"And he took a stick, gave divine power to it and threw it into the sky. It was transformed into millions of arrows and cut branches of the fruit-trees to pieces, thunder roared, lightning flashed, rain fell in torrents. In the midst of this conflict of the elements the voice of the yogin was heard:

" 'If I give more power the world will be in ruins.'

"The people implored him to calm this havoc. He willed and all ceased and the sky was calm as before.

"I do not," adds Max Müller, "say that the evidence here adduced would pass muster in a court of law. All that strikes me is the simplicity with which everything is told, and the unhesitating conviction on the part of those who relate this. Of course we know that such things as the miracle related here are impossible, but it seems almost as great a miracle that such things should ever have been believed and should still continue to be believed. Apart from that, however, we must also remember that the influence of the mind on the body and of the body on the mind is as yet but half explored; and in India and among the yogins we certainly meet, particularly in more modern times, with many indications that hypnotic states are produced by artificial means and interpreted as due to an interference of supernatural powers in the events of ordinary life."

I quote this long passage because all qualified to judge know that Max Müller is a scholar deserving the utmost respect in every matter relating to the philosophies of India, and is furthermore a scholar of extremest caution in all his statements. That caution will be seen in his treatment of the above events. I take issue with his use of the word "supernatural" in connection with the point of view of yogins in such matters, because no true yogin would admit for an instant that these or any such happenings could be supernatural. The word "supernatural" implies the breaking or suspension of a law, and that can never be. They would say they were supernormal—much above the common, naturally, but strictly in conformity with a higher knowledge of law.

I should not have quoted this passage but for its authorship, because very much clearer and more careful observations have been made by a European, a Frenchman named Jacolliot, who was chief justice of Chander- nagore, and spent many years in India in investigating the occult and recording his own direct observations and conclusions. I have given a full and exhaustive account of them in my book "The Way of Power" and cannot include them here. His own expression is that he records things as he saw them, without taking part in the dispute as to their cause.

I think it is not too much to say of Max Müller that he is not inclined to disagree with the chain of philosophy involved in Yoga, but that he shrinks, as a European would, from the conclusions to which it leads. That at least is the impression left on my own mind by close study of his works. As to the effect of Yoga in its form of concentration, in sharpening and strengthening the intellectual powers, I assert fearlessly that there can be no doubt at all upon the subject.

In reference to the conception of time in Yoga, I must give a very interesting passage, interesting because it is so closely related to some modern conceptions on that point

Vivekananda explains Patanjali's aphorism on the subject as follows:

"Patanjali speaks of the succession of time. Patanjali here defines the word 'succession' as the changes which exist in relation to moments while we go on thinking. With each moment there is a change of idea, but we perceive these changes only at the end of a series. This is called 'succession.' For the mind that has realized omnipresence, there is no succession. Everything has become present for it. That is to say, to that mind the present alone exists, and the past and future are lost. Time stands controlled by it, and all knowledge flashes into it in a second."

Vivekananda does not here put what he means very well, though his meaning is perceptible. He should not say "past and future are lost." They are only lost in the sense that they are perceived—past, present, and future— as unity—the eternal Now. Nor should he use the expression "a second." A second is as much a division of the phenomenal succession of time as a century.

However, I think the meaning of his comment on Patanjali's remarkable aphorism is clear enough.

It is desirable that I should give some passages from the Upanishads themselves that it may be seen on what the philosophy of Yoga has been built. The philosophy of Yoga, though inchoate, was ancient when these were comparatively young.

The Svetasvatara Upanishad says:

"Where fire is churned or produced by rubbing [for sacrifice], where air is controlled [by Yoga practices], then the mind attains perfection.

"Placing the body in a straight posture, with the chest, throat and head held erect, making the organs, together with the mind, perfectly established in the lotus of the heart, the sage crosses all the fearful currents of ignorance by means of the raft of Brahman.

"The man of well-regulated effort controls the *prana* with its other manifested forms, and when it has become quieted breathes out through the nostrils. The persevering sage should hold his mind as a charioteer holds the restive horses.

"By taking shelter in caves where there is not too much wind, where the floor is even free from pebbles and sand and fear of fire, where there are no disturbing noises from men or waterfalls, and in places helpful to the mind and pleasing to the eyes, the mind is to be joined in Yoga.

"Forms with appearances like snow, smoke, sun, wind, fire, firefly, lightning, crystal, and moon, gradually manifest the Brahman in Yoga.

"When the five-fold perceptions of Yoga, arising from [concentrating in the mind as] earth, water, light, air and ether, have appeared to the yogin, then he has become possessed of a body made up of the fire of Yoga and will not be touched by old age, disease, or death.

"The first signs of entering Yoga are lightness of body, health, thirstlessness of mind, clearness of complexion, a beautiful voice, an agreeable odor in the body, and scantiness of excretion.

"As gold or silver covered with earth, when cleaned, shine full of light, so the embodied man, seeing the truth of the Universal Self as One, attains the goal and becomes sorrowless."

Here is a quotation by Shankara from the Brihada- ranyaka Upanishad. The interlocutor is a woman named Gargi.

"Practicing the desired postures according to the rules, the yogin will become their conqueror. Seated on a deer or tiger skin and first worshiping Ganapati (the lord who removes obstacles) with fruit and sweetmeats, he will then resign himself to his care, take an easy posture, and place his right palm on his left. Then, accord-, ing to the prescribed way, he will sit facing the east or north, and hold his throat and head in the same line, with lips closed, body perfectly immovable, and eyes fixed on the tip of the nose.

"He should avoid too much food or fasting, in accordance with the prescribed way, for without it his practices will be fruitless. [The directions are here repeated.]...This should be practiced for three or four years or three or four months according to the instructions of one's master, in secret—that is to say, alone in a room—in the early morning, at midday, in the evening, and at midnight, until the nerves become purified. Lightness of body, clear complexion, and good appetite are the signs of purification of the nerves." Then follow the breathing directions, etc.

It must be fully realized that bodily health is made an essential of Yoga. As Radhakrishnan finely says the body can be made the basis either of animal incontinence or divine strength. This is a basic principle of Yoga. We are to control the body, not to torture it. Therefore we must abstain from stimulating drugs, foods, and drinks. As to the respiratory exercises, they are endorsed by eminent medical men, as a means of strengthening the heart's nutrition and action. But it must be remembered that Yoga, especially in its more advanced stages, calls for great endurance and should never be undertaken alone. A teacher is essential.

Lest this philosophy should be thought "Indian" and "emotional" let me quote another great European in whom "the leaven of the Indo-Aryan" evidently still persisted. I allude to Schelling, the German philosopher. In his "Philosophical Letters upon Dogmatism and Criticism" he says:

"In all of us there dwells a secret marvelous power of freeing ourselves from the changes of time, of withdrawing to our secret selves away from external things, and of so discovering to ourselves the eternal in us in the form of unchangeability. This presentation of ourselves to ourselves is the most truly personal experience, upon which depends everything we know of the supersensual world. This presentation shows us for the first time what real existence is while all else only pretends to be. At that time we annihilate time and duration of time. We are no longer in time, but time, or rather eternity itself, is in us. The external world is no longer an object for us, but is lost in us."

This is pure Yoga.

As I have said there are different aspects of Yoga for different natures and some are apparently born (India would say as a result of karma) with faculties in that direction partially or highly developed. I repeat that the powers are considered as of no spiritual value in themselves. The Buddha unfrocked a monk for using them, though on some special occasions, like the Christ, he permitted and used them. But Yoga does not recognize only one way of attainment. Besides the disciplined Yoga of which I have given a description are three other roads to perfect freedom of the soul. I will mention them very briefly for I have dealt with them fully in another book. There is *Karma Yoga*—to live a life of good deeds and devoted family and social service.

There is *Bhakti Yoga*—the life of utter love and passionate devotion, which, because love is the great breaker of the prison of selfhood and false individuality, must also lead to perfect freedom. And there is *Jnana Yoga,* the insight—the cold white flame of pure reason, which thrown upon the Mind will search out and destroy its weaknesses, blindnesses, and follies.

But the straightest, swiftest road to freedom in right hands is that of which Patanjali has compiled the guidebook.

Many will attribute much, if not all, contained in these two chapter on Yoga to self-hypnotism, or fraud. Only those can judge who have closely studied the subject; and it must not be denied or overlooked that in parts of India the ignorant have identified some of the Yoga detailed by Patanjali with the baser forms of the Tantric cult, and that the fraud and charlatan are always with us whether in East or West. But allowing for all these, my own convictions have brought me to the decision that as an integral and noble part of Indian philosophy, however tinctured with early superstition and later degradations, it would not be possible to omit it. It teaches that by faith and concentration we may transcend the normal limits of human vision, and realize that these do not limit the universe.

This subject of Yoga is a high and difficult one. At points there is symbolism that only the instructed can pierce and reach the truth behind. Remember also that Yoga is in many respects a key to the highest teachings of the Indian philosophies, including that of the Buddha. The Buddhism of Ceylon and Burma shrinks from this conclusion because Buddha asserted that he held nothing back "in a closed fist" from his disciples. True, but these disciples did not think that the meat for men is diet for babes; and in Tibet and elsewhere it is held that in the Buddhist faith are teachings "ear-whispered" from master to pupil from time immemorial; and these were studied at the great Buddhist university at Nalanda where the occult held its due place in the curriculum.

I end this chapter with a sentence from Radhakrish- nan which may serve to endorse the value of Yoga as a gift to the West. We are only beginning to realize what great gifts India brings us, gifts not to be feared but welcomed, as she will welcome the best of ours. With this saying of Radhakrishnan's I fully agree.

"It is good to know that the ancient thinkers required of us to realize the possibilities of the soul in solitude and silence, and to transform the flashing and fading moments of vision into a steady light which could illumine the long years of life."

CHAPTER 8

"THE SONG CELESTIAL" AND THE HIGHER CONSCIOUSNESS

Even in India are many misconceptions as to what is meant by the enfranchisement of the soul as taught in Vedantic philosophy—that enfranchisement by which the perceptions are cleared and the inward sight sees the universe as it is in truth. This subject begins to be touched in western philosophy. Dr. Bucke wrote a book chiefly upon western experiences which he called "Cosmic Consciousness"; and in books by other writers allusions to the subject are increasing, though for want of knowledge of Vedantic teaching they are not perhaps very well understood by the general reader.

In writing in this chapter of "The Song of the Lord," or "Song Celestial" (the "Bhagavad Gita"), this mystic state of consciousness cannot be passed over, because that famous and noble book offers one of the most remarkable descriptions of the way to it and the achievement.

In India exist two great epics in some respects comparable to the Homeric epics in that they embody the lives or legends of national heroes—or those who have attained to that position by reason of their place in these national epics. But there is a great difference. The Indian epics exist to represent not only history and patriotism but also the philosophy and religion of the people.

Like the Homeric heroes the Indian protagonists are often of immortal descent. The gods move through the pages at home with them. But moral and philosophic lessons are drawn which have the weight and sanctity of scriptures. And the Mahabharata and Ramayana may in consequence be said to be the Bibles of the people as well as their inexhaustible treasure-houses of story. The Mahabharata is sometimes honored with the title of the Fifth Veda.

A treasury of story indeed! I read almost daily in both, marveling at the vast fertility, the tropic splendor of romance unfolded in either, but still more at the nobility of ideals set forth, the great passion for the Unseen, the Beautiful, and Entirely Desirable, both in man and woman, which has always been the soul of India.

The Mahabharata is a vast poem, a world in itself. It consists of about 100,000 *shlokas* or stanzas. It comes from the hand of no one man. It is not even a compilation in the strictest sense of the word. It would seem to have grown by the force of accretion; legends, reflections, parables, fitting in here and there as if drawn by affinity.

It is thought that the nucleus of the story began about 3000 B.C. in the subject of a struggle between two clans for the mastery in the country now known as Sirhind, between the Jumna and Sutlej rivers. That in itself was as simple a story as the rape of Helen and the Trojan wars, but it grew and grew. Through its stages of growth I will not follow, for that would take volumes and I am concerned only with a part. In this vast and little-known epic—a series of gorgeously colored romances of lovely queens and mighty kings, full of a fascination that only those who care for true romance can realize—lies embedded a pearl of whose beauty and luster the world is aware. It is known as the Lord's Song—or the Song Celestial—and it represents one of the highest flights of the conditioned spirit to its unconditioned Source ever achieved. It is assigned to the fifth century B.C. though opinions as to dates vary.

William von Humboldt voices the opinion of many in describing it as "the most beautiful, perhaps the only true philosophical song existing in any known language."

The story is briefly this. It is a struggle between the powers of good and evil, of justice and injustice. The good is represented by the five Pandava princes, brothers —one of them the King Yudishthira—and their wife the Princess Draupadi, who represents all that is noble and desirable in womanhood. Evil is represented by their cousins the Kuru princes.

I wish I had space for the adventures and deadly insults which led finally to a great pitched battle for supremacy at

Kurukshetra. Of the five Pandava princes, Arjuna, the great archer, with his mighty bow Gandiva, is the most human and lovable. He is about to enter the fight, terrible in destruction as a god, and his friend the god Krishna, most beloved of all Indian deities, has honored him by acting as his charioteer. The air resounds with war-cries and drums and the furious roar of conch- shells, each called by its name as though it were a living personality.

> The High-Haired One [Krishna] blew Panchajanya. The Wealth-Winner [Arjuna] blew God's Gift. The Doer of Grim Deeds, Wolf-Bowel, [Bhima, a Pandava prince] blew the great conch Paundra.
>
> The wild roar cleft the hearts of the enemy and made the heavens and the earth to ring.

Arjuna shouts to Krishna:

> "Set my chariot, O Never-Failing, midway between the two armies, while I behold those with whom I must strive."

All is ready for the decisive battle. Arjuna looking over the battlefield perceives his brothers led by King Yudishthira the eldest. But on the other side, though he sees the hated Duryodhana and others who have insulted and trampled their rights, he beholds also beloved, reverenced, and kindred faces, the noble Bhishma and others, cousins and friends whom he loves and honors. Suddenly the horror of civil war and, above all, war between kindred rushes upon him and brings with it a crisis very well known to psychologists, which may be called the Dark Night of the Soul. Henceforth he represents the eternal question of mankind, as Job does in the Hebrew Scripture.

He turns to the god Krishna, his charioteer, who has already set his chariot midway between the opposing hosts, and speaks:

> "As I look, O Krishna, upon these kinsfolk meeting for battle, my limbs fail and my face withers. Trembling comes upon my body and the upstanding of hair.
>
> Gandiva [the bow] falls from my hand and my skin burns.
>
> I cannot stand in my place. My mind whirls.
>
> Contrary are the omens, O Long-Haired One! I see no blessing from the slaughter of kinsfolk.
>
> I desire not victory, O Krishna, nor kingship nor delights. What shall kingship avail me, O Lord of Herds, or pleasures of life?
>
> Teachers, fathers, sons, grandsons, kinsmen also! These though they smite me, I would not smite.
>
> O Troubler of the Folk, shall not we with clear sight see the sin of destroying a race?
>
> Ah me! a heavy sin have we resolved to do, that we strive to slay our kin from lust after the sweets of kingship.
>
> Better it were for me if these folk with armed hand should slay me unresisting in the fight."
>
> So spake Arjuna and sat down on the seat of the chariot and he let fall his bow and arrows, for his heart was heavy with sorrow.

This section is entitled "The Rule of Arjuna's Despair." The next is called the "Communion of the Blessed Krishna and Arjuna." Krishna speaks:

> "Why, O Arjuna, has come upon you this defilement such as is felt by the ignoble? Cease from this base faintness of heart, O Affrighter of the foe!"

Arjuna speaks:

"O Madhu's Slayer, how shall I contend against Bhishma and Drona who are worthy of honor?

More blest would it be to eat the food of beggary without the slaughter of noble masters.We know not which is best, whether that we should overcome them or they overcome us.

My soul is stricken with the stain of unmanliness; my mind all unsure of the Law, I ask you, 'Tell me clearly the more blest way.

I am your disciple. Teach me.'"

So spoke to Krishna the Terror of Foes.

> "I will not war!" he said to the Lord of Herds, and so made an end of speaking. And as he sat despairing the High-Haired Lord with seeming smile spoke.
>
> "You grieve over those for whom grief is unmeet. The instructed grieve not at all either for those whose lives are fled or for those who live.
>
> Never have I not existed. Never have you nor these princely men not existed. Never shall the time come when we do not exist.
>
> As the body's tenant [the soul] goes through childhood, manhood and old age in his body, so does it pass to other bodies.
>
> It is [only] the stirring of the instruments of the senses that begets cold and heat, pleasure and pain. It is they that come and go and do not stay. Bear with them, son of Pritha!
>
> But know that THAT which pervades the Universe is imperishable. None can destroy that Changeless One. It is the bodies of the Everlasting, Incomprehensible Body-Dweller which [only] have an end. Therefore fight!
>
> He who thinks one man a slayer and thinks the other slain is without perception. This [soul] slays not nor is it slain.
>
> This never is born nor dies, nor can it ever come to non-existence. This unborn, everlasting Ancient is not slain when the body is slain. As a man lays aside outworn garments and takes others that are new, so the

> Body-Dweller puts away outworn bodies and goes to others that are new."

(It may be interesting here to give Sir Edwin Arnold's translation of this passage:

> Nay, but as when one layeth
> His worn-out robes away,
> And taking new ones sayeth,
> "These will I wear to-day!"
> So putteth by the spirit
> Lightly its garb of flesh,
> And passeth to inherit
> A residence afresh.)

Krishna continues:

> "You do ill to sorrow for any born beings. To a warrior there is nothing more blest than a lawful strife.
>
> Happy the warriors, O son of Pritha, to whom such an unsought strife opens the door of Paradise. Holding in indifference pleasure and pain, gain and loss, conquest and defeat, make ready for the fight! Thus shall you touch no sin.
>
> Therefore do your deeds indifferent to gain or failure. Set yourself to the Rule. Skill in works is the Rule."

Arjuna speaks still pleading in doubt for knowledge of the Rule. How shall a man say in these matters? What do? Krishna replies. A strange scene for such an argument with the battle-field set, swords loosened, arrows on the string. Yet all pauses, as it were, for the end of this strange drama.

> "He who is without desire for anything and neither loves nor loathes whatever fortune befall him has wisdom securely based.

> When such a one draws in the feelers of his senses as a tortoise retracts its limbs he has wisdom securely based.
>
> Only he who entirely holds back his senses from desire of the sense-objects has wisdom securely rooted.
>
> The man who casts off all desires with no thought of mine or me enters the peace.
>
> This is the state of abiding in Brahman, O son of Pritha. He that has entered it is not confounded. If even at his last hour he enters he passes to absorption in Brahm."

So the soul is the only pure and untainted spectator of the struggles of mind and body. The idea of struggle, of right- and wrong-doing, is confined only to the world as the senses present the world. It is a dream—or rather a distortion. Let the prince rise above it to the Truth— the passionless impassivity of the soul! But yet Arjuna is not at peace, and still the battle waits. Again he questions the Troubler of the Folk what is the certain way by which he can win to assurance in this dreadful entanglement of right and wrong.

The god answers:

> "In this world the foundation is two-fold. There is the Wisdom Rule, and the Rule of good deeds without being hampered by good deeds.
>
> No man can be idle, therefore do your ordained deeds according to the Law, for deeds are better than idleness. Even the subsistence of the body cannot be gained from idleness.
>
> [But yet] the world is fettered by deed excepting in the deed which has sacrifice for its aim. Fulfil your deeds with this aim and stand free from attachment [to your deeds], O son of Pritha."

In the lines that follow the god points out how he also works in the world of appearances as man knows it, and how it would fall into ruin if he did not. Yet how he is Changeless, Unmoving throughout. Here is magnificently drawn the picture of the Personal God who is but an image cast on the mind of man—a distorted image— of the Unchanging Absolute. In other words, here He presents the Truth, and beside it the relative partial truth by which man must live in this world until he has attained the higher perception.

> "There is nothing in the Three Worlds that I must needs do, nothing that I have not. Yet I work.
>
> Deeds are done by the Moods of Nature. I created the Four Castes according to this Order of Moods and Deeds. Know that I am the Doer of that deed, yet I do no deeds. I am Unchanging.
>
> Deeds are done altogether [only] by the appearances of Nature but he whose self is confounded by the thought of T imagines 'I am the doer of these.'
>
> But the man who knows the truth of the two orders of aspects and deeds, O Mighty Armed One, knows that appearances dwell in appearances, and he has no attachment.
>
> Casting off all your deeds upon Me, fixed on the One Absolute Self, be without desire and without a 'me' or 'mine.' And fight!
>
> Those who fulfil My teaching are released from deeds."

But Arjuna, still seeing this serene blue dimly through the mists of earth's passions, must still question.

> "Then what moves a man to sin, dragged ever against his will as if violently?"

Krishna speaks:

> "Love and anger, sprung from fiery desire, mighty to devour, mighty to evil, these are the foe. As fire is smothered in smoke, as a mirror with soilure, as the germ by a membrane, so is the world observed.
>
> The knowledge of the wise man is obscured by this his eternal shape-changing enemy, hard to drive off and greedy.
>
> The sense-instruments, mind, and reason are called its seat. Through these it confounds the body's Tenant, hiding knowledge.
>
> But, knowing the Self to be higher than reason and leaning your self on Self, O Mighty One, slay this difficult foe."

Here follows a beautiful passage in which the Rule of Good Deeds, the Rule of Wisdom, the Rule of the discipline of the yogin, and that of loving devotion to the Divine are all gathered together like marshaled warriors for an attack on that conception of the world presented by the false report of the senses. Bliss consists in following in the spirit of true and joyous renunciation. There is bliss in doing these things, but beyond even these there is a higher bliss in renouncing them one and all, when the true perception is reached which transcends them.

> "Therefore arise, son of Bharata's race, and comprehend the Law, slaying with the sword of wisdom this unbelief in the Self, an unbelief which lurks born of ignorance in your heart."

And still Arjuna cannot understand. How is it possible there should be a state above good deeds? And still patient the Divine Charioteer expounds:

> "He who knows the Truth knows well that he does no deeds at all though he sees, eats, wakes, sleeps, breathes. For he remembers that the sense-instruments are the objects of the sense-inst-ruments."

(Therefore they are as illusory as the senses themselves.)

> "The Supreme accepts neither any man's sin nor his good deed.
>
> The instructed see indifferently a wise and accomplished Brahmin or an outcaste, knowing that I am He in whom sacrifice and austerity meet, the Sovereign of all, the world's friend of all beings he wins to peace."

Then follows a superb and mystic passage on the serene detachment of the yogin, "abiding alone in a secret place, utterly subdued in mind, without desire and without possessions, calm of spirit, perfect in the vow of chastity, given over to Me."

How great is the charm by which these thinkers of India, extinguishing every desire but the desire for the One, the Alone, draw the soul by a fascination irresistible as the music of Krishna's own Flute that whoso hears must follow! Magnificent are the teachings of the Upanishads, most wonderful the commentaries upon them of Shankara and the Sankhya—that other brilliant and akin system of high philosophy—but the Song Celestial, in which all these struggle, as it were, for agreement, is more divinely beautiful than all. It may be that its Setting helps it—the silent-waiting battle-field, the tortured soul of Arjuna, the serene presence of the conditioned deity, who yet in another aspect is the Unconditioned; but in all spiritual writing I know none that wins the heart and allegiance like this, or so overflows the soul with peace.

The unearthly music proceeds:

> "He who sees Me in all things and all in Me, he cannot be lost *to Me nor I* to him."

But still Arjuna trembles beyond the border of Realization. How can the fitful, fickle human mind stay itself on so great a certainty? Suppose he essays, but swerves from human appearances of good thought and deeds and the like, and so does not reach the eternal Truth; what then? Will he not have sold his birthright for a mess of pottage? Who can be sure of reaching so high, so terrible a goal?

There comes an assurance of eternal beauty in word and meaning:

> "Son of Pritha, neither here nor in that Other World is there *destruction* for him, for none that seeks righteousness, beloved, can come *to* harm.
>
> He that falls from The Rule [still] wins to the worlds of them that do right deeds and dwells there many years. And then he is born in the house of pure and well-doing people.
>
> There he is given the lordship of the knowledge which he had in his former body."

In other words he has not lost by his former attempt to scale the Unthinkable. He has made a blessed place for himself, whence he may renew the attempt.

> "For he is led onward (as it were) without will of his own by that former striving."

He will surely in the end know the Absolute Truth, for the Self in him is drawing him to Itself.

> "There is nothing higher than I, O Winner of Wealth. All this Universe is strung upon me as rows of jewels upon a string.
>
> I am the taste in water, the light in sun and moon, the A U M in the Vedas, manhood in man.
>
> The Might of the mighty and the Heat of the fire, the Wisdom of the wise, the Splendor of the magnificent.
>
> From me come the moods of goodness, fire, and melancholy. I am not in them but they are in Me.

> And bewildered by these three moods the whole universe fails in understanding that I sit above them and am Changeless.
>
> For my divine magic of moods is hard to see through, but they who cling to me transcend this magic."

Hearing this loveliness the prince climbs a step higher into the Void. He trembles now on the verge of discovery.

"What is this Brahman? What is this One Self?"

The Lord speaks:

> "It is the Imperishable; the Supreme. [But] the creative force that brings life into being wears the name of Deeds.
>
> The worlds pass and are gone, but for them who have come to Me is no rebirth.
>
> Now will I declare a royal mystery.
>
> By me, Formless, is this universe filled. When a cycle is ended, all beings reenter into my Nature. When a cycle begins again I remold them.
>
> Yet I am not fettered by deeds, O Winner of Wealth, for I am indifferent and unattached to deeds. But to those who desire me I give power to win and maintain.
>
> They who worship other gods, and offer to them with faith, in truth make offering to me though not according to ordinance.
>
> For I am He that has lordship of all sacrifices.
>
> If an eager one sets before me a leaf, a flower, water, I am content with this devotion.
>
> Even they that are born of sin turning to me enter the High Path."

So it proceeds and Arjuna, catching flame at fire, at last breaks into the cry:

> "Supreme art Thou, Supreme Glory, perfect in power and purity."

And, hearing as the mystic song proceeds, he is swept away, battle-field, himself, all forgotten; and he prays for the Vision of the Supreme Consciousness of the Supreme.

> "Show me Thy Changeless Self, O Sovereign of the Rule!"

And in a flash he sees:

> As if the light of a thousand suns should suddenly rise in the heavens.

Nowhere so greatly is the vision set forth as here. I have not space for it.

> Thereupon the Winner of Wealth, struck with bewilderment, hair standing on end, bowing his head, with clasped hands addressed the Divine.
>
> "God, in Thy body I see all the gods. As moths with exceeding speed seek a fire so Thou devourest and lickest up the worlds."

I cannot give what follows—the trembling speech of the mortal on whom the Divine breaks in a wave of thunder. It must be read uncondensed and as it is. The Lord speaks:

> "I am Time that works the destruction of worlds when they are ripe. How can these warriors live even if you strike not! By me they (and all) are doomed to death. Arise! Fight!"

So it proceeds and in the end fulfilled with understanding, Arjuna speaks:

> "Bewilderment is ended. By Thy Grace I have received wisdom. Freed am I from doubt. I will obey."

And like a mighty warrior he acquits himself in the battle, conquering and to conquer. And all is better than well.

Ended is this book of the Song.

What I have given is only the condensation of a few passages. Those who read the Song Celestial must not expect any logical solution of the problem of how the Absolute becomes for the moment the conditioned or personal God. Logic has no foothold in such spheres. The sole answer is that Arjuna has at first eyes only for that plane. He sees the deity from the human plane, and therefore sees him under—shall we call it—semi-human conditions. Later his eyes are opened: he realizes the Absolute, and all problems are solved for him or rather exist no longer.

There can be no higher expression of united religion and philosophy than the Bhagavad Gita—no more powerful expression of the four Yogas by which the spirit of man may live; the four roads which are yet one and indivisible. The word *maya* to which I have alluded before is often used in the Song Celestial. Perhaps the best translation in this case may be "partial consciousness," which of course results in distorted and therefore entirely misleading views as to the real constitution of the Universe. It is sometimes alluded to as the "magic" of the Supreme.

It will be noted that when Arjuna receives the flash of universal consciousness it comes in the form of more than mortal light. As it says in the Song Celestial:

> "Another sun shines there!—another moon.
> Another light, not dusk, nor dawn nor noon.
> And they who once beholding come no more—
> They have attained My peace—life's utmost boon."

But the light at first dazzles. Thus says one of the books on the Vedanta: "It is light inside, light outside, a light alone and holier than holy. It is the Light that lights all light, Uncaused. And it is the light of the Self."

So when the Indian saint Ramakrishna Paramahamsa, who died about forty years ago, received the higher consciousness, it is told that he was passing through the corn-fields near his native village when suddenly he beheld "glory" and lost all sense-consciousness. Afterwards he was able to describe it. He said:

"The Living Light does not burn. It is like the light of a jewel, shining yet soft, cool, and soothing. It does not burn. It brings peace and bliss."

Yet I think this varies in different experiences. In the case of St. Paul it was a searing, blinding flash, but this may be perhaps accounted for by his former violences and persecutions. The spirit may have been insufficiently prepared in certain directions.

In the case of Mohammed the experience is said to have befallen him in the solitude of a cave on Mount Hera, about three leagues from Mecca, where he was lost in meditation. As in the night he lay wrapped in his mantle he heard a voice calling, and when he uncovered his head, a flood of unearthly light broke upon him so intolerable that he swooned away. It was an illumination of the understanding also, and he "beheld the decrees of God."

Sometimes the revelation comes in the form of a flood of joy, which is described in India as "indivisible Existence, Knowledge, and Absolute Bliss." There can never be any more grief or perplexity for those who have once been submerged in this shining ocean.

In India, in relation to this consciousness, all roads lead home. A prayer daily repeated by millions says:

"As different streams, having different sources and with wanderings crooked or straight, all reach the sea, so, Lord, the different paths which men take, guided by their different tendencies, all lead to Thee."

In all who receive this consciousness appears the Vedantic realization that perception means wisdom as opposed to ignorance and that such phrases as good and evil are left behind and below.

I should like to point how small beside this attainment of the higher consciousness and true supermanhood (to which I should have given volumes instead of pages) appears the Nietzschean ideal of the superman, and yet how likely to catch the more superficial spiritual sense of Europe. It cannot even be said to be original in all that is of worth in it. Confucius had conceived the superman two millenniums before, and India in the Vedantic and Buddhist systems had given the world an ideal of what the highest form of manhood might be.

But neither India nor China had divested that ideal of what it pleases Nietzsche to call "slave morality." It still kept the chivalry of pity. A very good case for Nietzsche can be made if that side of his unbalanced teaching is omitted; but never if it is surveyed as a whole. There are sentences which seem to place him in the ranks of those who have perceived, but his pendulum always swings back into the darkness.

Nietzsche has the underbred scorn for the weak and sorrowful. The Vedanta, with the Buddha and the Christ, scorns self-pity and mercy to one's own weakness —for these there is no room in the morality of any of the three. And all three crave power, for a man must acquire much stored power before he can use it to guide and control others. They recognized that no blind man can lead another; but they never identify virtue with power, for they know that power is only a part of virtue —a part which if it is permitted command will result in what is called in Yoga the Lesser Samadhi, where excelling knowledge and intellect uncontrolled by love and wisdom will lead a man into the frightful excesses of absolute power, of which the world has seen examples.

There is no room in modern life for scornful supremacy of the Nietzsche brand. For this man, who was blind to the higher values, there is no place save as a historic memory in the coming synthesis of philosophy and science. Most truly he calls himself a decadent, he who enthrones the base individual selfhood in man.

The superman thus preached by a crazy decadent opposes the greatest philosophies of all time, and it was surely the reply of ironic Fates that the creator of the European ideal of the superman died helpless and broken in brain.

Having omitted the mention of other European philosophers, I have recalled Nietzsche only because in some respects he is Europe's answer to the Vedanta. It is to be wished that he with his great gifts had known and studied it more fully. We should not then have heard the blind statement that the superman is not yet born, nor have inherited the flat axiom: "Demand nothing of yourselves contrary to probability." He had never mastered the implications of evolution; an old-fashioned outworn mode was his, glittering with the lacquer of a brilliant modernity but no more. *Requiescat in pace,* and may Europe emancipate itself from the shadow of his "tragic optimism"!

Because it is not necessary to the understanding of the Hindu spirit, nor to any but students of philosophy, I have not dwelt upon all the six systems based on the Vedanta as I have on those of Shankara and the "Bha- gavad Gita." I have felt that the processes of reasoning were of less importance to the general reader than the large result. Yet, for those who care to study, all the six systems have deep importance.

How profound in the *Mimansa* is the thought that the whole universe is only the *meaning of words,* in other words, that only the idea is real! How great the *Vàishnava* with its insistence that the Divine may be adored *through* the senses, and that every earthly passion may thus be transmuted into divinity! Even where they appear destructive and contradictory the heart of them is clear of earthly taint. See compassion pushed even to the extreme by the Jaina system, or comprehend the brilliant, logical clearness with which the Nyaya fights what it considered the skepticism of Buddhism. It is not wonderful that it has been held to be one of the four limbs of the Veda and that Manu recognized it as holy. Even such a realistic system as *Nyaya* contributed, as do the other five, to the spiritualization of life.

Where Shankara outsoars it, is in his knowledge that the methods of reason cannot be applied to the higher flights of religion and philosophy, and the "Bhagavad Gita" breathes air in which the *Nyaya* dies. But that does not lessen its importance to students of philosophy— a subject on which I think indeed that none is competent to speak in East or West who does not know the six systems. I have not willingly omitted such men as Bad- arayana and Ramanuja and must beg remembrance of the fact that this is but a popular and bird's-eye view of a vast subject. Yet I am not without hope that it may send some seekers to the sources of a philosophy which regards this as a mind-born world, and finds its sustenance in ideas, not appearances.

CHAPTER 9

THE GREAT RENUNCIATION OF THE BUDDHA

In approaching Buddhism we are approaching not only one of the profoundest philosophies of the world but one of the greatest faiths. It has swayed the lives of uncounted millions. It is possible from its strange affinities with modern science that its future may be greater than its past. It is a child of the Vedanta, though in India (except in Nepal) it perished, killed partly by the skill with which the Brahmins manipulated certain likenesses to their own systems of thought, partly by monastic teachings, which those holding by the Laws of Manu could not but regard as antisocial in their tendency.

But great was its destiny. It was to spread far and wide, to capture the spirit of Asia in Tibet, China, Korea, Japan, Burma, Java, Siam, and Ceylon and elsewhere; and it is beginning to capture such minds in the West as cannot satisfy themselves with the dogmas and failing influences of the Christian churches. I do not speak of the teachings of Christ. That is another question.

First I will give a sketch of his life. Then I will exam- ine the philosophy.

The founder of the Buddhist philosophy was born, according to the best opinion, about six centuries before Christ in the district of Northern India now known as Behar. His father is said to have been a wealthy chieftain or prince of the city of Kapilavastu and was ruler of the Shakyas. Thus the Buddha was a member of the Kshatriya or warrior caste. His father's name was Sud- dhodana. His mother's name was Maya. She died seven days after his birth, and the child was nourished and fostered by her sister and co-wife Mahaprajapati. The word *Buddha* represents a title which may be translated "The Perfectly Awakened" or "Enlightened." His given name was Siddhartha, which means "He who has attained his aim." His family name was Gautama. He was heir to his father's princedom.

In the Buddha we meet with the only character which in spite of inherent differences can stand upon a spiritual parity with that of the Christ. Some would say, and perhaps not wrongly, that his intellectual power was mightier and stood higher.

For these reasons his personality has impressed itself upon the world's consciousness as none but that of the Christ has done. Both exhibited that indefinable power which mankind cannot resist because it appeals to the highest in them and summons them to the most cruel difficulties of renunciation and suffering with a promise of far-off peace as the ultimate.

Bacon perceived this strange anomaly in man, which is indeed one of his most spiritual qualities. Call a man to relinquish warmth, comfort, a good dinner, and he will grumble. Call upon him to die for an idea—his country, his faith—and he goes forth radiant to torture or death. And the Buddha asked none to travel by a road which his own feet had not marked with blood.

We find him first young, handsome, a prince of the noble Aryan race, with mental gifts that must have distinguished him apart from birth and beauty, an only son, heir to wealth and consideration. But we find him the prey of deep unhappiness. Love was his—for he had married a wife, whose beauty, according to tradition, was enhanced by all womanly graces. He had an infant son whom he had named Rahula, "a fetter," for already the spiritual leaven was working in him which compelled a sad prescience of the fragility of earthly ties. But neither wealth, nor intellect nor human love could shut out the black riddle of the universe—the sorrow of man—which pressed upon him and corroded all his joys with a black and bitter realization of senseless injustice and cruelty.

It is said that his father, terrified by his melancholy and aloofness, commanded that the triple secret of disease, old age, and death should be hidden from him and that, secluded in his palace grounds, he was not to be allowed to guess their existence, for the father feared that such knowledge would drive Siddhartha to the passion of the ascetic for solitude in the woods and mountains, and that not only would the son be lost but the princedom pass away into the hands of strangers. And around it lay Maghada and Kosala, great kingdoms, very willing to swallow their lesser neighbors.

It is told that the accidental sights of an aged man, of a man deadly ill with fever, and of a corpse followed by weeping mourners, enlightened the future Buddha as to the further miseries of the world and determined him to seek some Law, some understanding, which should account for these seeming caprices of most pitiless gods. Life became a nightmare of injustice and horror to him. He shuddered at its possibilities.

At about this time, now freed from palace trammels because he knew the worst, he went one day in his chariot to see the plowing of his father's lands, still fixed in sorrowful meditation.

The sights about him deepened his pain. In the great heat the laborers, young or aged, still must toil. He saw them, their bodies bent, struggling with all their might, wet hair falling about haggard faces, fouled with mud and dust. The plowing oxen—they also toiling so pitifully and with no reward—their lolling tongues and panting breath, the whip and goad indenting smooth flanks until blood ran. All those things tortured the heart of Siddartha as he sat, for the sufferings of our kindred the animals also wrung it. And he said:

"This world is built on pain, and its foundations laid in agony. If there be a Way, where is it? I am bound in the dungeon of despair."

So, nobly moved to sympathy, he sat alone, forcing himself to behold the suffering of man and beast and in all the universe could see no refuge or reason. Slowly, at length, passing down the road he saw a man carrying a bowl in his hand, wearing a coarse robe of yellow. And their eyes met. And it seemed to the prince that he had never before seen one who resembled this strange mendicant, and he rose, saying in his heart:

"Who is this person? For his face is calm, and his eyes bespeak a soul at rest. And what is this bowl in his hand?"

And even as he thought this the stranger answered him with grave salutation:

"Great lord, I am a religious mendicant, who, shuddering at the problems of life, seeing all things transient, have left the fetters of my home behind me to seek for some happiness that is trustworthy and imperishable, that looks with equal mind on friend and enemy and does not regard wealth or beauty. Such is the only happiness which will content me!"

Siddhartha in deep amazement at this repetition of his own thoughts asked eagerly: "And where, O wise man, do you seek it?"

"Great lord, in solitude, in the quiet of deep woods. There in the Quiet dwells Enlightenment. And I carry this bowl that the charitable may bestow an alms of food, and this is all I ask of the world. And now, pardon haste, for my way lies onward to the mountains where enlightenment awaits me."

And he passed on, but the prince returned to the city submerged in thought.

He sought his father and announced his resolve to seek the solitudes after the ancient fashion of the Arya, and there, deeply meditating, to find deliverance for himself, for those he loved, and for all the world.

I must not here dwell on the agony of his father and of the commands and lures put forth to restrain Sid- dhartha. I have told that piteous story in my "Life and Teachings of the Buddha," which I have called "The Splendour of Asia," for by no lesser name can this man be known.

He appears to have kept his resolution from his wife Yashodara, but to have prepared stedfastly for his escape from the trammels of sense which enclosed him. The tradition tells that on a certain night he heard strange voices borne on the wind, which convinced him that the time had come:

"Mighty One, O Mighty One,
There is a Way—a Way!
The wise of old have trodden it.
Rise now and go,
Finding the Light,
Share it with men.
Thou who in past lives Didst agonize for men,
Again go forth,
Riding to victory."

It is told that he called his charioteer Channa and bade him saddle his noble white horse Kanthaka, and that in dumb grief Channa obeyed. Then Siddhartha entered the little marble chamber where Yashodara slept with her child, all unconscious of the shadow of sorrow darkening above her. Twice he stretched his arms to clasp her and the child, and twice withdrew them lest he should waken her to agony sooner than need be. And it is told that at last he kissed her foot and stooped to breathe their breath but no more—knowing with anguish that he sacrificed her joy with his own for the world's sake, and so went forth leaving the two sleeping. His age was then twenty- nine.

He mounted his horse while Channa stood aside white as death, and he said to the horse:

"O brave in fight and fearless, put forth strength in a sterner battle, for tonight I ride far to seek deliverance not for men only but for your kind also. Therefore, for the sake of all, great horse, carry me far this night!" And as he passed out into the road beyond the gates the prince turned and said softly: "Never again shall I come here unless I conquer old age, disease, death, and sorrow."

And Channa followed. So they rode far, and at last on the edge of a great wood the royal horse stopped to drink, and the prince dismounted and looking into the horse's eyes he said:

"You have borne me well." And to Channa: "And you, O faithfullest—even before this night I knew you for a true man, but now I know more, for you have come with me utterly disdainful of profit, courting danger and rebuke. My heart will remember! Now take Kanthaka and return."

He gave a chain of jewels to Channa, He sent the crest-jewel of his turban to his father in remembrance. Of Yashodara he said no word, for that lay too deep. Channa pleaded all the relationships, the broken hearts, but in vain. The prince replied:

"What is relationship? For were I to die I must leave them. The kinships of this world are as a flock of birds, which settle on the same tree at night and disperse at dawn. When I have found the Way I shall return. Not otherwise."

He turned and stroked the head of Kanthaka, who bowed it to his master's foot.

"My horse, gentle and noble, your good deeds have gained their reward. No painful rebirth awaits you, this I know. Be content, for it is well."

Then taking his jeweled sword he cut off the knot of hair which he wore as an Aryan of high birth, and as he did it a hunter passed, clothed in coarse garments. Giving him his rich garments, Siddhartha took the hunter's in exchange and put them on. Then turning he looked into the eyes of Channa for the last time and, with no word said, made his way to the forest, parting the boughs with his hands, and so passing was seen no more. And this is what is called in Asia the Great Renunciation.

It is told that the prince was tempted in the wilderness by the regrets and desires of his own heart, taking visible shape in the melancholy beauty of Mara the Tempter, who is no devil but an epitome of all the heart's cravings. Resisting these he passed on to Rajagriha, the capital of King Bimbisara of Maghada. There, among the Vindhya Hills, lay many solitudes and caves wherein recluses assembled to consider and study the ancient philosophies of India, hoping, as did Siddhartha, for light upon the problems of life. And he betook himself to the cave where sat the Brahmin Alara, for this man's reputation was great in Aryan India.

He was lost in meditation, seated in the "lotus" posture, and at a respectful distance Siddhartha took his seat, wondering if this teacher held the key and waiting until it should please Alara to address him.

This done, the Brahmin agreed that the prince should study the Vedas and Upanishads under his guidance, and informed him of the rules of the various teachers and the fruits to be expected from their practices and asceticisms. He described the sufferings enjoined and the resultant births in Heaven, with millions of years of bliss before the soul should be launched again into the dreary round of *samsara*—or wanderings through births and deaths.

Siddhartha like the other ascetics took possession of a cave and set himself to study; and they marveled at the calmness and nobility of the young man who had forsaken the world for things spiritual. Once and again, his father sent officials to recall him, but though gentle and courteous as ever he would not hear. That life was dead.

Clad in the yellow garment of the ascetic he descended daily into the city of King Bimbisara to beg his food, extending his bowl for alms. On one of these occasions the king beheld him and said:

"Look on this man, lords; beautiful is he, great and pure, with all the signs of Aryan birth. His eyes do not wander. He is self-possessed, serene, and solitary. Ask where that mendicant goes."

It was done, and the king followed with his lords and inquired his story; hearing it he lamented Siddhartha's departure from the world, and implored him to return, offering him a share in his own kingdom, for he recognized his power and majesty. But Siddhartha replied: "World-renowned and descendant of Arya, I hear with veneration! Just and blessed is the way of a great king, but for me my Way is onward, and behind me lie the Five Desires. Would a hare rescued from a serpent's jaws return to be devoured? But you—return, O wise king, to your happy city. May all good go with you." And the king replied: "Great prince, that which you seek may you attain, receiving the fruit of your birth." And he followed him a little way in reverence, and then with his nobles returned to the city.

With Alara, Siddhartha studied so patiently that the ascetics who followed Alara besought him to become their master. But after some years had passed it became clear to him that the answer to the riddle did not lie, as the Brahmin taught, through ever-increasing spiritualization of the selfhood of man—though it was clear that this had been worth studying. Those great planes of spiritualization, lying one above the other, were as the medicament of a sore disease, but they were not its annihilation. There was left a spot of infection—though but a spot— by which the process of ever-recurring ignorance and consequent birth and death could begin again. Sorrowfully he betook himself to another teacher, Uddaka, and here again disappointment met him. He studied patiently until the pasture was eaten bare, and they had no more to offer.

Then he resolved to leave them and betake himself to Uruvela, there to practice a terrible asceticism, thinking that perhaps the soul might spring free from the almost utter wreckage and destruction of the body. This he did beside a pure river, entering upon the most cruel discipline of hunger and thirst and silence, with his end in view. But he was very weary, and he said in his heart:

"Long is the night to him who is sleepless, long is a mile to him who is tired, long is life to him who knows not the Law."

So he set himself to meditation, daily lessening his food until it became a morsel incredible to the mind of man, and after a while he spoke to no man, sitting mute and motionless, controlling even his breath. So still he sat that birds and beasts moved about him unafraid, and his fame as a great yogin spread far and wide. The greatest of all yogins.

Afterwards he said to his disciples:

"I remember when a crab-apple was my only daily food. I remember when I swallowed only a single grain of rice. Like dried reeds my arms and legs, my hips like a camel's hoof, like a plait of hair my spine. In the hollows of my eye-pits my eyeballs well-nigh disappeared. And yet with all this mortification I came no nearer to knowledge."

At last when he could think no longer, and dumb instinct awoke in him, as the brain almost ceased to function.

"If I could crawl down to the river the water, warm and kindly, would refresh me, and perhaps the power of thought would return."

And inch by inch he crawled to the water and lay in a warm shallow utterly fordone, and five ascetics with whom he had held counsel and who expected great results from his incredible sufferings said, one to another:

"He will die now. The ascetic Gautama will die."

At last supporting himself by a bough, he crept up the bank a little refreshed and could think once more. And he thought:

"This way of mortification has utterly failed. My body cannot support the intellect. I will eat and drink and strengthen it. It may be possible that my six years of struggle have prepared the way to Right Ecstasy."

Near by dwelt the young wife of a wealthy householder, owner of many herds; and she had vowed that if her prayer were granted and she became the mother of a son she would present every year an offering to the tree spirit of the wood; and now the little son was born and she was full of gladness.

So she took her best milk and boiled it with purest rice, herself making the fire and cooking it. This lady, Sujata, sent her maid Punna to see that all was prepared for her offering beneath the tree in which the spirit dwelt; and the maid ran, and beneath the tree was seated the Buddha-to-be. She believed him to be the tree spirit and rushed back to her lady; and Sujata put jewels upon her for a reward of good news, and placing the milk-rice upon a golden dish set forth, glad at heart.

A very beautiful account of this incident survives in tradition.

"So she came along the river-bank, glad in the dawn, robed in gray like a cloud before sunrise, and about her slender wrists were bracelets of white chalcedony, and the gray and white of them resembling the river bubble before it breaks, and she came as softly."

Seeing the prince she knew at once that it was no tree spirit but a holy ascetic in the last stage of exhaustion. Pity and reverence moved her heart, and raising the golden dish in both hands she offered it humbly; and he partook of the pure food, while she watched with such joy as that with which a mother watches her child eat. And the virtue of it flowed through him like oil to a lamp extinct, and seeing this and wishing him attainment she departed, caring no more for the golden dish than as if it had been a leaf upon the ground.

But the ascetics said angrily:

"The ascetic Gautama has failed. He has nothing to teach us and is a backslider. Come, let us go to Benares!"

But Siddhartha, strengthened, felt energy swelling in him like a great river in spate, and he set stedfast steps toward the tree whereunder he was to receive Enlightenment.

From a man cutting grass for his cattle he begged an armful of pure and pliant grass; and seeing before him a noble tree resembling a tower of leafage, he spread the grass beneath it and seated himself with folded hands and feet, resolving never to leave it until he had entered upon Enlightenment. And the night came softly down and veiled him from the sight of man.

It was a night of terror and temptation. Body and mind, apart and united, tempted him beyond human endurance. Visions of his life of love, luxury, and power, beset his body. Intellectual doubts and difficulties attacked his mind. Delirious dreams and delusions fell thick as snow about him. But love and deep compassion for the sorrows of mankind held him firm, and he clung to his purpose as a great ship plows her way through tempest and tossing billows to the haven where she would be.

And when the darkness thinned and the east became faintly gray he received Enlightenment. Not partial. Not intermittent, but clear, stedfast and perfect. He had attained the highest consciousness, and received it with a cry of "Light!"

He beheld past, present, and future as One. He beheld true causation and the secrets of birth and death and the passing on into new lives. He beheld the so-called individuality or ego of man unraveled before him into its component parts like the unwoven threads of a garment, beholding in them no immortality or durability. And he beheld the Truth—the Way of Escape. Illumined with all wisdom sat the Buddha, the Utterly Awakened, lost in contemplation of the universe As It Is, having entered the Nirvana of peace. About him day and night made their solemn procession unseen, for he was lost in bliss. And at last, lifting up his voice, he cried aloud in triumph his song of victory:

> "Many a house of life
> Has held me, seeking ever that which wrought
> The prison of the senses, sorrow-fraught.
> Sore was my ceaseless strife.
> But now,
> Thou builder of the body-prison, now
> I know thee! Never shalt thou build again
> These walls of pain,
> Nor raise the roof-tree of deceits, nor lay
> Fresh rafters on the clay.
> Broken the house is, and the ridge-pole split.
> Delusion fashioned it.
> Safe pass I hence deliverance to attain."

He had triumphed. For a while he sat in blissful contemplation doubting whether it were possible to convey his knowledge to the world. I quote here as I have done already from "The Splendour of Asia," for there I have already set this marvel forth.

"O bliss inexplicable, not to be confounded with others but singular, lovely, and alone; not in the heavens unattainable save by the strength of gods, but within reach of all who set their faces to the heights in true endeavor. For the little children of the Law as for the wise and noble. And at the last—not the dewdrop lost in ocean but the ocean drawn into the dewdrop. Thus, flooded with sunshine and bathed in peace, sat the Perfect One."

Here he received an offering of food from two Burmese merchants named Bhallika and Tapussa; the first whom he accepted into discipleship. Then rising, he determined to go to Benares to seek out the five ascetics who had scorned him and to open their eyes. His teachers, Alara and Uddaka, were now dead, otherwise his first duty would have lain there. On his journey to Benares he met a proud young Brahmin, who none the less was interested by the great personality of the mendicant who passed him. Hoping to trap him he cried aloud:

"Ha, master! What constitutes the true Brahmin?"

And the Exalted One replied: "To put away all evil, to be pure in thought, word, and deed—this it is to be a Brahmin."

The unexpected answer troubled the haughty man. He said with hesitation: "How is it that your face is so beautiful, shining like the moon in still water? Whence the peace that surrounds you? What is your noble clan and who your Master? Here in this country where all men struggle to find the Way, what is your Way?"

And He Who Has Attained answered: "Happy is he who has seen the Truth. Happy he who in all the wide world has no ill-will, self-restrained and guided. And highest is the bliss of freedom from the thought— *I am I.* No honorable clan have I; no Teacher. I go alone and content."

And the Brahmin's pride was hurt and he replied curtly, "Reverend person, your way lies onward," and struck into the opposite path, not knowing that opportunity had met and missed him.

So the Blessed One came to Benares, to the Deer Park of Isipatana where dwelt the five ascetics. Seeing him come, they said scornfully among themselves:

"Here comes the ascetic Gautama, he who eats rich food and lives in self-indulgence. Let us show him no respect nor rise to meet him. Let us only give him a seat as we would to anyone, and he can sit down if he likes."

But the nearer the Lord Buddha came the more did the majesty of his presence precede him, nor could they hold their resolution. They rose, and one took his cloak and alms-bowl, another brought a seat, a third water, and he sat and bathed his weary feet.

It was to these five that he preached his first discourse, and their eyes were opened upon joy. One, since called Kondanna the Knower, begged that he receive them as disciples, and he answered:

"Draw near, monks; well taught is the doctrine. Walk in purity to the goal of the end of all sorrow.

So they passed into perception and realization.

The news spread swiftly, and about him gathered very many young men of great family and high caste, wearied with the sensualities of life and its society, eager to hear of joy and the ending of sorrow. One story of such a rich young man is worth recording. His name was Yasas. His riches are detailed, his power of gratifying every wish directly it was formed. Also his satiate weariness of life, for the germs of nobler things were in him.

One night he lay among his women and sickening to nausea at pleasure, he rose and walked out into the quiet of the garden, glittering in pure moonlight, and he said aloud:

"O my heart, how oppressive it is! O my soul, the speechless weariness! Who in all the world shall show me any good?"

So wandering on he came to the Deer Park of Isipa- tana, and there in moonlight Gautama meditated and he heard what Yasas said. And he understood, for he himself had been a rich young man, and he said:

"Sir, you are weary, but I hold in my hand a life that is neither grievous nor wearying. This teaching is not afflicting. Nor is it oppressive."

And Yasas took off his gilded shoes and sat down beside the stranger. First the World-Honored spoke of the misery, worthlessness, and ruin of lust, of the strong calm of renunciation, the high way of the Law; and in place of burning disgust and weariness there flowed into the heart of Yasas the cooling streams of wisdom. Merit won in former births drew him to the Truth as a pure silken fabric is with ease dyed a noble color. And the Lord Buddha set the Way before him. Then in the dawn Yasas rose and said:

"It is impossible that I should return to a life which I now see to be unreal and foolish as a tale told by a madman. Receive me into the Order that I may spend my life in acquiring knowledge."

And the Blessed One answered: "Come, monk. The doctrine is well taught. Lead henceforth a new life." Presently his father, the rich guildmaster, came running to ask whether his son had been seen, and he too fell into talk with Him Who Has Attained; and the great teaching caught him, and he cried:

"Wonderful, great sir, most wonderful! It is a lamp set in a dark place. May the Lord take me as a lay disciple!"

He was accepted as a believing householder, and he looked upon his son, now divested of gold and jewels and clad in the yellow robe, and the Buddha asked him: "Is it possible, householder, that Yasas, the noble youth, should return to a life of lusts and pleasures?"

He replied: "Sir, it is not possible. It is gain to Yasas that he should be set free."

So after this fashion the wealthy and poor crowded about the Buddha, nor did he repel any, be his caste what it might. Nor yet did he repel women, not even those of light life.

Very strange is the story of Amra, the harlot, who came to visit him hoping that her beauty might plead for her, might even possibly deflect the Teacher, as in former days great sages had been deflected into desire by the beauty of the Maids of Heaven. But when she came, "within the shade was One seated with folded hands and feet, and lost in calm he looked out into the worlds."

And the rock-crystal that was her heart melted and flowed in a river of tears, and before his feet she fell and laid her face on the earth.

So, incited and gladdened with high discourse, this Amra entered into the highest knowledge and, attaining, wrote a psalm of victory that still survives.

Very fine indeed are the Psalms of the Sisters, the women who left all to follow the Light, having realized the impermanence of appearances taught by the senses and leaving behind them fear and grief. I cannot give them here, but they are deeply worth study.

So the people crowded about him, and at last he dispatched sixty disciples to carry his teaching abroad. Then, preparing himself, he set out on foot with certain of his disciples to visit his father and his home—the city of Kapilavastu.

In all the faiths and stories of the world there is scarcely anything more poignant than that return.

His father, having heard of his renown as a great teacher—an honored name in India—prepared to receive him with resignation; as one chastened indeed, far fallen from what his father as a wealthy ruler and man of the warrior caste had hoped, but yet endurable. The people, bewildered but more deeply impressed, had made their preparation of arches and garlands and offerings, for they thought:

"To what people has the like happened? He will return a glorious teacher."

Now as they thought this, and his father surrounded by his great men waited, looking along the dusty road they saw a young monk, yellow-robed, carrying an alms- bowl. He begged his food from house to house, receiving what was given in serene silence, passing on with patience when refused. And it was Siddhartha.

Then shame and love and anger contended in his father's heart and tore him like a whirlwind in the leaves of a tree; he clenched his robe across his breast and cried aloud:

"I am put to horrible shame. My son a beggar! Our race is beaten to the earth with shame."

"My father, this is the custom of our race."

He angrily denied this. "Not one of our ancestors has begged his bread."

And the Buddha answered: "Maharaja, you and your high race claim descent from kings, but my descent is far otherwise. It is from the Utterly Awakened of ancient days, and as they have done so do I and cannot do otherwise." And then, seeing his father still in grief and anger, the Perfect One said:

"Do I not know that the ruler's heart bleeds and that for his son's sake he adds grief to grief? But now let these earthly bonds of love be loosed, for there are higher. Let my father's mind receive from me such food as no son has yet offered to father."

And leading his father by the hand they entered the palace. Within it the Perfect One thought of another, but she was not there; for her very life beat against her body, as she thought: "I cannot go. If the mother of his son is of any value in his eyes he will come to me."

So the World-Honored rose and, attended by two of the mightiest of his disciples and followed by his father, he went to the dwelling of his wife; and he said to the two:

"Monks, if this lady should embrace me do not hinder her, though it be against the rule." (For no monk may be touched by a woman.)

Pacing beside him the two understood the Lord Buddha's compassion and bowed their heads.

So they entered the hall where stood Yashodara, her hair shorn, clad in a coarse robe of yellow. When she saw him, pride and love, each stabbed to the heart, strove within her, and with piteous eyes she watched him as he stood calmly regarding her with a look she could not understand. Then she ran to him and falling on the ground laid her face upon his feet and embraced them, weeping bitterly. There was silence, and none hindered her, and so she lay.

But after a while remembrance came to her of the distance wide as heaven and earth between them. She rose with majesty and drew apart, while his father declared to the Exalted One her griefs and patience and mortifications, and how she had resigned all, that she might resemble him in the austerities of her life. The Buddha heard and, speaking slowly with his eyes still fixed upon her, said:

"This is true. Great also was the virtue of this high lady the mother of Rahula, in a former life, which I remember with gladness and she will one day remember. Mother of my son, the Way that I have opened is for you also. Come and hear."

So, that evening seated by the river, the Perfect One taught the Way before his own people; and this high lady, seated, veiled that none might see her hidden eyes, heard also, and as she heard she knew and perceived the Unchanging, the Formless, the Beautiful. The illusion of time fell from her; she beheld her love no longer cast aside but eternal as the eternity of the Self that alone endures. And the imprisoning self, which alone can suffer, died within her and left her enfranchised and glad—and she knew the Truth.

And so it was also with the father of the Perfect One and with others.

Next day Yashodara called her son Rahula and said to him: "Go, now, beloved, and seek your father and ask for your inheritance." She led the boy to the window and pointed: "That monk—a lion among men—he whose face shines like to the sun in its strength, he is your father. Demand your inheritance."

He ran quickly and caught the robe of the Blessed One with tears of joy, asking his inheritance; but to test him the Exalted One for a while was silent, until at last, reaching the Nyagrodha Grove, he turned smiling to Sariputta, his great disciple, saying:

"Monk, what think you? For worldly wealth perishes, but this remains. Let us admit him to the Order."

It was done, and the heart of Yashodara sang within her for bliss.

In the caves of Ajanta there is a fresco, very ancient, more beautiful than the most beautiful if such a thing can be said. It is the great figure of the Perfected One returned to his own people, serene as the moon in the deepest solitudes of the heaven, when all the stars are dimmed in light; and looking up to him from far below are the figures of his wife and son, adoring with the love that transcends words, as to one who has given them all good.

So, leaving joy and peace behind him and measureless content in the soul of Yashodara, the World-Honored returned to Shravasti on the river Rapti, and to his work of making gladness and the defeat of sorrow known among the people.

CHAPTER 10

THE LIFE AND DEATH OF THE BUDDHA

There comes now an interesting passage in the life of the Buddha and this history of philosophic religion. About this time his foster-mother, she who had nourished him after the death of his mother, sent to the World-Honored a message from herself, from Yashodara and from other great ladies. It was to this effect:

"Full of hindrances is the household life, very free the life of the homeless for such as would walk in the Way! Let the Blissful One permit that women also retire to the peace of the homeless life, under the discipline taught by the Lord."

But he returned no answer; and a second time they asked, believing that women have much need of the Peace. His foster-mother Prajapati herself came and made this request with tears, and he answered:

"Enough, lady. Do not make this request."

So wandering and teaching he came to Vaishali, and Prajapati with shorn hair and yellow robes, followed by many of the Shakya ladies, journeyed there on foot and waited in the porch of the Pagoda Hall, very sorrowful. There the beloved disciple Ananda, cousin of the Buddha, met them and seeing their feet cut and bleeding from travel, and their faces covered with dust and tears, asked the reason. Having heard all he went to the Buddha and besought for these women and was refused. Again and yet again he besought—in vain. But pity urged Ananda to perseverance, and he said:

"Lord, if women retire to the homeless life, is it possible for them to attain Arahatship [the higher consciousness] ? Escaping from sorrow can they reach this?"

And he in whom is all truth answered: "They can attain."

Then Ananda gladdened (his name means Joy), and he said:

"Then let the Blessed One think of the Lady Praja- pati! She is sister to the mother of the Blessed One, and at her breast he was nourished. Let them be admitted. If they can thus end sorrow, should it not be permitted?"

And the Buddha answered: "I cannot refuse. If they will accept eight weighty rules in addition to those accepted by the Order and will be subject to the Order it shall be reckoned to them for ordination."

And when, standing patiently, they heard this, sorrow passed from them, and with joy they accepted the Rules.

Later, the Buddha meditating said: "If, Ananda, women had not accepted ordination under my discipline religion would have endured a thousand years in India. Now even with the eight weighty regulations it shall not endure."

And this is true of India, excepting Nepal, but elsewhere it has grown like a great tree.

It is needless to say that with his great discipline and his Enlightenment, the Buddha had acquired the supernormal powers; but he did not love their use and there are few records of his dealing in them or permitting those of the Order to use them. For in all the world is nothing but the flawless beauty of Realization; and the wise know there is no miracle, only a higher law unknown to the ignorant, which in its action appears to them strange and a miracle. Therefore, did Gautama teach that for those who have reached the higher consciousness the bonds of time and space and form exist no more. But he taught also that to expose these mysteries before the ignorant who see them with fear or greed is perilous and useless. Yet some records exist. As thus:

To the city of Rajagriha (the capital of King Bim- bisara) went with him his mighty disciple Kassapa, so great and wise that many of the people of Rajagriha were in doubt which was disciple and which master. But the World-Honored, willing to honor Kassapa and to demonstrate a truth, thus addressed him in presence of the king and people:

"Welcome, great master, welcome! Rightly have you won wisdom, and now as a wealthy noble displays his treasure to bring forgetfulness of sorrow to those who love beauty, so do you!"

Immediately Kassapa, composing himself into ecstasy, was raised up in the air, and this wonderful sight caused them to magnify the Buddha and implore his teaching. And he taught. So again also the Lord Buddha told this story while he rested once during the rains at Jetavana—that beautiful garden and dwelling presented to the Order by the faithful merchant Anathapindika.

There was a faithful, noble disciple who desired to hear again the words of Him Who Has Thus Attained; and he came in the evening to the river Acirivati, hoping to cross by the ferry. But the boatman had himself gone to hear, and there was no ferry. Then, joyfully meditating on the light and lost to all else, that disciple walked on the water of the river, and his feet made no holes and he went as if on dry land. But suddenly in the midst he saw the waves, and he remembered, and his joy sank and his feet with it—for he feared, and fear is a fetter of the world of form, where illusion is strong. But again he strengthened his inmost soul in meditation, and he walked on the water; and so came to Jetavana and saluted the Blessed One and sat respectfully beside him.

Gautama asked: "Disciple, did you come with little fatigue by the road? Did you lack for food?"

And he answered: "Lord, in my joyful meditation I received support so that I walked on the water and did not sink."

And the Buddha said: "So it also was in past lives."

We hear of his crossing a river in flood—standing suddenly on the other bank by use of the powers and enabling those who were with him to do likewise. At another time Gautama said (when he had grown old) :

"Now I call to mind, Ananda, how when I used to enter into an assembly of many hundreds of nobles I would instruct and gladden them, and they would say: 'Who may it be who thus speaks, a man or a god?' Having taught them, I would vanish away; and they would say in bewilderment: 'Who may this be who has thus vanished away? A man or a god?' "

Similar instances of all these powers will be recalled in the New Testament, but they are scanty in the life of the Buddha. All that department of knowledge was a side-issue and was not concerned with what really mattered. For he taught that though there are times and seasons for these things to be manifested to the ignorant they are very few; and for the man who has attained realization these powers are less than grains of dust blown along the face of the desert.

Here is a description of his person as age came upon him:

"When age came it was with beauty, so that all hearts fell at his feet and embraced them as a refuge. His face was worn and calm as in an image of royal ivory, his nose prominent and delicate, bespeaking his Aryan birth, his eyes of a blue darkness, and he carried himself as one of the princes."

Yet all this might be said of another, but for him Wisdom walked on his left hand and Love on his right and Light surrounded him.

For animals also, for all who draw the breath of life, he had love and pity. It is known how when King Bimbisara was about to offer a sacrifice of goats he stayed the priest's hands, pleading for their lives because he loved them and understood their karma and their striving and their upward path and the love and beauty in them. So since that time no true follower of the Buddha offers bloody sacrifices or will take life, for this he utterly forbade.

Also it must be told that having attained Enlightenment and being Utterly Awakened Gautama remembered all his past lives, many of them in the lower forms of life, and on these based parables wherewith he instructed his disciples and others. Of these I will tell one called "The Quail."

It so chanced that as he walked in the forest one day with his disciples a great fire came roaring to where they stood, and some of the monks not knowing his power would have made a counter-fire. But when it came within fifteen rods of the Blessed One it was extinguished like a torch plunged in water. And they praised him but he said:

"Monks, this was not due to my power but to the faith of a Quail. Hear this!"

And they said, "Even so, Lord," and Ananda folded a robe for him and he sat and told:

"In this very spot long ago was a young Quail; he lay in the nest and his parents fed him, for he could neither fly nor walk. And there came a great jungle fire, and all the birds fled shrieking away and even his parents deserted him. So the young Quail lay there alone, and he thought:

" 'If I could fly or walk I might be saved, but I can do neither. No help have I from others and in myself is none. What then shall I do?'

"And he reflected: 'In this world is Reality if it can be found, and there are the Buddhas who have known this and manifested it to others, and in them is love for all that lives. In me also is Reality (though but a poor little Quail) and belief that has power. Now it behooves me, relying on these things, to make an Act of Faith, and driving back the fire to find safety for myself and others.'

"So the Quail called to mind the powers of the Buddhas and the Truth, and making a solemn asseveration of his faith he said:

> 'Wings I have that cannot fly,
> Feet I have that cannot walk.
> My parents have forsaken me.
> O all-devouring fire, go back!'

And before this Act of Faith the fire dropped and died, retreating; and the Quail lived his life in the forest and passed away according to his deeds; and because of his faith fire dies forever when it touches this spot."

And the Excellent One summed up the story and made the connection thus saying:

"My parents at that time were my present parents, and I myself was the Quail."

So the unbroken chain of evolution of life and love runs through the universe, and no life is alien to another, from the highest to the lowest. So great, so fearless was the life of the Excellent One, stating all truth, supporting it with Socratic arguments, which none could foil, moving alone as all great souls must do, for the higher the path among the eternal snows the fewer the travelers! Let me quote the immortal charge to the soul in his *Dhammapada,* or Verses of Teaching.

> "Go forward without a path!
> Fearing nothing, caring nothing.
> Wander alone like the rhinoceros!

Even as the lion, not trembling at noises,
Even as the wind, not caught in a net,
Even as the lotus-leaf, unstained by the water,
Do thou wander alone like the rhinoceros!"

Since it is impossible that I should give all the incidents of the life of the Buddha (for few lives are more fully recorded in the words of disciples and in tradition) I shall pass on to his departure—that which is known as the Great Decease. It is full of beauty and instruction.

His life was passed in teaching, wandering from place to place, and resting during the rains in monasteries provided by those who loved that great Triad—the Lord, the Law, and the Assembly. The fetters he broke were those of ignorance, desire, the delusion of the individual self, doubt, belief in rites and ceremonies, the domination of the senses, and ill-will to others. But he compelled none nor threatened, for by a man's true Self comes his realization, and he said:

"He Who Has Thus Attained does not think that it is he who must lead the brotherhood or that the Order is dependent upon him." Only stedfastly pointing the Way, he rejoiced that men should follow it, casting out his light like the sun, but not compelling men to guide their steps by it.

Nor did he teach resignation to sorrow or its acceptance as a blessing and discipline. Far from it, for in the clear precipience of the Buddha sorrow is ignorance.

"One thing only, monks, now as always I declare to you—sorrow and the uprooting of sorrow."

Therefore of all philosophies and faiths his is gladdest and surest. This his followers knew and their song was: "We who call nothing our own, drenched with happiness, we in this world cast out light like the immortal gods."

There is a notable meeting at Alavi. By the cattle- path in the forest the Buddha, now very aged, rested on a couch of leaves, and a man of Alavi passing greeted him with respect and sitting beside him asked:

"Master, does the World-Honored live happily?"

He answered: "It is so, young man. Of those who live happily in the world I also am one."

Then, for his heart pitied the aging of the Master, the man continued: "Cold, Master, is the winter night; the time of frost comes; rough is the ground trodden by cattle; thin is the couch of leaves, light the monk's yellow robe; sharp is the cutting winter wind."

But the Buddha smiled. "Even so, young man. Of those who live happily in the world I am one."

But he was now eighty years old, and fatigues and years had had their way with the perishing body. To the last he taught, eager to shed the light of joy upon a suffering world. A sickness fell upon him, and sharp pains even to death, but mindful and self-possessed he bore them without complaint. And this thought came into his mind:

"It would not be right for me to pass away without addressing the disciples and taking leave of the Order."

And he struggled against the sickness, and it abated.

So when he began to recover he went out of the vihara (monastery) and sat down on a seat spread out for him. Ananda, the beloved, sat beside him, and said this:

"I have seen how the Blessed One suffered, and though at that sight my body became weak as a creeper I had some little comfort in thinking that the Blessed One would not pass from existence until at least he had left some instructions for the Order."

"What then, Ananda? Does the Order expect that of me? He Who Has Thus Attained thinks not that it is he who shall lead the Order nor that it is dependent upon him. I am now grown old and full of years. My journey is drawing to its close, and I am turning eighty years of age. And just as a worn-out cart can only with much addition of care be made to move, so I think the body of Him Who Has Thus Attained can be kept going only with much additional care. It is only when he becomes plunged in devout meditation that the body of the Enlightened One is at ease."

And the Buddha resumed:

"Therefore, Ananda, be lamps unto yourselves. Betake yourselves to no external refuge. Hold fast to the truth. Look not for refuge to anyone besides yourselves. And those who after I am dead shall be lamps to themselves, and holding fast to the truth look for refuge to no one outside themselves—it is they among my mendicants who shall reach the Height."

At this time the Blessed One had many discourses with Ananda. It was during one of these that he asserted one of the powers of the yogin taught by Patanjali, saying;

"Whoever, Ananda, has developed himself and ascended to the very height of the four paths to power [i.e., the four Yogas], thus transcending bodily conditions and using those powers for good, may if he desires it remain in the same birth for an age or that portion of an age which is yet to run."

Of this the Buddha would not take advantage, but the assertion is interesting.

So wandering on with ever-failing strength, at last he reached Vaishali with his immediate disciples, and there he commanded Ananda to assemble such of the Order as dwelt in the neighborhood. When they were assembled the Blessed One sat upon his mat and addressed them, saying:

"Practice the truths, monks, which I have made known to you, meditate and spread them abroad, that they may continue to be for the good and happiness of great multitudes.

"Behold now, monks, I exhort you. All component things must age and dissolve. Work out your salvation with diligence. At the end of three months He Who Has Thus Attained will die. I leave you. I depart, relying on myself alone. Be earnest, pure, recollected. Be stedfast in resolve. Keep watch over your hearts. Who wearies not but holds fast to the Law, shall cross this sea of life, shall make an end of grief."

So he spoke, and they dispersed silently.

Early in the morning the Blessed One robed himself and took his bowl and went into Vaishali for alms, and when he had eaten and was returning he gazed at Vaishali (a place of many memories) and he said thus:

"This is the last time, Ananda, that He Who Has Thus Attained will behold Vaishali. How beautiful art thou, Vaishali, city of towers and palaces! How pleasant thy slopes, how heart-gladdening thy meadows full of grain, how exquisite the sparkle of thy many rivers! I shall not see them more. Come, Ananda. Let us now go to Bhandagama!"

They went and he rested in the village, and there addressed the brethren, saying:

"It is through ignorance of the Truths that we have had to wander so long in this weary round of rebirth, you and I. But when the noble conduct of life, noble meditation, noble wisdom and noble freedom are realized then is the craving for Existence rooted out; the chain is broken and we return to earth no more."

And it was here he delivered a high discourse on the Four Truths. This done, he pressed on with Ananda and a great company of his own to Pava, and there he rested in the Mango Grove of Chunda, and Chunda was a smith by family.

So Chunda greeted him with joy and reverence, and the Blessed One gladdened him with talk of high things and he entreated the Buddha to honor him by taking a meal at his house next day with the brethren, and to this Gautama by silence signified his assent. And Chunda made ready excellent food, hard and soft, sweet rice and cakes and truffles, the food loved by boars, and notified the Lord Buddha when it was ready, and he took his bowl and went.

But after he had eaten there fell upon him a grievous disease and cruel pain, but he bore it without complaint and said to Ananda:

"Come, let us go to Kusinara." For there he was to die. And as they went slowly he thirsted, and a robe was spread and he rested and asked for water, and Ananda told him with grief that five hundred ox carts had passed through the river and it was turbid and foul. But still the Blessed One bade him take a bowl and go; and when he went the water flowed clear as light, and Ananda said:

"How wonderful, how marvelous! Let the Happy One drink!"

And even then, dying as he was, the Buddha received and taught the young Brahmin Pukkusa, and when the great teaching was ended, with gladness he joined the brotherhood. He presented two robes of cloth of gold as the teacher's gift according to the custom; and the Blessed One gave one to Ananda, and the other Ananda spread that Gautama might lie upon it. Now when he did this he observed that a light shone from the Buddha which dimmed the glory of the garment, and he said:

"Lord, it is marvelous that the color of the skin of the Blessed One should now be so clear, so bright beyond measure."

"It is even so, Ananda. For on the night when He Who Has Thus Attained achieves Supreme Enlightenment and also on the night when he passes away forever the color of his body becomes exceedingly bright and clear."

And they came near to Kusinara, and he said:

"Fold a robe for me, Ananda, for I am clean forspent."

And he lay on his right side and meditated, calm and self-possessed. And now comes a thing beyond expression beautiful, and worthy not only of a great saint but of the dignity and courtesy of a great prince. He called Ananda.

"Now it may happen that someone may grieve Chunda the smith, saying, 'It is evil to you, Chunda, and loss, that when the Blessed One had eaten of your provision he died.' But check this remorse, Ananda, by saying, 'It is good and gain to you that this should have been, for the very mouth of the Blessed One has said, "There is laid up for Chunda the smith a good karma of long life and good fortune and fame and the inheritance of heaven and sovereign power." ' Let this be told."

And rising once more he began again his pilgrimage of pain, and they came to the Sala Grove of the Malla people at Kusinara; and there they made a couch for him between twin sal-trees, and these dropped their blossoms upon him, for so it must be with a departing Buddha. And he lay with his head toward the eternal snows of the Himalayas. Then Ananda reverently besought the commands of the Lord Buddha as to the disposal of his mortal body and he replied :

"*Do* not hinder yourselves by honoring what remains. Be intent on good. There are men among the nobles who will do what is needful."

And hearing this Ananda could no longer endure his grief, and he went away to weep that the Buddha might not see his tears, for he thought: "Alas, I am still but a learner, and the Master is about to leave me—he who is so kind."

But the Blessed One called for him, and he came and the Lord Buddha said:

"Do not weep, Ananda. Have I not often told you that it is in the very nature of things most near and dear to us that we must leave them? How can it be possible that component things should not dissolve? For a long time you have been very near to me by acts of love, kind and good, never varying and beyond all measure, and also by words and thoughts of love. You have done well, Ananda. Be earnest in effort and you too shall soon attain the perfect percipience."

And the Blessed One repeated this to the others and said:

"Go now, Ananda, to the town of the Mallas and tell the people of the Mallas that in the last watch of the night He Who Has Thus Attained will die. And say this: 'Be favorable, O Mallas, and leave no occasion to reproach yourselves that you did not visit the Blessed One in his last hours.'"

And the Mallas heard this with grief and bitter weeping, and with all their families and servants they came to take leave of the Blessed One; and family by family they were presented to receive his blessing.

And one last work of mercy was left, and this the dying Lord Buddha accomplished, for he taught and received a mendicant named Subaddha, who came hastening to his feet that the opportunity might not pass away forever. And now the end was come and the Blessed One said:

"It may be that in some of you the thought may arise, 'Now that the word of the Master is ended we have no teacher!' This is not so. The truths and the rules of the Order shall be your teacher when I am gone."

And again:

"It may be, brethren, that there is doubt or misgiving in the mind of some brother as to the Buddha, the Truth, the Way. Ask freely, monks! Do not afterwards reproach yourselves with the thought—we were face to face with the Blessed One and we did not ask."

And there was silence, and again and a third time the Lord Buddha repeated thus. And in his care for them he said:

"It may be that the brethren will not ask questions out of reverence for the Teacher. If so, let friend communicate with friend."

And still they were silent and Ananda said:

"It is wonderful, Lord! I have faith to believe that in this whole assembly there is not one who has any doubt or misgiving."

And the Blessed One sinking into deeper weakness answered:

"You speak from the fulness of faith, Ananda, but I know of certain knowledge that none doubts, and even the most backward of all these brethren knows and has seen and will be born no more in suffering, but is assured of ultimate peace."

Then knowing the parting at hand, Ananda knelt and hid his face by the Blessed One. And there was deep silence and He Who Has Thus Attained lay with closed eyes, submerged in calm as in a great ocean. But after a while his eyelids opened, and for the last time his disciples heard his voice, strong in death:

"Behold now, brethren, I exhort you, saying, transiency is inherent in all component things. Work out your own salvation with diligence."

And they trembled kneeling about him.

Then the Blessed One entered into the first state of ecstasy, and rising from this entered into the second and into the third and fourth; and passing from ecstasy he entered the infinity of space, and from that to the infinity of consciousness, and from this to that of Nothingness, and thus arrived at the cessation of sensation and idea.

And in an agony Ananda cried out to the great Anu- ruddha, the Shakya prince.

"O my Lord, O Anuruddha, the Blessed One is dead!" But he, leaning above that Peace, said with calm: "Nay, Brother Ananda. He has entered into that state where sensation and ideas cease."

And all veiled their faces. And the mind of Him Who Has Thus Attained retraced the way downward again and upward, and passing out of the fourth stage of rapture he immediately entered the highest Nirvana. And at the moment of his dying the thunders of heaven broke roaring about them, and there was a great and terrible trembling of the earth, and the voice of Brahma, the personal creator, cried aloud:

"All beings must lose their compound selves and individuality, and even such a Master as this, unrivaled and endued with all the powers, even he has passed into the highest Nirvana."

And the voice of Indra, the king of gods, took up the tale:

"Transient are all component things,
They being born must die."

And the great disciple, the perfected saint Anuruddha said these words:

"When he, the Desireless Lord, lay in peace, so ending his span of life, resolute and with unshaken mind did he endure the pains of death, attaining his final deliverance from the Fetters."

But Ananda cried aloud, weeping in agony:

"Then there was terror, then the hair rose on the head when He Who Possessed All Grace—the Supreme Buddha—died."

So spoke all the voices of the phenomenal world, and those of the brethren who had not yet attained percipience wept in inconsolable grief. But the great Arahats (perfected in wisdom) bore their sorrow calm and self-possessed, saying:

"Transient are all earthly things. How is it possible they should not be dissolved?"

And all that night did the great Sariputta and Anuruddha, two of the mightiest disciples, spend in high discourse, but Ananda wept nor could be comforted. In the morning Anuruddha addressed them all:

"Enough, my brothers: do not weep. For those who have attained wisdom say, 'Transient are all component things. How is it possible they should not be dissolved? This cannot be.'"

And he sent Ananda to tell the true Mallas that the Lord Buddha had departed; and they came, lamenting, with great and costly preparation, and they encased the body of the Buddha in new cloth and folded sheets of wool and in a vessel of iron for the burning, and with devotion and spices and flowers they did what was needful; and the body of the Lord Buddha passed into gray ash, fulfilling all even to the uttermost.

Now when the burning was done, the true Mallas gathered the bones and they took them to their council hall, and because

Gautama was a man of the warrior caste they surrounded them with a latticework of spears and a rampart of bows; and there for seven days they did homage with solemn dance and music and garlands and perfumes.

And many sent, demanding portions of the relics, among them the King of Maghada, saying:

"The Blessed One was of the soldier caste and so am I, and I shall make a sacred monument and hold a solemn feast."

And the Shakyas of Kapila, Gautama's own people sent, saying:

"He Who Has Thus Attained was the pride of our race. We are worthy to receive a portion, and we shall put up a sacred monument and hold a solemn feast."

But at last the relics were divided and without contention, even as the Blessed One would have desired; and to this day they are honored in many lands. And the great Ananda, casting away the fetters of love and retaining only its radiance, became a mighty Arahat and laid aside all sorrow.

None but those who know the sources can know how scanty and poor an exposition this is of that most wonderful life and how much that is vital and lovely I have been obliged to omit. I can only refer readers to books named in the bibliography, including my own book "The Splendour of Asia," which is written not for scholars but for the general reader. Let me before passing on to the teaching quote the saying of a great Buddhist scholar, one which none who have studied the subject will controvert:

"Perhaps never while the world has lasted has there been a Personality who has wielded such a tremendous influence over the thought of humanity. And who recognizes this will also recognize that almost two and a half millenniums ago the supreme summit of spiritual development was reached, and that at that distant time in the quiet hermit groves along the Ganges had already been thought the highest man can think."

In the presence of the august beauty of the Life what more can be said save that the mighty Buddha was child of the mighty Vedanta. These thoughts have brought the soul of philosophy to myriads. They will bring it to many more. The conquest of the West is still reserved for the East.

CHAPTER 11

THE GREAT TEACHING OF THE BUDDHA LIFE AND DEATH

What then is the doctrine that not only produced a life of such majesty, love, and purity as to capture the adoration of all who know it, but has created one of the greatest of the world-philosophies, one which exercises the highest intellectual faculties of mankind, and besides all this is a religion of faith, truth, and love, within reach of the humblest? This philosophy accords also with the teaching of modern psychology and certain aspects of physical science so closely that it may be said to have been its precursor. This fact has given birth to hope in many minds that in the visible waning of the Christian dogma as presented by the Christian churches the highest form of Buddhism may be found to be a refuge from that materialism of western civilization which may be said to carry in itself the germ of death.

"Man cannot live by bread alone," though an attempt to exist on that meager diet is being made amongst some advanced thinkers of the West as well as the mass of careless opportunists. Let us take the philosophy first—that philosophy of which Rhys Davids says in commenting on the dialogues of the Buddha:

"In depth of philosophic insight, in the method of Socratic questioning adopted, in the earnest and elevated tone of the whole, and the evidence they afford of the cultured thought of the day, these discourses constantly remind the reader of the dialogues of Plato. It is quite inevitable that as soon as it is properly translated and understood this collection of dialogues of Gautama will be placed in our schools of philosophy on a level with the dialogues of Plato."

Here he alludes to one of the three divisions of the scriptures which, written in the ancient Pali language, constitute the canon accepted by what is called Southern Buddhism. The word Pali alludes to the language. A council was called at Rajagriha after the Buddha's death to decide what should be agreed upon as canonical. Books as yet were not. The great Kassapa, the most learned of the disciples, was called upon to repeat the metaphysical teachings of the Buddha. Upali, the oldest, recited the Laws and Rules of Discipline. Ananda, the beloved, repeated the stories and parables told by the Buddha. This may seem incredible, but such efforts of memory were in no way remarkable in India and can in certain cases be paralleled today.

These three form a collection known as the Tripitaka —i.e., the "Three Baskets"—of the Law. They were handed down orally until the year 80 B.C., when in a rock temple still existing, which I have visited more than once, they were for the first time committed to writing.

"The text of the Three Baskets and the commentary did the most wise *Bhikkhus* [monks] in former times hand down orally, but since they saw the people were falling away [from orthodoxy] the *Bhikkhus* met together, and in order that the true doctrines might last they wrote them down in books."

This information appears in the ancient history of Ceylon known as the Mahavamsa.

The Three Baskets are subdivided. In the first are five divisions, of which four consist of these arresting dialogues of the Buddha. It is on these and on the third of the Baskets that the attention of the student should first be fixed.

A fifth book named "The Questions of King Milinda" is sometimes included in the Pali canon. It is an account of philosophic dialogues between a shrewd dialectician named Nagasena and the Greek king Menander, who ruled the Indus territory from about 125 to 95 B.C. To this book I am not personally attached, nor do I consider it enlightening as to the doctrines of early Buddhism. Nagasena was a man who loved cleverness for its own sake, who delighted in glittering paradox, and whose hard rationalism excluded all understanding of the mystic and subconscious side of man's being. It is a material development for which some of the silences of the Buddha gave an opening, and in "The Questions of King Milinda" Nagasena takes smart liberties with the teaching of his august master which should not be admitted. His type of mind can easily be paralleled in the world of today. It is exceedingly modern, and it has its reward in the admiration of the many who will always be dazzled by dialectic skill. I mention this because the book is often accepted by scholars, and therefore by students, as a manual of the teaching of the Buddha; and in the monasteries of Ceylon it is granted an authority which I think it does not wholly merit. Its date is about four hundred years after the Buddha's death.

At the time when the Buddha was born, superstition was rampant, and the purer Vedantic teaching smothered under a mass of fables and subtleties. Rite and ceremonial were all. Wise men disputed about niceties of metaphysical meaning, as profitless as later Christian disputes over how many angels could dance on the point of a needle; and the people, in terror of the gods, conciliated them as best they could with sacrifices and penance. European parallels in the Middle Ages will occur to many minds.

A great doubt, a deep unrest, pervaded the air. The social position was that which I have set forth in the chapter on the Laws of Manu, though these were not yet codified; and the pride of the Brahmin already showed signs of menace to the well-being of the other castes. It was the very crisis which in all countries points to the need of a great man to restore the balance between the material and the ideal, and to harness reason to the service of morality. That cry for help is not always answered. It was answered gloriously in India by the Buddha.

And first he struck straight at the priestcraft, and at rite and ceremonial. What had that to do with the Eternal Verities? The ideal could be discerned in the interpretation of everything men see, hear, and do, if once the chain of causation were firmly established and understood. What need of the supernatural?—a word which indeed has brought disorder, derangement, and servility wherever it has been used.

Consequently he offered experience. He himself had fought doubt and dismay through a great experience. Others could do the same and judge for themselves. They could verify all he said. As in Yoga, experience verifies experiment, so also in the teachings of the Buddha. "Be a lamp unto yourself." None other can give the light by which a man must attain realization; and the blood of beast in sacrifice is no alternative for that perception.

In perception the faith of the Buddha was unalterable. If a man sees things as in truth they are, he will cease to pursue shadows and will cleave to the great reality of righteousness.

The Buddha must always be considered as the child of the Upanishads. Even the silences which have baffled some of his commentators may be interpreted by these. There were things he would not choose to say, for he had daily evidence of how they were misinterpreted; but Vedantists cannot doubt his meaning in broad outline. From Aryan India and the Upanishads he derived his belief in karma, his certainty of Nirvana.

He himself, a man of the princely Kshatriya or soldier caste, was eager to respect the Brahmin when the Brahmin could at all be respected. Therefore, when in any doubt as to the fundamental teachings of the Buddha the Upanishads must be considered. Not that he did not add to them and enlarge their scope, not that in the science of psychology he did not originate greatly. It could not be otherwise with one of the greatest thinkers who ever lived, but the Upanishadic attitude is fundamental.

The Buddha is often presented as the world's pro- foundest pessimist, but unjustly.

"Sorrow I teach and the uprooting of

There is no thinker but must allow the existence of bitter sorrow and disappointment in the things of the world, and in the cruelties of nature amongst men and animals and in insect and plant life. Every philosophy and faith rings with the grief of mankind, the attempt at solution of the mystery as

A thing, one shrinks
To challenge from the scornful Sphinx.

But the Buddha did not shrink. He diagnosed the disease in all its horrible details—how should the physician wince from the symptoms?—and he prescribed the remedy. He focused attention on the malady, for in the consciousness of its terrors lay a part of the cure. The statement which is perhaps most profoundly pessimistic runs as follows:

"The pilgrimage of beings has its beginning in eternity. No opening can be discovered, proceeding from which creatures, mazed in ignorance, stray and wander. What think you, disciples: is there more water in the four great oceans or in the tears which you have shed while you wandered sorrowing on this long pilgrimage and wept because what you abhorred was your portion and what you loved was not your portion? Every grief have you experienced through long ages; and were not your tears more than all the water in the four oceans?"

Can this be denied by any but the careless, the selfish, and the momentarily happy who close their eyes to surrounding horrors? Is it not true? and being true should it not be faced? And such joy as there is, is invariably menaced and ended by disease, old age, and death. Is this statement unduly pessimistic? But even if it did not make sufficient allowance for intervals of joy, it has a key, a solution, contained in it, and no statement which admits hope can be described as hopelessly pessimistic.

That key lies in the expression "mazed in ignorance." Can ignorance be dispelled? According to the teaching of the Buddha it can be, and peace and bliss are the resultants. Is this pessimism?

The philosophy begins with the statement of what he called the Four Aryan (or noble) Truths.

First: There is suffering.

Second: There is a cause for suffering.

Third: This cause can be eliminated.

Fourth: The Way to accomplish this end exists.

Mankind has almost abandoned the attempt to impute mercy to a personal omnipotent Being who could not only perpetuate but devise the horrors which we must see if we open our eyes. To be told they subserve a far- off divine event scarcely helps us, for surely Omnipotence might have devised some less cumbrous and bloody machinery to that end. Furthermore these cruelties have the air of blind experiment. Nature tries a type. It does not suit her purpose. She slowly murders the failure to substitute another type, which may in its turn fail. This we see; and below our perception lies a world of yet more sickening cruelty and horror in the insect world; and below that again the horrors of the microscopic world. He who reads such a book as the account of the termite ants by Maeterlinck is conscious of almost physical nausea. Can such things be? Yes, daily, momentarily, about us, and we are only happy when we are blind. Unless indeed we perceive causation and effect.

True, there is evolution—the evolution of orderly communities, but they still resemble the termite too nearly to afford us security. True, there is the intellectual life, but that is for the few. True, there is the spiritual life— but there the great mind of the Buddha paused in thought. That too was for the few. Could it be possible to make it the life-blood of the many?

To this end were his philosophy and dharma, or spiritual law, directed.

And first it was necessary to provide a foundation for morality to which the reason of all men could assent. Not that there are not higher flights and vaster consciousness than any which reason can provide, but where reason can conciliate, the rest may or will follow in its good time. The higher flights are the triumphs of psychic evolution. Reason is open to all. And there can be no despising reason because it cannot plumb the deeps of the universe. It is the handmaid of philosophy and much more. Therefore his aim—the chief object of his dharma—is to show that morality claims the allegiance of reason and of every quality that is inherent in the working of cosmic Law.

Conduct. That is the beginning and essential. The priests about him taught from the standpoint of supernatural religion, in which offended or jealous gods must be conciliated by sacrifices, penances, and liturgic rites. He, striking at the root of that deadly growth, taught a philosophy which gave birth to a religion where the gods were of no account, the priest nothing—sacrifices and penances vanishing in the larger conception of the universe as darkness dies in dawn. There must be liberation of the soul. Yes. But no man, no priest, no intercessor can accomplish that work for another.

Stedfast devotion to duty, high altruism, perfect self- control: these were the steps by which man might climb the Mount of Vision. Yet the Buddha was no materialist, no rationalist. In the very statement and building up of his system will be found the orderly development which leads reason to connections far beyond rationalism.

No one was better qualified to teach, for none had had deeper experience of ignorance, of earthly joys and renunciation, and also of the vanishing of ignorance in a light in which all contraries were reconciled. He *knew*. Was his knowledge communicable? At the first he doubted. After his own awakening it was only in deep and anxious consideration that it became apparent to him how he could open the Way for mankind.

The beginning of his philosophy consists in the mental attitude by which it must be approached; and here we come at once upon the great differentiation between the Buddhist and other systems. Pure reason at first. Nothing—no statement—must be taken on trust because it has authoritative backing. No word of his own is to be accepted on that ground. He lays down certain principles, which you can test by every test of reason; there must be doubt, induction, and comparison, before one of them is to be accepted. There must be close investigation and experience. Nothing is to be mere theory, and the judgment must be held in suspense until cause and effect are understood.

This indeed is the true scientific spirit. Reaching across more than two millenniums it connects the Buddha with such men as Newton and Einstein—all the patient apostles and disciples of the great Evangel of what we call modern science. This is the noble agnosticism that must eventually conquer knowledge, for it is in itself Wisdom.

But hidden in this agreement with the modern spirit of research lies the one great difference that was later to produce a world-religion from his philosophy. It is the fact that in the Buddha we have also a seer of the highest, most developed spiritual power; and in him the forces of intellect almost superhuman in might, fused with spiritual experience amongst the highest the world has ever known, were to produce a new and unique result in the extension of consciousness

Therefore those who have accepted his invitation to examine for themselves are not called by themselves Buddhists—as in the western world—for that would imply the possibly blind, certainly acquiescent followers of a great teacher. They call themselves *Sammaditthi,* which means "Those who understand rightly." Each, even if in a lesser sense, must be a Buddha—One who is Awakened; and the Buddha's own awakening is of no use to them as a means of realization except as laying down certain principles, which they are at liberty to test and approve by their own experiments. They are those who have revolted against sorrow and "evil" and have attained a life of finer quality from which these ingredients are eliminated.

Let us now consider the philosophy of Buddhist teaching.

The Buddha saw the world as a process of incessant change and becoming. Nothing ever All is becoming; however long or short the process of change, it is never arrested; nothing human or divine is permanent. This is a basis. It is well to quote a deliverance of his to a disciple; I clarify the expression a little for western readers :

"This world believes in a duality—either a thing is or it is not. But he who perceives with truth and wisdom knows there is no 'it is not,' there is no 'it is.' These are extremes. The truth is in the middle."

That is to say everything is at every moment passing into fresh forms of being, as a flowing river is ever and never the same.

The teaching follows that whatever arises is inevitably the effect of a previous cause, and therefore Law is the universe and the universe is Law. Does this apply to the body of man? Absolutely. To the mind? Again, absolutely. To what we call the soul? Absolutely. All these are forces, sequences, processes, as is everything in the universe. Nothing is unrelated.

What for instance is thought? A vibration, swiftly intermittent, a rapid flickering during the process of every thought It is always becoming, never become. It is never stationary—except in the state of meditation, ecstatic or otherwise, almost unknown in the West, and only possible under discipline and in a state of higher consciousness.

Then if this is so, and we ourselves are part of this constant flux of transiency, how is it that we are able to close our eyes habitually to processes and think of things as established and unchanging in any sense at all? There are more reasons than one. I should put in the first place the fact that in our sense-world, conditioned by the three bounds of length, breadth, and height, we have no real perception of the meaning of time, and that what I may call the "measurements" of time are very different in truth from what our senses report to us.

Another reason is that, as the Buddha points out in the speech given above, we think in opposites such as "whole and part," "good and evil," and so forth, whereas these conceptions are merely relatively true and operate only in the world of appearances presented to us by our purblind senses. If for a moment we could realize the processes of eternal change and becoming, we could not take seriously the conception of things set apart from change, isolated and abiding, to be worshiped, dreaded, desired— or what not. For when once these processes are realized we see that nothing we call "real" can excite any emotion whatever. It is gone while we think of it, even as in our conception of time, seconds are gone while we answer to the question, "What o'clock is it?"

Life is a flux and a continual passing into other forms. It is not extinguished, it is only passing on. Its energy is conserved, but in other channels. Yet a certain portion of energy is also dissipated in every transformation, and we cannot follow the disposal of every unit.

Then what becomes of human identity? Identity is only rapid continuity, just as in cinema pictures you get an impression of identity of action from swift continuity. Thus from the infant in the cradle to the old man is a series of states no more; and so it is with the mind also, even as a stick alight and whirled round produces the illusion of a circle of flame. And because it is useful we call this ever-changing human continuity "John" or "Mary"—which is as untrue as when we say, "It rains." What rains? It simply happens.

In this the Buddha largely followed the Upan- ishads, which had taught that the world presented by the senses was phenomenal and distorted. But he was to lay new emphasis upon certain facts and their results. Like the tolling of a great bell ring his sayings :

"Know that whatever exists arises from causes and conditions and is in every respect impermanent."

"Just as a chariot wheel in rolling rolls only at one point of the rim and in resting rests only at one point, so in exactly the same way the life of a living being lasts only for the period of one thought. As soon as that thought is ended that living being is said to have ceased." (And another begun.)

Yet underneath all these changes and becomings and passings lies something subjective that is, that does not change. Each change is caused by some inherence in itself, some law which it is compelled to obey. It is not arbitrary. It has a stedfast sequence. And too much emphasis cannot be laid on the fact that we find the Buddha making a statement more than once on this point, which he declined to analyze or explain.

"There is an Unborn, an Unoriginated, an Uncompounded. Were this not so there would be no escape from the world of the born, the originated, the compound."

In other words Reality, the Unchanging, underlies the world of appearances, of things as they are not.

All this is law. From this law nothing is exempt, from the mightiest of astronomical systems to the microscopic life of which science has only lately become aware. And all life is one in stone, plant, insect, animal, man.

What started the process? This is the everlasting question of all the faiths and philosophies. The Upan- ishads say, "In IT awoke Desire." The Buddha observes "the noble silence of the wise." He says that question does not matter, for two reasons. First—our finite minds could not grasp it even if any formula of words could be found (and it cannot) in which the truth might be presented to us. Second—what only concerns us is without loss of time to bring ourselves into accord with the Law, so that our own processes may be obedient and harmonious, and that suffering may cease. Following this process we shall reach the point of perfect cognition, as he himself and others have done.

It follows from this teaching of the processes that what man believes to be his individual ego is but a thing of shreds and patches of consciousness and sense-perceptions, which being put together, whirled together as it were in the vortex of becoming, must certainly dissolve and pass away, not only in the changes of life but in the final dissolution we call death.

"Our form, feeling, perception, disposition, and intelligence are all transitory and therefore evil, and are not permanent and good. That which is transitory, evil, and liable to change, is not the eternal soul. So it must be said of all physical forms whatever, past, present, or to be, subjective or objective, low or high : 'This is not mine. I am not this.' This is not the eternal soul!"

Very often the Buddha was and has since been reproached for declining to dissect and discuss this deep underlying Verity. Unreasonably reproached, for it is absolutely impossible to do so. Just in so far as it is a part of what the Upanishads call Brahman, so of it also must be used the negative. Is it loving, is it wise, is it eternal? Of every suggestion we can only say, "It is not that," for nothing describes it. We cannot understand. The attempt to do so must always be that of the man who falls back upon a Personal God, because his consciousness cannot stretch to the Absolute.

The wise and learned nun Dhammadinna, praised by the Buddha for noble intellectual grasp, says :

"The ignorant man regards the self [ego] as bodily form or something having a bodily form. Or else he regards the ego as feeling or something having feeling"— and so on through all the forms of sense-perception and consciousness. The "awakened" however know that all this is simply a complex to be dissipated at death. There is no permanent soul. There is nothing that is individual or separate or unchanging. And as to what universal principle underlies all this complex the Buddha is silent.

He loathed the ignorance which offered this bundle of perishable senses and qualities to be respected as an individuality and an immortal soul. The most burning words he ever uttered are invariably launched against this belief of individuality, which he considered the mother of all greed, selfishness, cruelty, and falsity. It was to the breaking-down of this base little prison that all his doctrine was directed; the hateful, the fettering belief in the individuality and immortality of the complex of perceptions and consciousness that we call man. It does not exist, for it is everchanging. It cannot persist, for it does not exist save as a process. The Buddha describes its phenomena as a doctor describes the symptoms of a disease. It is an actor posing as the Self—an actor of many moods and changes indeed but yet

> "a poor player,
> That struts and frets his hour upon the stage
> And then is heard no more: it is a tale
> Told by an idiot, full of sound and fury,
> Signifying—nothing."

That is the perfect Buddhist conception of the complex which man takes to be his self and his soul. And, taking it for that, he believes in it, obeys its impulses, takes its promptings for inspirations, and so miscomprehends and misuses his every faculty, and is submerged in the sea of sorrow.

Does nothing underlie all this mumming? Does death drop a black and final curtain on the stage? Now here we come to the very crux of Buddhist teaching, that about which scholars have wrangled and worshipers wept, that upon which great schools of Buddhism separated. To me, holding to the Upanishads (though with a difference) and accepting the silences of the Buddha in the light in which he himself set them, it has never seemed a difficulty. Take the famous approach of the wandering monk Vacchagotta, who questioned the Buddha.

"How does the matter stand, venerable Gautama? is there the ego?"

Silence.

"How does the matter stand? is there *not* the ego?"

Silence.

And, baffled, Vacchagotta went his way. The beloved Ananda ventured a question as to the reason for the silence. Summed up it was as follows:

"If I had said there is an ego it would have confirmed the [false] belief in the permanence of what is transient. If I had said there is no ego it would have confirmed the belief in annihilation [at death]."

He would countenance neither belief. In other words philosophy has its limits, and that which we attempt to describe is indescribable; we must let words alone. The subjective self eludes all description. He never denies it; he never explains it. And really, where the attempts made to do so and their results are considered, "the noble silence of the wise" may be welcomed, although on the other hand it may be owned that the Buddha's caution resulted in schisms and systems that were preventable. For if the Buddha accepted the Upanishad teaching of an Absolute underlying all appearances (phenomena), and in my opinion this cannot be questioned, he must have accepted that Absolute underlying appearances in every one of us.

But how was he to dissect or describe it if asked? The wise men of the Upanishads had given up that task as hopeless, because they knew no words could bind the Infinite. "Is It eternal, loving, just?" To each of these questions they replied, "Not so." For every one of these defines personality and is limited by it, and in the Absolute is neither limitation nor personality. Not even the giant intellect of the Buddha could declare the truth of *THAT* in us or of its state after death. Doubtless he knew, for he had attained cosmic consciousness; but how convey it to those who had not? Can a blind man distinguish between red and blue? Those of his disciples who also knew did not question what is beyond all human categories. This can be proved from many anecdotes; and all confirm the great teaching of the Upanishads, though giving it a different and more practical orientation and removing the abuses and superstitions of meta- physic which had gathered about it.

Thus there was a monk named Yamaka, who pondering on the teaching of the extinction of the ego believed that after death the righteous man is utterly annihilated and exists no more at all. His fellow monks in vain urged him to abandon so wicked a heresy and at last called upon Sariputta the Great (the Paul of the Buddhist dawn) to deal with him. He undertook it.

"Is the report true, Brother Yamaka, that the wicked heresy of annihilation has sprung up in your mind?"

"Even so, brother, do I understand the teaching of the Blessed One."

"Then what do you think, brother? is his bodily form the

saint? Are his sensations, perceptions, tendencies, taken separately the saint?"

"Certainly not."

"Then if they are not separately the saint, are they the saint when united?"

"Brother, no."

"Then if you cannot even prove the very existence of the saint in this world of forms (and yet you know he exists), is it reasonable for you to assert that at death the saint can be annihilated and does not exist?" In other words, can a thing be annihilated of which you cannot prove the existence?

And Yamaka held down his head for shame and abjured his heresy.

Also after the death of the Buddha, the King of Kosala met with the learned nun Khema, a great arahat (perfected saint), and asked her:

"Venerable lady, the Perfect One is dead; does he exist after death?"

"Great king, he has not declared that he does."

"Then does he *not* exist after death?"

"He has not declared that he does not."

"But, venerable lady, 'does and does not'? How is this?"

She answered him with a very beautiful illustration and ended thus: "So is it with the existence of the Perfect One if measured by any human category. For all statements of bodily form are abolished in him. Their root is severed. They can germinate no more. He is released from the possibility that his being can now be gaged in any human terms. He is now deep, immeasurable, and unfathomable as the ocean, and the terms of neither existence nor non-existence fit him any more."

And the king heard with approbation and went his way.

Thus there is something permanent, and the final Nirvana is not extinction, but timeless and unconditioned existence. Furthermore, the Buddha more than once used the word "immortal" or undying, in the sense of the Upanishads:

"I will beat the drum of the immortal in the darkness of this world."

Again:

"Hear, monks, the immortal has been won by me." But no immortality is promised to the complex of the non-existent *I;* and final deliverance from belief in it is the entrance to the Nirvana either here or beyond death.

"Being freed, he knows that he is freed. He knows that rebirth is exhausted . . . that there is no further return to this world."

Here it is well to use the Buddha's own pronouncement. He says it is only a fool who can believe that any manifestation of the ego depending upon the action of the brain and body can survive death. It cannot. This was and is the conclusion of distinguished European Positivists; and it shuts the door on any belief in any form of immortality. For them that question was settled. But the Buddha and some of his greatest followers teach that —allowing this—there still is something which does not die, but which cannot at all be expressed in any terms known to human thought.

With this view the greatest Vedantic philosophers and the scholars of the incipient western science of psychology may cordially agree; and certainly no true student of Asiatic thought could desire for a moment, much less for eternity, the persistence of that poor little brain- complex which the ignorant call "the self." But when this position of the Buddha's is fully accepted, his implications and silences still soar above us and leave us with questions that cannot be settled until we understand the Infinite because we have realized our own infinity.

I must dwell on this, because a part of the Buddhist world sets the Buddha forth as an atheist and nihilist, and treats any difference of opinion on this point as "heresy." That attitude in either religion or philosophy is a western importation which they should not permit themselves. The large philosophic tolerance of India from time immemorial, shown by her greatest thinkers, shown by such as the Buddhist emperor, Ashoka, should rather be their model.

But though the body was eventually nothing, the Buddha allowed no cruel asceticisms. He himself had trodden that road. He knew their uselessness well. The body must be cared for judiciously, because it is a factor in spiritual development. For the same reason it must not be pampered. He uses an excellent illustration here:

"When you were wounded by an arrow, you anointed the wound and bandaged it. Did you love the wound?" "No."

"In the same way true ascetics do not love their bodies, but they tend them that they may advance in the religious life."

His attitude to caste should be defined. He had no contempt for the laws of caste and was too much an Indo- Aryan nobleman to have it. I might say the same of the European of gentle birth in whom, whether in America or England, his caste-law is the breath of his nostrils. That is ingrained in the race, whether East or West. But the Buddha beheld it from the practically ethical standpoint.

"Not by birth is one a Brahmin nor by birth an out- caste. By deeds is a man a Brahmin, by deeds an out- caste."

Therefore, though the noble, wealthy, and intellectual gathered about him, the members of any caste were welcomed to his Order and could attain the highest rank. Yet he was no democrat. He desired an aristocracy of the Best; and the poor and lowly, like the high-born and wealthy, must be members of that aristocracy before they were acceptable. In so far, but no further, his teaching is open to the charge of intellectualism. True, there were heights in the Path, but also very lowly beginnings. This should never be forgotten and can be most truly realized in the happy countries where The Good Law rules, though in another connection the master's own words abide:

"Profound, O Vaccha, is this doctrine, deep and difficult of comprehension, good, excellent, and not to be reached by mere logic, subtle, and intelligible only to the wise. And it is a hard doctrine for you to learn, who belong to another discipline, to another persuasion, another faith, and have sat at the feet of another teacher."

CHAPTER 12

THE GREAT TEACHING OF THE BUDDHA THE WAY OF POWER

Buddhist philosophy is based as was that of the Upanishads upon the Law of Karma, though with a difference.

The Law of Karma regards death as a link in the chain of the experiences of the soul, and is in itself a mechanical law. It teaches that the consequence can as little evade its cause as a man can run away from his shadow. It is therefore the law of cause and effect in the world as we see it, and it conditions all life.

A man is the architect of his own fortunes in every relation of life. He lives in the house his former existences have built for him with his own hands; and inequalities and sufferings, otherwise inexplicable, are set before us as consequences. Yet they need careful reading. Wealth may be a test or a misfortune, poverty a blessing, and so forth. Each can be tested or considered only in relation to the innermost being of the man; and none can judge of its working but himself, who has the problem of working with and upon the stuff his thoughts and actions have provided for him.

I have already spoken of the teaching of the Upanishads upon karma, where it varies a little in the various systems of philosophy; but in that of the Buddha certain differences are so marked that it is well to recapitulate for the sake of comparison. He placed the Law of Karma upon a scientific footing which may be acceptable to modern psychology. In both his teaching and that of the Upanishads it is the law of conservation of moral energy, a force real as the power that drives the sun. It is mechanical in its working, but by no means mechanical in its genesis, for all its generators are creatures of growth, development, and perceptive consciousness, which can and will be developed to the highest. Each one is free. He is the captain of his fate. Self-control and discipline can be made his servants. Causation is a cosmic force and affects the whole tendency of the world as well as of the individual. The wave, small as it is, is a part of the ocean. No man can be righteous or unrighteous without affecting the universe, because he is a part of the universe, and we know that in the chain of consequence not an atom can move without affecting the march of the planets.

So far and even further is Buddhist philosophy a child of the Upanishads; but there is one especially marked and extraordinary difference, which I hope to make clear in the account that follows.

Let this be remembered. The Upanishads teach that "he who departs from this world without having known the Soul or its true desires, his part in all worlds is a life of constraint. He who departs from the world having known these, his part in all worlds is a life of freedom."

In other words his individuality persists in all lives until the final enfranchisement which extinguishes the last spark of desire and releases him from the sequence of births and deaths. It is the same man in a different garment of flesh. As says the Song Celestial, the soul discards a worn-out garment and takes another. This is the doctrine of metempsychosis as Plato received it, and (roughly) it may be called the teaching of the Upanishads on the law of causation which is as vital to the West as to the East.

But this is not the teaching of primitive Buddhism. Something indeed persists, but it is not the individuality. It is another man who catches up the torch, burning brightly or foully, which the dead man has laid down. Later in many Buddhist philosophies this teaching was modified—it had to be. Only the most exalted intellect could grasp all the implications or, alternatively, the most amazing docility accept it unquestioned. Yet it is of scientific interest to the West, and possibly more than that.

If the Buddha's teaching be accepted, and the complex which is called man dissolves at death and the underlying Absolute is always unconditioned, what is it that passes on at death to gather round it a new body and act a further part in the world of phenomena? This has always been a hard nut to crack in Buddhist philosophy, but it is extremely interesting and important. It explains many difficulties of modern agnostic science.

Now first we must remember that the Law of Karma is ourselves. We are a part of it, and because we are a part of it and of the universal no man's character concerns himself only. It is also a part of the universe and concerns the world at large. Is this difficult to realize? Then consider it a little. A man's character will be admitted to concern his family. If he is depraved it may tend to injure his children's character as much as if it were a poisoned cup from which all must drink. It is true that no man can sin or be righteous for another, and yet—as above—it concerns others profoundly. The character of each unit of a nation constitutes the national spirit. Stretching this further and to the world at large, believing with Paul that "we are all members one of another," though in a deeper sense than Paul possibly meant, we see that the upward or downward tendency of each man is of world moment.

Therefore in the path taught by the Buddha, which I shall define later, the struggle of the so-called individual to do right, to attain, is not a selfish one in any sense of the word. If it were he could not attain; the selfish desire would negative attainment. It is the aim to uplift the universal life in the sense in which the coral insect toils at his microscopic building in the reef. The reef will grow insensibly, be no longer submerged. Birds will drop seeds upon it. Trees and flowers will blossom. The individuality of the insect will have been lost, but his toil will have passed on into the life of others, and his work will have built up a better world for the advancing evolution of the race. That is the Buddhist karma. The individual dissolves, and another being succeeds him. Accepting as a part of himself the limitations and extensions made by his predecessor, he carries on the work in the world of phenomena to higher issues. Sometimes to lower issues temporarily, perhaps, but the work proceeds surely, even if slowly and with retrogressions. *You* cannot reform the world. You can as a unit reform only yourself, and being a part of the world thus do your bit and you cannot fail eventually.

But observe! The Law of Karma or causation is entirely concerned with the world of Appearances. It has no concern with the Absolute and Universal in each of us. For all we know, the Universal in us may sit apart, and smile with understanding at the earthly drama of karma and the spectacle of the successor taking up the burden of his predecessor's responsibility and carrying on the coral-reef work in his turn. We do not know. It is probably all a kind of maya, the truth seen distortedly by the senses. For the Self in us never comes or goes, is never born or dies.

Karma is the law of the world of phenomena and rules it utterly. It must be obeyed. It realizes all the noblest aspirations possible to our knowledge here. It accords with modern psychology and science. It echoes the hope of George Eliot that after death one may be the cup of strength to some soul in agony, because in one's deeds one did the utmost that one's sight made visible. It is true that others will reap where we have sown, but the harvest will be good and being universal will be our own also.

Thus, though by far the greater number of Buddhists accept the Upanishadic teaching of the doctrine of karma, this austerer one may seem to be neither incomprehensible nor unjust. It presents unanswerable reasons for doing the utmost that lies in us for the attainment of higher and higher consciousness and finally the highest. Every thought, every action, has this result for all, and we live according to the Law which benefits all, understanding that each ripple of good thought and action sends its impulse throughout the world and farther. And at last, when only pure good is left, when the Karma we pass on has become passionless and pure, so that no thirsty impulse in it attracts an inheritor to our summing-up of deeds upon the universe, then that cycle of births and deaths is ended. The state supervenes which neither the Buddha nor the Upanishads could or would describe, immeasurable, profound as the ocean; and of that we may imagine what we will, for eye hath not seen nor ear heard.

But why does the life-force or any impulse create birth and energy in another individuality? Why when we pass away and our complex is dissolved should another step into our shoes and "carry on"?

Because what we call our "individuality" is part of an immensely complex bundle of world-forces. Character is a force as real as heat or light. Deeds and thoughts generate energy, and all force is one. Therefore, when what we call "personality" is dissolved by death and the complex flies apart, as it were, the impress of deeds and thoughts upon the world, which may roughly be called "character," survives as a force. This "character" (as we might use the word in speaking of any chemical unit) survives, seizes what is nearest and akin to it for purpose of combination, and so produces a new form, that yet is certainly the old, speaking in a chemical sense—and a deeper. This is fitted by its affinities to carry on its being for good or evil, no injustice or favoritism being thereby involved. So in a sense, the child carries on the life- germ and aptitudes of heredity. He is not his father, yet is, and could not have been without him.

A Buddhist illustration of this passing on of qualities is a flame lighted from another flame. I prefer the Chinese one of a note sounded in one room causing a similar musical instrument in another to vibrate and to produce the same note in response. From that beginning a clearer or more jangled music may proceed, and so it is with the passing on of character.

I know all illustrations are futile in relation to this philosophy of the law of causation. Yet as symbols they may help realization. Such a conception certainly strengthens the sense of responsibility for deed and thought. Minds—and what lies deeper than mind—will find affinity in the interpretation either by the Buddha or by the thinkers of the Upanishads of this law of causation, according to the degree of psychic evolution they have attained in their wanderings through births and deaths. But, be it which it may, I think it is not too much to say that the West has had an almost irreparable loss in the absence of the doctrine of the law of causation from its philosophies and faiths.

If it inculcated what is ignorantly called the belief in "kismet," or destiny from which there is no escape, then we should be well rid of it; but since it is the doctrine of noble responsibility and free will, since it meets every logical necessity and what we call science is a part of it. since it demands no faith, nothing but self-control and experiment, I think it is very much to be hoped that—as philosophy is realized as a part of science—the West may accept a new basis for deduction of cause and effect in the doctrine of karma. No one knows better than I what a rough and incomplete statement I have made in this matter of a vast philosophy, but if it leads some to further examination of the world-responsibility of the "individual" it is enough. It will be seen that the teaching is very different from that of the generally understood "transmigration of souls."

What was the "Aryan Eightfold Path" by which the Bu-ddha taught that attainment of the higher consciousness and knowledge of the truth might be reached. That can be simply stated.

There are two extremes, which must be shunned. The one is a life of pleasure devoted to desire and enjoyments. That is base and ignoble, unworthy, unreal and is the Way of Destruction. The other is a life of self-mortification, gloom, and torture. This is unworthy, unreal, and leads to nothing. The middle way of wise temperance and recollectedness is the way which ascends the Mount of Vision.

Here are the eight stages:

First comes Right Understanding. Half-formed views and mere opinions must be laid aside. A man must perceive the distinction between the permanent and the transient. He must see truths behind hypotheses. Realization of the need of truth produces the right attitude for its reception.

Next: Right Resolution. This is the will to attain after it has been realized that attainment of wisdom is possible.

Third: Right Speech. This is the first grade of self- discipline. Indiscretion, slander, abuse, and bitter words are forbidden. All words which are not kind, pure, and true are forbidden in any concern in which a man may be engaged. To attain this practice is to have gone far in the Path.

Fourth: Right Conduct. Here the motive is all— the motive is the deed. Deeds actuated by likes and dislikes are forbidden. Having realized the law of causation all must be done for furtherance of that law in ourselves and others. In its highest this law is love and pity; therefore all must be in accordance with "love unmeasured and unfailing." Love is the very door of escape from the prison in which the base and transient little ego is our jailer, because it gives us wide hopes and joys and sympathy with all that is.

Fifth: Right Living. This includes choosing a right means of livelihood, for there are certain callings which a man cannot follow without "soiling his immortal jewel." Those involving cruelty to man or animal are forbidden. So also those which lead to any foulness. A man who has reached the fifth stage will know how to judge.

Sixth: Right Effort. Now, wise and enlightened, he will understand his deed and its aim, and will apportion his strength directly to the end. All that he does will now be in harmony with the law, nor does he need to consider his course, any more than a man in health need consider his heart-beat.

Seventh: Right Meditation. This is the state of a mind at peace, clear of perception, having laid aside distortion and illusion, and come face to face with the Reality of which it is a part.

Eight: Right Rapture. This is the Nirvana possible on earth, as distinguished from that which can be attained only after death. It is the peace which passes all understanding. It is the earthly attainment of the highest consciousness possible until death opens the way to mysteries not to be put in words.

This is the Noble Eightfold Path, based on the Four Truths of Sorrow.

There are ten Buddhist commandments. The whole ten are binding upon members of the Order. (These members may at any time return unquestioned to lay life, but this is very seldom done.) The first five alone concern the laity.

1. Thou shalt not destroy life.
2. Thou shalt not take what is not given.
3. Thou shalt abstain from unchastity.187
4. Thou shalt not lie or deceive.
5. Thou shalt abstain from intoxicants.
6. Thou shalt eat temperately and not after noon.
7. Thou shalt not behold dancing, singing, or plays.
8. Thou shalt not wear garlands, perfumes or adornments.
9. Thou shalt not use high or luxurious beds.
10. Thou shalt not accept gold or silver.

In closing this chapter and the account of Indian thought, it may be of interest to give the Buddha's famous and brief sermon of the false self, which masquerades in man as the true Self. I have simplified a little and have slightly shortened, but the meaning stands.

"The mind, the thought, and all the senses are subject to the laws of life and death; and when it is understood how all these are compounded there is no room left for the individual 'I' nor any ground for it; for it is this belief in 'I' which gives rise to all sorrows, binding us as with cords to the world of illusion. But when a wise man knows there is no such 'I' the bonds are loosened.

"And of those who believe in this false 'I' some say it endures beyond death, some say it perishes. Both are in error. It does not exist. But when a man has learned that there is no greedy 'I,' that it is an illusion, then he passes on in other lives, knowing he is the same but not the same, as the shoot springs from the seed, not one and yet not different. Learn therefore that the 'I' does not exist and the illusion of it conceals what is truly the Permanent."

There is a delightful scene in the life of the Buddha which recalls the life of ancient India in a clear picture before the mind and illustrates also how instantly the proud and high-born Aryan intellect leaped to the appreciation of his teaching. Not that there was not room for the poor, the slow-witted—for all were welcome— but there is a kind of austere beauty in seeing how the nobly-born in intellect as in rank, the selected castes, soared straight as eagles to the sun.

One of his five original converts, Assaji, had gone into the town to ask an alms of food. He walked in the shade clad in the yellow robe with bared shoulder, composed and with majesty, meditating as he went. A young Brahmin of noble birth named Sariputta saw him and was moved by the dignity of his serene presence.

He thought: "This man has attained the Law of Purity. I will question him. Not now, for he is seeking alms, but presently." And, after waiting, he approached and saluted him. "Friend your eyes shine. Your color is pure and clear. Great is your composure. In whose name have you renounced the world and who is your honorable master?"

"Friend, my Master is the Son of the Shakya House, a descendant of kings. I am a novice. I cannot tell the great heights of the law but I can give its spirit." And after musing a moment he said (and the words became a most famous summary): "The Awakened One teaches that existences which appear separate are dependent upon One Cause and upon one another, and that their apparent separateness springs from ignorance and illusion as to the Cause. And that these [apparently separated] existences can be ended and the truth of Unity appear."

When Assaji said this, suddenly all the implications were clear as light before the mind of Sariputta and he knew the truth:

"There is but One Unchanging, Permanent and Eternal, of which the true Self is a part."

Deeply moved he said to Assaji: "If the teaching were no more, it at all events makes an end to sorrow."

And he ran quickly to his friend Moggalana, who cried out: "Your eyes shine. Have you found deliverance from death?"

He answered breathlessly, "I have found it. I have found it!" And so told him.

On the great intellect of Moggalana also flashed the clear perception, and without an instant's delay they ran to the wood where the Perfect One sat in the shade surrounded by his Order. When he saw them hurrying he said to those about him:

"Welcome those two for they shall be my greatest; the one unsurpassed for wisdom, the other for supernormal power."

So they came and told him their case and he said:

"Come, monks, the doctrine is well taught. Lead henceforward a pure life for the extinction of sorrow."

It is interesting to know that it caused grave alarm among the people that so many men, young and noble leaders of the social order, should assume the yellow robe. They said:

"The ascetic Gautama has come to bring childlessness and the decay of families." And they made a verse which was sung in the streets. I render it thus:

> The great Monk has come through the *wood ways;* he sits on the hill.
> And whom will he steal from us next, for he takes whom he will?

His disciples repeated this angrily to the Buddha but he laughed, saying:

"The excitement will last only seven days. But, if they taunt you with that verse, reply with this."

And he made a verse of his own which I render thus:

> The heroes, the perfect ones, lead by the truth.
> Who shall call it amiss?
> If the Buddha persuades by the truth will ye blame
> him for this?

And in seven days it was forgotten; and still the great and lowly flocked to him.

A few words must be said about the Buddhist form of Yoga of which the master said: "Not to the clouded mind nor the foolish do I proclaim the meditation of the mindful breathing." And again, "Monks, if one who is ordained practices but for a short while the mindful breathing, he dwells with concentration. He is behaving in conformity with the ancient good teaching and my own practice. If such be its value when practiced for a short time, how great is its value if practiced for a long time."

I cannot here give the routine of the discipline nor is it necessary, for in my list of books will be found one which gives full details, "Anapana Sati." Among the objects to be attained are remembrance of former lives (on this the Buddha is very explicit), the power of instant reflection, that of instant attainment, that of instant emergence, that of bringing any desired thing to pass by sheer will-force, the psychic power of reviewing and investigation. The goal is the Great Awakening to cosmic knowledge, and beyond that the Hypercosmic. I strongly recommend the study of this system to those who would comprehend the psychic states.

Buddhism can never die, for it is a part of the eternal verities, but it was inevitable that it should be transmuted from its noble austerities for the use of those who can accept only a small portion of truth, which must always be relative wherever any high thinking is brought in touch with words and deeds. All men are not Sariputtas and Anandas. And so, in India, the sterner processes of the doctrine were gradually resumed into the rites and ceremonies of Brahminism, for those who could not advance without the support of the priest; the differences were softened, the Buddha was recognized as an Incarnation of Vishnu; and the astute Brahmin triumphed.

Buddhism was thus rather absorbed than killed, and being absorbed some of its value still leavens Indian thought, though the high intellectual perception and courage of intellect that would have saved Indian thought from many sentimentalities, follies, and degradations (which India has bitter reason to regret) had ceased to act. Remaining in Nepal in the form known as Northern Buddhism, it passed away to leaven and season the whole Asiatic thought, philosophy, religion, and art. Yet here too it underwent transmutation suited to the needs of the average man, for the knowledge did not as yet exist by which its high scientific value could be tested. That time has now come in the West.

In Tibet, China and Japan, the Teaching has thus undergone much change, save perhaps in the sect which is in Japan known as Zen; and that is dehumanized into pure intellect and certain highly austere forms of art. I shall refer to this later. In Burma and Ceylon (I write in Ceylon), though love and faith persist, the high philosophy is scarcely grasped except by scholars.

If philosophy and religion are not to be divorced, and the latter is to persist in the modern world, if West and East are to exchange and synthesize their gifts as they should for the good of all mankind, I predict a great revival for the finest forms of Buddhism in the West. But it may be that the disintegration of materialism has gone too far. Who can tell?

Such were the great philosophies of India—such is the heritage the Indo-Aryan mind has given to the world. Can the Indo-European mind accept it? But for those who have studied them with vision these philosophies are the highest flight to which the perception and intellect of man have attained.

India can speak with her enemies and calumniators when thought, wisdom, and spirituality are taken as values. She it is who has taught that man is a soul with a body, in contradiction of the western conception that man is a body with a soul. She it is who has taught how man may "spit out the body" and realize his divinity as the only reality. For this India, blinded with her own vision, a mighty place is reserved in the circle of the nations. Her feet are soiled and bleeding. Her brows are crowned with the eternal stars.

CHAPTER 13

TIBETAN TEACHING ON LIFE AFTER DEATH

It is impossible to omit Tibet and Mongolia in a survey of Asiatic thought, and this book would be incomplete indeed if I passed over the extraordinary and illuminative Tibetan Book of the Dead—or "Liberation by Hearing on the After-Death Plane"—which Dr. Evans-Wentz has lately issued in translation and to which I referred in a previous chapter. I hope my summary may send many to the book itself, for I regard it as one of the most remarkable gifts from East to West that have yet been given. There are people for whom it will reconstitute their thoughts on death.

The book is a translation from very early Buddhist documents in Tibet, so ancient that in some of the funeral ceremonies are unmistakable references to the original Bon religion of the Tibetans, which preceded Buddhism in that strange country and itself taught the doctrine of rebirth.

Buddhism was introduced into Tibet from two sources by the King Srong Tsan-Gampo, who died A.D. 650. He married a princess of the royal House of Nepal, which was a Buddhist country, and also a princess of the Chinese imperial family. These two princesses brought Buddhism with them, and the seed was sown. This king's powerful successor, Thi-Srong-Detsan, reigned from 740 to 786 A.D. and it was he—a powerful ruler—who invited "The Precious Teacher," Padma Sambhava, to come to Tibet and spread the Buddhist light. He was a Professor of Yoga in the great Buddhist university of Nalanda in India, and famous for his knowledge of the occult. It is from his original influence that Tibet has since been the home of the occultism of Buddhism.

He had many books on those subjects hidden with mystic ceremonies. They were not for the general reader. Some are preserved in the monasteries of Tibet. The book of which I write is supposed to be one of these, and should be regarded as having been compiled during the first centuries of Lamaism in the time of Padma Samb- hava or very soon after. It is believed that in addition to his own wisdom he was fortified by the assistance of eight gurus (teachers) in India, each representing a different aspect of the doctrines he taught.

The translation presented by Dr. Evans-Wentz was made by a very remarkable lama named Kazi Dawa- Samdup, who died in Calcutta in 1922. He was known to the British authorities for his learning and character, was attached to the political staff of the Dalai Lama when he visited India from Lhassa, and he later became lecturer in Tibetan to the University of Calcutta, where he died. Dr. Evans-Wentz and Sir John Woodroffe (Reader of Indian Law in the University of Oxford) speak in the highest terms of this young man and his attainments. Dr. Evans-Wentz modestly describes himself as the mouthpiece and "English dictionary" of this Lama Kazi Dawa-Samdup, of whom he was a recognized disciple; but those who read his powerful introduction to the book will allot him a very different position. His experience in Asia and among Asiatic teachers has been great and varied, and we must hope much more from his knowledge and the untranslated texts he still holds.

In my summary I shall not use the Tibetan Buddhist symbols, which though natural and beautiful to the oriental or scholarly mind are comparatively useless to western truth-seekers. In as plain English as possible I shall describe the various stages of this extraordinary and beautiful guide-book for the dead.

It teaches the art or science of death. A western writer has said:

"Thou shalt understand that it is a science most profitable and passing all other sciences for to learn to die. For a man to know that he shall die is common to all men; but thou shalt find few who have the cunning [wisdom] to learn to die. I shall give thee the mystery of this doctrine, the which shall profit thee greatly to the establishment of ghostly health and to a stable fundament of all virtues."

Such is the aim also of the Tibetan Book of Death. It is written for the guidance of the dead man during the forty-nine symbolic days which he must spend in the *Bardo,* or Intermediate State of the Dead, before reincarnation or ultimate union with the Divine.

Passages from this book are read in his ear during dying, following death, and afterwards, at intervals, for the forty-nine days. They are for the guidance of the deceased during the ordeal to which his past life has exposed him.

His time in the Bardo is divided into three stages, entirely conditioned by his own past thoughts and deeds. He passes into a swoon or trance, into one awakening and then another, until the third Bardo ends. In the second Bardo he meets in symbolic visions all the hallucinations he created for himself as the result of his earthly thoughts and deeds. His thought-forms now pass before him in a solemn and mighty panorama, which if he is not instructed he takes for real objective appearances. He still believes he possesses a fleshly body. Realizing at last that he does not, he enters the third Bardo of craving rebirth, and, this desire drawing him with passion to earth, he is reborn and the intermediate state ends.

With this explanation I begin the summary.

We are in a Tibetan home. The master is at the point of departing this life, and all about him know that the moment of the disintegrating process called death has come. The psyche is about to enter on a new life, the body to decay and to pass into other forms. Birth incarnated the soul-complex; death will now discarnate it. The proper steps must be taken to insure its happy departure and safe guidance through the mysterious state which precedes reincarnation or, possibly, the joyful and triumphant cessation of earthly births and deaths. The instructed lamas are summoned to give their aid.

And first, when breathing is about to cease, the jugular arteries are gently but firmly pressed that the dying man may be kept conscious with a rightly directed consciousness. The ebbing vital current is, if possible, to pass out through the suture of the head—for according to Yoga the head is the chief center of consciousness, regulating other centers in the spinal column—and when the vital current is thus withdrawn the lower parts of the body are devitalized, and there is concentrated functioning at the brain center. This being done the dying man recalls to mind the whole of his past life before he passes from it. He recalls it in every detail. In the West this is said to be the common experience of those who are virtually dead by drowning and who on being reanimated tell us that this was a feature of what has occurred. I have myself heard this at first hand.

The state of dying clarity and perception passes, and at the actual moment of separation of soul and body the consciousness of objects is lost. This state is known as "the swoon," and in it is perceived the Light of the Higher Consciousness, dealt with by the Vedanta and Buddhism as I have described in previous chapters. If the departing soul can now accept union with this high consciousness, he is a KNOWER and secure from future rebirths. If he cannot he is "an ignorant being" and is doomed to further pilgrimage on earth. All persons see this Light on dying, and therefore all have the opportunity of escape if they are qualified to accept it. This must be so, for the light is the emanation of their own Divinity.

The Light is spoken of in the Book of the Dead as such a dazzlement as is produced by an infinitely vibrant landscape in spring, an indescribably blissful inner experience. Yet the radiance is so great that it may inspire terror and flight to dimmer lights or shadows. Will the dying man, still perhaps the slave of his earthly experiences, recognize it as himself and so attain liberation from sad rebirth? Or will it dazzle him into flight toward the lesser lights which point the way to earth again? If he has reached the right point of development, if he is rightly supported, he may enter the Sea of Bliss, and all be well.

With this aim the lama seated beside him reads in his ear the *Thodol Bardo,* the guide-book to the Unknown Land.

> "O nobly born, the time has now come for you to seek the Path of Reality. Your breathing is about to cease.
>
> "Your teacher has set you face to face with the Clear Light, and now you are about to experience it in its reality, wherein all things are like the void and cloudless sky, and the naked spotless intellect resembles a transparent vacuum without circumference or center.

> "At this moment know Yourself and abide in that state." (That is, in the State of the Higher Consciousness.)

This must be read many times in the ear of the dying one, even before breathing has ceased. He must be turned over on the right side, which posture is called "the lying posture of a Lion" (the Buddha lay thus), and so composed. Then, still speaking in the ear, the lama says:

> "O nobly-born, that which is called Death being now come to you, resolve thus:
>
> " 'O, this is now the hour of death! By taking advantage of this death I will so act for the good of all sentient beings as to obtain the Perfect Awakening by resolving on love and compassion toward them and by directing my effort to the Sole Perfection.' "

This is repeated distinctly to impress it on the mind of the dying person and prevent it from any wandering. When the breath has ceased the instruction is to press the nerve of sleep firmly and thus exhort the dead man:

> "Reverend sir, now that you are experiencing the Clear Light, try to abide in that state. Recognize it. O nobly-born, listen!
>
> "Your present intellect is the Very Reality, the All Good. Recognize the voidness of your intellect, for that is Awakening, and so keep yourself in the Divine Mind of the Buddha."

And now, awakening in the first stage of the *Bardo,* the Intermediate State, and reviving from the Swoon, the dead person thinks: "Am I dead or am I not dead ?" He sees the weeping of his friends. He sees his body stripped for the shroud, the place of his sleeping-rug swept, for he will need it no more. The lama beside him reads in his ear:

"O nobly-born, listen with due attention.

"Death comes to all. Do not cling in fondness or weakness to this life. There is no power in you to remain here. Be not attached to this world. Be not weak. Remember the Holy Trinity of the Buddha, the Law, and the Assembly. Bearing these words in heart, go forward."

The following prayer is suggested to the dead man as suitable for his use:

> "Alas, when the uncertain experience of Reality is dawning upon me here, with every thought of fear or awe set aside may I recognize whatever visions appear as the reflections of my own consciousness. When at this all-important moment let me not fear the armies of my own thought-forms."

The lama resumes as guide:

> "When your body and mind were separating you experienced a glimpse of the Pure Truth, subtle, sparkling, bright, glorious, and radiantly awful; in appearance like a mirage moving across a landscape in springtime, in one ceaseless flow of vibrations. Be not daunted nor terrified nor awed. That is the radiance of your own *true* nature. Realize it!
>
> "From the midst of that Radiance, roaring like a thousand thunders, Reality will come. That is the sound of your own True Self. Be not daunted.
>
> "Since you have no longer a material body, sounds, lights, and rays cannot harm you. It is sufficient for you to know that all apparitions are but your own thought-forms.
>
> "O nobly-born, if you do not now recognize your own thought-forms, the lights will daunt you, the sounds will awe you, the rays will terrify you. Should

> you not understand this you will have to wander in rebirth."

Thus the spirit is visualized as within hearing distance and is exhorted and supported. After the funeral an effigy of the dead is made by dressing a block of wood or some such thing in his clothes and for the face substituting a printed paper, called the *chang-ku,* in which the central figure represents him in an attitude of adoration, legs bound, and surrounded by symbolical objects. Its inscription usually runs as follows:

> I, the world-departing one [here the name is inserted] adore and take refuge in my lama-confessor and all the deities both mild and wrathful, and may the Great Pitier forgive my accumulated sins and impurities of former lives and show me the way to another good world.

This is visualized as the spirit of the deceased in the readings which follow.

He must be instructed that he has been in a deep swoon of consciousness. Now he will awake with the formless blue of seeming space about him. Divine Appearances advance toward him. He is exhorted to look upon the blue Abysmal Light without fear and to remember that these mighty Appearances are only the thought-forms of his own past life, for in all the universe is in Reality nothing but himself and THAT of which he is a part. Let him not for an instant turn from the blue Light of his own highest being. For it is the light of one who is become a Buddha, the Light of Wisdom. The dead man must put his faith in it, believe in it firmly, pray to it with all his heart and soul and strength. He is to pray this prayer;

> May the Divine Mother of Infinite Space be my rear-guard.
> May I be led safely across the fearful ambush of the *Bardo.*

> May I be placed in the state of All-Perfect Buddhahood.

Let him shun the dull light of his mere intellect and lower perceptions, for they can lead him only into the pitfalls of rebirth, and hinder his reunion with the One. Here, in this world, must pass before him, assuming divine and fearful forms according to their nature, all the thought-forms of which he was the creator on earth. Beautiful and terrible, in awful procession, they move before him like pictures upon a screen; but the KNOWER in him, the divinity, is steadfastly exhorted to realize that these are phenomena and appearances of the earth, and that in all the Universe there is but the One and he himself is THAT. Realizing it he can pass safely through the psychic dangers of this transitional state, which will determine whether he is capable of seeing the Truth or whether he must still wander on earth, painfully evolving to the point where realization becomes possible. Let him see through these appearances to the Ultimate and be no longer deceived by their beauty or terror into belief that there is anything in the Universe but That which is the Universe and himself and ALL. This is repeated, enforced, driven home again and again.

Now the earthly ministrant, the lama, exhorts him to realize his own yogic powers. He is in the Fourth Dimension, no longer governed by the trammels of the flesh.

> "O nobly-born, your present body is not a body of gross matter. You have now the power to pass through hills, earth, houses, and mountains, straight forward or backward.
>
> You are endowed with the power of miraculous action, not as the fruit of discipline and ecstasy but naturally.
>
> You can instantaneously reach what place you will. Yet do not desire these powers of illusion and shape-shifting.
>
> Pray to the Teacher."

These powers only the yogin, and not the normal man, possesses in earthly life, and just as the yogin is warned against their use until he has attained pure spirituality, so is the traveler in the Twilight Land warned that until the perfect beauty of spirituality has flowered in him he must not use them, even though he thinks they would help him now. He is merely to be stedfast and unalarmed, and to realize in quiescence that all he sees is but the projection of his own heart or brain upon the screen of his own consciousness. He is to watch it as the spectator of a show, knowing that it will pass and he will step out into the clear air of Reality. But if he believes these hallucinations real, they will imprison him in earth's glamor once more and inevitably drag him earthward into the old snare of the senses, for they are the creation of his earthly life.

He is not to be misled even by the apparitions of angelic beings or deities. These too are only the phenomena of his own thought-forms. Steadily and fixedly he must focus with prayer and desire upon the One. In the next stage every lower instinct and craving is pulling him toward the desire of rebirth upon the earth he has left. Fierce is the struggle between this thirst of passion and the pure insight of the immanent spirit. Very few have reached the point where the latter is victorious over the greedy clinging yearnings of the forms, for all the familiar things of earth. Lonely are the stellar spaces, warm and desirable the hearth-fire. And the fierce wind of an imperfect karma drives him earthward again in spite of the struggles of the upward aspiring psyche. He must pray:

"O compassionate Lord of the Precious Trinity, Suffer it not that I fall into the unhappy worlds."

And still the lama exhorts:

> "O nobly born, listen.
>
> What you are suffering comes from your own karma [past deeds and thoughts and character].
>
> Pray earnestly. Think not of your worldly goods. Think that you are offering them to the Precious Trinity and your teacher.
>
> Create no impious thoughts. Pray!"

Then follow the instructions for closing the door of the womb, which offers itself as the gate of rebirth and draws him by some mysterious affinity. This is the last and hopeless struggle to escape rebirth, for insensibly and terribly he is drawing near that consummation once more. The Clear Light has become troubled and muddied, the earth-desires are strengthening their hold. Again the voice of the lama is insistent in the man's ear.

> "Be not distracted.
>
> The boundary-line between going upwards or downw*ards is here and now.*
>
> Giving way to indecision even for a moment you will suffer lengthened misery.
>
> *This* is the moment.
>
> Hold fast to one single purpose.
>
> Cling to the chain of good acts."

And now, still steadily declining toward earth, the discarnate one perceives the mating of men and women, and is still drawn downwards to the gateway of the womb. If he is to be born as a male the Knower (the soul) begins to experience the feeling of maleness, to be torn with a feeling of hatred to its future father, of love to its future mother (this is strangely Freudian) and vice versa if it is to be born as a female. Again the swoon takes it, but this time the swoon preceding birth; and it enters the embryonic stage in the womb with its doom pronounced by itself. Future wandering through births and deaths is to be its portion, until the time comes when on seeing the Clear Light it shall recognize it as Itself and its Own, and be one with it by instinctive knowledge and realization.

> Those who are voraciously inclined to this life or who do not at heart fear it—Oh, dreadful! dreadful!
>
> Thus is completed the Profound Heart Drops of the *Bardo* doctrine which liberates embodied beings.

Here are one or two of the Root Verses of the *Bardo*. The prayer of the soul.

Oh, now when the Bardo of the Reality upon me is dawning, Abandoning all awe, fear, and terror of all phenomena,

May I recognize whatever appeareth as being my own thought- forms.

May I know them to be apparitions in the Intermediate State.

Oh, now, when the Bardo of taking rebirth is dawning,

May the womb-door be closed and the revulsion recollected.

The hour is come when energy and pure love are needed.

And again:

When the cast of the dice of my life is exhausted

And the relatives of this world avail me not,

When I wander alone in the Bardo,

Let it come that the Gloom of Ignorance be dispelled.

When the shapes of my own empty thought-forms dawn upon me May the Buddhas in divine compassion

Cause it to come that there be neither doubt nor terror in the *Bardo*.

When the bright radiance of the Five Wisdoms shines upon me,

Let it come that I, neither awed nor terrified,

May recognize them to be of myself.

It is to be noticed that in this state of transition in the Formless World—the Twilight *Bardo,* there is no divine intervention whatever. Thought-forms of deities indeed are projected upon the screen of the man's consciousness, but they have no real existence. The Universe is One and he a part of it. It is said in Tibet that these forms will take the appearance of whatever the man has believed on earth—the Christ, if a Christian, Mohammed if a Mohammedan, the Buddha if a Buddhist.

The history I have given above is that of the normal man, who, having fallen short of the evolution which unites him with the One and unable to perceive his unity with Reality, is condemned by himself to rebirth. He reenters the womb—that entry being conditioned by affinity, and again begins his pilgrimage.

It will be observed how this northern Buddhist conception of karma in direct individual rebirth differs from the more subtle primitive Buddhist conception of the character of the dead being alone handed on to another being, as a torch is passed from one grasp to another in the torch race. Both are only symbols or earthly phenomenal conceptions of an infinite truth. So would the yogin say who has attained perfect cosmic perception. His own conception of death, and entry by that Gate into the Formless World, of *course* differs entirely from that of the average man.

The yogin, he who by training and discipline on earth was enabled even then to enter the formless, the fourth dimensional world and use its forces, he who has dwelt in the serene radiance of the Clear Light during his experience of living in the fleshly body, whose bounds he could so easily transcend—such a man has nothing to fear in the *Bardo*. No sights of forms, deific or otherwise, can mislead him; no horrors repel him. The Clear Light can be borne by his accustomed eyes. He enters and is absorbed in the One—into bliss unspeakable and incomprehensible to the man who does not possess his knowledge.

Can the man who falls into rebirth recall his former births? Here the Buddha is explicit, as I have said before.

"If he desires to be able to call to mind his temporary states in days gone by, so that he may say, 'In that place such was my name, my family, my caste,' . . . that object will be attained by the state of self-concentration. If the mind be fixed on the acquirement of any object that object will be attained."

In other words, by the discipline of Yoga the deep of the subconscious, which, in Professor James' words, "is the abode of everything that is sublatent," may be probed and the seemingly vanished memories be recovered. As says the Buddha:

"Thus he calls to mind the various appearances and forms of his past births. This is the first stage of his knowledge. Darkness has departed and light come; the result due to one living in meditation and subduing his passions."

It is interesting to consider this doctrine of hallucinations after death, derived from life-experiences. In this way we may account for the dream-cigars and brandies- and-sodas desired and enjoyed by the departed spirits if a medium can get in touch with their consciousness. We may therefore, knowing this, condone the follies they utter, their dreamed Christian or other heavens. There are indeed many developments of modern spiritualism to be accounted for by this Tibetan psychology.

Does the human spirit in its chain of rebirths ever assume an animal form? Naturally the Divine in a man cannot do so and need not, for the Divine is latent in all forms of life. But the Laws of Manu hold that the "vital spirit" in man, which is not divine, may by misuse incarnate in the lower forms of life. The belief of the higher occultists and philosophers is that even this is impossible and that just as the stedfast evolution or karma of a plant renders it impossible for it to change into any un-allied form, so, when the pattern of humanity is once stamped upon him, it is impossible for the man to unite with or manifest himself in any other form. He may degenerate into a savage man, but never into the subhuman.

Dr. Evans-Wentz quotes some interesting remarks of Huxley's, that famous scientist and warrior of the doctrine of evolution.

"In the theory of evolution the tendency of a germ to develop according to a certain specified type is its 'karma.' It is the last inheritor and last result of all the conditions that have affected a line of ancestry which goes back for many millions of years to the time when life first appeared on the earth. As Professor Rhys Davids aptly says: 'The snowdrop is a snowdrop because it is the outcome of the karma of an endless series of past experiences.' "

This has interest as coming from Huxley, for though it misses the spiritual meaning of the great philosophical conception of karma it recognizes its strong scientific verity. His statement does not walk in the regions of the *Bardo,* but it may very well define the blind impulses and yearnings impelling the man or the snowdrop to perpetuate existence upon earth so far as each is able, although in the case of the man the spirit strives against the material envelop and its desires "with groanings which cannot be uttered."

Other great faiths have aimed at this conception, but have not stated it clearly. It would seem that a new and most desperately urgent prayer might be added to the litany:

> From the thought-forms and illusions we create and mistake for Reality, good Lord, deliver us!

Yet most certainly this Tibetan teaching on death is a gospel of joy. These evils, these sins, are nightmares, dissolving like wreaths of mist in the dawn of Truth, for when a man realizes himself, they are not only gone— they never existed. He laughs as he goes on his way.

What an infantile science of psychology is that of the West compared with the clear, deep knowledge and experience of the East, the outcome of five thousand years' study. I have seldom felt it more profoundly than in reading this book of the strange lands guarded with snowy peaks, where so few penetrate, where life and death assume aspects very different from those of the crowded city life of the West. Yet, call it what we will, the *Bardo* lies before all, and life is the stair which ascends to it and to its infinite possibilities, from the city as from the steppe.

Tibet is a strange country. Its art reflects its stern and terrible outlook. Many of its pictures and deities are known to me, in brilliant and gloomy colors contrasting the hope of the virtuous man with the terrors awaiting him who has created the nightmares which will break his peace. "In that sleep of death what dreams may come?"—a question very terribly asked and answered in this book of the shadowy regions we shall all explore, and soon.

Traveling as I have done among the mountains of Little Tibet I have realized how in a country so desolate its imagery must necessarily take the shape of stark truth in all its terrors. The terrors indeed stand visibly about the way and demand their answer. But death and life are lonely whether among the mighty mountains or in the roar of great cities, and in the awful Tibetan solitudes or in the veiling loveliness of Ceylon where I write now the Clear Perception of Reality is apparent as the only guide for the blindness of man.

CHAPTER 14

THE MYSTIC LOVERS OF PERSIA

It is impossible—though I have purposely avoided dealing with the philosophies of the nearer East—to avoid the Sufi philosophy of Persia, partly because the Persians are a distinguished branch of the ancient family from which we and they alike descend, but still more because they had gazed into the same great mirror as the originators of the earliest Vedas, and had carried with them in their own wanderings a dimmer conception of that light. This is seen in the teachings of their prophet Zoroaster.

I have not written of this religion and its sacred book the Avesta, for neither can really lay claim to the title of philosophy, and high and ennobling as are the moralities, the framework is so Vedic that the distinctions are scarcely of importance except to the oriental scholar. The languages of the Veda and Avesta are more closely related to each other than are any other languages of the allied races, and may be described as dialects of the same tongue. For those who wish to study Zoroastrianism and the still more interesting worship of Mithra, a Vedic sun god, which at first bid fair to conquer Europe (and I strongly recommend the study of both) the names of useful books are given in the bibliography.

Nor do I enter into Mohammedan thought save in its development among the Sufis. But if a book on earth deserves study by those who are interested in religion and social organization it is the Koran, that great protestation of the Unity of God. As a philosophy it scarcely counts. It burns on—a fiery comet—to one end only. But since *it* is a faith of which much more will be heard in the future, especially as Africa develops her savage or semisavage races, it should be known and respected.

"In the name of the Merciful and Compassionate God, say: 'He is God alone. God the Eternal. He begets not and is not begotten. Nor is there anyone like to Him.' "

It throbs like the roll of war-drums. But in Persia, springing from the root of Islam like a rose set with thorns, came an astonishing development—that of a passionate mysticism evolving into a philosophy that was to influence the life and art of Persia and, through Persian culture at the court of the Mogul emperors, the Indian conception of art and its relation to life in a very high degree: the Sufiism of Persia.

Islam invading Persia had narrowed the Persians; it is a creed fenced with steel. They could not wholly assent to the most daring flights of the Vedanta; but in the close association of the two countries it was perceived that here was a conception which would modify the stern Semitic belief in a governing Oriental Sovereign —an Allah extreme to mark what is done amiss, slow to pardon, ruthless in justice. They had learned from India that the gods may be transcended—indeed Mohammedanism had led them thus far on the path—but Islam had not formed its own spirit, its central point of junction, where the Divine and man meet and blend in a love transcending the attitude of Ruler and subject, or father and son, and presenting a union only to be symbolized in that of the lover and beloved.

This is a most interesting chapter in the history of thought and that of Mohammedanism. Sufiism became a philosophy of life which reacted profoundly on the literature and art of Persia, producing such diverse fruits as the Rubaiyat of Omar Khayyam and the impassioned lyrics of Jellal-u-ddin and of Akbar's great poet Faisi. In no study of Asiatic thought can it be neglected, if it were but for its influence upon India.

The word "Sufi" is differently derived. Some trace it to *suf* (wool) a cloth used by early Islamic penitents, some to *sufiy* (wise, pious) some to safi (pure). Possibly the likeness of the word to all three decided its choice. It connotes a high mysticism.

The doctrine of the Sufis is that the human psyche differs infinitely in degree, but not at all in kind from the Divine. It is an atom in that infinite whole in which it will eventually be absorbed. They hold that God is immanent in spirit and in substance in the Universe, and that the only real love in the universe is that which relates us with that Perfection, all other love being a dream to vanish at dawn. Eternity has neither beginning nor end, its aim is bliss. Nothing exists in reality but mind or spirit; material substances, as the world calls them, are illusion, the false mirror of the Passing Show; therefore, nothing is worth a moment's consideration but the love which unites us to the Bridegroom of the Soul; and even in this illusory and miserable separation from the Beloved flashes of heavenly beauty and memories of divine love entrance us and remind us of forgotten truths. To quote an English poet, of these visitings and instincts it may be said:

> Harken, O harken, let your souls behind you
> Turn gently moved,
> Our voices feel along the Dark to find you
> O lost beloved!
>
> The yearning to a loveliness denied you
> Shall strain your powers.
> Ideal sweetnesses shall overglide you,
> Resumed from ours.
> In all your music our pathetic minor
> Your ears shall cross,
> And all good gifts shall remind you of diviner
> With sense of loss.

Christianity and the new Platonism of Alexandria, which influenced the Gospel of St. John, contributed their streams to the river of this passionate devotion; and it reacted upon the Moslems of India also in an ecstasy that produced there a form of Sufiism resulting, not only in a passionately beautiful form of verse, but also in art of which exquisite examples may be seen among the Mogul paintings.

Strangely—and yet why "strangely"?—the first famous Sufi was a woman, Rabia, who died a century and a half after the beginning of the Moslem era. Story after story is told of her ecstatic passion for the Adored— spiritual indeed, yet carrying the body onward with it like a flower borne on the bosom of a mighty torrent.

She declared that she reached God by losing in Him all else that she had found. Crying aloud that she yearned to see God, to draw nearer, nearer by any means, she was answered by the Voice in her heart:

"O Rabia, have you not heard that when Moses desired to see God only a mote of the Divine Majesty fell on a mountain and scattered it in fragments? Be content, therefore, with my name."

Asked by what means she had attained this intimate knowledge she answered:

"Others know by certain ways and means, but I without ways, without means."

A moth indeed, consumed in the flame of the Divine! When in sickness two famous theologians came to her bedside, the first said gravely:

"He is not sincere in prayer who does not patiently endure castigation."

And the second: "How can he be sincere in prayer who does not rejoice in suffering?"

But Rabia broke forth, radiant:

"How can he be sincere who seeing the Lord does not forget all chastisement?"

This spirit was to blossom and fruit in the music of Saadi, Rumi and Jellal-u-ddin.

Poetry was to dye her wings in celestial fires—was to soar so near the sun as to terrify those who still walked on earth and preached the doctrine that an enthroned Deity must be approached only with awful fear and rev- erence. And there was another fear also, sometimes justified, that this passionate flood of erotic symbolism and allegory might carry the body to earthly joys rather than the soul to those inhabiting the Paradise not built with hands, eternal in the heavens. But nothing could stay the ardor of the Sufis. Their love was a torrent.

"Glory be to Him who has removed from our eyes the Veil of Externals of form and confusion."

The fakirs of India are descendants of these men, and in the nearer east the dervishes (a word which signifies "poor"), performing their giddying whirlings, are all that are left to represent that jubilant outrush of soul and spirit to the Divine which made great saints, great poets in Persia and India.

They owned that what they had seen and experienced was beyond all human speech. In an image of Saadi's —the flowers which a lover of the One had gathered in the Garden of Paradise so dizzied him with their fragrance that they fell from his hand and faded. How could he share them with others? How could he tell in words what he had seen?

Jellal-u-ddin, the writer of that famous book "The Mesnevi," said of it: This book contains strange and rare stories, lovely sayings and profound indications, a way for the holy, a garden for the pious. It holds the roots of the Faith and treats of the mysteries of certain knowledge."

The miracle of this conquering love is that Islam, so hard and austere in its approach to a hard and austere Master, accepts this spiritual book as second only to the Koran! That Mohammed would have approved these later developments is impossible to suppose. He dwelt much on the outward aspects of the Faith and slightly on the inward. "Think on the mercies of Allah; not on his essence," was his teaching.

The Sufis, however, evolved what may be called a code of their own. This can be used in interpreting many of the Persian poets and restoring the inner meaning of much verse. It sets in their true light as mystics some poets whose fame has reached the West. They were men drunken with the wine which whoso drinks desires more even to infinity; they were God-intoxicated and not with wine.

In this code, *sleep* means deep meditation. *Perfume* the indication of the divine presence. *Kisses* and *embraces* are the mystic union of divine love. *Idolators* are not the infidels but men who in a lower stage of evolution do not recognize the One Immanent Presence, and who take Allah for the personal God and sovereign Creator with whom Christians are familiar in the Jewish Old Testament. *Wine* means spiritual knowledge, *intoxication,* ecstasy. The *wine-seller* is the spiritual guide (in India the *Guru),* and the tavern is the cell where the seeker becomes drunken with the drink divine. *Beauty* is the perfection of the Divine. *Tresses* are the expansion of His glory, and the *lips* of the beloved are his inscrutable mysteries. The *black mole* on the cheek of the beloved stands for the point of perfect union.

"For the black mole on the cheek of my beloved I would give the cities of Bokhara and Samarcand."

Throughout Asia, with the exceptions of China and Japan, the love of man and woman is the symbol of perfect union with the Divine, the mystic state where each is both. But only a symbol, for in human love there is always something which cannot be attained, some last unconquered peak of perfect amalgamation, whereas in the philosophy of the Aryan Asiatic races—and indeed in that of the western mystics—the Union is so transcendent, so absolute, that man, having recognized his oneness with the Divine, tastes perfection. "I am *THAT,"* says the Indian mystic philosophy; and no mystic East or West but echoes the cry of bliss.

Barrow, the well-known English divine, sums up the philosophy of the Sufis as though he had been one of them. I condense.

"Love is the sweetest and most delectable of all passions, and when by the conduct of wisdom it is directed in a rational way towards a worthy object, it cannot do otherwise than fill the heart with ravishing delight. Such, in all respects, superlatively such, is God. Our soul from its original instinct verges toward him and can have no rest until it be fixed on Him. He alone can satisfy the vast capacity of our minds and fulfil our boundless desires. He cherishes and encourages our love by sweet embraces. We cannot fix our eyes upon Infinite Beauty, we cannot taste Infinite Sweetness, without perpetually rejoicing in the first daughter of Love to God, Charity towards men."

Here East and West certainly meet.

It is the belief of the Sufi as of many mystics that such contact sets the soul above the earthly law of good and evil. This does not mean that this or any philosophy will permit a man to imbrute himself, but simply that he whose soul is exhaled into the Divine as the sun drinks up a dewdrop is no longer subject to what may be called the Ten Commandments, for he forgets and transcends them, being lost in that love of the Divine which can inspire nothing but passionate longing to resemble its object. His every instinct walks the divine Way. In this spirit the Christ dissolves the ten prohibitive commandments into the two affirmative ones: the love of God, the love of man. For whoso walks in that Light has outpaced the law of prohibitions.

There is a fine translation by Fitzgerald—the translator of Omar Khayyam—of "Salaman and Absal" by the Persian poet Jami, which expresses the conception that all earthly love and beauty are rays of this Sun

> That men suddenly dazzled lose themselves
> In ecstasy before a mortal shrine
> Whose light is but a shade of the Divine.
> Not till Thy secret beauty through the cheek
> Of Laila smite doth she inflame Majnun. . . .
> For loved and lover are not but by Thee,
> Nor beauty, mortal beauty, but the Veil
> Thy Heavenly hides behind. . . .
> To Thy Harim Dividuality
> No entrance finds—no words of This and That.
> Do Thou my separate and derived self
> Make one with Thine Essential! Leave me room
> On that Divan which leaves no room for Twain.

Yet in these beautiful words the student of the Vedanta sees one great difference between the two philosophies. Jami speaks of his "separate and derived self." That position the Vedanta cannot acknowledge. There is no separate or derived self. Sufiism postulates the approach to God and the passionate union with His Perfection—as of the lesser drawn by a magnet to the Greater and henceforth clinging to it indivisibly. In the Vedanta philosophy man has but to open the eyes of his soul to know that he was, is, and shall be Divinity itself, one and indivisible, not dividing the substance, if such a word as substance may be used. In Sufiism the attitude is that of the unity of a perfect marriage, husband and wife who in Homer's great words are "of one mind in a house." In the Vedanta, "There was One, There is One, and but One."

Mohammedanism needed this high conception to soften its masculine austerity. It is the garden of God that blossoms on the rocks of the mountain. It may be lamented that this spirit has not persisted and that it does not consistently inspire the Koran. Had it done so, the deep cleavage between Moslem and Vedantic thought in India might to a certain extent have been bridged.

It is interesting to consider the experience of Ibn-ul- Farid, an Arab born in Cairo in 1182, for it appears to coalesce with the Vedantic lore of Shankara and also with some European feeling after the supernormal modes of expression. (I refer the reader to Professor James's "Varieties of Religious Experience.")

Ibn-ul-Farid finds three modes: First, normal experience, which he calls "sobriety"; this is the common experience of man as distinguished from the consciousness of plant or animal life. Next, what he calls "intoxication"—the state of God—possession and the high rapture that follows realization of the Divine. Both these are normal though distinguished in degree. The third state is induced by "intoxication," but "intoxication" does not always produce it. This third state is the state now called cosmic consciousness—which Ibn-ul-Farid names "the sobriety of union." This naturally is rare. In it, as in a mystical, tranquil, luminous perception, the soul is wholly united with God. As Mr. Nicholson puts it—the mystic in the first stage is aware of himself as an individuality distinct in humanity from divinity, in the second every distinction between Creator and creature has vanished. In the third he is aware of himself as One with the Creator. In the famous poem of Ibn-ul-Farid he writes from this deific point of perception:

> There is no speaker but tells his tale with My words nor
> any *seer* but sees with the sight of Mine eye.
> And no listener but hears with My hearing, nor of
> any but grasps My might.
> And in the whole creation there *is* none but Myself
> that speaks *or* sees or hears.

Here is "the absoluteness of the Divine Nature realized in

the passing away of the human nature." For the writer speaks of himself as God.

There is a mystic of the Sufi order whose perception took so high a form that it must be remembered in any record of the mystic-philosophic side of Islam. An artizan, a wool-carder, and hence called Hallaj, he was credited with supernormal powers, and because of what was considered heresy by orthodox Moslems was tortured to death in the year 309 of Mohammed. "I am God," he cried, and devout Moslems were unable to attain these higher ranges of philosophy. That fatal sentence occurs in his book the "Kitab al Tawasin," which sets forth his teaching, and exercised undying influence in Islam.

> *I* am He whom *I* love and He whom *I* love *is I*.
> We are two spirits dwelling in one body.
> If you see me you see Him,
> And seeing Him you see us both.

Strangely, it is in Jesus, not in Mohammed, he sees the representative of God; and, still more singular, he sees in Iblis (the Satan of Islam) a witness to the Divine Unity. In the Koran it is told that Allah bid the angels worship Adam. Iblis, then named Azazil, refused:

"I am more excellent than he. Thou hast made me of fire and him of clay."

And Satan, or Iblis, was cast into hell—even as the emperors Akbar or Jehangir might have cast him into torture, for Allah is a true oriental sovereign. But Hallaj relates that Iblis cried aloud to Allah:

"Wilt Thou not behold me whilst Thou art punishing me?"

And Allah answered, "Yes."

"Then," said Iblis, "do unto me according to Thy Will. Thy beholding me will destroy all consciousness of punishment."

Such is love. And elsewhere, being reproached for disobedience as regards Adam, Iblis answers:

"It was no command but a test." A test of his unswerving devotion to the Divine. Therefore Hallaj makes Iblis declare:

"Even in refusing to obey Thee I glorified Thee." And he continues: "My friends and teachers are Iblis and Pharaoh. Iblis was threatened with hell-fire and yet did not recant. (How could he adore any but God?) Pharaoh was drowned yet did not recant, for he would not acknowledge anything between him and Allah. And I, though I am killed and crucified and my hands and feet cut off, I do not recant."

Yet it is interesting to observe how imperfect appreciation of the heights which may be scaled as in the Vedanta flung even a translucent soul such as that of Hallaj into the old dilemma of free will. He writes:

"God cast man into the sea with his arms tied behind his back. And said to him, 'Take care, take care, lest thou be wetted by the water!' " This will remind all of Omar Khayyam's sad statement of the same cruel difficulty:

> "Oh Thou, who Man of baser Earth didst make,
> And ev'n with Paradise devise the Snake,
> For all the Sin wherewith the Face of Man Is
> blacken'd—Man's forgiveness give—and take!"

It was natural that orthodox Islam could bear no such heresy; the man must die. Love, however, led Hallaj through the maze. "I cannot understand—I love" might have been his watchword. Thus it is told:

"When Husayn ibn Mansur al-Hallaj was brought to be crucified and saw the cross and the nails, he laughed so greatly that tears stood in his eyes." He knelt on the prayer-carpet of a friend and recited the Fatiha (the profession of faith) and a verse of the Koran, and then prayed a prayer so remarkable that though his friend remembered it only in part it should be remembered universally:

"I beseech Thee to make me thankful for the grace bestowed in concealing from the eyes of others what Thou hast revealed to me of the splendors of Thy radiant Countenance, which is Formless, and in making it lawful for me to behold the mysteries of Thine inmost conscience which Thou hast made unlawful to other men.

And these Thy servants, who are gathered to slay me in zeal for Thy religion, pardon and have mercy upon them; for in truth if Thou hadst revealed to them what Thou hast revealed to me, they could not have done what they have done; and if Thou hadst hidden from me what has been hidden from them I should not have suffered this tribulation. Glory to Thee in whatever Thou dost and wiliest." They did him to death with tortures impossible to relate, and so befell what he had spoken of to a friend: "And how will it be with thee, O Ibrahim, when thou seest me crucified and killed and burnt and that day the happiest of all the days of my life?"

The friend was speechless.

"Kill me," he said, "that you may be rewarded and I have rest; for so, you will be fighters for the Faith—and I a martyr."

It is easy to see how the way was prepared for this high thought by the Mithra-worship of Persia, and therefore how in one sense it derived directly from the Indian Veda, of which Mithra was a recognized deity. Even the close and almost passionate devotion which existed between teacher and pupil in India persists in Persia and in Sufiism. That worship of Mithra the sun god, the soldier, the beautiful, might at one time easily have become the worship of Europe. Europe indeed trembled in the balance between Christ and Mithra; but the former was to conquer and the latter to divide into many fertilizing streams of thought. One of these tinctured Sufiism, which in its turn gave to Mohammedanism a spirit and inspiration that it had lacked in the harsh realities and fatalism of the often noble teachings of Mohammed.

I give a specimen of the passion that broke on India from Persian Sufis, kindling a new fire in literature and music and affecting the devotion to the native gods in no small degree. This, though an Indian song and with purely Indian music, is a flower from the root of the Persian ecstasy.

I am mad for my Beloved;
They say, what say they?
Let them say what they will!
It concerns me not
Whether they are pleased or angry.

May One only be gracious to me!
Let them say what they will.

The Sheik walks round his holy place.
I offer myself at Thine altar,
Call it shrine or hovel.
They say, what say they?
Let them say what they will.
I have gazed on the glory of the cheek of my Beloved.
I am burnt as a moth in the flame.
I am as one drunken.
They say, what say they?
Let them say what they will.

Most of all is this seen in the heavenly songs of Kabir —he who wandered through India equally beloved by Hindu and Mohammedan—songs of union, of devotion and adoration so passionate, so tender, that even the colder western nature is swept by them to the height, where pure radiance dazzles the eyes and the unstruck music is sweeter than all sound. When Kabir died, Hindus and Mohammedans contested the possession of his body— each longing to do honor to the shell that had once contained the bird of God. And at last one lifted the pall, and there lay beneath it only a heap of roses; they divided these, and the Hindus burned theirs into pure ashes, and the followers of Islam buried theirs, that the perfume and color might pass into the earth to kindle the fire of other such roses; and both were content.

In the present day Rabindranath Tagore carries on the tradition of Kabir and the Sufis, united to the deeper depths and higher heights of the Vedanta.

"The way of truth is one," said Clement of Alexandria, "but into it as into a never-failing river flow the streams from all sides." And the Mithraic doctrines of the Incarnate Word, sacrifice, and above all communion had prepared the Persian mind for the inspiration of the Sufis, as a way to the highest consciousness, wherein the pearl of the soul is dissolved in the wine of God.

Thus Sufiism is another burning light of the great Aryan consciousness in the Orient; and a flame indeed was the philosophy of the Orient. There can be no doubt that the discipline which directed the eastern will in the direction of the spiritual and idealistic in philosophy and religion gave it a power almost unknown among the western Aryans, and enabled it to breathe in a rarefied atmosphere which they could not endure. Such enthusiasms and inspirations cannot be felt where the religion or philosophy is a foreign one grafted on an alien consciousness and not springing from the root itself.

Christianity was an imported faith, and its languor even as a militant impulse may be seen by comparing the Crusades with the fire and fury of an Islamic holy war. Taking another direction, as this force did in India, it permeated and molded a whole nation (many of them men of lower races, in whom, therefore, the lower racial characteristics still persist) into a faith and philosophy that but for some of the early native animistic beliefs colored all India. The rush of that wave was tremendous, and though its fighting strength was the force of the spirit rather than of the sword there is nothing like it in the history of Europe,' where philosophy and faith have rather been decorations than life itself as in the East.

CHAPTER 15

CHINA THE STORY OF CONFUCIUS

The first feeling of the average man on leaving the comparatively well-known ground of India and coming to the consideration of Chinese thought is that of entering a land strange and alien, shut away behind inflexible and rigid customs, peopled by men and women whose movements of mind and spirit have become almost automatic from the long discipline and constraint imposed upon them inwardly and outwardly. We expect no independence, no spontaneity, from the Chinese, either in philosophy, faith, or the conduct of daily life; all must be regulated by precedent and opinion. They are interesting because so far from our experience.

But we forget that the achievements of a nation in art —or, in other words, in beauty—are conditioned by its philosophy; and it has taken the West a long time to discover that China has probably made a larger contribution in beauty to the world's well-being, through her own achievement and the achievement of those she influenced, than any other nation known to us. We forget also that, highly as her philosophy is beginning to be appreciated in the West, it is still not known in its fulness, and cannot be until our familiarity with the Chinese and their literature and habits of mind is much greater than at present. We must be placed completely at their point of view before their thoughts can color our own in the mass, as those of Plato and Aristotle have done.

Yet it is quite as possible as desirable to understand China, and the writer who succeeds in humanizing Confucius to the level of western comprehension and brotherhood will have deserved more of the world than the most learned scholar who has translated his words into difficult English—for Confucius *is* China. Without him, she could never have been the China which demands our comprehension, and demands it as one of the pressing necessities of the time we live in.

On the Confucian ideal China has modeled herself with all her own patience and discrimination. Whether a man of her people is Buddhist or Taoist he will also be Confucian. He cannot escape it nor would if he could. And not only so. This mighty influence was accepted by Japan, and in a very subtle measure it molded the nascent character of that great people. Many Japanese have said to me, "Whether our people are Shinto or Buddhist we are still Confucian. It clashes with neither of the others. It is a part of our being."

And since all this cannot be denied it will be seen that the whole world has to reckon with this man who lived so long ago and with his ideals of government and of the individual "princely man." When present troubles are forgotten and we are brought more closely into relation with China, we and our posterity shall be constrained to own that no character in history is of more importance to us than his from its results upon two mighty nations and their reaction upon the civilization made and upheld by the white races.

Like all other philosophies this dynamic force has not been wholly advantageous to China's progress, for the very fulness of acceptance made it a drag on the wheel sometimes; but that it has been the most powerful means of holding the nation together and keeping the empire afloat, in the stormy seas of shock and change in which so many civilizations have gone down, can never be denied by those who know the facts.

It is necessary to learn to know the man and his times, before his teaching can be appreciated in its strong and simple verity. I tell his life according to the facts admitted by the greatest scholars as veridical, but I do not omit the ancient traditions which the Chinese themselves have believed and handed down. Such stories, divested of actual legend, are often truer than bare fact, because they give the imaginative point of view, which penetrates to the essential, as true imagination must in art and all else. This is the imagination which apart from actual historical record has reconstituted for us the figures of the Buddha and the Christ. It should not be disdained in striving to arrive at a living conception of the man who has influenced at least as many millions of lives and thoughts as either.

The greatest and most honored family in China is that of the K'ung, the descendants of Confucius, who himself is known in China as K'ung Fu Tsŭ (K'ung, the Master) —Confucius being the Latinized form of this name and title. They have enjoyed many privileges and immunities, and were the only subjects of the empire not of royal blood who were permitted a hereditary title of nobility. This family holds an authentic genealogy, which may well be older and more illustrious than any other in the world. Since the death of their great ancestor, each succeeding dynasty of China has striven to raise higher and higher the strain of praise in which the Master received due honor; and this redounded to the glory of his descendants.

By the contemporary prince of his own state of Lu he was addressed as the Great Father. The Han dynasty created him (posthumously) "the Duke Ne, perfect and illustrious." This became later "the First of Holy Men —the Royal Preacher"; and his statue was clothed in royal robes with a crown set upon its head. Later again the Ming dynasty saluted him as "the Most Holy, Virtuous of Teachers." The first emperor of the Manchu dynasty (now itself a memory) styled him "K'ung, the ancient Teacher, accomplished and illustrious, all-complete, the Perfect Sage." This style was later shortened into "K'ung, the ancient Teacher, the Perfect Sage," and so it has since stood.

But if the descendants of Confucius look back with pride to their glorious ancestor born in B.C. 551, he himself looked back with pride and joy to his own. Frequent genealogical tables trace the family to the inventor of the cycle, a man named Huang Ti, in the twenty-eighth century B.C. This is probably more or less legendary.

The account of his ancestry historically received gives his descent from a family related to the last emperor of the Shang dynasty, 1121 B.C. This emperor had an elder brother (the son of a concubine), who seeing that the tyranny of the emperor was dragging the dynasty to ruin left the court to its fate. Later he was created Duke of Sung—the eastern division of the present province of Ho-nan—by the second emperor of the Chao dynasty; and there his line dwelt in honor. After several generations the dukedom lapsed. It was the rule that after a title had lapsed for five generations the family should choose a new surname and under it merge from the nobility into the people. By the line of the former dukes of Sung the surname K'ung was chosen, which Confucius was later to make the most illustrious in China.

He had every reason, even from that time on, for the pride in a fine ancestry, which is universal but perhaps most marked in China. There was not one of his forebears, beginning with the imperial House of Shang, whom he could not mention with confidence; they had all been ministers, soldiers, and scholars. Of the women of the family, Chinese historians are likely to say little; but one at least has achieved remembrance, not only for beauty and noble courage, but because her tragedy led to the removal of the family into the state of Lu, where Confucius was born later. This lady's husband was master of the horse in the dukedom of Sung. The chief minister of state accidentally saw her and coveted her beauty. His intrigues ended in the murder of her husband and the reigning Duke of Sung. He sent in triumph to seize his prize, but when the litter reached his palace it held a corpse. The high-spirited beauty had strangled her self with her girdle. The affair obliged the K'ung family to flee to the state of Lu.

China at that time was a collection of small kingdoms under one more or less nominal head, the sovereign. The vassal states under him were held on feudal tenure, as they had doubtless been from the earliest time which can be traced. Wu Wang, the great ruler, had thus divided the empire, like Napoleon placing his own relations on the minor thrones—a system well enough at the time, but as family ties weaken unlikely to last.

It ended as such a system must, in disunion among the several states and disloyalty to the sovereign, who practically ruled only in so far as his own character and power enabled him to do. That was often to a very limited extent, and the state of China at the birth of Confucius was one of rapine and turbulence. Not only were the states often at war among themselves, but powerful families in some of them disputed the rule with the princes, just as in the Wars of the Barons in England. In the state of Lu where Confucius was born, there were three such families, and their head virtually governed the state, having made their prince or duke a mere cipher.

The father of Confucius, Shuh-liang Heih, was a soldier, who played a stirring part in the distracted times. He was a sort of Chinese Hercules, brave and faithful, distinguished by his height and strength; and an anecdote of him shows devotion of no small order.

In the year 562 B.C. he was besieging a place called Pei-yang. His friends made their way in at a gate left open to tempt them, and as he was following the portcullis began to drop. He saw the descending mass, and rushing forward caught it on the drop and with furious strength supported it, until his friends slipped under and escaped, and he followed.

Such a soldier was honored and feared, but a sorrow, heavy indeed in China, shadowed his private life. He had married as a young man, and his wife had borne him nine daughters but no son, though a concubine had given him two, one a cripple. This raised a question of the impossibility of performing certain religious rites at his death, and was in every way a grave matter. He was over seventy years of age when he resolved to marry again. It is uncertain whether he divorced his wife or no; but a failure to produce sons was ground for divorce in China —necessarily, because a son was needed for the observances due to a father's spirit.

He looked about him. The bride must be young and of good family, since such a son as he hoped for could be accepted only from a woman whose blood would mix on even terms with that of the highly descended K'ung; great requirements in a man who had passed his seventieth year! But the courage which had upheld the portcullis and produced so many other valorous deeds was still alive.

So he presented his suit to a gentleman of the noble house of Yen, who had three fair daughters; he little guessed that the beloved disciple of the son-to-be would afterwards spring from the same stock. Their father, perplexed, took the unusual step of summoning his three daughters to his presence and putting the case before them.

"Here is the Commandant of Tsao. His father and grandfather were only scholars, but his ancestors before them were descendants of the wise emperors. He is a man extremely tall and of high valor, and I warmly desire his alliance. Though he is old and austere you need not distrust him. Which of you will be his wife?"

It is possible in the strange blending of human qualities, so little understood as yet in its conditions, that the whole fate of a great people and therefore of the world might have been different if either of the elder two had responded. But they kept a submissive silence which meant rejection—in itself almost an act of daring in the presence of a Chinese father.

Ching-tsai, the youngest, came forward with deep reverence. "Father, why do you ask us? It is for you to determine."

It is allowable to wonder what wish lay behind the frank obedience of this speech, but that is a truth no one would have learned from the lips of a high-born Chinese maiden. Her father looked her in the eyes.

"Very well. You will do."

The scene may be imagined as in some Chinese picture of very long ago. The father, robed and stately, with wide falling sleeves concealing high-bred hands, the girls fair-faced as the higher ranks of Chinese women often are—I have seen them with complexions of lily and rose—black-haired and delicately browed, graceful as willows bowing in a breeze. The open windows give on a garden such as is described in the odes which Confucius was later to make a standard of preeminent excellence in beauty and doctrine.

> The wild doves coo to each other in the islet in the stream where lives in strict seclusion the pure maiden whom the prince has chosen. Lilies float on the surface and green grasses line the banks near which the beauty lives hidden.
>
> And the lilies and rushes grow luxuriant in the clear waters where she solaces herself in loneliness with her beloved harp and lute.

A bright picture seen for a moment through the veil of two and a half millenniums.

Ching-tsai married the old warrior, and gravely comprehending the reason of her marriage and the duty required of her threw herself on the mercy of heaven and the great spirits for help. There was a mountain named Ne-kiu within reach, holy because it was one of those which the great sovereign Shun in remote antiquity had dedicated in every division of his empire for the worship of their guardian spirits. And there the young Ching- tsai went up to pray for the blessing of a son. A natural simple story, carrying truth on the face of it, the more so because she commemorated the name of the mountain in her son's, when the blessing was granted. But marvels follow, as in the case of all supremely great men.

As Ching-tsai climbed the hills the leaves of the trees all stood upright and on her return bowed low. That night as she lay entranced a spirit appeared and made its annunciation.

"You shall have a son wise beyond other men. He must be brought forth in a hollow mulberry tree."

Again she dreamed and saw enter the hall five stately old men, who led a strange animal covered with scales like a dragon yet resembling a small one-horned cow— the sacred kilin, still to be seen sculptured outside temples in China, Japan, and Burma. Kneeling before Ching- tsai it dropped from its mouth a tablet of precious stone on which were cut these words: "The son shall be a throneless king." She tied a piece of embroidered ribbon about its horn, and it vanished. This vision is worth remembering, for it relates to a circumstance preceding the death of Confucius, which will be told in its place.

As the time drew near she asked her husband whether there was any place at hand known as the "Hollow Mulberry Tree."

Yes—a dry cave in the south hill.

"There shall the child be born," she answered; and there, as she wished, the great event took place. Confucius was born in October or November of the year B.C., thus being almost a contemporary of the Buddha in India.

A biographer of Confucius, G. Alexander, makes an interesting remark about these mythical animals—dragons, kilins, and others—which so often appear in the stories and indeed the histories of China. He wonders whether the accounts may not be traced to traditions of the last appearances of creatures belonging to extinct species, adding:

> Geological researches have not yet opened out the paleontology of Tartary and China; may it not be found that the last haunts of the ichthyosauri and plesiosauri were in the swamps and wilds of Chinese Asia?

This seems to be a curious anticipation of later American researches in Mongolia.

At his birth Confucius was given the name of Kiu and afterwards that of Chung-ne. It is said the first part of the name relates to his being a second son and the last to the sacred hill of Ne visited by his mother.

Of her it is unlikely that we should hear much, though in the case of the later philosopher, known as Mencius in the West, some charming stories of his mother survive. All we know of Ching-tsai may be briefly told. She was no small-footed, tottering creature, for that fashion did not appear in China till some centuries later. And she seems to have acted with discretion when she was left a widow three years after her son's birth. Certainly she won his affection. It is a Chinese tradition that she was a young woman of force of character, and perhaps that may be deduced from such an incident as I have told of her wooing. If so, she conforms to the almost invariable rule of the mothers of great men, and it is a pity so little is told of her.

A pity also that so little is known of the boyhood of Confucius, though what remains suits well with his later life, for we see him grave beyond his years, interested in the sacrifices to the spirits and the solemn rites accompanying them. It is recorded—and the same tale is told of his own grandson—that sitting one day with his grandfather he heard him sigh deeply as some sorrowful image crossed his mind. The boy looked up quickly:

"Sir, have I done anything to grieve you or shown any inclination which might cast a shade on your memory?"

Greatly astonished at such words from a child, the grandfather asked who it was who had taught him to speak so wisely.

"You, sir, for I have often heard you say that a child who behaves ill not only disgraces himself but brings disgrace upon his ancestors."

His grandfather was silent, but from joy.

This is a story that should be true, for it corresponds with the grave and formal atmosphere in which his life began and was to end. From the beginning he loved knowledge, and it is recorded that at the age of fourteen he had learned all his master could teach and indeed was able to help him with the work of the other boys. He himself told his disciples:

"At the age of fifteen the acquisition of knowledge was the one object which engrossed all my thoughts."

Perhaps he did himself a little injustice there, for he grew up a manly man as well as a scholar. He was regular in his gymnastic exercises, a skilful charioteer, a lover of the chase in its proper place and time, and above all a passionate devotee of music and performer on the lute. It is almost needless to say he was a lover of poetry in all its highest beauties, for that was and is a Chinese accomplishment with men of birth. In fact he may be taken as an example not only of the great Chinese gentleman (a type among the highest in the world) but of the great gentleman all the world over, stately-mannered, valiant, talented—and what more, this account of him will show.

It was natural that such a young man in such a country as China, where high intellect has always been honored, should soon find public employment; and it was urgent, for he and his mother were poor. It is said that his hunting and fishing were needed to supply a very thinly spread table, and later when the variety of his knowledge in these and other lines was praised he himself said :

"When I was young my condition was low, and so I gained ability in many things—but they were mean matters."

Scarcely mean, it is to be thought, if they forged the hard steel of a character which carried him nobly through so many misfortunes. Great men are not commonly cradled and reared in luxury.

He received an appointment in the state of Lu at about the age of seventeen, a subordinate one connected with the storage of grain and the charge of the public fields and lands. According to one of the greatest of his later followers, Meng-tzu (Latinized as Mencius), Confucius said at this time in describing his duties:

"My calculations must all be right. That is what I have to care about."

And again:

"The oxen and sheep must be fat, strong, and superior. That is what I have to care about."

He evidently succeeded, for he was held in evegrowing respect. There was that about the man which made him a personality and a presence to be noted, go where he would. It is easy to believe that at nineteen such a man would have no difficulty in winning a wife from a noble family. She gave him a son a year after; and it is a proof of the golden opinion he had won from the ruler of the state of Lu that the duke sent a courtier to congratulate him, and to present him with two costly and symbolic carp to be eaten at the banquet in celebration of the birth. Confucius acknowledged the honor by calling his son Li (the Carp), and added the name Pi Yu, which also relates him to the royal gift of the fish. The child thus became Pi Yu Li.

CHAPTER 16

THE GROWING POWER OF CONFUCIUS

When Confucius was twenty-four he lost his mother, the loving Ching-tsai, and that due filial honor should be paid to her memory he retired for nominally three years from public life, in reality two years and three months. To the western mind it is almost incredible that such a time can be given to the formalities of grief, but these things were done even by the supreme ruler the emperor, often to the great discontent of his people.

He buried her at the original home of his ancestors and removed his father's coffin that they might lie in the same grave. For as he said:

"We owe our being to both parents alike, and an equal debt of gratitude is due. We must express that feeling by rendering them the same homage, and it would not be just if those bound by such ties in life were separated in death."

That is a true instinct, honorable to parent and child. He remained in the neighborhood of the tomb for two years and three months fulfilling the command:

> Three years the infant in its parents' arms.
> Three years the mourner at his parents' tomb.

Then, laying his mourning robes on the tomb, he returned to life. Five days afterwards he took up his silenced lute again and tried to sing, but he had no heart for music. His voice choked in his throat, and it was five days more before he could bring himself to enjoy the music he loved so dearly. Song implied a forgetfulness in himself which wounded him. Beneath the surface of a grave ceremonious carriage, one can easily see that he was a man of quick nervous sensibility, very open to suffering, very tender of inflicting it upon others, except where high considerations demanded it.

It is related, though some cast doubt on the story, that he had a domestic problem of his own to confront, which is apparently not uncommon with philosophers; and it is possible to wish that Chinese historians had given a little more information on the cause inducing Confucius to separate from his wife. Nothing is alleged against her, but that of course does not prove that she may not have been intolerable for one reason or another.

On the other hand, it must be owned, there is something about philosophy that does not seem to harmonize with the feminine mentality. There have been too many examples of this to leave it in doubt. But there is the wife's side also; and if the reasons for divorce were and are many in China that may not always be to her disadvantage. It is not apparently realized of that great country that the wife is not always as reluctant to go as her lord may believe, and that in the seven causes for divorce she may easily find or create the means of an escape which she is not sorry to accept.

It becomes interesting, however, to learn the views of Confucius upon marriage. They have colored the whole ethic of China on that very important matter— more important there by far than in the West, where the family is now in practice a very discredited quantity, whatever it may be in the nobly conceived speeches of public men. In China it is still the unit and the safeguard of the land, and will so remain after the billow of Bolshevism has broken on the sands of time, though family-life many succumb later to the more insidious inroads of western example and education.

The ruling Prince of Lu had asked the opinion of Confucius on the subject of marriage. He replied: "Marriage is the natural condition of man and the state which best enables him to fulfil his destiny in this world. It is a state which dignifies those who enter it, but it must be seriously considered, that its duties may be scrupulously carried through. These duties are twofold—those which are common to the two sexes and those which belong to either respectively.

"The husband as master must command; but both are equally required to act in the way which best harmonizes with and imitates the relations between heaven and earth, by and through which all things are created, sustained, and preserved. The basis should be reciprocal tenderness, confidence, truth, and scrupulous consideration for each other's feelings; the husband ever leading and directing; the wife ever following and yielding, while every act is kept within the limits set by justice, modesty, and honor."

A beautiful ideal indeed if every husband were worth following and every wife right in yielding. In which did Confucius or his wife fail? He resumes:

"In every condition of her social life the wife is entirely dependent on her husband. Should he die she does not recover her liberty. Before her marriage she was under the authority of her parents or, should they have died, of her nearest relations. As a wife she lived in subjection to her husband, and as a widow is subservient to her son or, if she has more than one, to the eldest. And it is the duty of this son while serving her with all possible affection and respect to watch and guard her from those dangers to which from the natural weakness of her sex she may be exposed.

"Custom does not sanction a widow's remarriage. On the contrary it requires that she should remain in strict seclusion within her own home for the remainder of her days. She is forbidden to take part in any business external to it, and even in her own house is to occupy herself only with indispensable domestic matters. During the day she is to avoid all unnecessary movement from room to room, and at night a light is to be kept constantly burning in her chamber. She will be glorified by her posterity as one who has lived in the scrupulous performance of the duties of a virtuous woman."

He laid down also the rules for the suitable ages for marriage and pointed out the great need for care in the choice of husbands for daughters.

"No man should be thought eligible who has committed a crime or exposed himself to the action of the law, or who is suffering from a constitutional disease, or who has any mental or physical malady likely to produce distaste. Or a son, being the head of his family, who has lost both parents."

The last sentence is extremely difficult to understand. The annotation of a Chinese scholar upon it would be desirable.

Now come the reasons given by Confucius for the divorce of a wife:

"A husband cannot exercise this right without just cause. Of such causes there are seven. First, when a wife cannot live on good terms with his parents. Second, if she be found incapable of bearing sons. Third, if she be guilty of immodest or immoral behavior. Fourth, if she injures the character of her family by spreading unfounded or calumnius reports. Fifth, if she suffers from ailments which produce a natural feeling of repugnance. Sixth, if she cannot be restrained from using violent language. Seventh, if she secretly appropriates, no matter from what motive, anything belonging to the household without her husband's knowledge."

But yet pity must be remembered in the midst of judgment. A husband must not exercise his right under the following conditions:

"First, when the wife having lost both her parents has no home to return to; second, when on the death of the husband's father or mother the appointed three years of mourning have not been completed; and third, when the husband having married the wife in the days of his poverty becomes rich afterwards."

All this leaves large field for conjecture as to why Confucius separated from his wife. It seems likely that she could not have been a great offender, for many years after, he sorrowed on hearing of her death (though no etiquette commanded grief in such a case) and spoke of her with tenderness. Letting imagination play over the facts of history, I incline to think that she may have "appropriated no matter from what motive" some little household goods, perhaps even taking the liberty of considering it her own, and so met with her fate. Perhaps it was easier to forgive a very youthful crime in hearing of the death of the old woman who cared for none of these things now.

To the western mind these rules and regulations for marriage, even the formality with which they are set forth, may appear truly ridiculous and impossible. Yet let us remember that China is very old and very wise; we are very young, and perhaps foolish in spite of our precocious mechanical achievements—which really matter so much less than success in the social adjustments of life. As an old Chinese gentleman once said to me:

"In the West you think it of much importance to reach a place in sixty minutes rather than in sixty hours. In China we consider that what matters is what you do when you get there."

Based on the family and its pieties China has survived as a great nation during nearly two thousand, five hundred years of wealth and prosperity and storm and battle since Confucius uttered those words; and she may now be renewing her youth under our eyes. Who would dare to prophesy the same duration for the white civilizations? Do we yet understand all the implications of placing women in the same position as men judicially, socially, in every way?

It is not what Nature has done. She does not recognize the principles of equality and inequality in her work. She recognizes differences, which must be adjusted by differences of treatment. I have so great a respect for the wisdom of the Orient both in India and China that I cannot feel there is nothing to be said on their side in relation to their attitude toward women. I am certain also that the western peoples do not with a few notable exceptions in the least understand either the attitude or its reasons. And be it remembered there have been great empresses in China, poetesses, artists, women who have made themselves felt in every department of life. What China declined to lose in her women are the things which nothing else can offer in their place: sweetness, the wisdom of tenderness, delicacy, intuition, the home, the family—and much else more easily felt in Asia than expressed.

There is another feature in the character of Confucius, which because it bore an important part in his philosophy must never be forgotten—his passionate love of music and belief in it as a necessary part of good government. This is the more to be noted because it was a belief shared by some of the greatest of the Greeks. The very name of the collective Muses and the word "music" have the same derivation, expressing the rhythm and harmony upon which all creation moves. In China it had been a belief in remotest antiquity that even birds and beasts might be brought into docility and harmonious relations with mankind through the influence of sweet sounds; of all the arts it was the most powerful of humanizing forces and the best way of moving the hearts of a semibarbarous people to higher things. This reminds us of the western idea as expressed in the words: "Let me write the songs of a nation and I care not who makes its laws." For that way lies power.

"It is impossible," Confucius said once, "for a vicious man to be a good musician."

An interesting story is told of the love of Confucius for music. When he was still under the age of twenty- nine news was brought him of a musician named Siang living in the state of Kin and skilled in the ancient music, which Confucius venerated beyond all else. Eagerly he set out to visit Siang, though traveling through the distracted states was attended with many risks. Siang, seeing the quality of the young man, opened his heart and spoke with passionate enthusiasm of the glories of the art of music as one of heaven's best gifts to man, while Confucius listened enthralled. Then seizing his lute to illustrate his words Siang played a piece composed by the great Prince Wan Wang—most enlightened of patriots and one of the ideal heroes of Confucius. In breathless silence he listened.

For ten days Siang repeated and Confucius studied this music of the prince, and then Siang desired him to perform it with the other pupils for audience. He played it with such exquisite skill that Siang said with delight: "This piece is achieved. Let us pass on to another." But Confucius would not. He saluted with formality :

"Permit me to beg for delay. Thanks to your skilled instruction I have played the piece correctly, but I have not yet grasped the prince's intention. I am not content." "I give you five days to master it," replied Siang.

At the end of five days Confucius came, still doubting. "Allow me to beg for five days more. The great prince's intention in his music looms darkly on me through a thick cloud. If I cannot then see it clearly, music is too high a study for me, and I shall give it up." He returned on the fifth day, transfigured with delight.

"I have found it! I have found it! This morning waking I was a changed man. All I sought stood revealed. I took my lute and felt the meaning of every note I played. It seemed that I stood before the great Wan Wang, that I looked into his large and shining eyes and heard the sound of his sonorous voice. My heart expanded toward him, for now his thought was mine."

He had become an accomplished musician.

Siang heard him play in silence, then spoke:

"Sir, you are a man of such insight that I cannot act as your teacher. With your permission I enroll myself henceforward among your disciples."

It will be easily understood that neither Confucius nor Siang could have taken this line if they had regarded music only as an esthetic enjoyment. To Confucius it was one of the highest intellectual and moral forces, and as such it will find its place in my account of his philosophy.

The kin or lute, upon which he played is still used in China by the most elegantly cultivated Chinese, and many famous pictures of bygone days represent Chinese gentlemen playing it. Alexander describes it thus:

"It is about three and one-half feet long and six inches wide, with a curved, slightly tapering convex surface, over which the strings are stretched, and a flat undersurface, the space between being hollow. It had originally only five strings but two have since been added. They are of silk and vary in size. They are fastened to the two extremities of the instrument and kept in their places by a bridge fixed near the broadest end. The sounding-board is fitted with twelve mother-of-pearl studs to assist in the fingering."

Not long ago, in a voyage across the Indian ocean, I had the privilege of hearing more than once an accomplished Chinese gentleman sing some of the ancient songs of China to an inefficient substitute for the kin. But even then their pathos, fire, and ardor gave me some idea of what such music must have meant to "the princely man" of China, as he sat to delight his own ears and those of others with what moved his very soul. His kin was his pleasure in times of joy and his comfort in the many sorrowful hours which fell to his share. He is said to have played the harp also.

It was about this time that proof occurred of the notice attracted by his great personality. One of the ministers of the reigning Prince of Lu lay on his death-bed. He had been a student of the Rites honored from of old in China, and a great and necessary part later of the philosophy of Confucius. Thus waiting at the door of death he called to him his chief officer and spoke:

"A knowledge of the inner rule of conduct is the stem of a man. Without it he has no means of standing firm. I have heard that there is a man named K'ung [Confucius] skilled in this. He is a descendant of wise men, and it has been observed that if men of intelligent virtue do not gain celebrity themselves, distinguished men will certainly appear among their descendants. I think these words are to come true in K'ung. After my death tell Ho Kei to go and study the inner rule of conduct under this man."

Ho Kei was the son of the dying minister and with a son's obedience he enrolled himself as a disciple of Confucius. Others of the family followed, and so the number was swelled of the disciples already attracted by his wisdom. The wealth and standing of these new disciples brought him fresh celebrity, and his position as a famous teacher was assured.

We are now in the time when the rays of his great personality drew many into the atmosphere of what they felt to be almost unearthly wisdom. It was as though one of the mighty sages, seen dimly through the veil of time, had returned to bless the distracted empire with guidance from some higher sphere. And in the master, as we must now call him, this wisdom was combined with such courtesy, such love and reverence for antiquity and its semidivine heroes, that it might be said all the ideals of China met in this one man. He threw his house open to those who wished to learn, and gave teaching willingly to those who could afford to pay little or nothing for the privilege, feeling this to be a part of the duty to the state which he taught to each disciple in his measure. But he demanded intelligence and application, and anything less produced a haughty withdrawal.

"When I have presented one corner of a subject to anyone, and he cannot discern the other three from it, I do not repeat my lesson," he said.

But his was sometimes a peripatetic university for he loved travel. He had early described himself as "a man of the north, south, east and west," and he is to be pictured in his cart drawn by a single ox, moving about from one place to another, learning and teaching as he went. The disciples walked beside him, keeping pace with the slowfooted ox, and he would illustrate his discourse with any incident which accorded with his philosophy. Several of these stories shall be told later.

So for three years he worked, sowing good seed, but always with the hidden hope that the prince of his perplexed state might call upon him to help with more than advice, with practical power in its government. He knew his own gifts and longed to put them to the test, for as will be seen in the record of his philosophy its aim was to create and rule the Perfect State, in accordance with the inspired teachings of the men who had made the empire of China.

"I do not claim originality for my teachings. I am a transmitter," he said with the modesty underlying his utterances about his mission. And at first in that character, but later in a more exalted one as his unique greatness broke upon the people, his fame for knowledge of what constitutes good government and a happy nation spread through his native state of Lu. It grew the more because, from the dissensions and clashes of the various states, some of them paying little or no obedience to the will of the emperor, arose great miseries of battle and oppression, so that enlightened minds grasped eagerly at a doctrine which held out hope of peace and contentment. There were thirteen great principalities and many small dependencies, and in many of these the duke or prince was a law unto himself, and the misery or happiness of the people depended upon his personal character.

Here to the mind of Confucius was a great field for his wisdom and he lived in daily hope of a summons to the ruler of Lu. That was not yet to be. The weak and worthless Prince of Lu had not realized the scope of Confucius's great subject. Meanwhile as his consequence increased he was given a chariot with a pair of horses by the prince, and, with a band of his disciples about him, was permitted to make a visit to the court of the emperor, then established at the city of Lo in Ho-nan.

That expedition was one of the brightest spots in the outward life of Confucius. Even through the vast stretch of years between his time and ours can be felt the pleasure with which he set out, honored by his own sovereign. He was still in his prime, and it must have seemed that the world was at his feet, as he guided his chariot by the springing fields of rice and blossoming meadows of that land of flowers.

He prided himself upon being a skilful driver, an art which he thought part of the equipment of a gentleman. He was a sportsman too after a fashion, though so mercifully inclined that his disciples record of him that he never caught a fish by net and never shot a bird with his arrows except in flight, considering that they were entitled to a fair chance for their lives. It may have been on this very excursion to Lo that he saw a party of huntsmen and immediately got out of his chariot to join in the chase. One of the disciples was filled with horrified astonishment at such an undignified proceeding.

"What, sir! Can it be possible that you would do a thing so ill harmonizing with your great reputation? Surely your time should be spent in studying the sciences and fostering noble principles."

Confucius halted and looked at him, one may be sure with amusement.

"Really you are quite wrong. A wise man will consider everything within his purview. Besides, everything connected with the chase is interesting. It was one of man's earliest occupations. It not only fed and clothed him, but was the means of protection of life and agriculture from wild animals. For great kings it served as a relaxation, and for the scholar it is not only that but a means of restoring a wearied mind. And there is a still higher value. By the chase a man can best carry out the rite of offering up animals killed by his own hand, in honor of his ancestors."

And off he went with the sportsmen and remained with them for a week. Although these arguments can be effectively countered except in countries where protection is needed from dangers, I think one is glad to know that Confucius as a skilful charioteer and huntsman was something more than a sapless scholar.

Undoubtedly "the princely man" of his ideal will touch life at every point and know how to understand all its desires.

So he proceeded to Lo with his band of students about him, observing and commenting as he went. Those young men are to be envied, for there is no education like contact with a rich and fruitful mind, and personal affection and reverence kindle aspiration and understanding.

The account, traditional and historic, of his stay in the city of Lo is full of interest. The emperor did not honor himself by inviting Confucius to an audience, nor did any but one of the principal ministers. It is unknown whether this wounded Confucius or whether it was his choice to visit Lo as student of the usages of ancient days, preferring privacy with his disciples. But one result it certainly had, for it is recorded that he met the famous philosopher Lao Tsŭ, the Teacher of the Way, whose life and views I shall give in due course.

Surely the meeting of two such minds must have been a great occasion, for here face to face were Confucius, the man who considered that what man could know of the supernormal was most safely approached through the practical thoughts and acts of daily life, and Lao Tsŭ, whose beliefs centered on the Absolute, the transcendental, walking with his eyes fixed upon a glory which dazzled him. It may be compared with a meeting between Plato and Aristotle at their best.

It is said that Lao Tsŭ, then an aged man, spoke freely on the subject of what appeared to him the worldly aim of the teaching of Confucius. If so, it must be owned that he did less than justice to the great man before him. An Indian philosopher would have completely understood the Karma Yoga (the high evangel of noble deeds) which Confucius taught, and would have perceived that it was another road to his own goal. So great a mystic should have known that to all mystics the practical is the garment alone. But he spoke thus of the passion of Confucius for the wisdom of the ancient sages:

"Those men of whom you speak are dead, and their bones dust. Only their words remain. When the times suit the princely man he mounts aloft, when they do not his feet remain entangled."

Thus, as it were, indicating that there exists metaphysically a higher way than the practice of the stately virtues enjoined by Confucius. He objected also to the public life of Confucius and his following of disciples as ministering to self-sufficiency instead of to the solitary and impassioned search for wisdom. His own tastes were those of the true yogin.

"For," as he said, "the wise man loves obscurity. He avoids public employment, knowing that at his death all he can hope is to leave a few true maxims entrusted to a chosen few. He will not unbosom himself to the world, but regards time and circumstance. He who possesses a treasure guards it and does not boast of it to everyone he meets."

He is said to have dwelt also on the danger of the Confucian system of using dead forms as a means of giving life to China, insisting that slavish obedience to these would hamper the growth of the nation. He did not believe success could be thus attained. This could not have been acceptable to Confucius, who though so much the younger man kept his eyes fixed on the past golden age and incessantly used it for every example and illustration ; but his deep courtesy and reverence for age would enable him to hide any resentment, and he must have listened with profound interest if not with sympathy to the teachings Lao Tsŭ opened before him in speaking of the spiritual and universal Intelligence which he called "The Way."

The text of his discourse might have been: "The letter killeth; the spirit giveth life."

Here it seems there is much to be said on both sides and that the truth lies in the Mean, but those who have studied the philosophies of both must judge between two great thinkers.

It is said that Lao Tsŭ turned at last to Confucius with a searching question:

"And you—have you also learned to know the Divine Intelligence—the Way?" And that the younger man answered sadly:

"Alas, I have not. I have been a seeker for nearly thirty years and have not found it."

It is told that he remained troubled in spirit after the interview, and being questioned by his disciples answered thus:

"When I meet one whose thoughts fly upward like a bird I can aim an arrow and bring him to the earth. When I meet one whose thoughts range far and wide like the running deer, like a hound I can pursue and drag him down. When I meet one whose thoughts dive into the deeps like an angler I can bait my hook and pull him to shore. But when I meet one whose thoughts rush heavenward like the flight of the dragon and lose themselves in the Immensities, what power have I? So it is with Lao Tsŭ. When he speaks I listen with wonder. My mind is troubled and perplexed."

So met and parted two of the greatest minds of mortal men; and if a part of this story be traditional it is still of the profoundest interest, for it reveals the two great schools of Chinese thought in opposition. Its significance will be better understood when I come to deal with the doctrines of either and both.

CHAPTER 17

CONFUCIUS AND HIS GREAT DISCIPLES

During this important visit to Lo, Confucius was presented by his host Ch'ang Huang to one of the ministers of the emperor, who perhaps may have had orders to sound him before further honors were granted. This man asked:

"May I be permitted to know the nature of your doctrines and your manner of teaching them?"

Confucius replied—and a touch of pride may be guessed in his voice: "As to my doctrines they are very simple, being none other than those which were held by our unerring guides and ancient heroes Yao and Shun and are incumbent on all men to follow. I cite the examples of the ancients, exhort my hearers to follow the sacred books, and I emphasize the necessity of meditating deeply upon them."

"But how should a man begin who wishes to acquire wisdom?"

"A large question!" answered Confucius. "But certain propositions may be remembered when needed. Here they are: As the hardest steel is the most brittle, so that which is most solidly established is the easiest to destroy. Pride puffs up, and the ambition of the arrogant is boundless; but the proud man falls, and the claim of the arrogant is empty. The too complaisant man yields everything to gain his end and finds himself the dupe of his own facility. Now all this may seem trivial, yet the man who practices it will advance in the road of wisdom."

Here we have the warning that the oldest institutions are the most easily ruined and that personal conduct is the basis of all good government: the true Confucian note. One may wonder what were the thoughts of the minister as he retired, ceremoniously no doubt, to report on the new portent. But it is pleasanter to dream oneself back to the beauties of the ancient city and its magnificent temples, simple in comparison with later developments but beautiful in simplicity. In such surroundings Confucius was in high delight, as he wandered from point to point of interest with his eager disciples—explaining, commenting on what they saw and the value of its antiquity and power in forming the characters of men to reverence and obedience to just authority.

There is an account of one of these visits, when he and his followers entered the Hall of Light where audience was given by the emperor to the feudal princes of the empire. He walked about, examining with deep content all the arrangements handed down from antiquity, and sighed with pleasure.

"Now I know the great wisdom of the Duke of Chao and how his house attained to the imperial throne!" he said with deep satisfaction.

On the walls hung portraits of the sovereigns of China, from Yao and Shun downward, with words of praise or blame written upon them. Among them was a portrait of the Duke of Chao—the favorite ideal of Confucius—with the infant king, his nephew, sitting upon his knee, as he gave audience to the feudal princes. Then indeed joy dawned upon the master's face, as he turned to his watching disciples and said:

"As we use a glass to examine the forms of things so we must study the past to understand the present."

In the hall of the ancestral temple was a statue of a man with three needles fastening his lips. The disciples grouped themselves about it, while the master read aloud the inscriptions upon the back, of which I give a part:

Do not be overanxious for relaxation or repose. He who is so, will achieve neither.

If a man does not resent slight injustices he will soon be called upon to face giant wrongs

.Heed words as well as acts; thoughts also; and remember even when alone that the Divine is everywhere.

A sapling may be easily uprooted. With a tree an axe is needed.

Do not glory in your strength. There is always a stronger.

The masses and ordinary men have small prescience or power in dealing with the unknown and can only follow a leader.

Heaven has no favorites.

The ocean is full. Yet inflowing rivers do not overflow it.

My mouth is closed; I cannot speak. Do not consult me. I cannot solve your doubts and I have nothing to ask. My teaching is enigmatic and true.

I stand elevated above you, but no man can harm me. What mortal can say so much?

A house may be burned by smoldering fire, when a fierce flame would have shown itself and have been easily extinguished.

A river is the flux of many streams.

The union of many threads makes an unbreakable cord.

To him the silent voice might well seem inspired. He said afterwards: "In these words we have all that is most useful for knowledge, and he who studies and applies them will not be far from perfection. Observe them, my children. I shall do my best to use them and I hope you all are equally resolved."

Farther on, he led the way into the palace, and there another sight halted him.

By the throne among the silken and lacquered splendors stood an ordinary bucket such as housewives use for drawing water. Confucius understood its use but, willing to test the officials, asked for information. None knew. It had stood there from time immemorial, and that sufficed. So taking the bucket the master carried it to the cistern of a fountain close by and dipped it in. He bade the disciples notice that to fill it in equilibrium the exact degree of pressure must be used. With too little it floated useless, with too much it sank to the bottom.

"And this is a parable of good government, which never either exceeds due force or neglects it. Here is the lesson of firmness and moderation, and it was formally shown at the beginning of each reign that the sovereign might see and learn. My grief is that such a lesson should be disused!"

His host in the city of Lo was, as I have said, a gentleman named Ch'ang Huang, who not only treated him with the utmost hospitality, but being an authority on music gave the master an opportunity of much discussion and instruction on that vital subject. And Ch'ang Huang moreover has left a delightful description of his friend, which I give first in what may be called a literal translation—so far as literal translation is possible—preserving the Chinese flavor, and afterwards in ordinary English.

"I have observed about Chung-ne [Confucius] many of the marks of a sage. He has river eyes and a dragon forehead—the very characteristics of Huang Ti. His arms are long, his back is like a tortoise, and he is nine feet six inches in height [the Chinese foot was much shorter than ours]—the very semblance of T'ang the Successful. When he speaks he praises the ancient kings. He moves along the path of humility and courtesy. He has heard of every subject and retains a strong memory. His knowledge of things seems inexhaustible. Have we not in him the rising of a sage?"

Or in more ordinary words:

"He is a man with whom none other of our day can be compared. In person as in mind he is singularly gifted. You cannot see him without perceiving that he has supreme intelligence, which streams from his eyes in two broad beams of light. He is very tall, with rounded shoulders and long arms, and has a majestic presence. In conversation he constantly recalls the ancient royal sages, and every word gives rise to virtuous reflections. He presents the most perfect model for posterity to form itself upon."

It is recorded that Confucius when this was repeated to him exclaimed:

"I am entirely unworthy of such praise. It would have been nearer the mark if Ch'ang Huang had said: Here is a man who knows a little music, who wishes to obtain knowledge, and who tries to understand and give effect to the ever-holy Rites.' "

The Rites must have been very present to his mind at the time, for he was in the imperial city in the virtual presence of the sovereign by whom all the most important of those Rites must be performed, in circumstances of infinite solemnity. Each feudal prince could sacrifice and offer propitiation for his own subjects, but only the sovereign for the whole vast empire. There was then no professional class of priests in China; only the rulers and heads might offer these sacrifices. Those who know the Great Altar of Heaven in Peking alone can realize the profound and awe-striking position held by the emperor as representative of the people in this tremendous ceremonial. As I stood there it seemed to me that the weight of the ages and all the vast destinies of China, past and to be, descended upon the mind and rapt one away from common things and into full understanding of the attitude of Confucius toward these mighty matters. His declaration to his disciples on these points appeals to all who value truth and beauty:

"I love and reverence the ancients, for their writings are so far-reaching and comprehensive that I never weary of studying them. They are an inexhaustible mine of wealth, and so it is that when I write I care little to originate new ideas but confine myself as much as possible to compiling and elaborating everything taught by the sacred wise men of old."

It followed that he would set neither himself nor any other on the same level as the royal teachers and exemplars. As he said:

"The sage and the man of perfect virtue, how dare I name myself with them? It may simply be said of me that I strive to become such without satiety and teach others without weariness."

And now, returning to Lu and still continuing his teaching to rich and poor—for he would take those who brought even a little parcel of dried flesh for the fee, provided he saw they were in earnest—he began to turn his attention to collating the ancient classics, which recorded and embodied so much that he believed was necessary to the welfare of China. To some he added; all passed through his hands. These will be referred to in the account of his philosophy.

Since he was now famous and surrounded by disciples from different parts, even to the number of three thousand at times, material accumulated daily for the book that will always be most valuable to western readers— the account given by his disciples to their own disciples of the manners, appearance, and sayings of the great master. In these he lives and is as real to us as the Greek Socrates in the dialogues recorded by Plato; for though the utterances of Confucius are more gnomic they are as vivid with personality. This is the famous book known as "The Digested Conversations," or the "Analects," and it may be called his portrait drawn by himself and by those who knew and loved him.

On his return to Lu he found his native state in confusion from the aggression of the three noble families who held the ruling prince in terror, very much after the fashion of the great Earl of Warwick, known as "the kingmaker" in the reign of Henry Sixth of England. It came at last to war, and the prince, beaten in the field, fled into the neighboring state of C'hi for safety. Confucius followed to avoid the turmoil which disturbed his academic peace.

He may have had another reason for choosing C'hi as a refuge for he had already had messages from the Prince of C'hi, which he had dismissed with a certain curtness— messages demanding his advice as to how a troublesome people could be satisfied and ruled. He had answered:

"Tell your royal master that I know nothing of him or his people. How is it possible for me to be useful? Had he wished to know anything of the ancient sovereigns or how they would have acted, then certainly I could have told him, for I have a right to speak on subjects I have studied. But I am ignorant of the condition of his people."

Now that the events of his life pointed to C'hi it is probable that he may have imagined a possible future there for his great gifts of government, seeing that such a thing had become almost hopeless in Lu. There were other attractions also, for though the Prince of C'hi was in himself a weak voluptuary, he had a chief minister with a reputation for good sense and—still more attractive—a carefully preserved collection of music composed by the ancient sovereign Yun. This was irresistible to Confucius.

To C'hi accordingly he set out, with a little band of disciples. Little, for naturally the larger number were seldom all in attendance. They came and went as they needed instruction on some special point. Perhaps this is the time to picture some of these faithful men, who like planets on their orbits surrounded the great sun Confucius and whose spirit-tablets are still preserved with his in the Temple of Confucius in Peking. There I have seen them in the solemn shadows of that august place. I will give in the words of Confucius and their own the names and characteristics of one or two who stand out among the crowd. They are perhaps typical, each in his own way, of others who sat at the feet of their leader.

And first there is Yen Hui—dearest of all to the master, a scion of the same family as the master's mother. He wept inconsolable tears when Yen Hui died, saying: "Alas! God has forsaken me—God has forsaken me!" Yen Hui was a man, calm, silent, and simple, devoted to the master, devoted to the study of wisdom, whose whole life was passed in poverty which would have soured many a spirit, but could never touch the loftiness of his. He was so silently reflective that some of the more ardent disciples inclined to think him stupid, but said the master:

"I have talked with Yen Hui for a whole day, and he made no objection to anything I said as if indeed he were stupid. He has retired, and I have examined his conduct when away from me and found him able to illustrate all my teachings. Yen Hui? No, he is not stupid!" And again Confucius asked another distinguished disciple: "Which do you think superior? Yourself or Yen Hui?"

He answered: "How dare I compare myself with Yen Hui? He hears one point and knows all about a subject. I hear one and know only a second."

The master said: "You are not equal to him, I grant you! No, you are not equal to him."

And again the master said:

"Such was Yen Hui that for three months there would be nothing in his mind contrary to perfect virtue. The others may attain to this once a day or a month, but no more. Admirable indeed was the virtue of Yen Hui! With a single bamboo dish of rice, a single gourd dish of drink, and living in his mean, narrow lane, while others could not have borne the distress he never allowed it to trouble his joy. Admirable indeed was the virtue of Yen Hui!"

This man stands out as a living figure even, so to speak, in death. We see the master's bitter tears at his death and hear the disciples, amazed at the break-up of his stately calmness, assert:

"Sir, your grief is excessive!"

"Is it excessive? If I am not to mourn bitterly for this man, for whom am I to mourn?"

And so, doubtless touched themselves, they proceeded to give the true-hearted Yen Hui a sumptuous funeral, very little in accord with the pinching poverty of his life. Confucius had buried his own son very simply, because his strong sense of fitness revolted at the unnecessary and foolish cost of the funeral rites, though no one laid more stress on true mourning and honor, and he was displeased at this ostentation. He said with grief:

"Yen Hui behaved to me as a son yet I was not able to [bury] him as I did my son. The fault is not mine; it is yours, O disciples!"

It is one of the tragedies of true greatness that often it is so little comprehended by those who stand nearest to it. But Yen Hui had understood and he had his reward. Even while he lived Confucius knew and recorded it:

"There is Yen Hui. He has nearly attained to perfect virtue. He is often in want."

That such a man could be happy in this poverty is the meaning. Another of the disciples described him as "empty-hearted"—or, as they would have said in India, "desireless"—free from all vanities and ambitions and utterly devoted to the master. Once when they were making a dangerous journey the master missed him, and on his coming up again with the party said anxiously: "I thought you had died!"

Yen Hui answered with love which shines through the formality: "While you were alive how could I presume to die?"

And this man of simplicity and poverty receives great honors from a country which has never forgotten his virtues and never will. In his master's great temple at Peking his spirit-tablet has the first place east among the Four Assessors, and the title of "The Second Sage, the Philosopher Yen." And there his gentle spirit is believed to descend at the time of solemn offering and laudation,—a man of many griefs, white-haired at the age of twenty- four, dead at thirty-three, dear to his country and to all who esteem true greatness of soul. I cannot raise the image of the master in my mind without Yen Hui at his shoulder.

Then there is Tsŭ Lu—a very different character yet lovable in his way—rash, impetuous, brave to a fault, hasty and mistaken in some of his judgments, a soldier given to dashes and excursions in philosophy as on the field of battle. Confucius early predicted of him that he never would die a natural death, nor did he, for he fell fighting gallantly in one of the ferocious little battles that disturbed the warring states. The master was often obliged to check him and to rebuke his rashness gently.

"Shall I teach you what knowledge is?" he said to Tsŭ Lu one day. "Well—it is when you know a thing to hold to the fact that you know it, and when you don't know a thing to allow that you don't. This is knowledge."

No doubt—but a difficult approach for Tsŭ Lu, who had much confidence in his own powers. But Confucius loved him also, though with far less respect than Yen Hui had won from him. He said one day:

"My doctrines make no way. I had better put myself aboard a raft and drift out to sea. And the one who will come with me, I dare to prophesy will be Tsŭ Lu." Tsŭ Lu ventured a little exultation on this compliment to his fidelity, upon which Confucius said (and one can see the smile):

"Tsŭ Lu is fonder of daring than I am, but he does not exercise his judgment upon things." And later when another asked whether Tsŭ Lu could be called perfectly virtuous, Confucius answered a little discouragingly:

"I do not know. In a kingdom of a thousand chariots [a small principality] Tsŭ Lu might be employed to manage the military levies. But I really do not know whether he is perfectly virtuous."

Yet he was an eager soul. It is recorded that when he heard any teaching he had not carried into practice his one terror was lest some other great apothegm should come crashing about his ears before he had mastered the first. He could not appropriate it fast enough. There is a very instructive little scene when the master invited Yen Hui and Tsŭ Lu to reveal their inmost ambitions for his consideration. In broke Tsŭ Lu first:

"I should like having chariots and horses and light fur robes to share them with my friends, and I would not care—not I!—though they should spoil them. I would not be displeased!"

Yen Hui said reflectively:

"I should wish never to boast of my excellence nor to make a display of my right deeds."

In broke again the audacious Tsŭ Lu: "I should like, sir, to hear your wishes."

"As for my wishes: in regard to the aged to give them rest; in regard to friends to show them sincerity; in regard to the young to treat them tenderly. Those are my wishes," the master answered.

One may see the three with this beam of the bright light of memory falling upon them through the dark of ages. Tsŭ Lu's courage never failed him. When the master gave the honor of a visit to a lewd woman (Nan- Tsŭ, wife of the reigning Prince of Wei) Tsŭ Lu was highly displeased at so great and misplaced a favor, insomuch that where no one else would have dared to criticize he stirred Confucius to unwonted emotion and asseveration. He cried aloud in answer to Tsŭ Lu:

"If I have done wrong in this, may Heaven reject me, may Heaven reject me!"

This lovable rashness and audacity cropping out in Tsŭ Lu are seen on every occasion, and always this wakes what Browning calls "the sympathetic spasm," and the reader half smiles, half acknowledges the justice of the master's rebuke.

Confucius said to Yen Hui: "To undertake the duties of office when called to them; when not so called to live retired and content: it is only you and I who have attained to this."

Tsŭ Lu put in, evidently eager of praise and determined not to be left out: "If you had the conduct of the armies of a great state, whom would you have to act with you?" One can hear the "Aha! that would not be Yen Hui!" in his mind.

The answer came coolly:

"I would not have that man to act with me who unarmed would attack a tiger or cross a river without a boat, or would die without any regret. My associate must be the man who proceeds thoughtfully to action, who adjusts his plans and then carries them into execution."

Tsŭ Lu seems to have been silent. But nothing could silence him when his love for his master was awake and watchful. Thus when Confucius was once very ill Tsŭ Lu asked leave to pray for him—i.e., to recite his excellences as the ground for entreaty.

"Is there a precedent for this?" asked Confucius.

"There is," replied the eager Tsŭ Lu. "In 'The Eulogies' it is written 'We pray unto you, O Spirits of Heaven and Earth.'"

The master said: "My prayers began long ago."

He meant that a life lived in harmony with the Good, the True, is in itself a prayer. This anecdote, for which we may thank Tsŭ Lu, gives much insight into the inner calm of a great soul. But this disciple's eagerness led him into excesses later, when Confucius was suffering from serious illness and Tsŭ Lu proposed that his disciples should act as ministers to him. This was after he had held and abandoned office; and the idea in Tsŭ Lu's mind was a consolatory measure to surround him with the shadowy pomp of the time past, when ministers attended him at the court of Lu. He should have known the master better. Confucius broke in:

"Long has the conduct of Tsŭ Lu been deceitful. By pretending to have ministers when I have none, on whom should I impose? On Heaven? Moreover I would sooner choose death among my disciples than among ministers."

Yet the master loved Tsŭ Lu and speaking of him could say with joy:

"Dressed in a tattered robe quilted with hemp, yet standing not ashamed by the side of men dressed in furs— ah, it is Tsŭ Lu who is equal to this! He dislikes nothing, covets nothing! What does he do which is not good?" A brave and generous soul! and we see the firmer mind forming in Tsŭ Lu in spite of all his haste and vanity. Truly Confucius was a great teacher. As he said himself he knew when to urge Yen Hui forward and when to hold Tsŭ Lu back. But he derived much quiet amusement from the excursions and alarms of the latter. He turned to him one day as some of the other disciples sat with them, saying with humor:

"Almost daily you are saying, 'We are not known.' Now what would you do if some prince were to know you?"

Tsŭ Lu answered hastily and lightly:

"Now let us suppose the case of a state of ten thousand chariots: [a large state] let it be pinched between other large states; let it be suffering from invasion; and to this let there be added a famine in corn and all growing things. Well, if I were entrusted with the government, in three years' time I could not only make the people courageous, but teach them to recognize the laws of righteousness."

The master smiled. He was not likely to believe that his teachings filtered through such a medium could produce such a miracle. That was one side of Tsŭ Lu; but of the other his teacher could say:

"Ah, it is Tsŭ Lu who can settle litigations with half a word."

He had reason to know his teaching had not fallen on dry ground. To Tsŭ Lu was awarded the noble praise that "he was one who never slept over the fulfilment of a promise." And we ourselves have cause to thank him, for he had the gift of wholesome irritation—of drawing forth some of the finest sayings of Confucius by unnecessary questions. Thus on his asking for a brief precept for good government he had the answer:

"Go before the people with your own example and be laborious in their affairs." And Tsŭ Lu, unsatisfied and still persisting, got with stern emphasis the repetition, "In these things never weary."

Again we find him one day insisting in his usual hurry:

"The Prince of Wei has been waiting for you that he may administer his government with your help. Now what will you think the first thing to be done?"

"Why to rectify names!" said the master.

Tsŭ Lu was seriously upset at this irrelevance. Indeed he permitted himself to assure the master he was quite wide of the mark. Instruction immediately fell upon him like an avalanche.

"Tsŭ, how unmannerly you are! When a princely man does not know a thing he shows reserve. If names are not correct, language cannot be in accordance with the truth of things, and affairs cannot succeed. When they cannot succeed, rules of conduct and the art of music cannot flourish, punishments are not rightly dealt out; and when this is so, the people do not know how to move. Therefore the instructed man knows it is needful that the names he uses should be appropriate, so that what he speaks may be carried out in truth."

Here we have I think one of the wisest of the utterances of Confucius. Apply this rule to the storm of words let loose in our parliaments, by our so-called statesmen, and note the result. Apply it to certain men of our own race such as Cromwell and Abraham Lincoln, and note with what stern rectitude they observed it, and how in them the inevitable word was father of the inevitable deed not only in themselves but in others. Such are usually men of few words but those unforgotten— unforgetable.

Again, Tsŭ Lu, who always concerned himself with great persons and matters, asked how a sovereign should be served:

"Do not impose on him," said the master, "and moreover, withstand him to his face."

This is the doctrine of utter sincerity which forms such an important part of the Confucian philosophy.

Of these two disciples one might say much more and also of the others, but perhaps enough has been said at present to give a glimpse of the men who learned from and loved Confucius and the great lesson of personality that was ever before them. So we leave them with some last words, describing a group which often gathered about him:

"The disciple Min stood by his side, looking bland and precise; Tsŭ Lu looking bold and soldierly; Yen Hui and Tsŭ Kung with a free straightforward manner. The master was pleased!"

Let us go forward now with these men we know on their pilgrimage to the neighbor state of C'hi.

CHAPTER 18

THE RECOGNITION OF CONFUCIUS

There could have been little hope in his mind as Confucius traveled slowly to the state governed by a prince of whom it was said later: "He had a thousand chariots of four horses each, but when he died none praised him for a single virtue."

The journey there must be pictured as the master sat in his little ox-cart calm and observant, certain of the seventy disciples beside him, Yen Hui and Tsŭ Lu among them. Some of the incidents of the way survive. As they passed the T'ai mountain they saw a lonely grave with a solitary woman weeping bitterly beside it. Confucius halting sent Tsŭ Lu to question her.

"You weep as though you had known sorrow on sorrow," he said with sympathy.

"And so I have," she answered. "Here on this spot my husband's father was killed by a tiger. My husband also, and now my son."

Confucius leaned forward in his car. It was his custom in such cases to bow forward to the front bar as if to do homage to the majesty of grief. Then he spoke: "If this is so why do you not leave this terrible place?" She answered with streaming eyes: "Here there are tigers but at least the government is not harsh."

He turned to the disciples standing about him. "My children, hear and remember. Oppressive government is fiercer than a tiger."

And revolving this they passed on slowly and left her weeping.

Another curious incident is referred to this journey. They had entered the borders of the state of C'hi, when from a grove hard by were heard choking cries and struggles as if from a dying man, and on searching they found one in the agonies of death from strangling. Confucius rushed to the rescue and unknotted the cord about his throat and when he could speak asked what cruelty had brought him to this. The man sobbed aloud and told them he had intended to die by his own hand.

"For I began life well. I loved knowledge and studied with zeal. Soon I outdistanced my masters, and then I resolved to travel and see the world that I might gain knowledge of men. Far and wide I traveled, and after many years returned home and married. But within a very short time my father and mother died; and then too late I realized with horror how naked I had been of filial duty, how I had done nothing to repay them for all their tender love. It bowed me with remorse, yet I hoped I could make amends by other duties. I was full of knowledge and experience. I offered my services to my prince, and he would have none of me—would not even grant me an audience.

"Still, I would not despair. I hoped much from the affection of my friends. There too I was wrong. I found nothing but cold and careless indifference. And my only son, whom I loved with all my heart, followed my own example and wandered the wide world over, and still does so—disowning his miserable father and pretending to be an orphan."

He broke down into tears and then continued: "Well I know that I have not performed the most ordinary duties. As a son I have failed utterly. As a citizen I have done nothing for my prince and state. I could not keep my friends' affection nor win my son's. Therefore I would have ended my life if you had not prevented me."

Confucius listened with deep sympathy.

"And yet you were wrong," he said, "very wrong. Despair only adds to a man's ills. Certainly you brought this misery upon yourself, and to your neglect of the greatest of all duties—filial piety—all your ruin may be traced. But everything is not lost. Go home. Act as if today for the first time you had learned the true value of life and use every moment of it rightly. Even now you may attain to the wisdom you missed so long ago." He turned earnestly to his disciples. "Mark what you have heard. Apply it, each one of you, to his own needs."

Thoughtfully he continued the journey; and quietly one by one his followers dropped off, until by the end of the day thirteen had gone back to their homes that they might fulfil the duties which they had learned must not be laid aside even for the pursuit of wisdom. That result must have pleased Confucius, to whom words at all times meant less than the spirit of practical obedience to conviction.

It seems probable that the following pronouncement from "The Analects" may have been suggested by this experience:

"The master said: 'While his parents are alive the son may not go abroad to a distance. If he does go abroad he must have a fixed place to which he goes.' " That is to say a place where the needs of his parents can reach him.

As he entered C'hi in honor—for the prince had come out to meet him—he declared he could tell from the bearing and refined manners of a lad who passed them carrying a pitcher that the influence of the music of the great King Shun was abroad in the land. He hastened his ox that he might not lose a moment in reaching the capital and sharing the delight of the stores of ancient music hoarded there. And hearing its beauty he was so transported beyond the limits of the senses that it is said he tasted no flesh for three months, and that he cried aloud, "Little did I know that music could be so surpassing."

The indwelling spirit of this harmony confirmed his belief that music is an essential basis of a nation's civilization, and he keenly noted its influence in C'hi.

But more than music met him there. Opportunity. The prince might be weak and worthless, but not so much so as to forget that the wisest man in China was within his gates. He sought his advice, putting, as he thought, difficult questions on the science of government, and very likely expecting easy panaceas and flatteries in reply. Those days were not the far more dangerous modern days of flattery of the people; but sufficient harm might be done by flattery of the princes to make it an obvious and profitable task for a philosopher of the baser sort. Confucius, however, had no temptation to waver from his doctrine of sincerity as a mark of the gentleman.

He amplified the remark he had made when Tsŭ Lu demanded a definition of good government. He had then said, "What is necessary is to rectify the names of things." Now he answered, "Good government is present when the prince is prince; the minister, minister; the father, father; and the son, son," meaning that nature in the laws of the family and society lays down the unalterable pattern of good government, which needs only development from the right government of a family to the paternal government of a great state, and that when the prince is truly a royal man as the father is a paternal one, all is achieved, for the little is the condensing of the great, and the great the amplification of the little.

The wisdom and personality of his great guest must certainly have impressed the Prince of C'hi, for he desired to keep the master as the adviser and ornament of his court, with an assignment of land for his support. It might have come to pass had not his chief minister intervened on grounds which are interesting and to be expected when an unusual man is likely to interfere with mediocrity.

"These scholars," he said, "are impracticable and cannot be imitated. They are proud and vain and must have the best positions. They value ceremonies and give way to grief, wasting money on great burials, all of which injures the outlook of the people. The master K'ung is truly a most peculiar person. Certainly he knows all about the Rites, but this is not the time for bothering about his rules for what is fitting. If your Majesty employs him to change the customs of C'hi you will not be considering the people's best interests."

It was easy enough after this to put the weak prince out of love with his adviser.

He said to Confucius, "After all I am old. How can I use the new teaching?"

Yet he tried to make what seemed to him amends, offering the master the lands of Ni Ki, with their revenues as an income.

But these Confucius refused with pride, saying:

"A naan of high instinct will take rewards only for service rendered. I have advised the prince, and he has rejected my advice. Very far indeed is he from understanding me!"

So, wearied in heart a little more because he saw no way of realizing his high vision among men, he set out on his ret urn to the much perturbed state of Lu, to hasten his resear ches into the poetry, music, history, and Rites of the ancient civilization of China, with his disciples aiding him, and in their going and coming spreading the seeds of his ethic of government and social life to germinate in other states.

For fifteen years he occupied himself in these researches, which the Chinese people have accepted as invaluable, combining his work with his teaching. About him and his disciples disorder seethed. Every day was forced upon his mind the deadly peril of neglecting the rule of virtue and the science of government. Selfishness and cruelty in the rulers struggled with brutality and ignorance in the people, and no way out of the confusion was apparent to any mind except his own. For him the light fell on one straight path, and he could not doubt.

Occasionally some distracted chief or ruler would send to him for advice; but those who asked were incapable of profiting by it; and he went his way digesting, collecting, editing, emitting wisdom, which he believed would have saved them all if they could only have applied it. But that was beyond them.

Very little is known of the relation of Confucius with his son Li—who was to die so long before his great father —but one anecdote which survives is interesting.

One of the disciples came up one day to Li as he stood alone and, filled with curiosity as to the son's advantages, asked:

"Have you had any lessons from your father differing from those given to us all?"

"None. He was standing alone once when I was hurrying along the court below and he said to me, 'Have you yet read the Odes?' [The book of ancient poems on which he set such store.] I answered, 'Sir, not yet.' He replied, 'If you do not read the Odes you will really not be worth talking with.' Another day in the same place he asked, 'Have you studied the Book of Rites?' I replied, 'Sir, not yet.' He added, 'If you do not learn the Rites of Behavior you will have no stability of character.' I have heard only those two things from him."

The delighted disciple said:

"I asked one thing and behold I have got three! I have heard about the Odes. I have heard about the Rites. And I have also learned that the higher type of man has no secrets even with his own son."

Possibly Li needed a measure of restraint, for we hear that on the death of his mother—the separated wife of his father—he insisted on wailing aloud for her long after the allotted time for such demonstrations. So much so that Confucius asked what the noise was about, and on hearing said, "Pshaw, it's too much!" and sent a message reminding the weeper that it was quite time he subdued his sorrow. Whereupon Li dried his tears and wept no more.

We come now to the time when public affairs in the state of Lu, going from bad to worse, fell into such a condition that however averse the prince may have been to the teachings of Confucius there really seemed no other choice than to give them a trial. The chief troubler of the peace had fled, and the way was open for "the princely man" to try his hand at public affairs if he could be induced to come forward at all.

Confucius was away from home when the prince's message reached him, but he hurried at once to the capital, glad at heart that the moment had come.

The time for words was past. Deeds were at hand. He was made chief magistrate of the town of Chung-tu. A beginning, if no more.

It is of great interest to see him at last in a public position. On a smaller scale we may see the result predicted by Plato if the philosopher became king. He threw himself into his work with the utmost ardor, holding in his mind the idea of the ruler as father of a great family. And as in the family nothing can be too small or great for the father's notice so it was with the chief magistrate of the city of Chung-tu.

He made rules for the feeding of all the people, for what father can see a child starve? Rules also for due observances to the dead, for on this the ancestral honor of a family is based. Different foods are suitable to the children and to the aged in a well-ordered household. This too was his care. Men and women were debarred from intercourse in the streets—he considered that sex and its differing occupations demanded this rule. And under this paternal care extending into every branch of life, a great and astonishing reformation took place in the manners of the people.

A thing of value dropped in the road lay there, for none would steal it. There was no fraud. Since Confucius considered that valuable agricultural land should not be wasted for the making of graves they were now made on grounds useless for agriculture, no mounds were raised nor trees planted about them.

He said:

"Grave-places should never resemble pleasure gardens. They should harmonize with the feelings of the mourners, and to give way to mirth in such places insults the memory of the dead. Far better is some lonely height, unfitted for the plow, without enclosure, planting, or adornment, where true feeling takes the place of frivolities. Let us in this fulfil the inmost spirit of the Rites as they were set forth by the wise ancients." A saying which required some courage at the time; which is worth attention now.

In short such great results flowed from his wise and kindly rule that the princes of neighboring states wished nothing better than to imitate his methods.

His own prince asked eagerly: "Doubtless this is the way to rule a city but can it be applied to a state?"

Confucius assured him that it could, and to the empire also.

He was immediately appointed assistant superintendent of works, and thereupon gave his mind to improvement in agriculture, for which no doubt his early experience fitted him. From this he was promoted to minister of crime, and it is said his success was so great that it was no longer worth while to be a criminal. Prevention by wise rule was better than cure by punishment. If there is exaggeration in these accounts, they are yet most valuable.

Instances of his human feeling shine through all his life, like gold woven in a rich tissue, for Confucius had a tender heart, not easily to be recognized in the formal figure generally presented to the West. A little instance from the Book of Rites gives touching evidence of this, and draws him nearer to us across the ages.

"The dog kept by the master having died he employed Tsŭ Kung to bury him, saying: 'I have heard that a worn- out curtain should not be thrown away, but may be used to bury a horse in, and an umbrella should not be thrown away, but may be used to bury a dog in. I am poor and have no umbrella. In laying the dog in the grave you may use my mat; and do not let his head get buried in the earth.' "

I like this anecdote the more because it dates from the days of his poverty and wanderings, so soon to follow the brief sunshine of his official position.

But he was now to be tried in a sterner issue:

It was arranged that the princes of Lu and C'hi were to meet and form a pact of alliance and friendship, and Confucius was called to attend as master of the ceremonies, which would certainly not be abridged at his hands. Meanwhile, the chief officer of the Prince of C'hi, despising Confucius as a mere scholar easy to frighten and overcome, had advised his master to attack the Prince of Lu during the conference, make him a prisoner and force him into any terms desirable for the state of C'hi. Confucius suspected the trap and was prepared for it.

He boldly addressed the Prince of C'hi: "You have brought a band of savage vassals to disturb the conference. What have these barbarians to do with our Great Flowery Empire? In the eyes of the spirits this conduct is ill-fortuned. It is contrary to social virtue."

And he walked out of the conference taking the Prince of Lu with him and leaving the enemy astonished.

The conference proceeded, however, to the terms of the proposed alliance; and here again the men of C'hi mistook Confucius. They read aloud:

"And so be it to Lu if it does not contribute three hundred war chariots to the help of C'hi when its army crosses its borders."

The delegate of Confucius wrote against this:

"And so be it to us if we obey your commands unless you return to us the fields south of the Wan."

Still hoping to entangle Confucius and his prince, the Prince of C'hi proposed a great banquet to conclude the meeting; but Confucius, knowing well the design on his ruler, refused this on the ground that the Rites would not allow such a conclusion. The men of C'hi went off, furious and disgraced by "the man of ceremonies," and the lands stolen by the state of C'hi were returned to Lu.

And still Confucius pursued his shining course as minister of crime. When an important matter came up, he would take the opinions of a group of wise and sensible men and would say, "I have decided according to the view of So-and-so." Legge points out that there is a hint of our jury system in this plan, Confucius intending to carry opinion with him, and, it may be added, to inspire general confidence. One incident very striking in view of his resolute insistence on parental power and filial obedience must be told.

A father brought a charge against his son. Confucius kept both in prison for three months and then dismissed them. The chief minister was dissatisfied and said: "This is trifling with me. You have always insisted that in a state filial piety is paramount. Why not put to death this unfilial son as an example?"

Confucius replied, sighing: "When superiors fail in their duty should inferiors die? This father had never taught his son to be filial. To act upon his charge would be to kill the innocent. The manners of this age are sinking. Can we expect people not to break the law?"

So he went on his high way—the wise man no longer hidden from the world but acting in and on it. He made his sovereign great and created a transforming government. "Loyalty and good faith became the characteristics of the men, and chastity and gentleness those of the women. Far and wide went his praises, and the people all but worshiped his name."

And then came the Unforeseen. An opportunity of very different action.

The state of C'hi had nursed its jealousy since its failure to blind the watchfulness of Confucius, and the Prince of C'hi trembled, possibly also with rage, at the chance he himself had lost.

"With Confucius at the head," he said, "Lu will become supreme among the states, and C'hi, which is nearest to it, will be swallowed up. Let us court it by surrendering territory."

One of his ministers, knowing the Prince of Lu, proposed that they should first sow bitterness between Confucius and his sovereign. They knew the way well enough. They chose eighty girls, irresistibly beautiful and skilled in all the arts of music and dancing, and added a hundred and twenty horses of the noblest strain. This great gift they sent to their enemy.

The prince was captivated. What were the dull lessons of Confucius compared with this living joy and beauty? How should it matter what the great Yao and Shun, now so long dust, had taught? He spent all his time with the women, and neglected Confucius. For; three days he saw none of his ministers, lost in the delights of the inner chambers.

"Master," said the brave Tsŭ Lu, ever on the watch, to Confucius, "the time is come for you to be going!"

But still Confucius hoped against hope. The great Sacrifice to Heaven, uniting the whole empire would soon take place. Surely that high solemnity when Earth prostrated herself at the feet of Heaven in the person of her rulers would bring the prince to his right mind! It did not. The ceremony was hurried as a thing to be done with, and the share of offerings given by custom to the various ministers was forgotten. The women had con- quered, and though he did not then know it had con-demned the master to thirteen years of sorrowful wan-dering.

CHAPTER 19

THE GREAT DOCTRINES

With a heavy heart Confucius departed, going slowly, hoping at each stopping-place for a recall. But beauty was stronger than wisdom, and it drove him out to wander homeless for many sad years.

He went westward to the state of Wei. He was a man now fifty-six years of age and very sorrowful, his life's work torn from him by the rough hands of folly when at its brightest flowering. As he went he thought aloud in verse:

"I would still look toward Lu if I could,
But the Hill of Kwi stands between.
With an ax one may cut through forest,
But against hard rock man is helpless."

And again, seeing a young bride's litter borne to her new strange home, her own forever left behind, the bitter grief broke out of him:

"Cold rain falls thick and fast,
And a freezing wind sweeps the valley.
I see a young bride borne from her home:
Never again shall she see it.
And I—I too am driven from my home,
Doomed to wander.
O azure Heaven, look down and pity my grief!
All is dark; and who among men cares for worth and honor?
There is no light upon the way that leads me to the grave."

His disciples went sadly beside him. On the borders of the state of Wei, the warden came out to meet him, and they talked together. Afterwards the warden called the disciples about him, speaking cheeringly to raise their drooping spirits:

"Friends," he said, "why grieve at your master's loss of office? Long has the empire lacked the principles of truth and light. Now you will see that Heaven will use him as a bell with a wooden tongue that must needs be heard."

Perhaps a better consolation was their master's own saying when asked for a definition of the noble man:

"The noble man knows neither grief nor fear. If on searching his heart he finds no guilt, why should he grieve? Of what should he be afraid?"

And yet he might well grieve on nobler grounds than self-pity that such an opportunity was lost to his state and to China. So wandering on, he came to the capital of Wei and there, very wearied, he took up his abode with a high-minded officer. The Prince of Wei was a listless voluptuary and husband of that very worthless woman Nan-Tsŭ; yet so great was the fame of Confucius that the prince could not neglect him without shaming himself, and he gave him a revenue of grain sufficient to support him.

But in Wei his heart could not rest. An evil woman influenced the prince, and the master left Wei soon to go for a while to Ch'in, speeded by an incident which gave great scandal at the time. One day the prince invited the master to make an expedition with him into the country, and drove through the capital with the infamous Nan- Tsŭ displaying herself in the light of day by his side, while Confucius followed in another carriage. The very people in the streets cried out:

"Look! Vice goes in front, and Virtue follows behind!"

Again he set forth upon his wanderings. The anecdotes showing the master on his human side are very precious to those who would see one of the greatest of men as he really was and not as the formalists have made him. It was on a journey to Ch'in that he passed a little house where he had once stayed, and hearing the master was now dead went in to condole with the family. Coming out he spoke to his disciple Tsŭ Kung:

"Take one of the horses from my chariot and give it as a help toward the funeral expenses."

"But it is too much—far too much," remonstrated Tsŭ Rung. "You never did such a thing at the funeral of one of your disciples! Surely on the death of a host this is excessive."

Confucius answered only this:

"When I went in, my coming brought a burst of grief from the chief mourner and I wept with him. I should hate it if my tears were not properly evinced. Do this, my child."

It was also on his way to Ch'in that, attacked by a band of ruffians as he sat under a tree, Confucius made one of his greatest utterances. He said to the frightened disciples:

"Was not the cause of truth lodged in me? If Heaven had wished to let this perish, then I, a mere mortal, should not have been related to it. What can these people do to me?"

Dispersed and wearied, all made their escape; but Confucius was somehow separated from the others and reached the east gate of Ch'in alone. One of the disciples who had got there before him was told by a man of Ch'in:

"There is a man standing by the east gate with a forehead like Yao [the ancient sage], tall and majestic, but for all that looking just like a lost dog!"

The disciple guessed who it must be and hurried to him with his story to tell, and Confucius laughed aloud:

"The description matters little, but to say I was like a lost dog—that's capital! Capital."

He was little better so far as peace and comfort went. He returned to Wei, found it impossible, returned again to Ch'in, and lingered there hoping against hope for return to his native state of Lu. On one of their expeditions he and his disciples even wanted for food. A sad record of sufferings and cares! But courage never deserted him. A noble man was never more noble than in adversity, and though they suffered Confucius could at times forget his sorrows in the music which was one of his inspirations. His lute appears to have accompanied all his wanderings.

It was about this time that a rebel chief asked Tsŭ Lu how one should think of the master. Confounded by the magnitude of the question, Tsŭ Lu really could not reply. He put it before Confucius himself, who answered with touching simplicity:

"Why did you not say, 'He is only a man who in his eager pursuit of knowledge forgets to eat, who in the joy of attainment forgets his grief, and who does not perceive the approach of old age.' "

There is something dignified and worthy of the greatness of China in the way in which rulers sought the counsel of the wisest man they knew. In the West that would be impossible; but Asia sought and seeks the counsel of a wise man, recognizing that he has climbed peaks inaccessible to the ordinary person, and free from passion and vain opinion, looks out from them over an unbounded prospect. In this manner Japan begged the advice of Herbert Spencer on some of her more intimate and complex problems, and though one may not wholly agree with his views it was given and received in a manner worthy of both the man and the nation.

Trouble and disappointment went beside Confucius, yet he was not wholly uncomforted. Such thoughts as his could not leave him altogether desolate, though sorrow and age were darkening down upon him. His disciples still surrounded him, some dying and passing on, others growing up to take their places. And their talk was of high things, each being permitted to ask his question at the fount of wisdom. The Analects are indeed mines where men may dig for gold and jewels to this day.

There is recorded how in a noble flash Confucius anticipated the Golden Rule of Christianity, to be pronounced by the Christ under other skies and centuries later. One of his disciples, Tsŭ Kung, had asked him:

"Is there any one word which may serve as a rule of practice for daily life?"

One may well picture the eager watching eyes as Confucius turns his serene face upon them.

"Is not 'reciprocity' such a word? What you would not have

done to yourself do not to others. Tsŭ, you have not attained unto that."

And in another great out-flash:

"Lay down your life rather than quit the straight way. In a state governed on right principles, poverty and low station are things to be ashamed of. In an ill-governed state, riches and rank are things to be ashamed of."

There speaks the very voice of eternal verity.

And here is another jewel from the mine which has been condemned most unwarrantably, as I think, on the ground that it falls short of Christian benevolence. He was asked:

"What should be thought of the principle that injury should be recompensed with kindness?"

He answered at once: "With what then will you recompense kindness? Recompense injury with justice and kindness with kindness."

It appears to me that this is true wisdom. The man who has met you with kindness can be trusted to appreciate all its bearings and neither to presume upon it nor to undervalue it. The man who has done you an injury should be made to realize the strict application of the universal law he has broken; and this for his own sake, not for yours. Confucius had the highest interest of the wrongdoer in mind, realizing that a man who has done an unjust thing requires the lesson of being met with perfect justice, by no means in itself unkind but in its nature a revelation. Then, if he is touched to kindness, the latter part of the injunction comes into play, and he must be met with kindness. This seems a point of high wisdom—nobler than practicing a virtue which he has shown himself so far incapable of understanding.

There comes, however, a pronouncement that must not be ignored in presenting a portrait of a great man. His disciple Tsŭ-hea asked him what course should be pursued by a son in dealing with the murderer of one of his parents. He answered instantly:

"The son must sleep upon a matting of grass with his shield for his pillow. He must decline to take office. He must not live under the same heaven with the slayer. When he meets him in the market-place or the court he must have his weapon ready to strike him."

"And what is the course on the murder of a brother?" "The surviving brother must not take office in the same state with the slayer. Yet if he go on his prince's service to the state where the slayer is, though he meet him he must not fight with him."

For the first of these two answers Confucius has been universally condemned in the West, but I think with little realization of his reasons. In the first place the appeal to law was almost useless in the struggling feudalities of China in the days when he spoke. In the next the son, in such a case, was avenging no merely private quarrel but justifying a principle on which the Chinese Empire was founded—namely, that filial duty must carry a man to and beyond any limit of consideration for personal safety. The injunction is not universal, nor can it apply to other countries and times; and its urgency is accentuated by the different teaching given on the question of a murder of a brother. *There,* there is no question of any gratification of a blood feud, though the inclination may be as strong in the one case as in the other.

We find a noble note struck in his view of the responsibility of the ruling powers, which statesmen would do well to remember, and here the injunction is neither local nor temporary. It relates to the light by which a great soul enlightens others in all times and places. The chief Ki K'ang asks for instructions as to wise government, and Confucius replies:

"To govern means to rectify. If you lead the people with rectitude, who will dare to break the rule of rectitude?"

"But in the state are many thieves? How is it possible to do away with them?"

The master answered:

"If you, sir, were not covetous, they would not steal even if they were paid to do it."

"And what do you say to killing the unprincipled for the good of those who obey the social laws?"

It is possible to realize the answer Ki K'ang expected and to contrast it with that he received.

"Sir, in carrying on your government killing need not be necessary. Let your evinced desires be for what is good, and the people will be good. The relation between superiors and inferiors is like that between the wind and the grass. The grass must bow when the wind sweeps it."

In other words it may be said that Confucius believed with Plato in the rule of the philosopher as king. It is to be wished very earnestly that he had had the chance of demonstrating its benefits personally among a race so susceptible of influence as the Chinese. Fate made the experiment once in Rome, when Marcus Aurelius was emperor; but either the European race was hastier and fiercer than the oriental, or example weighed light against their hurrying passions, for Marcus Aurelius passed, and left the world pretty much as he found it, except among those already elect of spirit; and the empire was bequeathed to his vicious son Commodus. Whereas the example of Confucius though shown on lowlier levels has enlightened and uplifted uncounted millions, and had it been displayed upon a throne might have done for China even more—if more can be conceived.

So the master went on his way, learning and teaching, courteous and calm. In the Discourses and Dialogues, Tsŭ Kung the well-known disciple says:

"Our master is benign, upright, courteous, temperate and complaisant, and thus he gets his information. The master's mode of asking information is not different from that of other men."

That description has a gracious beauty borne out by many anecdotes and traditions. It supports also the descriptions of his own inward beliefs and feelings, rarely given by Confucius and contrasting sharply with the dogmatic superiority ascribed to him in the West. He is not so misunderstood in China. Hear this:

The master said:

"How should I be afflicted at men's not knowing me? I will rather be afflicted that I do not know men."

And again:

"At fifteen I had my mind bent on learning. At thirty I stood firm. At forty I had no doubts. At fifty I knew the decrees of Heaven. At sixty my ear was an obedient organ for the reception of truth. At seventy *I could do what my heart desired without transgressing what was right.*"

Always is to be seen the fine spirit pointing straight to the inward and spiritual.

His disciple Tsŭ Yu (now among the "Wise Ones" who form the spirit court of Confucius in his great temple in Peking) asked him concerning the duties of filial piety, and he replied:

"Filial piety now means the support of one's parents. Yet this is something in which even our dogs and horses likewise can share. Reverence also is needed. Without that what distinguishes the one case from the other?"

Another disciple, the recurrent Tsŭ Kung, asked what constitutes the superior or perfected man. The master answered:

"He acts before he speaks, and afterwards speaks according to his actions."

Some of his sayings are gnomic, wonderfully condensed and needing long and deep reflection. Among those I would set this:

"It is only the truly righteous man who can love or hate others." And again that strangely wise saying which few countries but India in her wisdom have comprehended :

"Riches and honor are the desire of men. If they cannot be gained rightly they should not be held. Poverty and meanness are the detestation of men. If they cannot be gained rightly they should be avoided."

It is the fashion in the West to call Confucius merely a moral philosopher, and to dismiss him at that. True, that would be much in itself; but he aimed higher, though he shrank from casting the spiritualities into the arena of ignorant discussion. Probably development on the spiritual side had not reached the point where his aims could be profitably discussed. But now and then come sentences in the Analects of searching insight. Here is one which aims at the heights indeed, though the man to whom he spoke did not perceive the full implication.

The master said:

"My teaching is that of one all-pervading principle."

Tsang the philosopher replied, "Yes."

The master went out, and the other disciples asked, "What do his words mean?"

Tsang replied: "The teaching of our master is to be loyal to oneself and charitable to our neighbors and nothing more."

Thus Confucius summed up the two great commandments in a spirit not distant from the Two Commandments of the New Testament. For he who is loyal to the Divine in himself obeys the first, and the second inculcates the love of our fellow men. Truly he himself may be described as the noble man whose virtues he set on high as a standard for his people.

CHAPTER 20

THE SORROWS OF CONFUCIUS HIS DEATH

Events were now drawing Confucius back after long and sorrowful wanderings to the state of Lu. "Let me return. Let me return!" he had said long years before, little knowing for how long Fate could compel him to wait. His course had been disapproved alike by those who wished to see him in power and believed he shrank from taking office and those who (with the great philosopher Lao Tsŭ) considered the life of solitary meditation the higher way. Confucius had chosen the middle way—the Mean—and had pleased few. An example of the ascetics' opinion was that of one known as the Madman of T'su, who meeting the little carriage of Confucius sang scornfully aloud as he passed it:

"O Phoenix, O Phoenix, how is your virtue fallen! Reproof for the past is useless, but the future is still yours. Give up your vain pursuit!"

Confucius, who may have himself had the moments of self-distrust that assail all great spirits, and probably remembered Lao Tsŭ and his exhortations only too painfully, got down hurriedly and would have spoken with the man; but he rushed off and was seen no more.

Time went by and old age darkened over him and his high hope of usefulness to his country. It is likely that at this time no one would have expected less than he the stupendous future which awaited the least of his sayings and doings. It is true that Prince of T'su distinguished him when he entered his state and listened gladly to his wisdom. To him was spoken the summary which has come down the ages:

"It demonstrates good government in a state when those who are near are given happiness and those who are far away are attracted."

But again as always came disappointment.

The Prince of T'su would have given him great territory and its government, and fixed him to his court; but once more a minister intervened, seeing his own power threatened by greatness.

"Consider well, your Majesty. Have you any such great men about you as this K'ung has in his three disciples, Yen Hui, Tsŭ Lu, and Tsŭ Kung? You have not an officer to stand beside them? With himself and these three how can you suppose he will work simply for the good of your kingdom and not for himself? Remember how Wu and Wan long ago made themselves masters of the empire! Be warned!"

And because intellectual power seldom prospers in a world of little men the prince was frightened. He drew back, and Confucius left his state and returned to Wei. Like others of his fiber he had to pass into the cold atmosphere of death, where hatreds and envies die, before he could assume his rightful throne.

Yet there were still moments of hope. The prince whose connection with the infamous beauty Nan-Tsŭ had driven him out was dead and his grandson sat on a tottering throne, defending it against his own father, who had been driven out of the kingdom because of an attempt on his mother Nan-Tsŭ's life. The young prince felt that if he could gain the approval of Confucius and thus the support of the great apostle of filial piety, his position might be secured despite his plight; and such overtures were made that when Confucius reached Wei, the brave disciple Tsŭ Lu could meet him with the offer of power in his hand.

"The Prince of Wei is waiting for you, that with you he may administer the government! What will you do first?"

What Confucius considered the first thing to be done was to reject such offers. How could he support a man in rebellion against his father? or support that father, who had himself been guilty of slaughtering a mother, however wicked? Let them go their own way—fight their own battle! Here he would not intervene. Therefore he remained in Wei continuing his private work and seeing hope ebb daily.

But as I have said events were shaping for his return to Lu. He was to see the hills of home before the ages claimed him. His beloved Yen Hui was to do him one more service before the disciple's early death. Yen Hui had returned before to Lu, on the invitation of the ruling power, and distinguished himself in some military operations. He was asked how he had learned such skill and had replied that he owed that and everything else to Confucius. Who could compare with him? His listeners, deeply impressed, declared that they must bring the master home to Lu. Yen Hui listened and answered with his own serenity, suggesting scorn of the past and hope for the future:

"If you do so, see at least that you let no mean men come between him and you!"

Three officers were sent bearing rich gifts to beg the master's return to the state that is remembered only as his birthplace. And he went, now sixty-nine years old and hoping for the last time that his ripened wisdom might once more benefit his native land. But it was grief, not success, which was to test his great heart to the end.

In the very year of his return, the beloved disciple Yen Hui, who had brought about that return, died, and the master was left desolate indeed, weeping as one uncomforted. I have told some of his lamentation. This also survives:

"Yen Hui is dead and lost to me forever, and where is there another to fill his place? He never lagged, he never wearied. His face was set forward as a true lover of knowledge, and to him toil was pleasure. He is gone and I cannot find his equal. Heaven is destroying me."

There are moments of terrible solitude for the highest of men. Wisdom cuts them off from fellowship and sets them apart on more than Alpine peaks uplifted into cold and starry skies. But those who study the utterances of Confucius will realize that Yen Hui by the very force of love and devotion had climbed the snows and sat at the feet of his master, warming them with the glow of love. That companionship was now withdrawn, and henceforward he walked to the end in a great loneliness of spirit.

Yet another shadow was to fall upon his life in the death of his long unseen wife. Years had passed since their separation, but memory moved him.

"Yes," he said, "her life is done, and it will not be long before mine is done also."

Then his only son Li died. That could not move him as the loss of Yen Hui had done, for little is known of Li and that little is colorless. Yet he left a son in whom Confucius might hope with a hope that was not to be disappointed. His grandson K'ung Kei's name is esteemed and with reason as that of a philosopher whose work on the classics honorably follows that of the master.

And now the end was drawing near, and the master, working at the great classics—which were to be one of his priceless bequests to China—conscious of the lengthening shadows of night, toiled with unwearied energy at the only task his country would permit him for its benefit.

For no power, no share of government, was offered to him in Lu. He had attained the plane of wisdom in which as he said of himself: "I could follow what my heart desired without transgressing what is right." But though the prince and his ministers would talk with him now and again and raise questions of good government he was not needed at the helm of the ship of state. It is said that he interrupted his labors to make a last pilgrimage to T'ai Shan, the holy mountain, and that the disciples who attended him allowed themselves to hope for many years more of his wisdom, so strongly he climbed the steep, so keenly did he look from the summit over the wide country below. According to tradition he offered a sacrifice on his return to commemorate the end of his literary work, and then calling his disciples together bade them a solemn farewell, declaring that his mission as a teacher was now ended, he was no longer their master but a friend—for that bond between them no time could sever.

It is to be wished that some master of the greatest age of Chinese painting could have immortalized that moment in the life of the teacher with those men who had been faithful to him in so much disappointment and sorrow—a moment of grief and gratitude and of the pro- foundest sense of mighty gifts given and rightly accepted in so far as their lesser capacities permitted.

There is another anecdote of this time which has beauty of perhaps more human order. The teacher was present at a little village festival—one of gratitude to the spirits of the elements at the ended toil of harvest. The poor people rejoiced with noisy gaiety, and Confucius stood watching them with a pleasure some of the more priggish of his companions could not approve.

"How far better," said they, "if instead of rejoicing in this boisterous unmannerly way they had solemnly expressed their gratitude and hopes in prayer!"

"Not at all!" replied the master. "Why cannot you see that they are expressing both in their own simple way? They cannot share in the higher points of view. Their life is one of unceasing toil, and surely these poor fellows may have one day of untrammeled enjoyment after their own fashion. A bow never unbent is useless." If his long and sorrowful wanderings had taught him nothing but this sympathy for the neglected life of the suffering peasants of China, he probably would have felt they had not been wasted. But they had taught him the ruin and misery following evil government, and the passions and jealousies which divert man from the only road to peace and wisdom. He had learned the desperation of disunity which set state against state; and travel as he would from one to another in hope of better things he found betterment impossible in one and all.

He had seen the brotherhood of man—the pattern of the perfect family repeated in that of perfect government —all his ideals for the good of suffering humanity, set as a dying rainbow against black clouds, dissolving as a rainbow does; and the only comfort left to him was still to love human nature, to sympathize in its struggles and believe that the way was there if men's blinded eyes could be opened to the truth.

One last heavy grief awaited him before the end— the death of his brave, impetuous disciple Tsŭ Lu. He had remained behind with a disciple named Ch'ei. A revolution broke out in Wei, and these two were caught in its meshes, Tsŭ Lu following his master's principles and defending the prince against the rebels.

This was told to Confucius. He said sadly:

"Ch'ei will come here, but Tsŭ Lu will die."

Too true! Tsŭ Lu fought gallantly for the prince and was killed; and Confucius mourned in the last great sorrow earth had in store for him.

According to tradition a warning was now granted that he might prepare even more solemnly for the end.

It is told that in the spring of 480 *B.C.* a huntsman *of* the Duke of Lu captured in hunting an extraordinary animal, which immediately died. It is described as four- footed, scaled like a dragon, with fleshy protuberances instead of horns. It was thrown down in a public place near the palace, and crowds went to see it, the news flying far and wide. Confucius also went, but seeing it, showed signs *of* consternation. As it is recorded by Kung-yang, he recognized it as the marvelous animal that had appeared before his birth to whose horn his mother Ching-tsai had attached a ribbon.

"It is the kilin, the kilin!" he cried. "For whom have you come? For whom have you come? That sacred animal, typical of all that is good and holy—behold, it is dead! What evil does not this foretell to the empire? Living, it gave notice of my approaching birth. The course of my teaching is run."

It may be supposed that he redoubled his work in consequence of the portent, for about this time he completed "Spring and Autumn." In this book, written from the standpoint of the state of Lu, he sets forth in brief the chief events occurring throughout the empire, "every term being expressive of the true character of the actors and events described." His own estimate of the book sets it high for he said:

"It is 'Spring and Autumn' which will make men know me, and it is that book which will make men condemn me."

It was of this that the great Chinese philosopher Meng-Tsŭ (Mencius) said later:

"Confucius completed 'Spring and Autumn,' and rebellious ministers and villainous sons were stricken with terror."

With failing strength he could still testify to the right. The Prince of Ch'i was murdered, and though this was not his own prince, Confucius thought it his duty to make a solemn protestation to his sovereign the Prince of Lu. He bathed, robed himself in his dress of ceremony, and went to court. There, coming before the prince, he said:

"Ch'in has slain his sovereign. I beg that you will undertake to punish him."

The prince hesitated, saying that Lu was a weaker state than Ch'i, but still the master persisted:

"One-half of the people of Ch'i are not consenting to the deed," he said. "If you add to the people of Lu one- half of the people of Ch'i, you cannot be overcome." But all was useless, and he returned home in sadness, believing as he did that the slaughter of a sovereign was a terrible and dangerous form of parricide and a ruinous example to the empire. So the rulers picked his brains for aphorisms and suggestions to guide them in their tortuous course, but power they would not give him. And slowly the light that was to light China, that might have lighted it more immediately, flickered down.

One morning in the dawn he rose, and with his hands behind his back clasping his dragging staff, he moved listlessly up and down before his door murmuring to himself:

"The great mountain must crumble,
The strong beam must break,
The wise man must wither like a plant."

He returned to the house and sat down silently facing the door. One of the disciples, Tsŭ Kung, heard and said to himself:

"If the great mountain crumble, to what shall I look? If the strong beam break and the wise man wither away, on what shall I lean?"

He hurried into the house, and the master said:

"Tsŭ, why are you so late? According to the rules of Hua the corpse was dressed and coffined at the top of the eastern steps, the dead thus treated as one who receives his guests. Under the Yin dynasty the ceremony was performed between the two pillars, thus making the dead both host and guest. I am a man descended from the royal house of Yin, and last night I dreamed that I sat with offerings before me between two pillars. No wise sovereign arises; there is none in the empire who will make me his master. My time is come to die."

These are his last recorded words. He fell into a deep lethargy and so gradually sank into death in the year 479 B.C.

It was natural that his disciples should attach the utmost importance to the burial rites. His grandson K'ung Kei was too young to lead the rites, and two of the disciples acted for him. They robed the master in ceremonial robes, with the cap of ceremony, and the official badge on a cord of colored twisted threads. Three small portions of rice were placed in his mouth. The body in a double coffin, adorned with the insignia of great houses of old times, lay under a rich canopy.

They bought a plot of ground to the north of the capital, and there raised three cupola-shaped mounds—the central one for the grave. A great procession of disciples and friends followed the relics of their master, and by the grave Tsŭ Kung, the most famous of the disciples, planted a tree of which it is said traces can still be seen.

It was decided by the disciples that the time of mourning should be the same as for a father, but Tsŭ Kung did more. By the tomb he built himself a hut, and there led a hermit's life for six years.

The death of Socrates though man-inflicted was happier in its circumstances and carries a nobler ring down the ages; yet not even Socrates was to light such a beacon in the world as the great man who passed away so quietly and with so heavy a sense of failure in the state of Lu. In the beneficent influence he shed upon mankind two only can stand beside him: the Indian prince known as the Buddha and the Christ. Some might include Mohammed; but though I yield to none in admiration and reverence for his mighty work I cannot class his doctrines nor his life so highly as those of the Three. The mountains lift their peaks into the blue, but Gaurisankar (Everest) outsoars them all and mingles with the stars. So, the Three.

Before we turn to the spirit of the man as represented in his philosophy, it is well to consider his manners and customs and the impression he made on those who knew him best. These his disciples treasured and handed down with minute and loving care, realizing that they presented the standard for the highest type of human being that China at that time, and for ages afterwards, could present for general admiration.

They knew in their own hearts, even if it were not generally admitted as yet, that here was the great man, he whom intellect enthroned and goodness crowned and stately manners adorned. All could not be like him— that was true—but all could measure themselves by that ideal and mourn their failure; all could rejoice when some small ray of that light shone upon their darker path. Therefore in the Analects—that most lovable book—we find little personal details which endear the master to us, even where it is difficult for nations whose leaders have never made an ideal of dignified behavior to follow the symbolism of some of the traits. Many are beautiful to all who read.

We see a man stately in presence—for he was often spoken of as "the tall man"—rather dark in complexion, with the broad Mongolian nose and keen eyes. There are portraits which it is held in China give the traditionary likeness, but to those no real importance can be attached.

The dress of his day was more like the Japanese kimono than that worn in modern China, with loose flowing sleeves covering the hands. He would turn up the right sleeve to free his hand. In summer his robes were of linen. Linen was then more costly than silk. His cap was of silk. His winter robes were lined with fur— the yellow ones with fox fur, the white with fawnskin, the dark with black lambskin. Red and brown were colors he disliked, nor would he allow his robes to be trimmed with green, purple, or red, the reason being that the approved colors in the Book of Rites were blue, yellow, carnation, white and black. Thus we have the mental portrait of a distinguished gentleman, one who attached self-respect to dress as to all that concerned him, considering it as the part of manners and revelation of personality that it undoubtedly is.

When his work was laid aside, he was always cheerful and smiling, yet with gravity as a background, attentive to all who spoke, serene in manner.

If a man who was in mourning for his parnets sat beside him at dinner, it appeared to Confucius courteous not to ignore his grief, and therefore he ate slightly and sparingly as though to curtail his own enjoyment.

Four things were the special subjects of his teaching, as forming the necessary equipment of a gentleman (using that word in its deepest truest sense): literature and the arts, with special emphasis on music; conduct; a conscience trained to unerring instinct; and sincerity in word and deed.

When he saw a person in mourning or dressed in robes of office, or one who was blind, he would at once rise from his seat even though the other were his junior, thus marking his sympathy with sorrow, his respect for rank, and his tenderness for the afflicted. Another instance of this tenderness may be given.

A blind musician having come to see him, Confucius guided him with his own hand up the steps and to the mat prepared for him. He told him where all the visitors were sitting and who they were. After the guest had left, one of the disciples asked, in some astonishment at the stiff rules of rank in ancient China having been thus infringed: "Is it the right thing to speak thus to a [mere] musician?"

The master answered: "Very certainly it is right to give help to a blind man."

Yet no man was more punctilious as to the forms and ceremonies antiquity had taught and he believed necessary as a safeguard to the intercourse of man and to his social well-being. At some of these, those will smile who cannot perceive the underlying spirit that characterizes intercourse between educated and often between uneducated people, not only in China but throughout all the great countries of Asia.

If in illness he received a visit from his prince he had his court robe thrown round him and wore his girdle. He entered the palace for an audience by a side door as if to avoid the undue honor of using the great entrance, then with bent head, gathering his robe about him with both hands, he went on to the dais in the inner apartments, bowing right and left with clasped hands to the officers who lined the approach; and as he passed the prince's empty chair he hurried as if in awe. Returning from the audience he let his expression relax as if with satisfaction. He advanced rapidly to his place for the public audience, spreading out his robe on either side like a bird's wings. When he carried the jewel-badge of authority of his prince it was with bent body and an air of deep awe and apprehension.

These were the ceremonies for the feudal courts. At the imperial court much more state would have been required.

When fasting he wore his clothes brightly clean and made of linen.

In eating he would always have his rice carefully clean and his meat finely minced. The meat he took only in due proportion to the rice. With wine he was more liberal, but never to the extent of confusing himself. Ginger was served to him at every meal. He ate sparingly and in silence. Even if his food was only coarse rice and vegetables, he reverently offered a little of it in sacrifice to the ancestral spirits. When a rich banquet was provided for him he would rise to return thanks to his host. When the villagers were feasting he would not precede the ancients of the village but followed them; and when they held the ceremonies for driving away evil influences and entered his house noisily for the purpose, he would put on his court dress and receive them standing on the eastern steps, as a host does with guests. When any friend died without relations who could be depended upon to perform his burial, the master said:

"I shall bury him."

In a word Confucius was careful to fail in none of the pieties and duties of life; and more so because, as will be seen in the next chapter, the duty of right example was an essential part of his philosophy.

Of his disciples, ten, divided into four classes of differing attainments, are known as the Ten Wise Ones. Of their love of their master and devotion to his teachings little need be said, but it is interesting to know how they viewed him. The beloved Yen Hui, sighing, said of the master's doctrines:

"I looked up to them, and they seemed to become more high. I tried to penetrate them and they became harder. I looked at them before me and suddenly they were behind. By orderly methods he leads men on skilfully. He enlarged my mind with learning and taught me the rules of conduct. If I wished to give up the study of his doctrines I could not; and yet after I have exerted all my powers something seems to stand up high before me, and though I wish to follow and grasp it I cannot."

Another disciple said:

"Our master's teaching really comes to this: loyalty to oneself and charity to one's neighbor."

Another:

"Let me use the simile of a house surrounded by a wall. *'My* wall rises only to the height of a man's shoulders, so that anyone can look over and note the excellence of the building within. But my master's wall is many fathoms in height, so that one who cannot find the gate cannot see the loveliness of the temple nor the noble adornments of the priests within. It may be that only a few will find the gate."

And another, on hearing Confucius disparaged:

"It is no good. K'ung Fu Tsŭ is proof against detraction! The wisdom of other men is like hills and mounds, which can be stepped over. But he is like the sun and moon, which man's foot can never reach. True,a man may refuse to receive their light, but that leaves the sun and moon untroubled. It only demonstrates that he has no notion of the measurement of capacity."

With this summing up the Chinese Empire has concurred. There are few places in the world which convey such a profound impression of antiquity and solemnity as his great temple in Peking. The air breathes the serenity of wisdom enshrined in the worship of the ages. China appears to prostrate herself in this august place and thus to honor herself as well as the greatest of her sons.

It may be seen in the dim light of the Hall of Perfection that there is a hall behind, containing the tablets and images of certain of his ancestors and other distinguished men. In the Great Hall is his own tablet, the tablets of his chief disciples and of others who have spread his teaching. On the first day of every month are made offerings of fruits and vegetables, and on the fifteenth an offering of incense. But formerly twice a year came a solemn ceremony of worship. The emperor then invariably attended as the chief officiant.

Twice he knelt and six times bowed his head to the earth in the invocation of the spirit of Confucius.

"Great are you, O perfectly wise man.
Your virtue is full; your doctrine complete.
None among mortal men has equaled you.
All kings honor you.
Your statutes and laws have come down gloriously.
You are the model of the Imperial School.
Reverently we have set out the sacrificial vessels.
With awe we sound the bells and drums.

"I, the emperor, offer a sacrifice to the philosopher K'ung, the ancient teacher, the perfect sage, and I say:

"O teacher, in virtue equal to Heaven and earth, whose doctrines embrace the past and present,
Transmitter of the six classics,
Hander-down of lessons for all generations,
Now in reverent observance of the old statutes with victims, silks, spirits, and fruits, I carefully offer sacrifice to you.
With you are associated the philosopher Yen, your continuator;
The philosopher Tsang, exhibitor of your fundamental principles;
And the philosopher Meng, second to you.
May you enjoy the offerings!"

Confucius died comparatively unnoticed and with a sense of failure. He could not have foreseen the outburst of glory so soon to follow his death and to continue to the present time. What man could foresee such triumph? It holds in it something superhuman and awful. So men spoke of the ancient gods. In the words of Dr. Legge:

"Confucius is in the empire of China the one man by whom all possible personal excellence was exemplified and by whom all possible lessons of social virtue and political wisdom were taught."

CHAPTER 21

THE SOCIAL ORGANIZATION OF ANCIENT CHINA

There was no good news for the masses in the worship practiced by the wealthy and educated classes headed by the emperor. There were moral precepts, and none who know will undervalue their work among the toilers of the empire; but the atmosphere about them, associated as they necessarily were with reverence of the dead, was cold and chilling, and lacked the spiritual warmth which draws the love of men as well as their duty. As will be shown in due place it gained glow from India and enforced the precepts with added incentives and hopes unknown to ancient China. Yet though Confucius was an aristocrat in all his instincts he had true democratic sympathies, and government worthy of the people was his principal aim.

I shall now briefly allude to the books which he edited and added to, wrote or partially rewrote, and then sum up their teachings.

The books of highest authority are the five canonical works known as the "Book of Changes," the "Book of Historical Documents," the "Book of Poetry," the "Record of Rites," and "Spring and Autumn." Confucius is credited with the compilation of all these and the authorship of one of them; but it is known that much of the Record of Rites is from later hands.

This is indeed an amazing book. If a book of etiquette can be imagined directing manners and behavior even to facial expression in every possibility of life, yet imbued with deep religious and ancestral feeling, it is here. There are moments when to those unused to Chinese habits of thought an impression of calculated insincerity may be given, but unjustly; and there are certainly moments when the injunctions may seem as absurd to the West, as those of a western book of etiquette seem to those who are born to the manner and need no teaching.

But like many other customs of antiquity and of foreigners the thing needs understanding. Confucius taught that with a gentleman of the highest type the use of ceremonies is "to give proper and becoming expression to his feelings." That he should do this for the benefit of all is an integral part of the philosophy of Confucius, and a highly important one. His definition of ceremonial runs as follows:

"Without the rules of becoming behavior, respectfulness becomes toilsome bustle; carefulness, timidity; boldness, insubordination; and straightforwardness, rudeness."

Were ever truer words written? And let it be remembered that the first sentence of this book begins, "Always and in everything let there be reverence"; and that, apart from the general questions raised, this classic presents as has been said, "the most exact and complete monog- raphy which the Chinese nation has been able to give of itself to the rest of the human race."

Agreeing with this, I would add that both in its strength and its littleness we have no way of understanding the natural and trained sense of decorum in the Chinese people. We are alert, hasty, sudden, rough, where they are unhurried, courteous, foresighted, and stately. Yet nearly all our own habits also are ceremonies. Without them society would crash; and if we consider that the Chinese go too far, who are we to enunciate the perfect mean? It is certainly better to be extreme on the Chinese side than on our own.

The Book of Rites does not encourage grimace. It states throughout that ceremony without the reverence of the heart is worth nothing. Not that we need suppose that everyone who practiced these forms sincerely felt them. Undoubtedly that high standard was not always attained. But the man who did not attain knew and in his own heart admitted that he had fallen far. And probably then and certainly now the Chinese nation has a level of manners very much above our own, and in its perfection often very beautiful.

Still some of the injunctions have a humorous aspect to the western mind, and some occasion the profoundest astonishment that constraint could go to such length and especially that such rigors of mourning could be endured by human beings. Here are a few examples of prescribed behavior from this famous book:

> When a father has just died, the son should appear quite overcome and as if he were at his wits' end. When the corpse has been laid in the coffin he should cast quick sorrowful glances this way and that, as if seeking for something which cannot be found. When the burial takes place he should look alarmed and restless, as if looking for one who does not return. At the end of the first year's mourning he should look sad and disappointed, and at the end of the second year he should have a vague and unre- liant look.

There is the advantage that three years of this experience might produce a very finished actor, but it must be remembered that less would have been thought deeply disrespectful to the dead. It was said by the ancients that even a dying fox would lift its head and look in the direction of the mound where he was born. Could a gentleman show less feeling for a parent?

As a matter of fact they all showed much more, and there was a spirited competition in the display of proper feeling. When one (who seems to have made a new record) was mourning for his parents, "his tears flowed like blood for three years and he never laughed so as to show his teeth. Superior men considered that he did a difficult thing."

And most people will agree with them. One trembles to think how an epidemic in any virtuous family might have resulted for those who had to escort the victims courteously to the tomb!

A singular ceremony is that the vessels made for serving the dead must not be such as could be actually used. They were made so that they were useless. The earthenware vessels could not be used for washing, the lutes were unevenly strung, the pipes were out of tune, the bells had no stands.

"They are called vessels to the eye of fancy. The dead are thus treated as though they are spiritual intelligences," says Confucius.

The point was that they must not be treated as though they were dead, for that would hurt their feelings and show a want of affection. But they could not be treated as if they were living, for that would show lack of wisdom. The happy mean of vessels nominally practical but unusable would exactly meet the case.

The wedding etiquettes are also curious. Confucius, who believed that all these observances promoted and preserved right feeling, dwelt at length upon marriage customs.

> The family that has married a daughter away does not extinguish its candles for three nights, for it is thinking of the separation that has taken place. The family that has received the new wife for three days indulges in no music, remembering that the bridegroom is now in place of her parents. After three months she presents herself in the ancestral temple and is styled "the new wife that has come."

But I must not linger on these etiquettes, though so conservative is China that many in the Book of Rites still hold sway.

Of the Book of Changes I dare say little, for though Confucius loved and studied it, no clear explanation of its mysteries has been given to the West. It is dear to those who have studied the geomantic knowledge determining auspicious or inauspicious moments for the great crises of life, death, and burial. Systems of divination have been built upon it. But the key is not in the hand of the West, and though many western scholars have made attacks upon its mysteries, I do not even know whether the ancient Chinese system of divination, which I have seen practiced, is based upon it. In the Book of Changes there are again additions said to be by Confucius in the shape of appendices; but "Spring and Autumn" is the only one of the five canonical books that can be approximately described as actually composed by Confucius himself.

Of the four famous books which follow the five, the first is the Analects (which I have quoted so often), i.e., the Conversations and Observations of Confucius, the next is "The Great Learning," attributed to his distinguished disciple Tsang Sin. The third is "The Doctrine of the Mean," ascribed to K'ung Kei, the famous grandson of Confucius. The fourth is written by the great Meng Tsŭ or Mencius. But all these books, if the work of Mencius is excepted, are so saturated with the personality, the teaching, and even the words of Confucius, that it must be said that all emanate from the Confucian school, and are "faithful reflections of his teaching." From these books then, his philosophy may be confidently deduced, for all these men and books are mouthpieces of the great Confucius system.

His view of the nature of God was never given, yet it must not be supposed that he had not deeply reflected upon the subject and that in observing silence it was from want either of words or thoughts. It may be safely asserted that he felt discussions or speculations on this point were not suited to the condition or powers of the average man. Who that has studied the theological dogmas and speculations of the West but must feel some sympathy for his point of view? Dr. Legge is inclined to think Confucius doubted much more than he believed, but silence is not necessarily a symptom of doubt. There are other ways of accounting for it in so great a moral teacher. The man who said, "He who has offended Heaven [the synonym for God] has none to whom he can pray," was not without his beliefs and reflections on the Divine. And consider the following:

"Alas," said the master, "there is no one that knows me."

Tsŭ Kung answered: "What do you mean by saying that no one knows you?"

He replied: "I do not murmur against Heaven. I do not grumble against men. My studies lie low, and my perception rises high. But there is Heaven—*That* knows me."

Dr. Legge complains that not once in the Analects does he use the personal name of Deity, and he calls him "unreligious rather than irreligious." My verdict would be that he was neither, but rather that a deep sense of reverence prevented him from using the personal name, which was considered too great for use, or from dragging into discussion high things that he did not believe the mind of man was competent to settle.

Dr. Legge brings the charge of insincerity against Confucius— the teacher whose system of development of moral character and all the virtues of the true gentleman and "princely man" was based on the fundamental virtue of sincerity! On what are these charges founded? On the fact that he excused himself from seeing an untimely visitor by saying he was ill. In the first place it must be considered that the courtesy of China would by no means permit the blunt truth on such an occasion and that true kindness saves the visitor's face also by permitting him to assume that nothing but illness would stand in the way of his reception. In the next place such excuses were and are as well understood in China as the "not at home" of the West. Nothing but an overstrained Puritanism can object to either. He instances also the case of Meng Che Fan, who when the army of Lu was defeated brought up the rear of the retreat, and being praised for courage replied:

"My horse was slow. There was nothing more in it than that."

Confucius commended this reply. Dr. Legge asserts that it was weak and wrong. Would he have had Meng say, "It was my gallantry which placed me in the danger zone"?

No, Confucius and all China understood that here was the grace of a gentleman and a brave man, who disclaimed praise with a smile. No question of insincerity for a moment comes into the question, which is one of what the West calls "good form," conduct perfectly well understood in China.

But Dr. Legge has a graver charge of insincerity— indeed untruth. The case was as follows: Confucius was returning to the state of Wei in circumstances of danger and tumult. A rebel officer of Wei stopped him and compelled him to engage that he would not go on to Wei— an engagement he had of course no right to exact. When released, the master proceeded to Wei, and when his disciple Tsŭ Kung asked whether it was right to violate the promise he had made, he answered:

"It was a forced oath. The spirits do not hear such." This is treated as a deliberate lie, but it is difficult to allow that even the tenderest conscience can treat it as such. It may not be praiseworthy—that is one thing— but to treat it as a betrayal of truth is a very different matter. It is a question of expediency, which only the man himself in those circumstances and at that moment can settle, and the whole teaching of Confucius and the array of his conduct as known to us must be considered in relation to that charge. If anyone wishes to allege that he was a man inconsiderate of the truth such a charge must awaken ridicule, because he himself placed truth as the basis, and his view of human nature and its possibilities of self-discipline must be put first.

In "The Doctrine of the Mean" we have K'ung Kei, the grandson of Confucius, declaring the teachings of his august grandfather often in his own words. The scope is set forth by another well-known philosopher thus:

"First it [the Doctrine of the Mean] deals with one principle. Next it spreads this out and takes all things into its circumference. All these returning, it gathers under the One principle. Spread it, and it brims the universe. Regather it, and it is in the background, though concealed."

What is this all-sufficing principle?

"Man has received his nature from Heaven."

That is the first proposition. It follows that it is essentially good, inevitably drawn toward the Better.

It will be noticed that this is the same teaching (though far less advanced) as that of the Yedanist in India, who proclaimed that man is one with the Divine. Confucius proceeds:

"Conduct in accordance with that nature constitutes what is right and true. It is pursuance of the true way. The cultivation or regulation of conduct is what is called instruction. . . .

"The path may not be left for an instant and the man of high virtue is cautious and careful in reference to what he does not see and on his guard against what he does not hear. There is nothing more visible than what is secret, nor more manifest than what is minute, and therefore the man of high instinct is watchful over his *aloneness.*"

Here is the teaching that nobility cannot be attained but by considering that in the spiritual—or as Confucius would have called it the moral—life nothing is a trifle. The infinitely little may prove to be the infinitely great in relation to the real issues of life, and therefore his *aloneness*. The innermost chambers of the heart are what the man who travels toward the heights will watch.

Then because this book deals with what is called the Mean we have the doctrine of equilibrium and resulting harmony of nature.

"While there are no movements of pleasure, anger, sorrow, joy, we have what may be called equilibrium. When these feelings have been moved and all act in due measure, we have what may be called the state of harmony. This equilibrium is the root of the world, and this harmony is its universal way."

Here we have indicated what is called in Vedantic teaching in India the "desireless" state of mind, in which no state can arise where one emotion predominates unduly. One may use the analogy of an ocean sleeping in calm; a wind comes; a wave is raised; all is tumult. So perfect will the harmony and equilibrium of the emotions of the ideal man be that no wind of circumstance can disturb the complete serenity of his emotions, for each balances the other and none can sway the rest.

Finally:

"Let the states of equilibrium and harmony exist in perfection, and happy order will prevail throughout heaven and earth, and all things will be nourished and flourish."

Undoubtedly. Such happy order as in the revolution of planets and procession of the season proceeds in silence and complete harmony, making no noise about it, yet developing all life and beauty. As a great disciple of Lao Tsii says:

"Beautiful is the universe, yet it does not talk. The four seasons abide by a fixed law, yet they are not heard. All creation is based upon absolute principles yet nothing speaks."

These paragraphs give the heart of the book of which the rest is an amplification, yet much flows from these brief passages, which are, as it were, the text of the discourse. Purify the heart according to the nobility that is in you, and its influences will flow far and wide, for though the path of duty carries a man into the world and its doings, the mainspring of all is at home in the citadel of being. All is in truth one, for the path itself is a part of the man, being his effluence. Well does Confucius say "The path is not far from man." "In hewing an ax- handle the pattern is not far off," says the Book of Odes, which he helped to transmit to posterity. True, for on the pattern of the ax that hews must the new ax-handle be wrought. They are the same though apparently apart. And the man who is born to rule and attains rule by the virtue in him will know that men must be governed by the nature that is in them, and according to the stages of development they have reached—no more and no less.

Their feeling must be considered and consulted as far as possible on the Golden Rule which the master enunciated :

"Reciprocity. What you do not like when done to yourself do to no other."

But yet the man of high virtue will neither weakly nor complaisantly give to others what he knows is bad for them. He will temporize. Chuang Tsŭ, a later philosopher, illustrates this point with a delightful fable. It contains the essence of wisdom in peaceful dealings with others in a few words.

> A keeper of monkeys said with regard to their rations of chestnuts that each monkey was to have three measures in the morning and four at night. But at this the monkeys were exceedingly annoyed, and the keeper therefore said they might have four in the morning and three at night, with which arrangement they were all well pleased. The actual number of the chestnuts remained the same, but there was an adaptation to the likes and dislikes of those concerned. Such is the principle of putting oneself into subjective relations with externals.

This little parable, which is uncommonly useful for either household or imperial ends, sets forth one aspect of the wise and great man's dealings with those who have not reached his own moral and intellectual plane. He will not change the rule. That rule is for their welfare, for he knows better than they; but he will adjust it to their satisfaction.

Practically, there are four primary obligations upon the man who is earnest in pursuing the path, and neglecting these he cannot attain. He is to serve his father as he would wish his son to serve him. That is the root-virtue of China; and some say that her days as an empire have been long in the land because she made that filial virtue peculiarly and nationally her own. But in the hands of Confucius it did not preclude reasoning with unworthy parents, and he himself in a celebrated instance, which I have given in the details of his life, set free a son who had offended against the canon of filial behavior on the ground that the father who had so ill taught him was the one to blame. One saying of his on this point should be quoted:

"In serving his parents a son may remonstrate with them, but gently. When he sees they do not follow his advice he shows an increased degree of reverence, but does not abandon his purpose. Should they punish him he does not allow himself to murmur."

Submission therefore was not to be unreasoning, but it was to be submission for the sake of higher good to the son and to the nation than could be gained from breaking away into revolt. The next requirement was that a man should serve an elder brother (the second head of the family) as he would choose his younger brother to serve himself. A part of the reason for this command is to be found in the family and clan system of China, where the elder brother may at any moment be called upon to take the father's place and with the same right to obedience.

The next essential is that a man should serve his prince as he would require a minister to serve him. In other words a man should be as faithful, loyal, and obedient to the government of his country, as though he himself formed a part of that government and every item of its laws had been imposed by himself. And the last essential is to behave to a friend as a man must hope a friend would behave to him.

But in addition the man who loves the right will be earnest in practicing these and the other ordinary virtues and sparing in talking of them. He must be vigilant in exertion to attain, and if his words tend to be excessive in quality or quantity he must curb that license. "For his words are related to his actions and his actions to his words—and complete sincerity must mark the man." But Confucius distinguishes between two sorts of sincerity— the first is inborn in some and practiced without effort; the second requires discipline and practice. He asserts that some men (certain of the old sages among them) are born naturally perfect in nobility and virtue—a belief which would in India be held as justified by the natural result of many previous incarnations and struggles—and he taught further that those not so born still have it in their power to attain that status, though with struggle and pain. In this doctrine of innate nobility we have a sharp cleavage with the doctrine of original sin as taught by a Christian philosopher like St. Thomas Aquinas—the Angel of the Schools. It would be impossible that any teacher trained in the Confucian methods should assert that the heart of man is naturally deceitful and desperately wicked; and the best friends of the doctrine must own it is not encouraging.

This fundamental difference has formed a bar to the full appreciation of the greatness of Confucius in the West, where, filtering through the missionaries of all the Church sects in China, it has been considered a heathenish and presumptuous way of looking at the relation of man to God. On the other hand the way was smoothed for the reception of the philosophy of Buddhism when it came down the steep passes and along the terrible deserts from India to China.

It followed from these teachings of Confucius that he set the utmost store on two things: altruism and example. The true gentleman, the man born to guide others whether in the day of small things or great, must be one whose personal interests can be subordinated without hesitation to the needs of others, in whatever relation they stand to him. And not only this, for active energy on others' behalf is also expected of the man who understands the secret of life.

"A man of perfect virtue, wishing to be established himself, seeks to establish others; wishing to be developed himself, he seeks to develop others and to be able to judge others by what is nearest in ourselves: this may be called the art of virtue." Not the science—that word might connote something cold and aloof. No—the welling joy of creative art, which is virtue on the esthetic side as it is also in perfect beauty of character. Every faculty must be so trained and disciplined that it would never obtrude itself to the destruction or shaking of the equilibrium of perfect harmony.

One of the reasons (for there were many) why Confucius loved music was that he felt it to be a symbol of varied interests, blending in the harmony which can also be observed in the well-ordered unit of the family and the state as the aggregate of the family. It will not be forgotten by students of Plato that he also in "The Republic" attaches the same importance to that strange art of music—the most inspirational of all and the very cry of Nature in her inanimate (to use a contradiction in terms) and animate life.

Again and again Confucius insists on the importance of esthetics but more especially music and poetry—for he placed the starry Muses side by side—in the formation of a great people. We do not hear of the glyptic art nor that of the painter's brush in the same way, but other reasons may be assigned for that omission. By precept and example he drove it once for all into the soul of the Chinese nation that beauty—beauty in small things as well as in great—was to be their formula of life. "Man does not live by bread alone" is a saying which might have sprung from his own lips, as in other forms it did; and well was it accepted and acted upon, as those who know China can testify, and those who know only her great arts can echo, with a gratitude due to few other nations.

He saw also that accomplishment in these kingdoms of Beauty must be based on the human duties. They come first. He says:

"A young man when at home should be dutiful, when abroad reverent to his elders. He must be earnest and sincere. He should overflow with charity for all and cultivate the friendship of the good. When he has time and opportunity *after these things,* he must employ them in study of accomplishments of a gentleman—i.e., music; the rules of courteous behavior, which imply knowledge of the fitness of things; archery; horsemanship; writing and numbers; the knowledge of literature and poetry and the study of history." In a word, his must be an all-round character developed like the themes in a great fugue, which meet in sublime and perfect union-in-difference at the close. Confucius himself used such an illustration.

"How to play music may be known. At the commencement of the piece all the parts should sound together. As it proceeds they should be in harmony, while severally distinct and flowing without break; and thus as one to the conclusion."

A description which applies to his ideal man as well as to the art. For such a character these rules are enunciated.

"Hold fidelity and sincerity as first principles. Have no friends not equal to yourself. When you have faults do not hesitate to abandon them."

Luxury too was forbidden to the gentleman (I use the word as Confucius took it—a word of deep meaning). Luxury could not delight a soul so finely tempered or moved to such high issues. To sum up; the development of perfect manhood at once valorous and humble, wise and serene, must be based on the retention of a tender conscience, the habits of a simple life, the spirit of humility, and the strengthening of constancy, be it in study, in action, or in moral endeavor. And these qualities must be maintained by self-examination. As the master says in "The Doctrine of the Mean":

"The poets say that though the fish sinks and lies at the bottom it may be seen. Therefore the noble man examines his heart that he may have no cause for selfdissatisfaction."

And in the *Lung Yu* (the Analects) :

"When self-examination discovers nothing wrong, what is there to be anxious about and what is there to fear?"

The master said: "He who aims to be a man of complete virtue, in his food does not seek to gratify his appetite, nor in his dwelling-place does he seek the appliances of ease. He is earnest in his undertakings, careful in his speech. Such a man may be said to be an ardent student."

Tsŭ Kung, his famous disciple, replied: "It is said in the Book of Odes, 'As you cut and then file, as you carve and then polish.' I think the meaning is the same as that which you have just expressed."

The master said: "With one like Tsŭ Kung I can begin to talk about the Odes. I told him one point, and he knew its proper sequence."

The praise was deserved. Never was there a more apt quotation, for the ode quoted by Tsŭ Kung is one very ancient in the day of Confucius, in praise of the great Prince Wu, who had dealt with himself as a lapidary who first cuts the gem and then with many tools and infinite art polishes it until all who see it must rejoice in its radiance. In other words, work and example. On the examples given by such characters Confucius based his hope for family and state.

The seven steps of ascent would be in this order for the individual: The investigation of things and their causes; the completion of knowledge; the truth and sincerity of the heart; the cultivation of esthetics, the regulation of the family; the government of the state.

In the family will shine the virtues of the man who has thus attained, with a light as sustaining and nourishing as that of the sun. Such examples will spread like the vibrations of water from a stone dropped into a pool. The master believed goodness and nobility to be infectious, and he saw in the enforced bonds of the family a most powerful urge to goodness, both on the grounds of imitation and emulation. From the seed of the family virtues will spring the Tree of the State. The humbler virtues applicable to family life will not be changed in essence, but will widen in their scope. In the classic known as "The Great Learning" we are told that filial submission will in state matters appear as loyalty to that state and its ruler. The reverence for an elder brother will be transmuted into reverence and ready obedience to elders and those in authority. Family kindness will appear as universal courtesy. It is said:

"From the loving example of one family a whole state becomes loving, and from its courtesies the whole state becomes courteous."

From the example of such a man on the throne all might be hoped. Here again we have Confucius according with Plato. Passage after passage from the Analects strikes that lesson home to people and ruler. K'e Kang, distressed at thieving in the state, asked Confucius for a precept. He replied:

"Sir, if you yourself were not covetous they would not steal—no, not even if you paid them to do it."

"And what is your view about killing the wicked for the sake of the good?" was the next question.

The master replied:

"Sir, in carrying on your government why use killing? Let your evinced desires be for what is good, and the people will be good. The relation between governors and governed is like that between wind and the grass. The grass bows when the wind blows over it."

And again he said:

"If good men were to govern a country in succession for a hundred years they would transform the violently bad and dispense with capital punishment."

How fine is this realization of collective responsibility for crime!

He dwelt much too on the necessity of education for all. It was not to be a monopoly of the classes. Even for war he would have an educated people. An ignorant and uneducated poeple are neither worthy nor fitted to fight for their country.

It may be said: "Is this practical? Can so much be hoped from the personal characters of those composing a government? While admitting that such influences would be more directly felt in a feudal government like that known to Confucius, where the example of the king would percolate through the feudal princes to the lowest official, I still answer:

Yes ... It is practical even now and from two points of view. If we can imagine a government of gentlemen, using the word in the Confucian sense, one may say that in the complication of modern government there are many more channels and therefore a much wider opportunity of spreading honorable example and teaching than in his days. Consider a present-day government with its titulary or elected head, its cabinet, its lower ministers, the representative houses, the judiciary, the systems of education from high to low, the hundreds of thousands of officials who in the least degree represent the power of the state; is it possible to deny that if in such a state the Confucian ideal were set before the people in every movement of the government, it might bear mighty fruit in their lives?

It will be replied, "That dream could never be realized." And I own that looking upon the present-day governments in all the countries of the earth one might well despair if one did not share the Confucian faith in the innate goodness of man. It must at least be admitted that when he ruled a city he himself made a fine success of it, even if we allow for natural exaggeration. And I think we must also admit that there is not one single government in the world at the present moment where his elementary precept has been followed: "Employ the upright and put aside the crooked."

Until we have learned the alphabet we can scarcely expect to read the classics.

CHAPTER 22

THE HEROES OF CHINA

We turn now to the philosophy of Confucius. It leads us, as he would have it, directly to the wisdom of the ancients, the springs of pure water that he like a skilful irrigator collected, divided, and formed into a network of flowing streams to fertilize the thirsty empire. This is an illustration he would have approved, and none the less because on the material side and literally such had been the work of one of his ideal heroes, and his was the example Confucius followed on the intellectual and moral plane. "I am the transmitter of the wisdom of the ancients" was his own too modest claim.

It is hopeless to understand his teaching unless a view is taken of a China very ancient even in the days of the master, who was born five hundred and fifty-one years before our era.

Before our knowledge of China becomes historical and concrete, there stretch away into the past what may be called the traditional and legendary periods. Of those, though their interest to students of a certain order can scarcely be overrated, I shall not speak here except to say that, in so much as legend and tradition mold belief and therefore philosophy, they are more valuable than the modern world is willing to admit, even as the idea is often more valuable than what is called the fact. But according to Chinese opinion, Chinese history may be said to begin about four thousand five hundred years ago or two thousand six hundred years before our era.

Record of Chinese dynasties begins with the time of the Five Rulers 2852 *B.C.* It is said that the first of these invented what are known as the Eight Trigrams—a hidden writing never since solved but used in China then and now as a decoration. He is also said to have written a record and to have fixed the calendar. If there is any approximate truth in these statements civilization was highly developed even at that time.

Of this extraordinary people it seems that almost anything may be true. Here is the monumental democracy, controlling its monarchy, dismissing dynasties as easily as unsatisfactory servants, accomplished in literature when Europe had scarcely begun its alphabets, despising war as mad folly; a nation of philosophers, yet prepared to defend their rights and liberties with the sword from internal and external foes. All must approach the thoughts which guided the destinies of such a people with the same sense of awe as that felt in presence of the Sphinx's brooding silence. Fortunately the Chinese were not silent. They formed schools, as has been seen in the story of Confucius; and from these we may know what molded and will mold their history.

According to Dr. Legge, the great Chinese scholar, the religious belief of the Chinese was monotheistic at that time. The earliest character for the name of God symbolizes "Lordship and Government." In his opinion the name *Ti* represented to the ancient Chinese what the name "God" represented to our own ancestors. One of the Manchu emperors of China confirmed the belief of the Jesuits that this represents the Supreme Ruler and that any other expression was used by the Chinese to avoid what was considered a disrespectful direct mention.

Round this idea crystallized another belief in subsidiary spirits. One class of these was related to heaven, a second to earth, a third to the spirits of dead men. The ancient Chinese therefore believed that death did not extinguish a man's being.

The heaven and earth spirits were invoked as serviceable to men under the Divine Sovereign. Dr. Legge gives a prayer from "The Statutes of the Ming Dynasty" which though in itself comparatively modern he considers as faithfully representing the ancient tradition of the position held by spirits in relation to God and man.

> To the spirits of the Cloud-Master,
> The Rain-Master,
> The Lord of the winds, and the Thunder-Master!
> It is your office, O spirits, to superintend the clouds

> and the rain and to raise and send abroad the wind as ministers assisting the Supreme Ruler.

And to the earthly spirits—

> The spirits of the mountains and hills,
> Of the four seas and four great rivers of the imperial domain,
> And of all hills and rivers under the sky!

it is said:

> Yours it is, O spirits, with your Heaven-confirmed powers and nurturing influences,
> Each to preside as guardian over one district
> As ministers assisting the great Worker and Transformer,
> And thus the people enjoy your meritorious services.

Roughly this seems to correspond to the lesser deities of other faiths and to have presented a model for the imperial court of the empire, including the ruling sovereign, his ministers and prefects in charge of various territories and districts—benefactors of the people, who can only approach the sovereign through these intermediate rulers.

The spirits of the dead were and are believed, when evoked for state and ancestral worship, to descend into small rectangular wooden tablets, inscribed with the characters "Seat of the Spirit" or "Lodging-Place of the Spirit" and with the surname, name, and office of the dead man. These are set up before the worshiper. At other times the spirit is absent, and the tablet, which is laid aside until the next occasion, is not holy.

In very early times living members of the worshiping families were chosen as vessels to receive the ancestral spirits. Thus a boy and girl might represent their grandfather and grandmother as though they were their spirits. They then ate the sacred foods prepared for the ancestors, sat in state to receive homage from the family, and the grandson pronounced words of blessing. Such a service ended with a song to the following effect:

> Thou comfortest me with long life, giving me many blessings so that I am become great.
> I offer this sacrifice to my meritorious father and to my accomplished mother.

No doubt in ancient times human victims were sacrificed to accompany the dead into the unseen world; but as civilization advanced it was recognized that the immaterial idea was what constituted the true value of this offering and from that time paper representatives of beautiful or necessary objects have been burned on the occasion of Chinese funerals—the educated Chinese of the present day respecting the custom as traditional.

We now come to the venerable "Shu King" (the word *"King"* means "classic"), the Book of Historical Documents. This collection is the oldest of Chinese books. The first two parts of it extend over one hundred and fifty years, and give the events of the reigns of two sovereigns, Yao and Shun—names never to be forgotten by those who wish to understand anything of Confucius and his system. Dr. Legge records that a Chinese gentleman of intelligence and education said to him, "We have nothing in China the roots of which are not to be found in Yao and Shun." A statement which I have heard myself and which yet has profound meaning though no longer wholly true.

A Chinese commentator, Tsei Chin, who wrote a preface to the Book of Historical Documents about 1210 *A.D., says:*

"I labored at it assiduously for ten years. This classic contains the acts and ordinances of the two great sovereigns Yao and Shun, together with those of the founders of the three succeeding dynasties; and these acts and ordinances must be regarded as the rule and pattern for all future ages. Their importance is such that they cannot be dealt with superficially. ... Every act of these five gifted rulers was based on sound principles originating in personal rectitude. . . . But whether we find them exhibiting these principles in their own persons or impressing on others the value of benevolence, reverence, truthfulness, or valor it will be found that what these great men did was the exhibition of personal rectitude."

Of the book a European translator, W. A. Medhurst, observes (I condense):

"The lessons of practical wisdom contained in the 'Shu King' are applicable to all times and nations. Even in enlightened Europe something may be learned from it, and so long as the world retains the distinction between high and low, rich and poor, so long will the principles of reciprocal justice, affection, respect, and obedience, laid down in its pages, keep their ground."

It will be seen that the admiration of Confucius was not misplaced. For the rulers were his models alike in philosophy and the practical science of government.

The first chapter breaks dramatically into praise of the great sovereign Yao—he who corrected the calendar, restrained the floods and irrigated the land. He began his reign at the age of sixteen and lived to be a hundred and six.

"He was kind as Heaven, wise as the gods. He wore a yellow cap and dark tunic and rode in a red chariot with white horses. The eaves of his thatch were not trimmed, and the beams had no ornamental ends. He drank his lentil broth from a clay dish with a wooden spoon. He did not use jewels, and his clothes were simple and without variety. In summer a simple garb of cotton, in winter deerskins. Yet was he the richest, wisest, longest-lived, and most beloved of all that ever ruled." On him the comment of Confucius is: "Heaven alone is great and none but Yao could imitate Heaven."

The time had now come that he should appoint a successor; he is seated among his ministers and nobles for that purpose. And first he speaks to his prime minister, known as the "President of the Four Mountains." "Harken, President of the Four Mountains! I am old and infirmity has clutched me. Seventy years have passed since I ascended the jewel-throne. You can carry out my commands. I shall resign my place to you."

The chief said: "I have not the virtue. I should disgrace your place."

The sovereign said: "Show me one among the illustrious or put forth one among the poor and mean."

All said to the sovereign: "Among the lower people there is an unmarried man called Shun of Yu."

And the sovereign said: "Yes, I have heard of him. What have you to say about him?"

The chief minister said: "He is the son of a blind man. His father was obstinately wicked, his mother insincere, his half-brother Hsiang arrogant. Yet he has been able by his filial piety to live in harmony with them and to lead them gradually to self-government, so that they are no longer filled with great wickedness."

The sovereign said: "I shall try him. He is unwed, and I shall wed him to my two daughters."

Thus he determined and sent down his two daughters to the north of the Kwei to be wives in the family of Yu. The sovereign said to them:

"Be reverent."

Thus tested, the lowly bom Shun did not fail, and he first became coruler with the mighty Yao. In the next chapter his accession to sole power is recorded. The ancient book describes him as a man of great force of character and energy, wise and vigilant for the welfare of "the black-haired people." He improved the methods of astronomy, made a ritual for the worship "when sacrificing to the Supreme God and presenting offerings to the presiding spirits of the land."

In the Canon of Shun are recorded several acts of worship, beginning with his inauguration in the Temple of the Accomplished Ancestor. A solemn sacrifice to God followed, "according to the ordinary forms," so it appears, as Legge points out, there was even at that remote time a representative worship of God by the ruler of China.

Shun instituted a uniform system of weights and measures; adjusted the musical scale; codified the criminal laws and established fines for lesser offenses. Not only thus, but the lowly born sovereign set forth rules of conduct for all those who administered the country. His charge to his surveyor general is immortal:

"Be careful, be cautious in the administration of the law. Offenses of ignorance and misfortune must be freely pardoned, and in all matters of doubt let your judgment incline to the side of mercy."

He divided the empire into twelve states and fixed their boundaries. He was great in the reclamation of land and the drainage of floods and marshes. China, always democratic in spirit though reverent to authority, has no reason to be ashamed of her sovereign chosen from "the lower people," as his reign is described in the Book of Historical Documents.

Shun lived to a great age and was succeeded by his surveyor general, who had been chosen as successor in his lifetime on account of his great practical powers in establishing boundaries, controlling floods (always the sorrow of China) and driving the waste waters into the rivers.

The third chapter describes these great works to their conclusion, and gives details of the distribution of lands and titles among the nobles, with the regulation of their tenures.

Then comes a very interesting part of the book, giving an address of the sovereign to his soldiers before battle with a rebel vassal. He recounts the reasons which have decided him to "execute the judgment of Heaven [God] upon the rebel," and the speech proceeds:

"And now, spearmen and archers, I warn you. Take heed that you obey my orders, and you, charioteers, see that your horses are well guided. I have great rewards for welldoers, to be given before my ancestral temple, and death for the man who earns my anger—death for him and his children."

Passing on we come to the (possibly) supreme hero of Confucius, Fa, afterwards the Duke of Chao. Old customs had fallen into disuse, and a brutal tyrant, the last sovereign of the Yin dynasty, sat upon the throne with a beautiful wife, Ta Ki, whom the people considered a devil incarnate from her acts of cruelty. "She invented the trial by fire, the hot brazen pillar, and the punishment of the roasting-spit. And the people repined with shuddering."

But the sovereign and his wife heeded nothing, drinking from cups of crystal and eating the paws of bears and the wombs of leopards. He was a drunkard, a man of ferocious strength, and appeal after appeal was made to him in vain. His was the right to tax the people almost to extinction for his pleasures, so he replied.

Of all the tributary princes the greatest and best was the Duke of Chao. His state was the model for an empire, and to him all hearts turned—to him and to his son Fa, who was worthy of his father's great soul. The duke ventured to rebuke the sovereign. He was seized and cast into prison, and there, because

> Stone walls do not a prison make,
> Nor iron bars a cage;
> Minds innocent and quiet take
> That for an hermitage,

he spent his time in writing a part of one of China's famous books.

But his escape was necessary to China, and his son Fa temporized. He sent a beautiful woman, instructed in her part, with a large gift of money to the tyrant. She pleaded and wooed, and in an evil hour for himself he released the duke, who returned to his son Fa and his state. About them gathered the angry nobles and the unhappy people; and every day came in more horrible tales of the tyrant's evil deeds, and every day men's hearts turned more steadily to the hope that the duke might displace him and extend his merciful rule to the whole empire.

From prince to peasant all saw it with wonder and delight. Some years before, two princes of neighboring states who had quarreled as to their boundaries had resolved to ask the good duke to arbitrate, and came to his state for that purpose. There great amaze possessed them, for in that state each man appeared to consider the general good rather than his own. The farmers helped one another, fields had no landmarks, travelers moved about with courtesy and consideration, and there was a law that no old man should carry a heavy load. The princes marveled. In the palace all was the same. Cooperation reigned instead of rivalry. There was fine emulation instead of competition. One prince turned to the other;

"And why should we weary these good men with our affairs?"

Why, indeed! They would not trouble the duke, whose whole life was given to the good of others; and so they went home at peace with each other, and settled the business and the boundary without more ado.

Such was the man to whom the hope of China turned. It was not to be realized in him, but in his great son. He died, ninety years old, and Fa, now Duke of Chao, seeing his father dead, his uncle murdered by the tyrant whom he had dared to rebuke, and the people driven to madness by cruelty, knew that the time had come.

He addressed his army:

"The sovereign squats on his heels; he cares nothing for the worship of God or of his ancestors. He says, 'God made me king, who can disturb God?' "

And the duke marched to battle, saying, "I have offered sacrifices to God. I lead you all to execute the will of Heaven." In one hand he carried his battle-ax, in another a flag of the royal white. And as the chariots charged, the sovereign's troops gave way, and there was a mighty slaughter and victory.

The sovereign fled to the Stag Tower. There he adorned himself with pearls and jewels and when he saw all was hopeless set fire to the tower and died in the flames; and he and his beautiful, abhorrent empress went to their own place.

The great duke ascended the throne and made wise and healing laws for the suffering—such as Confucius studied night and day with delight and hoped to perpetuate in China. He gave to his dead father the title of Wen Wang—that is to say King Wen—and he himself took the title of Wu Wang, or King Wu. Among the greatest and best of the sovereigns of China their names are loved and honored; and none ignorant of their story can understand Confucius.

"The king sent back the war-horses to the Flowery Mountain. The weapons of war he wrapped about with tiger-skins, and covering the chariots and armor he stored them away. Thus he made an end to war."

When Confucius was a very old man, failing in health and hope, he said one day:

"Extreme is my decay. For a long time I have not dreamed of the Duke of Chao." So constantly had that presence been with him in his meditations.

It is natural that "Spring and Autumn"—the book which is most truly his own, and therefore profoundly venerated in China—should be a history of a period in the Chao dynasty. There he could permit love as well as intellect to guide his hand. It is said that in that famous book he sets the example of meticulous care in the art of "rectifying terms"—that is, using the words which express to a hair the finest shade of thought in dealing with his great subjects. For example: If a king is slain by his subjects Confucius used the word "murder" to express the deed. If a tyrant meets the same fate Confucius employs the word "kill," with the implication that a tyrant has ceased to be a king in any reasonable meaning of the word. Each word and phrase is given an ethical as well as literary value.

This is a book whose appearance, it is said, struck rebellious ministers and villainous sons with terror, so directly was it aimed at the conscience, so clearly did every word perform its office in distinguishing truth from falsehood and good from evil. There men might learn that a government departing from virtue ceases to be government in any real sense. In that book, as in all his teaching, stands clear the fact that the world's good depends upon the individual, and he who would hope to reform it must begin at home—a truth at once cheering and awe-striking. A world in which this truth is realized—is called by the master "The World of the Great Identity." That name would have been understood by the Indian philosophers. They would have said: "Though this teacher does not know it he has realized that the Manifold is the Appearance. The One is the Truth. And duty done to others is done to ourselves."

The Book of Historical Documents contains many stories of old, unhappy, far-off things, human yet almost diabolical in cruelty, but it also contains stories of noble things and of the Golden Age of simple and generous government which could never be permitted to die. It is the dearer to the Chinese heart because the hand of Confucius is everywhere apparent about it. It has not survived intact, for the tablets on which it was written narrowly escaped extinction (with many other books of ancient times) in the famous or infamous "Burning of the Books" by that foolish emperor who was first of the Ts'in dynasty; and the scholars of the Han dynasty, who came later, found the books—such as they could retrieve —mutilated and in disorder. The account of this burning given in the Historical Records cannot be left out. It took place in 212 B.C. and would have broken the heart of Confucius if he had lived to see it. (I condense.)

> The emperor returning from a visit to the South gave a feast in the palace when the great scholars [men of official rank] to the number of seventy appeared and wished him long life. The superintendent of archery came forward and praised him, saying:
>
> "Your Majesty by your spirit-like efficacy and intelligent wisdom has tranquilized the whole empire, so that wherever the sun and moon shine all appear before you as guests, acknowledging subjection."
>
> The emperor was pleased with this flattery.
>
> The chief minister said:
>
> "At the risk of my life I say that now when your Majesty has consolidated the empire, scholars still honor their own peculiar learning, and combining together they teach men what is contrary to your laws. They discuss every ordinance. They are dissatisfied in heart. They keep talking in the streets. And so they lead on the people to be guilty of murmuring and evil-speaking. If these things are not prohibited, your Majesty's authority will decline.

> "As to the best way to prohibit them I pray that all the records in charge of the historiographers be burned excepting those of Ts'in [the state of which the emperor had been prince before he became emperor]. Also that, with the exception of officers belonging to the board of great scholars, all throughout the empire who presume to keep copies of the Book of Odes or of the Book of Historical Documents or of the Books of the Hundred Schools be required to go with them to the officers in charge of the several districts and burn them. Also that all who dare to speak together about these two books be put to death and their bodies exposed in the market-place, and that those who praise the past so as to blame the present shall die along with their relatives.
>
> "I propose also that officers who shall know of the violation of these rules and not inform against the offenders shall be held equally guilty, and that whoever shall not have burned their books within thirty days after the issuing of the ordinance shall be branded and sent to labor on the building of the Wall. The only books which should be spared are those on medicine, divination, and husbandry. Whoever wants to learn the laws can go to the magistrates and learn of them."

The emperor's decision in this wise counsel was "Approved"! Here were Radicals indeed—their only regret that a past which mutely reproached them could not be burned with the books. But they went as far as they could. Next year on the discovery that over four hundred and sixty scholars had hidden their books they were all buried alive in pits, and all who were suspected were degraded and banished. In vain did the emperor's eldest son Fu Su remonstrate. He was himself banished to the care of the general who was superintending the building of the Great Wall, and the emperor might at last hope that the destruction of the banned classics was complete.

The whole story is a mighty tribute to the influence for good of the ancient sovereigns and of Confucius and of the classics, as viewed from the angle of a fool and a tyrant. He and they could not exist together. Three years later he died, and twenty-two years later his dynasty was extinct, the emperors of the Han dynasty doing all in their power to retrieve part of the miserable calamity he had brought upon Chinese literature.

There is an account of the efforts in the Han dynasty (201 B.C.-A.D. 24). Thus it is written:

"After the death of Confucius there was an end of his glorious words, and when his seventy disciples passed away violence began to be done to their meaning. Amid the disorder of the warring states a sad confusion marked the words of various scholars. Then came the calamity inflicted under the Ts'in dynasty, when the literary monuments were destroyed by fire to keep the people in ignorance. But later arose the Han dynasty, which set itself to remedy the evil. Great efforts were made to collect slips and tablets [on bamboo, for there was no paper], and the way was thrown wide open for the bringing in of books. In the time of the Emperor Hiau Wu [189 *B.C.],* portions of the Books being wanting and tablets lost so that the Rites and Music were suffering great injury, he was moved to sorrow and said, 'I grieve for this.' "

He and succeeding emperors and scholars earnestly labored to retrieve the injury done to knowledge and wisdom. Much was regained, but terribly mutilated and in disorder. It was also found that during the war of the states the feudal princes had destroyed the records of the golden age of government, the very existence of which condemned their own ill-doings. Of the priceless Analects—the conversations of Confucius and his disciples—appeared first two copies, one from the state of Lu, the native land of the master, and one from the adjoining state of C'hi. These were confusing inasmuch as they differed considerably.

It was not until 150 *B.C.*—when one of the emperor's sons, appointed King of Lu, in enlarging his palace demolished the house of the K'ung family where Confucius himself had lived—that copies of the Book of Historical Documents, the "Spring and Autumn" and the Analects were found. They had been hidden there in the wall at the time of the Burning of the Books, and were all written in the ancient and then disused "tadpole characters."

This copy of the Analects agreed with one of the others, save in one important matter, and so what may be called the canonical copy can be relied upon. A poetic story is told to the effect that the king could not after all destroy the sacred house in which the wisest of the sons of earth had lived, for as he reverently ascended the steps leading to the ancestral hall the air was thrilled with the joyful sound of singing stones and of lutes—the music beloved of old by the master.

But it may easily be realized through what dangers the great books of China have come. It was to insure their safety in a more permanent form that in *A.D.* 175 the classics were cut upon slabs of imperishable stone after the text determined by the scholars. Later, between the years *A.D.* 240 and 248 this was done again, and the slabs preserved together.

The philosophy of Confucius had two aims—the production of individual character, generous and noble in itself, and its effect upon society and especially upon the science of government.

The chief importance of the development of individual character lay in its influence upon the world at large, not in its result of happiness on earth and a blessed eternity for the virtuous man himself. With any future which lay beyond death the teachings of Confucius were not concerned. Several times his disciples pressed him upon a point on which they were naturally anxious, especially as all round them were sacrifices and offerings to the spirits of departed ancestors. They would gladly have learned what he believed of the abode of these spirits. But it was not a subject on which he is known to have expressed any opinion. On the contrary, it is recorded that there were four things of which he would never willingly speak: extraordinary things, feats of strength, rebellious disorder, and spirits Like the Buddha he held to "the noble silences of the wise."

And he held to this stedfastly. A disciple once asked him for light on the question of the service of the spirits of dead ancestors. He answered:

"While you are not able to serve men alive, how can you serve their spirits?"

"I venture to ask about death," persisted the questioner.

"While you do not know life, how can you know about death?" was the answer.

But the disciples, perhaps unpossessed of the philosophic calm of the master, could not leave it there. They knew well that in and from the times of those sovereigns most reverenced by Confucius for intellect as well as every virtue, solemn offerings had been made and prayers offered to the spirits of the noble dead. They wanted to know what was in the mind of their great instructor on these dark questions, and Tsŭ Kung asked whether the dead knew or did not know of the offerings made to them. Confucius answered:

"If I say that the dead know, I fear that filial sons and grandsons would all but ruin themselves in such observances, and if I say otherwise, I fear that the un- filial would leave their parents unburied. You need not care to know. The point is not urgent, and later you yourself will know."

Like the Buddha, Confucius was aware that for general humanity the Infinite is too transcendent. His mission was to lead men by the path of duty and discipline to the point where a diviner apprehension awaited them. He who faithfully follows "the Way of man" will in due time find that it merges in the Way of Heaven. The reserve of Confucius is not hard to understand. Yet later in the Record of Rites he said:

"All living must die and return to the ground. But the spirit escapes and shines on high in glory. The vapors and odors that produce a feeling of sadness are those of the subtle animal essence."

But here also he declined to be explicit, and China both anteceded and followed this position. They allowed by word and gesture the existence of the spirits of their ancestors in a happy place. This is certified again and again by late and early prayers. The ideal man of Confucius, the famous Duke of Chao, "carried up the title of king to his grandfather and great grandfather and sacrificed to all the former dukes of the line with the observances due to the Son of Heaven" (the emperor), their wives also being honored, and each pair of tablets placed side by side. And here are fully explicit prayers used by the emperor during the Ming dynasty.

I think of you, my sovereign ancestors,
whose glorious souls are in heaven.
As from an overflowing fountain run the happy streams,
Such is the connection between you and your descendants.
I, a distant descendant, having received this appointment,
Look back and offer this bright sacrifice to you,
The honored one from age to age for
hundred and thousands and myriads of years.

Now brightly made manifest,
Now augustly hidden,
The movements of the spirits leave no footprints;
In their imperial chariots they wander serene wherever they pass.
Their souls are in heaven:
Their tablets are set up in the hall.
Sons and grandsons remember them with filial love unwearying.

Confucius in one great passage of the Doctrine of the Mean had struck a higher note, where it was not easy for the general Chinese mind—nor for any racial mind save that of the Indo-Aryan—to follow him, either then or now.

"How generously does the Divine display His good. We look for Him but do not see Him; we listen to Him but do not hear; yet He enters into all and without Him there is nothing. Like overflowing water He seems to be over the heads and on the right and left of His worshipers."

The practical Chinese mind paused below this vision and sought no ultimate issues until Buddhism entered China *in* the year *A.D. 65.* Great and noble is that mind. It produced an uplifted and ordered civilization with forms of beauty which India never equalled except in the spiritual realm. It preserved that civilization intact, almost uncolored by invaders who thought they had mastered China when the spirit of China had wholly mastered them. Esthetics were a part of its policy. None who do not know China can realize how beauty in all the arts was a part of her daily bread. But when it came to the relation of man to the Divine, India soared on eagle's wings to the empyrean, and to the feet of India China was compelled to come suing for that bread without which the spirit of man cannot live—that light which kindled the flame of Greece, Persia, Japan, Ceylon, Siam, Burma, and Java and others, and may yet strike fire from the West.

CHAPTER 23

THE SOUL OF CHINA

What then is the summing up of the unique personality and position of Confucius as leader, shaper, and—it may almost be said—deity of the great Chinese people? One may lay aside the somewhat ineffectual missionary position of comparing his labors with those of the Founder of the Christian faith and finding in differences a reason for condemnation. That point of view is not likely to commend itself in the future, and he will be judged on his own merits and results.

His death was darkened with a sense of failure—a common enough doom of great men; and when it took place his followers, however sensible of his magnitude, could hardly have foreseen how his figure would dominate every other in China. He had hoped for the reformation and purging of the feudal princedoms under the emperor, and this appeared to be the great means of making actual his dream of ideal government. But it was not to be. The feudal system passed away in blood and revolution after his death; and no one could then have predicted how the future of China would develop.

But the words of Confucius, his example and teachings, his sublime faith in the lightward striving heart of man, had kindled a beacon-fire which drew all noble souls as surely as flame draws the moth. They could not escape the fascination of that high evangel even if they would. In himself they beheld the ideal man, the princely man, the man of perfect virtue, whose portrait he had drawn so often and so lovingly as the hope of China. A hope not heavenly and out of reach, but practical and to be visualized on earth. It brought to birth the ideal commonwealth, presided over by a ruler whose personal attainment and example should be his sword and shield; one who should make throned virtue so beautiful and desirable as to win the love and fealty of all who saw, not only for himself but for the Divine which dwelt in him.

They believed with the master that in the Golden Age of China such men had lived and reigned. Confucius had carried on the continuity of these supermen. Was it too much to hope that his precepts and the examples given by him in the classics might yet bear fruit in a people who accepted these truths and lived by them? No, it was not too much. The hopes of the master, whose teaching was based on altruism and cooperation, were to be largely realized by the union of the warring states, in the harmony of an empire, noble in peace, diffusing beauty in all her arts, and setting an example of just dealing and filial piety throughout Asia.

Undoubtedly there was failure also—here and there abundant failure of which the teaching of Confucius cannot wholly be acquitted. Though he himself perceived great spiritual truths he had not the will—perhaps not even the power—to clothe them in words easily to be understood by the people. He left the highest spiritual attainment of man a mystery to be solved, as no doubt it will be in each individual case by stedfast advance in the road of right thinking and right doing—a road he constructed as a skilful engineer lays his roads and rails over primeval swamps beneath. Still the kindling force of mystic emotion was wanting; and though the light shone brilliantly it shone somewhat coldly.

Yet China had never more cause than now to return to the teachings of her uncrowned king and to pray that his hopes for her may be realized in a mighty future. That there is greater teaching is possible, but if greater exists, let her live up to the full measure of the Confucian ideal, since there is no height for which it cannot prepare her. The western nations may learn much also from this calm and practical ideal of the noble life, with its concentration on statesmanship and public as well as private good—the ideal of a character in which all the graces of heart and intellect meet.

Is there a better ideal known for young men who must take their place in the family and in the world? For my part I would have the Analects made a study for every young man who goes through a university; and if it be true that the greatest thoughts of the greatest men of every nation are the world's common riches, copies of that book should be within reach of every man and woman to whom individual and national progress in the highest ethics are dear.

CHAPTER 24

A GREAT CHINESE MYSTIC LAO TSŬ

We turn now to the teaching of the great rival of Confucius—Lao Tsŭ (pronounce "Loudza"); he who is said to have met and discussed the higher wisdom with the master on his memorable visit to the royal city of Lo. His doctrine could not hope to rival that of Confucius in the sense of popularity. The Confucian ideal was certain to conquer by the dynamic of sheer obvious visible beauty, as undeniable as that of Greek sculpture. No one with eyes and reason could deny its charm or it may be said its life-and-death value to China. Its consecration of the national heroes must alone have won it devotion.

But there are different forms of greatness, different points of perception; and while Confucius built for the average man of high attainment, the cloudy foundations of Lao Tsŭ were laid for the habitation of that man who must dwell in spiritual places, where the mists drift beneath his feet and the lights are the sun and moon and hierarchy of the rolling planets.

Confucius stated his precepts so that all could understand if they would. Clear and plain as a guide-book are his directions for the fundamentals of his system. Lao Tsŭ, wrestling like Jacob with the Divine, cannot always find words to express his full meaning, for the reason that they are called upon to convey the Infinite, which transcends all human languages. Yet for those who can feel and can attain realization—even as glimpses of light in a troubled sky—the doctrines of Confucius will have a tendency to seem somewhat trite and obvious beside this voice of unearthly beauty, with its promise of a serenity the world neither gives nor can destroy.

For with Lao Tsŭ we enter the realm of the Indian realization of Union with the Divine, the Buddhist Nirvana, the Christian Peace of God. He might have achieved clearer expression of the mighty thoughts overcharging him had he paid that mythical visit to India with which some legends credit him. But though he probably did not, his brief book of some eighty chapters, each consisting of but a few words, sets China among the nations whom the mystic light has dazzled and gladdened.

Of his life little is known. In thinking of him he sits aloof like one of those Immortals (as China calls them) who have attained wisdom among the precipices and pinnacled rocks, where towering pines rival the peaks and downward-thundering rivers shout for joy upon their way to the profounder harmonies of the ocean. So vague, so spiritual is his figure, that some have even attempted to deny his existence. As an Immortal may be seen in those supreme pictures known to the happy student of great Chinese art, here sits Lao Tsŭ, lost in contemplation —his breath exhaling in divine shapes among the kindred mysteries of nature glimpsed in drifting sunshine, drowned in sweeping mists—alone, contented, absorbed in the ecstasy of supernal wisdom.

But that wisdom is not for all the world. You must have eaten the bread of the mystics and drunk their wine before you can behold those midnight skies where Lao Tsŭ revolves, a moon about the sun, reflecting light to be beheld by earthly eyes only in clear dream and solemn vision.

Every circumstance connected with Lao Tsŭ has the mystic aura. He is described as the son of a virgin mother, conceived under the influence of a falling star.

The name by which he is known to us signifies the "Ancient Child," but may also be read as the "Venerable Philosopher." His surname Li represents the plum, and he is said to have been born under a plum tree—the symbol of immortality.

From the account of the places connected with him, given by the historian Ssu-ma Ch'ien, Carus translates: "He was born in the hamlet of Good Man's Bend, in Grinding County, in the Thistle District, in the State of Everywhere."

However much of this is legendary, it has value as giving an estimate of his figure and teachings. In *A.D.* 666 he was canonized by the then emperor, with a rank among divine beings as Great Supreme, the Emperor God of the Dark First Cause. Later he received the title of the Great Exalted One—the Ancient Master. He must have been a man of great learning and intellect, for he received a state appointment while still comparatively young, and was imperial historiographer and as librarian was keeper of the royal archives in the city of Lo at the time when Confucius paid his well-known visit there.

It is possible that a man holding such a position and having access to such records may have seen documents relating to the beliefs of the earlier philosophers of India —which were by his time being developed by Pythagoras in Europe—for the likeness between his points of view and those of the great Indo-Aryans is startling. Some, unable to account for these coincidences, declared that in a late period of his life he left China and traveled in India—a thing often done later by Chinese scholars in search of the truths of Buddhism. In any case his famous book the "Tao Teh King" ("The Moral Code" is one rendering of the title) was written before he could have made such a voyage, so that unless documents had reached him he must have journeyed the mystic road alone and formulated his own conclusions.

Ssu-ma Ch'ien, the famous Chinese historian, furnishes the account of the celebrated meeting with Confucius which I have given in previous chapters, and adds to it as follows:

"Lao Tsŭ cultivated the following of the Way and of Virtue, the chief aim of his studies being to keep himself concealed and remain unknown. He continued to dwell at the capital city Lo, but after a long time, seeing the decay of the dynasty, he departed, going by the gate leading out of the state on the northwest. Yin Hsi, keeper of the gate, said to him:

" 'Sir, you are about to withdraw yourself and far out of sight. I pray you first to compose a book for me.' "On this request Lao Tsŭ wrote a book in two parts, setting forth his views on the Way and Virtue in five thousand characters."

It is told that he and the friendly officer departed in a little cart drawn by one black ox, and so vanished into the dim horizon of myth. Nothing but the book remained.

' "He was a man of princely virtue," continues Ssu-ma Ch'ien, "who sought solitude."

Great is the contrast between his life and that of Confucius. This strange and fascinating book is our only real hold upon Lao Tsŭ. We are in full possession of the life of Confucius so far as all its leading events go, and the Analects place him before us as a living man. He remained stedfastly at the post where he conceived duty had set him. That attitude could never have been possible for Lao Tsŭ. He could contemplate nothing but the vision, and finally it absorbed him. It was reserved for his great disciple Chuang Tsŭ to make it as practical as such teaching can be made. I will return to him later.

The wisdom of Lao Tsŭ is extremely condensed in style, full of hint and suggestion. The Jesuit fathers in China, quick to observe its mysticism, ransacked it for passages which might be interpreted as referring to their own interpretation of the Christian dogma, and naturally found a few—which scholarship has entirely disproved. There are versions in English, French, and German; and as the West learns to know the treasures of the East many more will be made.

It is written in a kind of meter and with a rugged grandeur difficult to express in English. It is the outline of a high system of transcendental philosophy, perfectly new so far as China is concerned. This system is known in China as *Tao*—the Way, a word which some translate Reason (in the highest spiritual sense) and some the Word—in nearly the same sense as that in which it appears in the first chapter of the Gospel of St. John. "The Way" or "The Law" is perhaps the most satisfactory of these renderings. It begins thus:

> The Way which can be expressed in words is not the eternal Way; the name which can be uttered is not the eternal name.
>
> Conceived of as Nameless it is the cause of Heaven and Earth—conceived of as having a name it is the mother of all things. Only the man eternally free from passion can contemplate its spiritual essence. He who is clogged by desires can see no more than its outer form. These two things, the spiritual and material, though we call them by different names, are one and the same in their origin. This sameness is a mystery,

> the mystery of the mysteries. It is the gate of all that is subtle and wonderful.

Here we have in plain terms the statement made by the Advaita philosophy of India—the doctrine of Unity of all in the Universe, which leaves no room for any dualism. To those familiar with this Indian gate of knowledge the difficulties of Lao Tsŭ vanish away. He proceeds:

All in the world know the existence of beauty.
The obverse of beauty is ugliness.
All men know the existence of love.
The obverse of love is hatred.

Here we have the Indian statement that the Divine sits above good and evil, and from that height regards them as indistinguishable or combined opposites. Where love exists there must be its shadow—hate; and beauty cannot be perceived as beauty without its foil of ugliness. So it is that existence and non-existence are interdependent one upon the other.

"Length and shortness fashion out each one, the figure of the other."

The universe is thus in truth a system of combined opposites. We may say that good and evil cannot exist without each other. In real truth these things are not opposites, but are only perceived as such by finite knowledge.

> This is why the wise man teaches not by words but actions. Things grow, and no claim is made for their ownership. They go through their processes and expect no reward for the result. The work is accomplished but there is no finality in it as an achievement.

Thus the Way is exemplified in all natural processes and neither is greater nor less than another.

This may convey the thought expressed by Walt Whitman:

> I believe a leaf of grass is no less than the journey-work of the stars . . .

> And the running blackberry would adorn the parlors of Heaven... And a mouse is miracle enough to stagger sextillions of infidels.

He and the wise man of China would have understood one another at this point.

It may be easily understood how opposed were these views to those of Confucius, who set such store on rightspeaking and the importance of active and incessant labor in all the spheres of man's endeavor. A still deeper cleavage follows in the next chapter, where Lao Tsŭ presents his singular doctrines on government.

The way to keep the people from rivalry is to refrain from exalting brilliant men above them. Not to show them what will exalt their desires is the way to keep their minds from disorder.

Therefore the wise man in governing empties their minds but fills their stomachs, weakens their wills but strengthens their bones.

His endeavor is to keep them unsophisticated and without desire, and where there are those who have knowledge to keep them from presuming to act upon it. Where there is this abstinence from action good order is universal.

This declaration has been a great difficulty to many commentators, but I think it need not be. Lao Tsŭ shares the Indian belief in reincarnation, and realizes that the great majority of people are in an early stage of intellectual and spiritual evolution; they are unfitted for the right use of that very two-edged weapon Knowledge. They cannot understand any but the simplest first steps of the Way. The best the wise man can hope is that they will follow the simplest virtues. He will secure for them the good things that it is in their scope to understand and will withhold the so-called benefits that their ignorance would misuse to their own detriment. Therefore he will attend to their bodily needs. He will live simply himself that they may not covet what they have not got, and he will withhold the knowledge of the schools that they may not provoke calamities to themselves by acting ignorantly upon it. With Pope he considers, "A little learning is a dangerous thing." This system leaves room for the rugged and simple virtues, which grow in the earlier stages of civilization and seldom later.

If wise men, in secret conclave, undeterred by public and democratic expectation, were to express their opinions candidly to each other, with which would they agree: the confidence of Confucius in the force of example on the masses and the high goodness of their natures or Lao Tsŭ's blunt recognition of what he considers scientific and evolutionary fact?

His next chapter has grandeur:

> How unfathomable is the Way—like unto the emptiness of a vessel, yet, as it were, the honored Ancestor of all. Using it we find it inexhaustible. Deep and unfathomable. How pure and still is the Way! I do not know who generated it. It may appear to have preceded God.

This is very interesting. Here we have the pure Incomprehensible Essence, the First Cause of India, from which all deities later take birth, the Absolute, the Supreme Brahm.

Lao Tsŭ continues:

Heaven and Earth do not act from the impulse of any wish to be benevolent; they deal with all things as the dogs of grass are dealt with.

This is again the Indian teaching. The Supreme Law sits above any benevolence or partiality. The dogs of grass were made of straw in ancient Chinese sacrifices, and when the sacrifice was over were discarded and uncared for. So with the Law. Man himself is a part of it. He rues it if he contravenes its processes, but in obeying and going with them all is harmony and the great peace. I think the meaning of Lao Tsŭ would be far more easily understood if the word "Law" were used in preference either to "the Way" or "Reason"—or the Chinese "Tao" which some translators prefer.

Heaven is long enduring and earth continues. This is because they do not live of or for themselves. Therefore they endure. He who is wise puts his own person last, yet it is found in the foremost place; He treats his person as if it were foreign to him and yet that person is preserved.

Here we have the note of the Christian mystic, "He that loseth his life shall find it," and a thousandfold with it. The man who meditates upon the Supreme Law, what has he to do with the individual self?

Lao Tsŭ proceeds:

The highest excellence is like water. Its excellence is seen in its benefiting all and occupying without dissent the low place which none chooses. Hence it resembles the Way. And when the virtuous man does not wrangle over this none can find fault with him.

Here again we have a root-thought of Christianity and India: "He that humbleth himself shall be exalted." Then comes a saying of pure Indian yoga.

When the mind and spirit are at one they can be held in unity. When a man concentrates upon the vital breath and brings it to perfect pliancy he can become as a little child. When he has purified the most mysterious channels of his perception he may become flawless. In loving the people and ruling the state, can he not go on without purpose of action?

In opening and closing the nostrils, can he not do so like the brooding of a mother bird? While his intelligence penetrates in every direction he need not therefore display knowledge.

The Law gives birth and sustains all. Yet it does not claim them as its own. It works in all yet does not boast. It presides over all yet does not force them. This is called "The Mysterious Quality of the Way."

This chapter has the interest of setting forth a prominent detail of the Yoga system in India—the learning and practice of deep breathing as a means of concentration before the great vision. It seems at times almost impossible to suppose that Lao Tsŭ had not been in direct touch with Indian mystic teaching, and yet on the other hand no place can be found for any visit to India, and no records survive of any meetings with any Indian sage who could have instructed him. The alternative is that perception of such quality as his must have seen the "Way" by direct intuition.

We look at it [The Law—the Way] and it is invisible. Its name is "The Equable." We listen and cannot hear it. It is the Soundless. We grasp and cannot hold it. It is the Subtle. With these three qualities we cannot analyze it. Hence they are blended and are the One. Ceaseless in action it yet cannot be named, and again it returns to non-existence. This matter is called the form of the Formless and the semblance of the Invisible. This [matter] is called the fleeting and indeterminable. Meet it, its face cannot be seen. Follow it, its end cannot be seen.

Here we have spirit and matter. Cause and phenomenon. This is the statement of the mystics—of whom Lao Tsŭ is a master—throughout the world. As said by a modern poet—Francis Thompson:

O world invisible, we view thee,
O world intangible, we touch thee,
O world unknowable, we know thee,
Inapprehensible, we clutch thee!

Lao Tsŭ proceeds:

The skilful masters [of the Law] in olden days with a subtle and exquisite penetration comprehended its mysteries, and their profundity eluded men's knowledge. I shall endeavor to describe of what sort they seemed to be.... They look reluctant like men who wade a winter stream. Cautious like those who dread an attack from any quarter. Circumspect as guests before the host. They efface themselves like melting ice; are unpretentious as unfashioned wood. Those who keep the Way desire not to be full [of themselves]. It is because they are empty of themselves that they can afford to seem worn and not new and complete.

Again, in modern words:

If I could empty all myself of self,
Like to a shell dishabited,
Then might'st Thou enter in And fill it with thyself instead.

We cannot if we are brimmed with intense individuality make room for THAT which is One in all and All in one. But in emptiness it is possible. Lao Tsŭ describes the method:

The state of emptiness should be brought to perfection and that of ultimate Quiet guarded. All things go through their processes of activity and return to the Root. This is what we call the State of Quiet, and this stillness is the reporting that they have fulfilled their eternal end. To know the infinite is to be perceptive, to ignore it leads to wild movements and evil issues. To know the Law is to be great of soul, and to be great of soul leads to sympathy with all things. From this sympathy comes the ruling soul, from rulership comes spirituality.In spirituality the Way [the Law] is possessed. He who possesses it endures long and is not liable to decay.

Here we have the picture of the ideal man as seen in the teachings of Confucius but lifted to a far higher plane. The Confucian ideal is always the man who walks on his way, shone upon by the approbation alike of the world and of the Divine. He had not conceived the man drunk with God, alone with God, careless of the world's opinion, a part of all that he surveys, a realization of unity which needs not to reason about good and evil but leaps with passionate intuition to the very heart of things.

Now comes a crucial point of Lao Tsŭ's teaching, the famous doctrine of outward inactivity and passivity—to be further and most interestingly developed by his great disciple Chuang Tsŭ with a sense of humor and shrewd observation, which I will deal with in due course. It must be remembered that Lao Tsŭ thinks in paradox, and paradox until it is grasped is apt to bewilder the unwary. Here he writes:

> If we could renounce our sageness and discard our wisdom it would be better for the people a hundredfold. Could we renounce our benevolence and discard our righteousness, they would again become filial and kindly. Could we renounce our artful contrivances and discard our scheming for gain, there would be no thieves and robbers.
>
> He who stands on tiptoe does not stand firm; he who stretches his legs does not walk easily. So he who displays himself does not shine, and self- asserters lack distinction. The boaster does not find his merit

> acknowledged and the vain man will not find his superiority allowed. Such things in comparison with the Law are like excreta or a tumour on the body. Therefore he who has the Law has no place for them.

This is an exhortation to return to the simplicity of the Law and to *be* without seeming or striving.

Except ye become as little children ye cannot enter the Kingdom of Heaven—of the Peace. Fuss, righteousness and dogma have no place in the passionless and immutable Law—which is everywhere and all in all.

There must be no fixed purpose. There must be abandonment to the Law with a wise passivity. The wise man must, as it were, lean over the pool of eternity, viewing himself as in the First Cause, in rapt and endless contemplation; and then only will virtue go out of him in radiance and world-wide benevolence, and accomplish in this seeming inactivity all that the fussy dogmas, ceremonies, and precepts of the world can accomplish—and infinitely more. Humility, the obliteration of the imagined ego, profound simplicity—these are the landmarks of the Way.

Gravity is the root of lightness. Quiescence is the Master of motion....

> That is why a wise prince marching all day does not go far from his base. Though magnificent sights lie before him, he remains still with a free mind. How should the lord of a myriad chariots carry himself lightly before the kingdom? If his conduct is light he is severed from his root. Hasty in action, he will fail as a ruler.

This of course applies to the inner princedom, the Kingdom of Heaven where every man may be "a prince with God." Much of the difficulty in comprehending Lao Tsŭ lies in persistence in translating his teachings into the outward sphere of action. He lives in the World of Ideas. True they mold the outer worlds, in truth they *are* the outer world, but only the man of deepest perception can understand this. Therefore for ordinary readers Lao Tsŭ must be taken as an Indian yogin speaking from the point of view of the man to whom the drama and mirror of phenomenal life are meaningless. The want of understanding this has led his disciple Chuang Tsŭ into great extravagances as to the conduct of the outer life.

He proceeds:

> If anyone should wish to rule and effect by action I see that he cannot succeed. The kingdom is a spiritual thing. It cannot be gained by action. He who would so win it destroys it. He who would hold it in his grasp loses it.

In the words of our own Scriptures the Kingdom of Heaven cannot be taken by violence. The heavenly towers cannot be stormed, for the kingdom is within the deep realizations and secrecies of the spirit. It follows that, in the eyes of the man who has attained, war is a terrible and loathsome sin against the Law—the Way.

> Among the tools arms are unblest. He who would assist a lord of men in harmony with the Law will not assert his mastery by force of arms. Such a course only invites reprisal. Where armies are quartered briers and thorns take root. The followers of great armies are evil years. A wise commander strikes a decisive blow and halts. He strikes as a necessity not from the desire of mastery.
>
> In the feasts of peace the left hand is the place of honor; in mourning, the right. The place of the general commanding in war is on the right as in the ceremonies of mourning. He who has killed many men should weep with bitter tears. Therefore he who has conquered in battle should stand in the place of mourning.

The world will today acknowledge the sharp truth of these sayings. In France all may see the fact well illustrated that briers and thorns take root where great armies are quartered. Lao Tsŭ perceives the better way and declares it in the chapter which follows:

> To him who holds fast the Law the whole world repairs. Men flock to him and receive no hurt, but rest, peace, and the ultimate calm. When music and dainties are set forth, they win the passing guest for a time. But though the senses cannot perceive the Law and it transcends the ears and eyes, by using it is known to be inexhaustible.

This of course proclaims the transcendence of the Law, the deceit of the senses. The great Way puts forth no lures for them, but its feet are set on Eternity and infinite is its habitation. In the next chapter Lao Tsŭ proclaims the scientific and spiritual law of alternation:

> If you would breathe deeply the lungs must first be emptied. Desiring strength you must first weaken. If you will overthrow you must first exalt. If you would take, you must first give. This is called "Hiding the light." This is how the soft vanquishes the hard and the weak the strong.

Truly in this ancient book dating from the seventh century B.C. are deep knowledge and wisdom worthy of the profoundest study in the modern world. When India and China unite their voices on things spiritual, man does well to listen.

The next chapter has a majestic simplicity. It must be always remembered that the Way, the Law, means the first Cause, the Self as it is called in India, in distinction to the false, ignorant, crouching self—the ape-self, which abides in the uninstructed man.

> The ancient things that hold the Unity are Heaven, which by it is bright and pure, and Earth, which thus

> is firm and sure. Spirits who are devoid of bodily form. Valleys full in their emptiness. All creatures which through it do live. Princes and kings, who are its models diffused to all. If Heaven were not pure it would rend asunder. If Earth were not thus established it would disintegrate. The life of spirits would fail. Drought would parch the valleys. Creatures would miserably perish. Princes and kings would decay.

For the Way is the Universal, and in its circumference all things live and move and have their being. But harmony with it must be no effort. The moment it is an effort it becomes self-conscious and flawed with the ape-like individuality of the ignorant man. Lao Tsŭ, like the Christ, leans on the instinctive, the intuitive—choosing for illustration, as Christ and others have done, the utter simplicity and instinctive humility of the little child. Therefore in a very famous sentence he declares:

"He who knows the Way cares not to speak of it. He who is ever ready to discuss it does not know it."

And indeed in no human language can it be told. His analogy of the little child follows:

> He who has his foundation in the Law is like a little child. Poisonous insects pass him by. Fierce beasts spare him. Birds of prey do not strike him. His bones are weak and his sinews, yet he can grasp. He is ignorant of sex yet full of virility—showing the completion of his physical essence. All day long he cries or sobs without hoarseness, showing his harmony of construction. To him in whom is this harmony, the secret of the Eternal is known, Wisdom is throned upon it.

This needs no comment. It is the vision of all the faiths. Here follows Lao Tsŭ's views on statecraft in relation to the Eternal. The secret may be summed up in one of his unforgettable sentences: "Govern a kingdom as you would cook a small fish." That is do not overdo it. Mark what follows:

> A state may be ruled by correction. Weapons of war may be used with cunning dexterity, but a kingdom is truly conquered only by freedom from action and purpose. How do I know this? By these facts. In a kingdom the multiplication of prohibitive enactments increases the poverty of the people. The more implements the people possess to add to their profits the greater disorder is there in state and clan. The more arts of cunning dexterity possessed by men, the more do startling events appear. The more active is legislation, the more do thieves and robbers increase. Therefore a wise man has said: "If I act from the inner life the people will be transformed of themselves. I shall desire quiet, and the people will become righteous. I shall not labor and fidget, and the people will grow into riches. I shall manifest no ambition, and the people will regain the primitive simplicity."

Here we perceive points of agreement with Confucius upon the force of example and its radiating power. We perceive that the way of commercial prosperity is not the road to peace nor to true attainment. Indeed it may be that the round of civilization, as we understand the word in the West, is fated to increase in complexity and crime until it shatters itself against the Nature of Things, and recommences at the primitive simplicities. There are blind alleys upon which the gates of evolution are closed.

> The rivers and seas are lords of a hundred valleys. This is because their strength is in lowliness; they are kings of them all. So it is that the perfect ruler, wishing to be above men, must in his speech be humble. Wishing to lead them, he follows. Thus, though he is above them, men do not feel him to be an injury. And therefore the

> world delights to exalt him and tires not in serving him. And since he will not strive none strives with him.

"Gentleness is victorious," says Lao Tsŭ in another place. He would carry this principle far indeed; hear him on capital punishment:

> The people do not fear death. Of what use is it to frighten them with death? If they always feared it, and men could always seize those who did wrong and slay them, who would dare to offend? But there is always One who presides over the infliction of death. He who would inflict death in the room of Him who so presides may be described as hewing wood in the place of a master-carpenter. Seldom is it that he who undertakes this in the place of a greater carpenter fails to cut his own hands.

Here in ending my account of this great and ancient book—a quiet voice reaching us across more than two thousand five hundred years I quote the words of a great Chinese emperor, founder of the Ming dynasty in the year *A.D.* 1368. They relate to Lao Tsŭ.

> At the beginning of my reign I had not yet learned the principles of the ancient wise rulers. One day, reading through many books, I came across the Canon of Wisdom and Virtue. I found the style simple and the thoughts deep. At length I found this text: "If the people do not fear death, how then can you frighten them by death?" At that time the empire had only begun to be united; the people were obstinate and the magistrates corrupt. Almost every morning ten men were executed in public: by the same evening a hundred had committed the same crimes. Did not this justify the thought of Lao Tsŭ? From that time I

> ceased to inflict capital punishment. I imprisoned the guilty and imposed fines. In less than a year my heart was comforted. I recognized then that in this book is the perfect source of all things. It is the sublime Master of Kings and the inestimable Treasure of the people.

These are true words. I much regret that it is impossible to give more of this great book of Chinese mysticism, so pregnant with suggestion for all time. I turn now from this to the great disciple of Lao Tsŭ—a man wise and humorous, but standing on a lower pinnacle than the perfect selflessness of the master.

CHAPTER 25

A MASTER OF THE MYSTIC WAY CHUANG TSŬ

In dealing with Chuang Tsŭ, the most famous disciple of Lao Tsŭ, we are confronted as in the case of his master with a difficulty in the title of his book. The Chinese use not letters but idiograms, and the complicated composite characters frequently convey different ideas to different minds, just as when a picture is gazed upon, the same thing may happen, and the impressions received differ. For this celebrated and extraordinary book Dr. Legge suggests the title of "Rambling at Ease"—of course, in the intellectual and spiritual realms. Let us take it at that. Its fascination partly consists in the ease and humor with which the author moves among vast subjects. I know no book more companionable, more calculated to induce calm or cynical reflection on life as it is. The little stories and parables are delightful. The style is said to be the perfection of literary Chinese, and the man is a master of paradox.

Chuang Tsŭ, born and living in the third and fourth centuries before Christ, is a man (as were Confucius and Lao Tsŭ) of the feudal age of China, when the wrangling tumultuous states were under the nominal sovereignty of the royal but weak dynasty of Chao. The historian Ssu- ma Ch'ien, whom I have already quoted, gives an account of Chuang Tsŭ (pronounce Chwongdza), who was born in the province of An-hui. He says:

"Chuang Tsŭ held a petty official post in Men. His erudition was most varied, but his chief doctrines are based upon the teachings of Lao Tsŭ."

Yet none the less he developed views of his own, and his fine poetic imagination, combined with the mystic sense and the unusual blend of cynicism, makes him a most interesting writer, abounding in excellent stories and illustrations of his point. He was perfectly disinterested and entirely loyal to the faith that was in him. The ruling prince of the Ch'u state, hearing of his great wisdom, sent officers to him with noble gifts and an invitation to become prime minister; such an opportunity as it is impossible to imagine Confucius refusing. Mark the difference of the Lao-tsian influence! He was fishing in the P'u River when the two high officials arrived, doubtless with all the pomp and circumstance which Confucius would have approved.

Chuang Tsŭ went on fishing without turning his head, and said :

"I have heard that in Ch'u there is a sacred tortoise which has been dead now some three thousand years and that the prince keeps this tortoise carefully enclosed in a chest on the altar of his ancestral temple. Now would that tortoise rather be dead and have its remains venerated, or be alive and wagging its tail in the mud?"

"It would rather be alive," replied the two officials, "and wagging its tail in the mud."

"Begone!" cried Chuang Tsŭ. "I too will wag my tail in the mud!"

On another occasion the prime minister of the Liang state, hearing Chuang Tsŭ was in Liang and terribly afraid lest he himself might be dispossessed from office, searched with warrants all over the state to find the intruder. Chuang Tsŭ walked in to see him and observed:

"An owl which had got the rotten carcass of a rat looked up as the phoenix flew by and screeched to warn it off. Are you not screeching at me over your kingdom of Liang?"

It will be seen that such a man would go his own way and enjoy his own freedom of comment everywhere; and this he did fully and freely even to the extent of caricaturing the sacred, the venerated Confucius by making him a figure in many imaginary scenes and placing opinions in his mouth that he never could have held. This was a peculiar delight of Chuang Tsŭ, and it is interesting to find Confucius in all sorts of plights of argument and paradox, either confounded, or extricating himself by the pronouncements of a school in many respects so opposed to his own. In the long run all good men tend to the same goal, but the roads are often very different, and to find the exalted Confucius traveling in that of Lao Tsŭ, or rather that of the cool cynicism of Chuang Tsŭ, is extremely amusing. Here is an example, and it is pleasant to reflect alike on the feelings of Confucius if he could have read it, knowing that some people would take it as historic, and on the sly humor of Chuang Tsŭ in penning it.

Tsŭ Sang Hu died, and Confucius sent Tsŭ Kung, a chief disciple, to take part in the mourning. Two friends sat by the corpse, and one had composed a song which the other accompanied on a lute.

> "Ah, will you come back to us, Sang Hu?
> You have already returned to your God,
> While we still remain here as men, alas!"

Tsŭ Kung hurried in and said: "How can you sing beside a corpse? Is this decorum?"

The two looked at each other and laughed. "What should this man know of propriety?" [Meaning the inward and spiritual propriety of the soul.] Tsŭ Kung hurried back to Confucius, greatly shocked. "Who can these men be who sit by a corpse and sing unmoved? What are they?"

"These men," said Confucius, "travel beyond the rule of life. I travel within it. So our paths do not meet, and I erred in sending you to mourn. They consider themselves as one with God, knowing no distinction between human and divine. Though admitting different elements, they take their stand on the unity of all. They ignore their passions. They deny their senses. Looking backwards and forwards through eternity, they admit neither beginning nor end. How should such men care what people think of them?"

"But if such is the case," said Tsŭ Kung, "why should *we* stick to the rule?"

"Heaven has condemned me to this. Nevertheless you and I may perhaps escape from it."

"And how?"

"Fishes," said Confucius, "are born in the water, Man is born in the Law. If fishes find ponds they thrive. If a man lives in the Law he may live his life in peace [apart from the world]. Hence the saying: "All that a fish wants is water. All that a man wants is Tao—the Way."

As if this were not impertinence enough he introduces Confucius constantly as a kind of lay figure on which to hang his own and the opinions of Lao Tsŭ. Yet Chuang Tsŭ could never think of Confucianism as a merely practical system. He knew that Confucius went further and deeper than that, but that rightly or wrongly he studied expedience and gave to the average man what he believed he could take. This being so, Chuang Tsŭ felt that the deep concern of Confucius for tradition, ceremony, and the search for prosperity even though it might be of a high order had been an influence in swelling the tide of materialism which he saw rising round him and threatening to submerge all spirituality. Mencius, the great follower of the Confucian ethic of whom I shall presently give a sketch, had contributed to strengthen the hold of a spirit that saw its goal in this world's gain and all such things as men consider "proper" "desirable" and "becoming." To Lao Tsŭ such words had no meaning, nor had they for Chuang Tsŭ, who fiercely rejected their implications. Skeptical of all else, he was a true believer in Lao Tsŭ's teaching that the world was well lost if a man should gain his own soul; and he believed the way to that end was through simplicity and deep contemplation. These things once achieved and become habitual, intuitive power would not only be inherent in a man but radiate from him and subjugate others.

Therefore Chuang Tsŭ was the true metaphysician— and China has not produced his like in that sphere. For him righteousness was no dogma. It was spontaneity grown instinctive by long use, and, to use his own phrase, man "becomes embraced in the obliterating unity of good." His famous illustration of the cook of the Duke of Chao points this well.

Prince Hui's cook was cutting up a bullock. Every blow of his hand, every heave of his shoulders, every tread of his foot, every thrust of his knee, every *whshh* of rent flesh, were in regular cadence. Movements and sounds proceeded as in the Dance of the Mulberry Forest and were simultaneous as the blended notes of the *Ching Shou*. The Prince said: "Admirable that your skill should have become so perfect!"

The cook laid down his knife and replied:

"What your servant loves is the method of the Tao [the Law]. When I first began to cut up an ox I saw nothing but the whole carcass. After three years I ceased to see it as a whole. Now I deal with it intellectually and never use my eyes. I discard the use of my senses, I work by eternal principles. Observing the natural lines, my knife slips through the great crevices and slides through the great cavities, taking advantage of natural openings. So my art avoids membranous ligatures and much more the large bones."

The duke reflected on this and the cook went on: "Now a good cook changes his knife every year in cutting and an ordinary cook every month. My knife has been in use for nineteen years. It has cut up several thousand bullocks and yet is as sharp as if new from the whetstone. There are the interstices of the joints, and the knife edge has no appreciable thickness. When that which is so thin enters the interstice, it remains only to move it easily along. By a very slight movement the part is easily separated and drops like a clod on the ground. Then standing up I look all round in a leisurely way, with satisfaction, wipe the knife clean and put it in its sheath."

Prince Wan-Hui said:

"Excellent! I have heard the words of this cook and learned from them the rule of our life."

And how? He had learned that spontaneity may become instinctive, a true second nature, and that a man has but to will, and practice what he wills, to make it his own and one with him and he with it.

The cook of Prince Wan Hui understood the doctrine of relativity and turned away from skill and knowledge as acquired through the fallible and superficial senses to the inward sight which cannot err. Spontaneity is the essence of true righteousness.

In Chuang Tsŭ we get the high doctrine of the reconciliation or rather the identity of opposites.

He knew that from the highest view all is One. To quote Heraclitus, the great Greek: "God is day-night, winter-summer, war-peace, repletion-want." And in a practical and magnificently written chapter Chuang Tsŭ deals with that astonishing conclusion—the identity of opposites.

"There is nothing which is not objective; there is nothing which is not subjective. But it is impossible to start from the objective. Only from subjective knowledge is it possible to proceed to objective knowledge. The true sage rejects all distinctions of this and of that. He takes his refuge in God and places himself in subjective relation with all things."

Undoubtedly this is the road which science must tread if it would not forever involve itself in the contradictions we see today.

"And," he goes on, "as the subjective is also objective and the contraries under each are indistinguishably blended, does it not become impossible for us to say whether subjective and objective really exist at all? They have not found their point of correspondence, which is the very pivot of the Law [the Way]. When that point is found, it is the center where all the Infinities, affirming and denying, converge into an infinite One. Therefore, there is nothing like the true light [of the spirit]."

This is indeed a clear statement of a difficult subject. One may smile when one hears the Chinese spoken of as a race who need our civilization, in reflecting that such writing was possible there in the fourth century *B.C.* Chuang Tsŭ continues:

"Therefore it is that—viewed by the light of the Law —a beam and a pillar [the horizontal and perpendicular], ugliness and beauty, nobility and wickedness, may all be reduced to the same category."

For our knowledge of these things is relative only, and we can never see them as they really are until we have attained the height of cosmic perception.

"Separation leads to completion, from construction ensues destruction. Yet all things in spite of their construction and destruction may again be perceived in their identity. Only the wise understand this, and they can place themselves in subjective relation with the ordinary way of looking at things. Wherefore, the truly wise man while regarding contraries as identical adapts himself to the laws of Heaven and follows two courses at once."

That is to say, knowing the truth that nothing is as the senses reports it to be, he yet acts outwardly according to the relative knowledge of those with whom he has to deal. Chuang Tsŭ illustrates this by the delightful fable of the monkeys and their keeper which I have quoted elsewhere. He ordered the monkeys three measures of chestnuts in the morning and four at night. The monkeys were indignant. He changed the arrangement to four measures in the morning and three at night which delighted the monkeys who could not perceive it was the same thing under another name. The keeper smiled as the man smiles who knows that the Divine Law is One and sees all in unity yet obeys the popular view, for this is the law of Heaven as manifested in the phenomenal world.

He has a delightful dialogue between a disciple and a tutor of the ancient days. The disciple asks:

"Do you know for certain all things are subjectively the same?"

"How can I know?" answers the master, speaking from the objective point of view. "But I will try to tell you. How can I know that what I call ignorance is not knowledge? A man sleeps in a damp place. He gets sciatica and dies. A man lives in a tree, and his nerves are all a-quiver. But how about a monkey? Can anyone say absolutely which is the right place? Men eat flesh; deer, grass; centipedes, little snakes; owls and crows, mice. Can any of these pronounce on which is the finally right taste to possess? Mao Ch'ang and Li Chi were divine beauties in the eyes of men, but at the very sight of them fish would dive and birds soar and deer scurry away. Which had the correct standard of beauty? In my opinion it is the same thing with the standard of the first principles of human virtue. They are so obscured and mixed that how can I discriminate?"

"But then," persists the bewildered disciple, "if you, sir, do not know what is good or bad is the Perfect Man equally ignorant?"

And now comes the outburst from the man who has perceived the ultimate Truth.

"The Perfect Man is a spiritual being. Were the ocean scorched up he would feel no heat. Were the Milky Way frozen, no cold. Hurrying thunderbolts might split the mountains and winds storm the ocean, and he would not tremble. Being what he is, he rides the clouds and passes beyond the external and the sun and moon. Since death and life have no dominion over him, how much less can thoughts of advantage or injury?" But Chuang Tsŭ is equally delightful in his practical and somewhat sardonic mood, and in his consummate impertinence to Confucius. Chuang Tsŭ takes part in this imaginary discussion which is supposed to be between himself and a scholar of the ancient days. Note that anachronisms matter nothing to him when he has a point to make. The scholar begins with Confucius as a lay figure ventriloquized by Lao Tsŭ.

I heard Confucius say: "The really wise man pays no heed to mundane affairs. He neither seeks gain nor avoids injury. He adheres without questioning to the Law. Without speaking he can speak. He can speak and say nothing, and so he finds his happiness outside the mundane dust and dirt. But these," added Confucius, "are wild words." Now I think them a fine setting forth of the mysterious Way. What, sir, is your opinion?

"Where the Yellow Emperor doubted how should Confucius know?" [The Yellow Emperor is a legendary sage.] But you go much too fast. You have your egg and see the chicken. You see the bow, and immediately expect the roast pigeon. I shall say a few words at random. Listen at random.

"The wise man keeps his mouth shut and blends everything into the All, rejecting the confusion of the manifold. The manifold pursues its course before him.

"How do I know that the love of life is not a delusion and that the man who dreads to die is not like a child who has lost the way home? The lady Li Chi was a daughter of the border warden of Ai. When the Prince of Ch'in first got possession of her,she wept until the bosom of her dress was drenched with tears. But when she came to his palace, shared with him his luxurious bed, and ate his grain and grass-fed meat, she regretted that she had wept. How do I know that the dead do not repent of their former craving for life? There is the Great Awakening, after which we shall know this life was a dream.

"Confucius was bigoted! He and you are both dreams, and I who say you are dreams—what am I but a dream? This is a paradox. After ten thousand ages a sage may arise to explain it. Since, then, you and I and man cannot decide, must we not depend upon Another? But such dependence is not in truth dependence.

We are embraced in the obliterating unity of the Divine. Take no heed of Time nor right nor wrong, but passing into the Infinite there take up your position.

"Once upon a time, I Chuang Tsŭ dreamed I was a butterfly hovering here and there, to all intents and purposes a butterfly. I did not know that it was Chuang Tsŭ. Suddenly I woke and was myself again the veritable Chuang Tsŭ. Now I do not know whether I was then a man dreaming I was a butterfly, or now a butterfly dreaming I am a man. Between a man and a butterfly there must necessarily be a barrier. This is a case of what is called the Transformation of things."

The point is that ordinary life and perception may mislead us into any false and dreamlike conception of the universe, which it is impossible to prove either right or wrong. The truth is both and neither.

We are next indulged with a conversation between Confucius and Ai, the ruling prince of the Lu state, in which Confucius as usual is made to say exactly the opposite of certain utterances of his in the Analects; and a better exposition of the tenets of Lao Tsŭ can scarcely be imagined than the rule for governing a state. Yet one is conscious that in the depths of his own heart, with the weltering ruin of the warring states about him, there may have been moments when Confucius himself realized that the best-laid schemes of human provision have an ugly way of letting their projectors down at unexpected moments, and that far above all sits an immutable Law "which shapes our ends, rough-hew them as we may." He *may* have had the intuitions Chuang Tzu puts into his mouth, though in practice he would have thought it madness to preach them.

According to Chuang Tsŭ, Duke Ai of the Lu state says to Confucius:

"In the Wei state is a leper named Ai T'ai T'o. His father-in-law, who lived with him, thought so much of him that he could not do without him. His wife when she saw him said to her parents, "I had ten times rather be his concubine than any other man's wife." He never preaches at people, but always feels what they feel. He has no power by which he can protect people's bodies and no revenues by which to satisfy men's cravings. He is ugly enough to scare the whole world. He sympathizes, but does not argue. His knowledge is limited to his neighborhood. Yet men and women are of one mind about him in his presence. Seeing he must differ from other men, I called for him and saw him. Certainly he was ugly to a degree. But we had not been many months together when I was drawn to him, and before he had been with me a year I had full confidence in him and as the state lacked a prime minister I offered him the government. He responded sorrowfully, hesitating as if he would have declined it. I was ashamed of myself but finally gave it to him. In a little while, however, he left me and went away. I grieved for him as for one dear to me and as though there were none left with whom I could rejoice. Now what do you make of a man like this?"

How, he means, could a man triumph over such natural handicaps? Confucius as usual is made to solve the problem exactly as he never would have done. He replies:

"Once when I was sent on a mission to the Ch'i state I saw a litter of young pigs trying to nourish themselves from their dead mother. After a little they looked at her with quick glances and all left her and ran away. For she looked at them no more and seemed to be no longer akin to themselves. What they had loved was their mother—not her body but that which made it live. This man was believed by men though he says nothing. He caused a man to offer him the government of his state, and the only fear was lest he should refuse. He must have been a man whose spiritual powers were perfect though his realization of them was not manifested in his person."

Ai asks: "What do you mean by perfect powers?"

Confucius is made to answer:

"Death and life, failure and success, poverty and wealth, hunger and thirst, and many other things—these are the operation of our appointed lot. Day and night, they succeed one another and no man can trace their source. But they cannot be allowed to disturb harmony and they must not enter the spiritual kingdom. To cause this harmony to radiate without interruption day and night, so that it is always the happy springtime in a man's relations with the world, is to be ready for all seasons; and this is characteristic of the man who possesses these perfect powers."

"But," persists the duke, "what do you mean by his not manifesting his powers in his person?"

Confucius answers:

"There is nothing so level as a pool of still water. All in its circuit is in peace, and nothing without can agitate it. Righteous efficiency is the perfect cultivation of equilibrium, and even though it does not appear in the outward form its fascination cannot be resisted."

Chuang Tsŭ cannot sufficiently insist on this doctrine of *being* and not *acting*. In other words there is a mighty universal rhythm with which, if man can once become conscious of it, he is in full accord. Its unspeakable power possesses him—he reacts to all its processes. What need he do—what think for himself, with *That* pouring through him? This occurs in the Christian Scriptures also. "Take no thought for the morrow." The disciples are instructed that it "shall be given" them when they need to speak. Why should they prepare? They too have become channels of the Universal. Chuang Tsŭ has a magnificent illustration of this:

A disciple said to Lu Chu: "Master I have got hold of the Way. I can heat the tripod under my furnace in winter. I can make ice in summer."

Lu Chu said:

"That is only using the negative and positive principles in nature. That is not what I call the Way [Tao]. I shall demonstrate it to you."

He tuned two lutes and placed one in the hall and one in the adjoining room. And when he strung the *kung* note on one, the *kung* note on the other responded. When he struck the *chio* note on one, the *chio* note on the other sounded, because they were tuned to the same pitch. But if he changed the interval of one string, all the strings jangled. The sound was there, The influence of the key-note was gone.

More perfect analogy there could not be. What is vital will always tune such a man and those who know him. What he is, so often overpowers what he says or does—however plausibly he speaks or acts—that his outward personality is stricken dumb by the reality within him, either bad or good as we describe it.

"We must have transcendent men and we shall then have transcendent wisdom," is ever the cry of Chuang Tsŭ. And he describes the transcendent man (who differs very much from the "princely man" of Confucius) in terms that accord with the Vedantist conception of the Indian yogin:

"What is a transcendent man? These men of old acted without calculation. They laid no plans. So, failing, they had no cause for regret, and succeeding, no cause for congratulation. Thus they could scale heights without fear; enter water without becoming wet; fire without burning. So far by their wisdom had they advanced on the Way. Their breathing came deep and silently. The breathing of the transcendent man comes even from his uttermost deeps; the ordinary herd breathe only from their throats."

Chuang Tsŭ describes the process by which one sage instructs a man in the Way of Peace:

"I imparted as though withholding, and in three days for him this sublunary state ceased to exist. I withheld again, and in seven days the external world had ceased to be for him, and after nine days he became unconscious of his own existence and finally entered the state where there is no distinction between life and death, where dying does not destroy life and the prolongation of existence is not living. And in that state he is even in accord with his environment [i.e., the requirements of daily life]. The Law is tranquillity amidst disturbance, and disturbances lead to its perfection." This is the Nirvana of the Buddha and the Upanishads.

As Chuang Tsŭ says later:

"Man has ever given way to God. Why then should I be afraid?"

In other words: "Let God have His way with us."

He has curious and interesting passages on the bodily safety of the man who is a part of the Law [the Way].

"A drunken man if he falls out of a cart, though he may suffer, does not die. His bones are the same as other people's, but he meets his accident differently. His spirit is in a condition of security. He is not conscious of riding in the cart or of falling out of it. Ideas of life and death fear, etc., cannot penetrate his mind, and so he does not suffer from conatct wtih objective existences. And if such security can be got from wine how much more from Law? It is there the wise man has his refuge and is safe from harm."

He points this with one of his graphic stories.

Two men are at archery together. The one a skilled archer sets a cup of water on his elbow and steadily lets fly arrow after arrow, standing like a statue. Wonderful! But the other cries: "Why, this is shooting under ordinary conditions. Come; stand on the edge of a precipice a thousand feet deep and see how you can shoot."

He leads the way, himself standing on the edge of the terrific precipice, his back to it, until one-fifth of his feet overhang the precipice, and beckons the archer to come on and shoot thus. The archer, with the sweat pouring off him, falls prostrate.

"The perfect man," says the other serenely, "soars up to the blue sky, dives down to the regions of death, or flies to any extreme point of the compass without change of countenance. But you are terrified and your eyes dazed. Your way of looking at things is defective."

There follows later a striking passage bearing on the "identity of opposites." It relates to a famous bandit of whom I shall speak further on.

An apprentice of Robber Chi asked him: "Can the Law be found in thieving?" [meaning of course the transcendent Law of Lao Tsŭ and Chuang Tsŭ, which they taught swayed all things.]

Robber Chi replied:

"Pray tell me of anything in which there is not the Law! There is the wisdom by which booty is located. The courage of going in first, the heroism of coming out last. The insight of calculating the chances of success. And justice in dividing the spoils. There never was a great robber who was not possessed of these five."

Yes, the Law is in thieving, in all. Even thieving needs its virtues. And Chuang Tsŭ clinches it thus: "The doctrine of the Wise is equally indispensable to the good man and the robber." Why? Because it is the Way of Power, and can be used impartially. "But good men," he adds, "are few, and bad men plentiful, so that the good done by the wise to the world is little, and the evil the other do is great."

Like Landor, who also excelled in imaginary conversations, Chuang Tsŭ provides us with one between the two protagonists Lao Tsŭ and Confucius, which deserves to head another chapter.

CHAPTER 26

CHUANG TSŬ HIS IRONY AND HUMOR

Says Chuang Tsŭ:

Confucius went to the West to deposit his writings in the library of the Imperial House of Chao, and Tsŭ Lu counseled him, saying:

"I have heard that the officer in charge was one named Lao Tsŭ, who has resigned his office and lives privately. As you, master, wish to deposit your works, why not go and gain his help?"

Confucius said, "Good," and went to see Lao Tsŭ, who refused his assistance, whereupon the other began to give a summary of "Spring and Autumn" with the view of convincing Lao Tsŭ. But Lao Tsŭ interrupted:

"This is all nonsense. What are your fundamentals?"

"Charity," replied Confucius, "and duty to one's neighbor."

Said Lao Tsŭ: "And do you think charity and righteousness constitute man's original nature?"

"I do. Without charity the princely man could not be what he is. Without righteousness he would be of no effect. These two belong to the original nature of the superior man."

Lao Tsŭ continued:

"Tell me what you mean by charity and righteousness?"

Confucius answered:

"To be in one's inmost heart in sympathy with all things, to love all men without selfishness—this is the characteristic of charity and duty to one's neighbor."

Lao Tsŭ exclaimed:

"What stuff! Does not universal love contradict itself? Is not your elimination of self a positive manifestation of self?"

[Meaning that if everyone loves everyone there is nothing to set forth love as love—no background against which it can be perceived. In the same way absolute unselfishness awakens absolute selfishness as a necessary result of its practice. It must be owned that Confucius is in a difficulty here! He does not answer, and Lao Tsŭ goes on triumphant:]

"Sir, if you would cause the empire to be rightly nourished, think of heaven and earth, which go their way undeflected! Think of birds and of beasts, who collect in their dens, and of trees and shrubs, which grow upright without deviation. Be like these. Follow the Law and you will reach your end. Why must you make such a pother about charity and duty to one's neighbor as though beating a drum for the hue and cry after a fugitive? Alas, master, you have brought much confusion into the mind of men!"

Some dispute that this conversation is from the hand of Chuang Tsŭ, possibly because they are surprised to find him allowing Confucius his own opinions, if even for the purpose of putting them to flight; and yet it may very well be a part of the actual discourse which took place at the meeting in Lo.

The story of Confucius and Robber Chi that I give now is certainly spurious in that it was not written by Chuang Tsŭ; but it is so well written, so entirely in the manner of his philosophic stories, and it so perfectly illustrates a favorite point of his that it was long supposed to be his; and I think this a highly appropriate place for such an ancient and valuable effort in the art of transcendental philosophy. I give it condensed as follows:

Robber Chi had nine thousand followers. He ravaged the empire, plundering nobles and people. He lifted cattle. He stole women. Family ties were nothing to his greed. He had no respect for parents or brothers and neglected ancestor worship. Where he passed the greater states flew to arms, the smaller to refuge.

Said Confucius to the elder brother of Robber Chi:

"An elder brother should admonish his junior. If it is not so, there is an end to the value of these relationships. Now you, sir, are one of the scholars of the age, and your brother is Robber Chi. I blush for you. Let me go and exhort him on your behalf."

"As to what you say, sir," replied the brother, "if the junior won't listen to his elder brother, what becomes of your argument? Besides Chi's passions are like a whirlwind. He can argue until wrong becomes right. He is free with abuse. Keep away from him! I strongly advise you."

Confucius paid no attention but with Yen Hui [his favorite disciple] for charioteer and Tsŭ Kung [a famous follower] on his left, went to Robber Chi. The robber was engaged in devouring a dish of minced human liver; Confucius alighted and addressed the doorkeeper.

"I am Confucius of Lu state. The high character of your captain has reached me."

He then twice respectfully saluted the doorkeeper, who went in to announce him. When Robber Chi heard the name he was furious. His eyes glared like stars. His hair raised his cap.

"What? that crafty scoundrel—Confucius of Lu? Go, tell him he is a mere word-spinner! That he talks nonsense about the ancients. That he wears an extravagant cap with a thong from a dead ox. That his lips patter, and his tongue wags, and he throws dust in the eyes of rulers and prevents scholars from reverting to the original Way. That he makes a great stir about filial piety, glad enough himself to secure some fat fief or post. Tell him if he does not take himself off, his liver shall be in my morning stew!"

Still Confucius repeated his wish, burning to evangelize the offender.

"I am anxious to set eyes upon your captain's shoestrings." (A polite form of address.)

He was admitted and hurried in, avoiding the place of honor and making two obeisances.

Robber Chi, flaming with fury, straddled out his two legs, laying his hand on his sword, and roaring like a tigress with young, said:

"Come here! If what you say suits me you shall live. Otherwise you shall die."

"I have heard," said Confucius, "that there are three sorts of virtue. To be tall and beautiful and thus the idol of all. To be possessed of all-embracing wisdom. To be possessed of valor. A man with any one of those may rule, but you, captain, unite all three. You are stately in stature. Your expression is radiant. Your lips are vermilion, your teeth like a row of shells. Your voice is sonorous as a beautiful bell. Yet you are known as Robber Chi! Captain, I blush for you! If you listen to me I will go south, north, east, and west for you. I will have a great wall built for you many in length, enclosing a state which you shall rule. You shall disband your men, gather your kin about you and join in the worship of your ancestors. Such is the behavior of the true sage, and such is what the world needs."

"You come here with offers!" cried Chi in a rage royal. "Those who are squared by offers and corrected by preaching are the stupid, vulgar masses. The height and beauty you praise, my parents gave me; and do you suppose I am not well aware of them? All you promise about this fine state is simply squaring me, as though I were one of the common herd. And of course it would not last.

"Even with the empire and the heroes of old their posterity reigns no longer. In the olden days men lay down without caring where they were, and got up without worry as to where they would go. A man knew his mother but not his father. He lived among the animals, tilling the ground for good. He wove cloth to cover himself. He had no thought of injury to others. These were the results of an age of virtue. Since then we have had nothing but disturbers of the peace.

"And now *you* come along, preaching the old dogmas and palming off sophistries to teach posterity; you wear patched clothes and talk big and act falsely, while all the time you yourself are aiming at wealth and power! You are the biggest thief I know; and if men call me Robber Chi they should certainly call you Robber Chiu [the personal name of Confucius].

"As to the sermon you propose for me—if it is on spiritual subjects they are beyond me, and if on human affairs, I know it already. Now I'll tell *you* a few things!

"The lust of the eye is for beauty, the lust of the ear for music, the lust of the palate for flavor, the lust of ambition for power. Man's greatest age is a hundred years. A medium age is eighty. The lowest estimate is sixty. Subtract the hours of sickness, death, mourning, and trouble, and there remain no more than four or five days a month in which a man can laugh. Heaven and earth are eternal; man must die. Seen against the Eternal, the mortal is a mere flash, like the passage of a white horse seen through a crack. And those who cannot gratify their ambition and live through their span in doing so, are men who have not attained the Law.

"All four teachings are nothing to me. Go home! Say no more. Your doctrine is full of falsity. It can never preserve the original purity of man."

Confucius made two obeisances and hurried off. As he rode in his chariot he sometimes dropped the reins. His eyes were so dazed he could see nothing. His face *was* the color of slaked lime. With downcast head he grasped the bar of his chariot. Arrived outside the eastern gate of Lu, he met the brother of Robber Chi, who said:

"I have not seen you for some days. From the look of your chariot I guess you have been traveling. Can you have been to see Chi?"

Confucius looked up to heaven and sighed. "I have!" "And did he not rebuff you as I said he would?"

"He did!" said Confucius. "I am a man who has cauterized himself without being ill. I hurried away to stroke the tiger's head and cut his whiskers and I nearly fell into his jaws."

Here again we have the doctrine of inaction, and the assertion that even in an evil life consistently and gallantly carried out its strength is based on the maxims of the Law and can be no other. And yet there are moments when the suspicion haunts me that the whole is an early Chinese parody on the teachings of both Confucius and Lao Tsŭ, and that if Chuang Tsŭ did not write it he would at least have read it with a smile in those deep eyes of his and with laughter on those very ironic lips. He has certainly no use for those who set out to "uplift" others.

But his triumph in beauty of language and in philosophy is in a chapter known as "Autumn Floods," considered by those in China who are best qualified to judge as one of the loveliest things they own in philosophic literature. As usual I must condense; but since I hope to send many to the company of Chuang Tsŭ, who is my own constant companion, this will matter the less.

It was the time of autumn floods. Every stream poured into the river, which swelled in its turbid course. The banks grew so far apart that it was impossible to tell a cow from a house.

The spirit of the river shouted for joy that all the beauty of the earth was gathered to himself. Down with the stream he journeyed east until he reached the ocean. There, looking eastward and seeing no limit to its waves, his face fell. And as he gazed over the expanse he said to the spirit of ocean:

"A common proverb says that he who hears half the truth thinks no one equal to himself. And so it is with me. When formerly I heard people decrying the learning of Confucius or the heroism of Po, I did not believe, but now that I see your vastness—Ah, if I had not reached your dwelling I should forever have been a laughing stock to those who know better!"

To this the ocean spirit replied:

"You cannot talk of the ocean to a frog in a well —the creature of narrow bounds. Nor of ice to summer flies—the ephemera of a day. You cannot speak of the Law to a pedant. His limits are narrow. But now that you have emerged—that you have seen the great ocean, you know your narrowness, and I may speak of great principles.

"Nothing beneath heaven is greater than ocean. All water flows into it, yet it does not overflow. It is drained, yet does not empty. It knows no floods or droughts and thus is greater than mere rivers and brooks—though I, its spirit, dare not boast, for I get my shape from the universe, my vital power from the negative and positive principles governing all. In the universe I am as a little stone or a bush on a vast mountain. And of all who inhabit the earth man is but one. Is not he compared with all creation as the tip of a hair on a horse's skin?"

"Well, then," replied the spirit of the river, "and am I to consider the universe as great and the tip of a hair as small?"

"By no means. Dimensions are limitless. Time has no bounds. Conditions vary. Terms are not final. How then can one say that a tip of hair is the last word on littleness or the universe the last word on vastness?"

Relativity again—the Buddhist philosophy in another form of relative truth which humanity can grasp (again relatively), with absolute truth forever beyond its reach. The whole chapter is a magnificent exposition of this and the other doctrines of the

Way written with exquisite discrimination from the literary point of view. Those who can should read it in the translation of Dr. Herbert Giles. That of Dr. Legge is more difficult to follow, except for those used to Chinese modes of expression. But it should be read.

Chuang Tsŭ is not only one of the great thinkers but one of the great writers of the world, and he carries conviction to those who read him that the Chinese can make their philosophies more interesting than any other people. The difficulty is that behind his ironic mask it is difficult to know whether there are smiles or tears—unless, indeed, one is of the same way of thinking. How is his anecdote of his wife's death and the effect on himself to be taken? Was it pure invention? was it based on belief? was it merely another flout and jeer at the Confucian attitude to death? Did it ever happen? Here it is— told, as it were, in the third person:

When Chuang Tsŭ's wife died a friend went to condole. He found the widower squatting on the ground, singing, with his legs spread out at a right angle and beating on a basin between them.

"When a wife has lived with her husband," cried the friend, "and your eldest son is grown up and she dies, not to shed a tear is surely enough! But when you go on drumming on this basin and singing, it is surely a most excessive and singular demonstration!"

Chuang Tsŭ answered:

"It really is not. When first she died I could not help being troubled by the event. But then I remembered she had already existed before birth. She had neither form nor substance then. Substance was added to spirit and substance took on form, and she was born. And now change comes yet again, and she is dead. The relation between all this is like the procession of the four seasons. There now she lies with her face turned upward, sleeping in the Great Chamber [of Eternity]. And while this is so, if I were to fall to weeping and sobbing I should think I was ignorant of the law of nature. I therefore restrain myself."

So the book goes on to its wise close, giving many of the teachings of India seen through a brilliant Chinese mentality, which falling short of the soaring spirituality of India yet saw the universe luminous with a many-colored humor not easily to be found in the great Indian writings. Side by side with the ironic story of the pigs is set the lovely story of the old fisherman, rejected by some but accepted by Dr. Legge as true Chuang Tsŭ. Here are the pigs. Note the subtle irony What is there to choose between the pigs and the officer of sacrifices, when all is said and done?

The officer of prayer in his dark and square-cut robes approached the pig-pen and thus addressed the pigs:

"How can you object to die? I shall feed you on grain for three months. Then for ten days I shall fast, and keep vigil for three days, after which I shall strew white grass mats and place your members upon a carved sacrificial dish. Will not this please you?"

Then, speaking from the pigs' point of view, he said:

"Really it is better to be fed with bran and chaff and live on in our pen."

So, considering for himself also, he very much preferred to enjoy while he lived his carriage and cap of office, and after death to go to the grave in state with an ornamented carriage and canopy. But in what was he different from the pigs?

I can give only enough of the old fisherman to kindle the desire for more. It begins with a picture beautiful as any in the range of Chinese art, and that is saying much.

Confucius and his disciples have been journeying in the Black Forest. They are a little weary and stop to rest a while in the heat of the day by the Apricot Altar. The disciples get out their books. Time is precious, and life is short, and a wise man trained in the Confucian ethic will be up and doing every moment. His intellect shall not rest even if his body must. He is all for incessant improvement. Confucius elevates his soul with playing on his lute and singing to its accompaniment. He reflects with pleasure that this music of the ancients is a truly uplifting delight and that only the wise of heart can love it as it should be loved. Such is the scene.

Half-way through the song an old fisherman stepped out of a boat and advanced toward them. His beard and eyebrows were snow-white. His hair hung loose, and his great sleeves flapped. He came up the bank and stood with his left hand on his knee and the right to his ear listening. When the song ceased he beckoned to Tsŭ Kung and Tsŭ Lu, both of whom went to him. Then pointing with his finger he said:

"What is that man?"

Tsŭ Lu answered, "Why, that is the wise man of Lu!"

"Of what clan?"

"Of the K'ung family."

"And what is his business?"

"He devotes himself to loyalty and sincerity. He conducts his life with charity and righteousness. He cultivates the ornaments of ceremonies and music. He pays special attention to the social relationships. Loyal to his ruler he seeks the transformation of the masses, his object being to benefit the empire."

"Is he a territorial lord?" asked the stranger, "or a minister?"

"Neither," said Tsŭ Kung.

The old man laughed and turned away. "Yes— charity is charity, yet I fear he will not escape the wear and tear of mind and body which imperil the true nature. Alas, how far has he wandered from the Way!"

Naturally Confucius must speak with him when he hears this. He is persuaded the old man is a sage, and he follows and finds him as he is drawing his boat in with a staff. He prostrates himself twice before the ancient wisdom and begs instruction. He is met with the doctrine of the immutable peace of the Way as compared with his own fussy little activities. And when he laments the sorrows of his life. . . .

"Dear me!" says the old man in a vexed tone. "How slow of perception you are! You are like the man who was so afraid of his own shadow that he was always running away from it. He pelted along without resting, and his strength broke and he died. It never occurred to him that by going into the shade he could easily get rid of the shadow."

And from this the teacher leads on to the great teaching of the Peace. "Leave externals. What are ceremonies? The invention of man. Real mourning weeps in silence." The true essentials are there always. The Kingdom of Heaven is within. You have but to recognize it and look upon the beginnings of peace.

So it is expounded, and Confucius prostrates himself twice, then rising entreats to follow the mysterious stranger as his servant.

"I have heard," says the old man, "that if a man is a fit companion one may travel with him into the very heart of the Way. But if not— Excuse me—I must leave you!"

He gets into his boat, pushes it off and is lost among the tall reeds. Confucius, himself an old man, returns sorrowfully to his disciples, to be reproached for such amazing submission. He replies with solemnity:

"The Law is the source of all creation. Men have it and live. They lose it and die. The old fisherman had the Law. Dared I presume not to show him reverence?" And they stand thinking, pondering, while the boat drifts slowly away far and far among the reeds, which sway in unison with the Law.

We shall end, where in reality a story begins, with the death of Chuang Tsŭ. It has his old irony mingled with the grandeur that never forsook his thoughts. His disciples, determined to give him a grand burial, seemed to have essayed to gladden him with the pospect. He replied:

"I shall have heaven and earth for my coffin and shell, the sun and moon for my two jade jewels, the great and ancient constellations for my pearls, and all creation to lead me to the grave. Are not the provisions for my burial made?"

But the disciples were not satisfied. "We fear lest the crows and kites should devour the body of our master." To which Chuang Tsŭ rejoined: "Above ground the crows and kites will devour me. Below, the moles, crickets, and ants. To take from those and give to these is scarcely impartial."

Thus like the old fisherman he fades into the mists of time, remote, yet the most modern-minded of men, the highest follower of Lao Tsŭ, the great master of the Law One should not conclude with death but with the living and immortal words he wrote:

"O my Exemplar, Thou who destroyest all things and dost not account it cruelty; Thou who benefitest all time and dost not count it charity; Thou who art older than antiquity and dost not count it age; Thou who sup- portest the universe and dost not account it skill; this is the Bliss of God."

For such a man the word "death" has no meaning. Would he not have smiled with even finer irony had he known the relative fates of his teaching and that of Confucius, at whom he often mocked so subtly but always with a humor precluding unkindness? There is an irony of destiny even more subtle than that of Chuang Tsŭ.

The Confucian teaching made its appeal to the average man. It set before him a standard that he could console himself by attempting to follow even if he were not likely to master its full perfection of ceremony and emotion. He could feel that it was emphatically the right thing—good form—a thing all decent men must commend and to decry which partook of the nature of sin; and also that if rightly followed it would lead, as a famous don once said of the study of Greek, to positions of emolument in this world and the next. The higher flights of spirituality in it were likely to escape him, because it was so heavily robed and shod with the ceremonial garments of this world.

It spread over China—a great light but also a great gospel of respectability. It was perceived by teachers and literary men to be a bulwark of law and order, by emperors to be a guarantee of empire. And so the ethic of Confucius was absorbed into China, and he became her life-blood and her soul. As for the teachings of Lao Tsŭ and Chuang Tsŭ—they were for the few, the seers, the dreamers of dreams. Of these there is a world-wide company throughout the ages, but not many at any given time. Those who love the Way love it with a passion that outflares all else, but they will be mostly silent—not even expansive to each other. The cup of their lips will be the chalice of the grapes of God; and that cup stands in the sanctuary and is the Grail whether in China or the West. In this manner and in such hands the flame of the Way was and is kept alive in China. But it had another great development.

The aim of the teaching of Lao Tsŭ and his great disciple was to fuse the spiritual and what we call the material; and this being also one of the aims of Art the influence of Taoism on art in China was enormous. It appeared as a revelation to Chinese artists. Reinforced later by the cognate teachings of Buddhism, it created the mighty schools of landscape and portraiture in which China sits supreme. It thus perpetuated the perfect spiritual rhythm which all who experience it will perceive in the Way—reacting to it as the seaweed reacts to the motion of the vast swell that lifts it. That is life; that is vital rhythm. That is the gift of the great Taoist school of thought in China. Volumes might and should be written on this magnificent subject, which I can only touch in passing. Spiritually Lao Tsŭ and Chuang Tsŭ molded the greatest in China and through China, in Japan. They had drunk the milk of Paradise, and it became the food of nations.

Yet there was another side to the teaching of the Way, one fatally certain to popularize itself in the hands of the baser sort. Chuang Tsŭ had dwelt on the powers open to the attainment of the man who became a conscious part in the rhythm of the universal. He spoke as the Buddha, the Christ, and other mighty teachers have spoken—with a profound sense of the selfless truths he uttered, but not perhaps so necessary a sense as theirs of the danger of such a teaching in the hands of the uninstructed. The Christ was no lover of "miracles"; the Buddha foresaw and dreaded their results. Chuang Tsŭ issues no caution that I can remember.

The inevitable happened. Notions of magic multiplied like blotched fungus in the fair soil of Taoist teachings. The charlatan, the sly priest, the fanatic, the lunatic—all the brood we know very well in the West staked out their claims on that ground, and according to their powers cheated emperors and people, until today that degraded Taoism is an officially endowed superstition in China. The best perverted is certainly the worst. It cannot be said there is no good even in that. Such salt could not wholly lose its savor, nor such high spirituality wholly decay.

But once as I sat in a Taoist temple watching the priests, gloriously habited in crimson with golden dragons and symbols embroidered on cope and robe, gliding to and fro, performing their fantastic charms, evocations and exorcisms, "with woven paces and with waving hands," the fumes of incense and the dim gliding possessed my brain; and for a moment I saw through them the little boat of the old fisherman drifting away into the reeds, and beheld his face radiant with understanding of the simplicity and unity of the whole universe and the Beyond, as he rowed to its rhythm, God-possessed, himself a spirit of nature.

What these yellow-capped Taoists believe and teach now can have no place here. It is far indeed from philosophy. And yet it must be said there have gone with it through the centuries poetry and romance that have done much for Chinese literature. It has made a fairyland of myth and legend—full of loveliness, sometimes perverse, sometimes grim, always immaterial. Thus it still holds aside the curtain of the world invisible, and the Three Precious Ones—the three giant images in the Taoist temples—have a glimmer of the beautiful and even the spiritual to minds unfitted for more.

The work of Lao Tsŭ and Chuang Tsŭ was not wasted. The seed is living, and the fruit will take its place in the great treasury of thought that Asia is now opening to Europe.

CHAPTER 27

MENCIUS THE GUIDE OF PRINCES

It is impossible to leave Chinese philosophy without reviewing the work of the great disciple of Confucius who is known in Europe as Mencius. Just as it would have been impossible to do justice to Lao Tsŭ without a full account of Chuang Tsŭ, so when Confucius is discussed Mencius cannot be ignored.

"Mencius" is the Latinized form of Meng Tsŭ—"the philosopher Meng." He sprang from one of the great and turbulent noble houses of the state of Lu, whose rebellious spirit troubled Confucius and so often caused his exile. He also was born in Shan-tung, in 371 *B.C.,* one hundred and eight years after the death of Confucius, and he lived to be eighty-four years old. Dr. Legge points out that his life synchronized with the last half of Plato's and that Aristotle, Zeno, Epictetus, Demosthenes, and other great Greeks were his contemporaries. It is singular that spiritual and intellectual light appears to come to the world in rhythmic waves, like the rising and ebbing of tides, differentiated into the various colors of the white light that is alike Art and Truth. Thus Confucius was contemporary with the Buddha and Lao Tsŭ. The explanation of this fact would be interesting.

Mencius had a remarkable mother, and since this is recorded in Chinese chronicles she must have been remarkable indeed. She is still honored in China as the example of what a mother should be. Her name was Chang-shi. The stories tell us that his father died when Mencius was three years old and that his mother was left in narrow circumstances—the right training for a thinker if rightly turned to account.

Their first house had a burial place in full view, and the child, imitative as a monkey, amused himself with acting all he saw—the ceremonial, the formal grief, and so forth. To this his mother strongly objected.

"This is no place for my son!" she said, and changed her house to one in the market-place. But with no improvement. The chaffering and trading caught the boy's fancy, the untruthful boasting of the wares by the seller and equally untruthful depreciation by the customer. Those who know the Orient can very well figure the scene. Again the boy's fancy was caught, and he imagined it the purpose of life.

"And *this* will not do," said his mother, and patiently moved again—this time to a house close by a school. Here the little Mencius observed the gravity of carriage and formal ceremonial ritual which the scholars were taught according to the Confucian ideal.

"This will do," said his watchful mother. "This is the proper place for my son."

And there they settled.

It is to be imagined from the following story that they could not afford meat for their food. Not far from their house was a butcher, and Mencius asked his mother for what reason they killed the pigs. She answered:

"To feed you." But on reflection she did not find this a perfectly truthful answer. She thought: "While my boy was yet unborn I would not sit down if the mat were not placed square. I would eat no meat which was not properly cut. I taught him before birth. And now that his intelligence unfolds I deceive him. This would be to teach him the spirit of deceit."

Therefore she went out and bought a piece of meat to make good her words, and that day the little Mencius feasted.

In China this belief in influencing the unborn child was highly commended. There is a book by Chu Hi which begins with the education of the unborn child by the mother. If a mother's thoughts are fixed and directed to the one goal it is difficult to believe the child will not be influenced during that time of union. I have known a few—a very few—Western mothers who held this creed, not only from the physical but from the intellectual and psychic point of view, and who were rewarded. It may be said this was heredity—that the woman who could argue thus must have a character likely to be transmitted. Possibly, but who can gage the dynamic of conscious will? We understand its marvels very little as yet.

In his schooldays Mencius' wise mother was somewhat disappointed wtih his progress. He came in one day as she was spinning, and when she asked how far he had gone he answered carelessly that he was doing well enough. Instantly she took a knife and cut her thread. This startled him, and he asked timidly what she meant.

"What I mean is that what I have just done you are doing, cutting the thread which makes the web of life, destroying all hope of utility and beauty. That is what neglecting education means. No less."

It went home. He realized her meaning, and she had no need to complain again of his carelessness.

We see the same wide point of view later on in this remarkable Chinese woman, and this time in a path where many women fail. Mencius married, and apparently, as seems to be the way of philosophers, his wife did not wholly please him. Perhaps the philosophic ideal of perfection is higher than the average man's. At all events he came in one day unexpectedly and found his wife in her own room sitting on the floor, and resenting this informality and carelessness in a woman who should be acquainted with the Rites, went straight to his mother and told her that he meant to put his wife away, as one who did not value the rules of propriety. No doubt he expected full sympathy from a mother who not only loved her son but was herself an example of all a Chinese lady should be. But he was disappointed. She was one who could look from the particular to the general. She answered:

"It is you who have no sense of the fitting and not your wife. What do 'The Rules of Propriety' say? When you are about to enter a hall raise your voice. When you enter a room keep your eyes low." And the reason of this is that people may not be caught at a disadvantage. Now, you walked into the private room without raising your voice, and so caused your wife to be caught. The fault is yours, not hers."

And Mencius saw the truth of this, and his anger was at an end.

One day she noticed the grief of her son's expression as he stood leaning against a pillar, and asked him the reason of it. He answered, as I think, in a way likely to wound a mother who had been all to him:

"I have heard that the princely man should hold the place that suits him, taking no reward which is not justly his and being not covetous of praise and riches. Well, what I teach is not practiced in Ch'i, and I long to leave it; but I think of your old age and I hesitate."

There is a touch of love, a little hurt in her dignified reply:

"It is not a woman's part to determine anything of herself, for she is subject to the rule of the Three Obediences. When young she must obey her parents. Married, her husband. As a widow, her son. You are a man in full maturity. I am old. Act as your conviction of righteousness directs and I shall act according to the rule that is mine. Why should you be anxious about me?"

It is clear that Mencius had thus the best education at home in fitness for his great career. As for his outer education he himself says he studied with the disciples of Confucius, and the Chinese historian whom I have mentioned before (Ssu-ma Ch'ien), says he worked with the disciples of that famous philosopher who was the grandson of Confucius. This being so it is no wonder that he held and carried on the Confucian tradition in perfection, nor can it surprise any to miss in him the infinite speculations and beliefs of Lao Tsŭ and Chuang Tsŭ.

But the Confucian teaching needed much renewal, and Mencius came at the moment when he could do vital work in practical reconstruction of a very high ideal. For China had gone through nightmares of civil war and dissension since the death of Confucius. The feudal system had sunk into chaos, from which it scarcely seemed society could be reconstructed. The imperial dynasty of Chao had weakened so that it was helpless, while the larger states devoured the smaller. Two ruling princes would unite to ruin a third, then dissolve the bond in quarrels between themselves. Bands of robbers roamed the country. Adventurous men sold their swords to whoever would pay most. What room was there for philosophy or for any consideration of the bases of life? It was hard enough to live at all. Wild doctrines gained ground and the Confucian ideal was half forgotten. Mencius comments upon all this, and his voice is almost the voice of despair.

"Wise kings arise no longer, and the ruling princes give rein to their lusts. Scholars indulge in foolish discussions. Yang's principle is, 'Every man for himself.' Mih's principle is to love all equally, which certainly does not acknowledge the special love due to a father."

He felt that vague principles of universal benevolence (the Mihist teaching) are often a very easy way of compromising with non-fulfilment of the special and primal obligations of duty to parents and to the ruler. And as to the principle of "Every man for himself,"Mencius points to the result in burning words. In those of another wise man he describes the rulers:

" 'In their kitchens there is fat meat. In their stables are fat horses, but the people are famine-pinched, and in the wilds lie the starved bodies of the dead.' If [says Mencius] the principles of Yang and Mih are not checked, and the Confucian principles set forth, these perverse teachings will delude the people and block the path of benevolence and righteousness. Beasts will devour men and men will devour one another."

Accordingly, to reform vice was the task Mencius set himself, and following to a certain extent the example of Confucius, he resolved to influence the ruling princes where and when he could. It is a difficult task to touch pitch and keep clean hands, as Chuang Tsŭ had pointed out again and again. Mencius could not stand the ordeal wholly unspotted. There were occasions when he laid himself open to the charge of inconsistency and even of flattery, for though on the whole his character stands, out in bright light against a stormy background, there were littlenesses also which made him human. As they illustrate the life of ancient China, they are sometimes amusing and worth recording. Here is one that might have happened yesterday, and I give it because his entry into the state of Ch'i, invited by the ruling prince, is typical.

"The Illustrious," as this prince is called, had sent to make private inquiry as to what manner of man the new philosopher might be. This was followed by an invitation, but the outlook was so hopeless that Mencius, though he remained and took office, kept his hands free by declining any salary. This movement was evidently viewed with alarm, for the prime minister sent him a handsome gift to ingratiate himself. Mencius accepted the gift but made no visit of gratitude according to usage. "There was a gift," he said, "but no corresponding respect." Why should he step out of his way to acknowledge it?

But the Illustrious received him honorably and held many long conferences with him on the means of good government. And here one may doubt the wisdom of one of his methods in dealing with these people of importance. It would have been scarcely possible to Confucius and absolutely impossible to Lao Tsŭ and Chuang Tsŭ. The prince in stating his difficulties said frankly:

"I have a lust for beauty and surely that stands in the way of my attaining to the royal government you advocate?"

Mencius replied with philosophic calm:

"Not in the least. Gratify yourself, only do not let your doing so interfere with the people's similar pleasures."

Even the most devout of his disciples were a little startled by this. Naturally his aim was to bring the prince to recognize the claim of the people, when it might be hoped his own reformation would follow. But the sequence is rather more than doubtful. Perhaps it was the natural consequence of this system of compromise that suspicion characterized the relations of the Illustrious and the philosopher. There does not appear to have been real confidence and respect. Here is an amusing instance of the wariness of two formalists, each trying to get the better of the other:

Once Mencius was dressing in the robes suitable for a visit to court when the prince sent word that he had intended to receive him but had taken cold. Would Mencius come to the audience next day?

Instantly Mencius suspects that cold. It is a carefully laid plan of the prince's to evade the courtesy of receiving him, and philosophers have their dignity to keep up and must not be slighted. He sends back word that he is unwell and cannot have that pleasure; then carefully and ostentatiously goes out next morning to pay a visit of condolence, supposing the prince will send to ask after his health and receive the wholesome snub of hearing he has gone out visiting. But mark how all this carefully-built house of cards tumbles at a breath!

The prince sent indeed, but a blundering, good-natured cousin, willing to smooth the matter for the ear of royalty, said eagerly to the envoy:

"He was better and so he hurried off to court. I doubt whether he has got there by now." And runners were sent rushing after the peevish philosopher to urge him to go to court at once. But still his wounded dignity stood in the way, and still this important matter agitated the court circles. The indignant Mencius avoided both home and court at last, and betook himself to sleep at the house of a great official, who dashed into the fray by accusing Mencius of calculated disrespect to the prince. He angrily rejoined:

"Not so. It is I and I only who bring high and royal subjects to his notice."

"That isn't what I mean at all," said the other. "The rule is that when the prince's order calls the carriage must not wait. You were going to court, but would not when you heard the royal message. This does not seem in accordance with the Rites, I think."

Mencius replied on general principles that a ruler who did not honor the virtuous was really not worth having anything to do with—illustrating his position by examples from history which drowned all remonstrances, and so remained victorious.

The storm in a teacup ended but had left its mark, and before long he prepared to depart from the state. Then the prince made another proposal, conscious that an insult to such a sage would not reflect any honor upon himself. Would he stay if he were given a house large enough for himself and his disciples and an allowance of ten thousand measures of grain to support them? A very handsome allowance indeed, but an insult in the philosopher's opinion. They had not understood him. They believed wealth could buy wisdom—a thing impossible in its very nature. Mencius rose in true and worthy anger. Could they suppose he would sell himself, he who had already refused a salary worth a hundred thousand measures of grain? Not he!

So he left Ch'i, but slowly, sadly, as Confucius had once left Lu, hoping against hope to be recalled upon honorable terms. Some of his disciples thought even this hope unworthy of his dignity, but he replied:

"You do not understand. The Illustrious is a man with good in him. If he were to use me it would be for the happiness of more than the state of Ch'i—even for the empire. I am hoping he may change. Daily I hope this. I will not be little-minded. Little-minded people get angry and go off in a huff. So will not I!"

But he was not recalled, and he settled for a while in Ho-nan. There a distinction awaited him—a visit from the heir apparent of T'eng, who had made a long journey for the purpose. They talked at length and earnestly on the antique wisdom and the teachings of Confucius, and still the prince admired, and still he doubted whether such exalted views were applicable to daily experience. But he went away almost persuaded to be a philosopher, and later invited Mencius to T'eng and lavished large gifts on him (as did other princes), and yet could not at all use him. The net result appears to have been a magnificent display of mourning ceremonial when his father died, in which the profound knowledge of Mencius as to ceremonial was strictly followed. This obtained great reputation for the prince, but can hardly have bettered the condition of his people.

Thus the saddened philosopher wandered through more than one principality, scattering seeds by the way- side, which fell upon barren ground. There was little public opinion to support him, and it was easier for the princes to follow the line of least resistance and lose themselves in sensual pleasures and in war, when it became inevitable, than to climb the heights which few understood. He met with censure here and there, sometimes because his spirit of compromise offended consciences formed in the Confucian school, sometimes unjustly because his disinterestedness was real and profound.

Then his mother died. She had followed him to the state of Ch'i, and he took her coffin with such magnificent ceremony to Lu to bury it near his father that even his disciples remonstrated at the cost. But he was not likely to lose such an opportunity for displaying both knowledge and affection, and his reply was:

"The noble-minded man will never be niggardly to his parents. And since I have the means and the will, why should I not do all I can to express my feelings?" One is conscious of an opinion that Chang-shi's own calm good sense might have rejected such extravagance. But it is not for the West to judge China in such matters. The springs of "filial piety" differ there and here.

A triumph was to come however which gladdened him, so that for joy he could not sleep. A disciple of his, Yo Ching, was given the administration of the government of the state of Lu, the state famous as the birthplace of Confucius; and Mencius rejoiced in the hope of seeing his ideals translated into action. He followed Yo Ching to Lu, impatient, eager, and transfigured with joy. The ruling prince was stepping into his carriage to welcome the coming philosopher, and all the horizon was roseate, when a worthless favorite dissuaded him. "Do not go to him, my prince." And the prince, no doubt glad to get out of it, ordered his carriage away, and the visit was never paid.

After his long wanderings and fleeting hopes Mencius took this as a definite ruling from Heaven that the time was not come when his work should be established.

"Heaven does not yet wish that the empire should rejoice in tranquillity and good government," he said, and knew as he said it that life does not stand still and that he was growing old. He had given his best to effort, and effort had failed. Heaven knew best. He would submit and would toil no more with the ungrateful princes. "Ephraim is joined to idols. Let him alone!" as said a prophet of Israel. And then and there suddenly and pathetically Mencius disappears. No more is known of him among the great courts and officials. He had tried the world, and it had tricked him; and this though he had given of the best that was in him, and the flaws in the jewel of his purpose were small indeed in comparison with its radiance. He might at least console himself with the reflection that Confucius, whom he almost worshiped, had fared little better at the hands of men.

Therefore he withdrew, probably, it is thought, to calm reflection and teaching among his disciples. The last years of such a man could hardly fail to be serene and to influence others profoundly; but there all knowledge of him ends.

China has marked her gratitude to a great son. The man fifty-sixth in descent from Mencius was made a member of the great Han Lin College and of the board in charge of the five great classics. This honor was made hereditary in his family, and after his death he was created Duke of Tsao. His tablet stands in the Temple near that of Confucius. But far more than this are the honors received from those who knew and could appreciate the value of his influence in the empire.

"It is owing to his words," says one, "that learners now know how to revere Confucius, to honor benevolence and righteousness, to esteem the sovereign and despise the mere pretender."

"The merit of Mencius in regard to the teaching of the great sages is more than can be told," another says.

And to his undying glory it is Mencius who enunciated the great principle:

"The people are the most important element in a country. The ruler is the lightest."

That may seem a truism. It was very far from being a truism in China in his day. He went further, and with amazing courage.

The Prince of Ch'i once asked him, "May a minister put his sovereign to death?" instancing the case of the great Prince Wu who slaughtered his sovereign, the last of the House of Chao, a most unworthy ruler, an abandoned tyrant, the very essence of wickedness.

Mencius replied:

"He who outrages benevolence is called a robber. He who outrages righteousness is called a ruffian. In the case you mention I have heard of the cutting off of a robber and a ruffian—the fellow Chao; but I never have heard that Prince Wu put a *true* sovereign to death."

Such was the ruling of Cromwell and his associates when confronted with only incapacity in Charles I. Such also was the ruling of the terrorists in the French Revolution in dealing with Louis XVI. Such again was the decision of the Bolshevists in dealing with the tsar. It is not difficult to realize what Mencius would have decreed in such cases, but in all three the result has been to exalt the man from sovereignty to martyrdom. It is evident there are arguments on both sides.

Yet his conclusion was: "Heaven sees according as the people see. Heaven hears as the people hear."

This is the teaching of democracy. Lao Tsŭ and Chuang Tsŭ would have questioned it sharply, but theirs was a high and spiritual gospel, above the reach of any but highly evolved spirits.

CHAPTER 28

THE GUIDE-BOOK FOR PRINCES

Such was the life of Mencius. His philosophy, while founded upon the rock of Confucius, was nevertheless so far original that it built its own castle, especially in relation to good government and to certain aspects of individual character. One of these was the tender and paternal love a ruler should bear to all his people, and this was developed by Mencius with illustrations that would not have occurred to Confucius. Here is an example from one of those celebrated conversations, which might indeed be called "Lessons for Princes." This especial one was with the ruling Prince of Ch'i, who had asked:

"Is such a one as poor I competent to love and guard the people?"

"Undoubtedly, yes."

"And how do you know this, sir?"

"Because I have heard the following story. Your Majesty was sitting in the hall when people led past a bull. Your Majesty saw it and asked where the bull was going, and being answered that they were going to consecrate a bell with its blood said: 'Let it go free. I cannot bear its frightened face as if it were an innocent person going to the place of death.' They asked whether the consecration of the bell should be omitted. Your Majesty said: 'How can it be omitted? Take a sheep.' I do not know if this really happened?"

"It happened," said the prince.

Mencius replied:"

The heart seen in this is sufficient to carry you to royal heights. The people supposed that your Majesty grudged the animal. I—your servant—know surely that it was your Majesty's pain at the sight of the creature's distress."

"You are right. How should I grudge a bull? Indeed it was because I could not bear its terror."

Then said Mencius:

"Let not your Majesty deem it strange that the people grudged it. When you changed a large animal for a small one, how should they guess the reason? If you felt pained, what was there to choose between a bull and a sheep? It was an artifice of benevolence. You saw the bull and had not seen the sheep. So is the man of high virtue touched with the suffering of animals. Having seen them living, he cannot bear to see them die; having heard their dying cries, he cannot bear to eat their flesh." The prince was pleased and said:

"The Ode says:

> 'What is in other men's mind I can guess by reflecting.'

And so it is with you, my master. When I turned my mind inward I could not analyze it. But as you spoke now the movement of compassion stirred in my heart. But what has my heart in it equal to the royal heights?" Said Mencius:

"Here is kindness extended to animals, yet no benefit to the people! How is this? The mercy is not used for them. Your Majesty's falling short of the royal heights is because you *will* not climb, not because you cannot." The prince asked how these things should be done. Mencius answered with an echo of his idol Confucius. "Treat with reverence the aged in your own family, so that those in the families of others should receive reverence. Treat with kindness the young in your own family. Do this and thus, and the kingdom may be encircled in your palm. It is said in the Book of Odes:

> 'His example swayed his wife,
> It spread abroad to his brethren,
> And was a guide to all Clans and States.'

Thus it tells us how the good King Wu simply realized his kindly heart and used it for the service of all. Now if your Majesty will institute a government whose action shall all be benevolent, there is not an official but will wish to stand in your court, not a farmer but will long to plow your fields, not a merchant, traveling or stationary, but will wish to store his goods in your Majesty's market-places. And all under heaven who suffer from their rulers will wish to lay their wrongs at your feet." The prince said: "I am not quick in intelligence. I cannot advance to this. But, my master, assist my intentions. Teach me clearly. I should like to try."

Said Mencius: "The livelihood of the people is now so regulated that they have not the wherewithal to serve their parents nor to support their wives and children. Their only hope is to escape from death, and they fear they cannot do even this. What leisure have they for manners or virtue? Turn back then to the practical steps.

"Let mulberry trees be planted about the homesteads with their five acres, and people of fifty years can be clothed in silk. In keeping domestic birds and animals, let not their proper times of breeding be neglected, and old people can taste flesh. Let not there be taken away the time necessary for cultivation of the field allotment, and a family of eight mouths will not suffer from hunger. Let careful education be given in the various schools, and let repeated emphasis be laid upon the filial and fraternal duties, and we shall no longer see gray-haired men upon the roads bent under the burdens on their backs and heads. It is impossible that the ruler of a state where the aged could wear silk and taste flesh, and the blackhaired people did not suffer from hunger and cold, should not have attained to the royal heights."

Note the tact and grace with which the prince is led on to realize the virtue in himself if he will but use it. Here Mencius fills the office of a true courtier, for he lacks neither rightful courage nor courtesy. I give another example of real philosophy.

"Will you allow your servant to speak to your Majesty about music? Your Majesty is having music here. The people hear the sound of your bells and drums, the sweetness of your reeds and flutes; and they all with aching heads frown and say: 'That's how our prince loves music! But why does he reduce us to this extremity of misery? Father and sons cannot see one another; older and younger brothers, wives and children, are scattered abroad.'

"Again your Majesty hunts here. The people hear the noise of your carriages and horses and see the beauty of your plumes and pennons, and they all with aching brows say: 'That's how our prince loves hunting, but we are miserable!'

"And this is because you do not care for the people's happiness as well as your own. Your Majesty has music here. Now if the people hearing the music could say with joyful looks, "That sounds as if our prince were rejoicing in health. What splendid music! What splendid hunting!" it would be because you considered their pleasure as well as your own. So if your Majesty will make happiness a thing common to the people as to yourself, royal heights await you."

Thus Mencius draws a lesson from the prince's passion for music, as he drew it later from his passion for valor, and in this is seen the true democracy of the Chinese spirit. There have always been fearless men to tell the sovereigns home truths, even when their own lives were at stake and not infrequently paid the forfeit. Even the terrible old dowager empress of the Boxer riots had high-minded courtiers who, following the great examples of Confucius and Mencius, placed before her the ancient way, those laws of which Sophocles wrote:

"The power of Heaven is mighty in them and groweth not old."

The great learning of Mencius, described as "infinite," gave him an advantage before which the prince trembled, knowing that all China venerates the sage, even if his birth be the lowliest of the lowly. Therefore, with very few exceptions Mencius spoke his mind fearlessly, and was at his best and highest in so doing. He delighted after the manner of Confucius in the Odes, and enriched his discourses with frequent quotations from them, regarding music and poetry as integral parts of the government of a cultured state. But all was used to drive home the lesson of caring for the good of the people, and in so doing he often gives a most interesting picture of ancient China. For instance, the prince said, as another had said:

"I have a weakness. I am unluckily devoted to beauty."

Said Mencius: "Long ago King T'ai was devoted to beauty and loved his wife. It is said in the Book of Odes:

> 'The ancient Duke T'an Fu
> Came in the morning galloping his horses Along the bank of the Western River,
> And there he and the Lady Kiang
> Came together and looked out a site on which to settle.'

At that time in the seclusion of the house were no discontented women and abroad no unmarried men. If your Majesty is fond of beauty let the people be able to gratify the same love, and what shall stand between you and the royal heights?"

But here again the disciples were inclined to look a little askance at this compromise. He could, however, rebuke like a Jewish prophet when there was need, or rather—what is better—compel a tyrant to rebuke himself after this fashion:

"Suppose one of your Majesty's servants trusted his wife and children to the care of a friend and went a long journey in Tsŭ, and on returning found the friend had caused them to suffer from cold and hunger—what should he do?"

The prince said, "He should cast him off."

"And suppose the chief criminal judge could not regulate the officers of justice under him, what then?" "He should be dismissed," said the prince.

Then said Mencius: "And suppose that within the four borders of your kingdom there is no good government, what then?"

The prince looked to the right and left, and spoke of other matters.

Thus we see in Mencius a touch of the heroic, which was perhaps a little lacking in Confucius. Confucius hesitated, for instance, to declare boldly what the doom of a worthless sovereign should be. He dwelt on the virtues of Yao and Shun, and permitted those who heard to draw the inference. Mencius had no such scruples. He was an Elijah denouncing doom to Ahab, and whatever the risks might be he took them. He stated clearly what the means of removal should be. The Prince of T'sui questioned him on that point:

"I beg to ask about the chief ministers, who are noble and relatives to the ruler? What should they do in such a case?"

Mencius replied: "If the ruler has great faults they should remonstrate with him; and if he do not listen to them when they have done so repeatedly they should appoint another in his place."

The prince on this looked moved and changed countenance. Mencius noticed it; he said:

"Let not your Majesty think what I say strange. You asked me, and what could I do but reply truthfully?" But because in him as in all deep thinkers there must needs be a strain of the mystic he envisaged another solution—the belief that in the last resort Heaven would provide the right man to fill the place of a degraded ruler. He might be of humble birth. He must not raise the flag of rebellion but of righteousness; and Mencius with his belief in the innate goodness of human nature was assured that men would flock to him. Therefore, since in his time the Imperial House of Chao had so debased itself, his effort was to stir one if not more of the feudal princes to noble revolt against a weak licentious tyranny, exactly as the kings Wen and Wu, the heroes of Confucius, had done in the great old days. He could not succeed but the effort remains memorable.

So he preached nobility of life, and love of the people, believing that greater results would follow from this than the rulers could gain by oppression, and that following this rule one of them would develop power and strength to trample down the Chao dynasty.

"If among the present rulers throughout the kingdom there was one who loved benevolence, all the other rulers would aid him by driving their people to him. Even if he did not wish to exercise the royal sway, he could not avoid it," he said.

But first the people must have comfort. They must be raised above the rank of beasts to that of the natural hopes of humanity. And then they must be educated. Without the latter, the former must be a danger. In the view of Mencius the goal of education is only to illustrate the human relationships. "Book-learning" was the last thing he sought. He was certain that those who needed and were capable of that would naturally gravitate toward it. For the mass of the people, the interlocking of human social relationships was all that was needed. That was the true education, to lead men from a selfish individuality to consideration of the good of others as part of their own. He knew that when life is brutal in its surroundings there is no room for these possibilities; and therefore material necessities came first with him. Chuang Tsŭ would have said:

"Yes, but man can relinquish these *voluntarily* and gladly when he has reached a higher stage of spiritual development."

This Mencius did not affirm, but it is almost implicit in his teaching.

He was extremely modern in appreciation of the fact that everywhere must be a division of labor, each man doing that for which he is best fitted—the gospel of specialization.

"The business of the handicrafts, man can by no means carry along with that of husbandry. Great men have their proper business, little men, theirs. Hence the saying: 'Some labor with their hands, some with their strength. Those who labor with their minds govern others. Those who are governed by others support them; those who govern others are supported by them.' This is a universal principle."

Mencius, like Lao Tsŭ and Confucius, insisted upon the Golden Rule; and surely it may be taken as a strong testimony of its universal truth in human nature that teachers so far apart in time, place, and race as Confucius, the Buddha, the Christ, and others, should all have borne witness to its vital necessity to any true life of the spirit. Benevolence to others is the key-note of all the teaching of Mencius.

His doctrine of what he calls "the passion-nature" is interesting also. Man has the driving force of his passion-nature, but the will—the active force of the will-to- goodness—is to guide and direct it. He does not desiderate the suppression of the passion-nature as do some of the philosophies of India. He considers it a useful horse for the chariot of the soul if it is drilled, disciplined, and tamed by the Heaven-directed will. There is a difference here which, though it may appear small at first, may be what has rendered India weak and passive even in her own great teachings, and China virile, haughty, dignified, in holding and proclaiming her own views in the face of the world.

On great example he dwelt as Confucius had done and as all the faiths must needs do:

"The sages, perfectly exhibiting human relations," were the model. Let men form themselves on that. Just as no skill of hand could form circles and squares without compass and square, so without great examples virtue could not survive. And again, in a strangely beautiful sentence, anticipating the teaching of Christ and the mystics, and joining hands (though that he could not know) with his great countryman Chuang Tsŭ, Mencius says: "The great man is he who never loses the heart of a child."

That sentence will bear much pondering. With it we may leave one of the greatest of the philosophers of China —a man not perfect, but wise with a great wisdom; a seer with percipience which was to enkindle vision in his own people, in days when many supposed it dead and burned with the ashes of Confucius.

CHAPTER 29

BUDDHIST THOUGHT AND ART IN CHINA AND JAPAN THE TEACHINGS OF ZEN

A Few words on the position of Buddhist philosophy in China and Japan must end our survey.

In the philosophies of Lao Tsŭ, Confucius, Chuang Tsŭ, and Mencius, no one charted road was indicated that could lead a man beyond earthly hopes to the hope man will never relinquish. Confucius had marked a path that promised the best type of prosperity in this world, but he, like Virgil with Dante, was obliged to lay down his guideship at the portals of heaven. There he did not attempt to enter.

It was the same with Mencius. Both conceived they had done all that was possible in setting men on the road which must lead at last to Knowledge of the Truth. They did not realize with Lao Tsŭ and Chuang Tsŭ the sudden flash that strikes some men awake in an instant to all the issues of life and death; and indeed it was true that such teachings were fitted only for men so highly evolved that they needed no guidance, and that for others of the lower type they must be dangerous. So it proved. The rebound of mysticism is magic, and in baser hands the teachings of Lao Tsŭ and Chuang Tsŭ degenerated into superstition. They too had indicated no certain road. The truth was vague as a mountain in mists.

China accordingly needed a middle way her own teachers had not given, a faith which should incorporate the spiritual with the material, the world as they saw it with the world as it might be believed to be. She desired spiritual sanction for the moral teachings her sages had given her, and most of all she craved for spiritual romance. That, to the world at large, is the essence of the great faiths. Their philosophies lie beyond the reach of the masses. Their romance invites all to the spiritual adventure.

There lie the flowery ways, the cloud-capped towers not built by mortal hands; there, beyond the utmost starry peaks, lies the City of God.

Religion and philosophy can never be dissevered. Religion is alike the philosophy of the highest and the romance of the lowest, according to their different stages. It is the comment of Everyman on life, and inevitably much more than that to great minds. For this reason Buddhism was welcomed in China.

It is said to have come first in the dream of an emperor. He beheld in sleep the golden image of a Man, and on inquiring learned that such a religion as it symbolized existed. But apart from all this, Buddhism was certain sooner or later to pass along the trade-routes, which have been the conduits of so much beside trade. It was sure of a reception in independent democratic China that would contrast with the slowly chilling Indian belief—damped and wounded as it was at every point by what may be called the strong trade-unionism of Brahmin interests, which knew so well how to exploit its affinity with them.

When it arrived it was under the two forms already described in the section on Buddhism—the *Hinayana* (Lesser Vehicle) and the *Mahayana* (Greater Vehicle). The first was the stern, august philosophic system set forth in the Buddha's great teachings, impervious to scientific attack, drawing to itself the highest spiritual forms of mentality that could be founded on the doctrines of the Upanishads divested of their earlier and more childish speculations.

The second was the decorated palace which the mindsof schoolmen and theologians had built on the rock of the Buddha. They had perceived in some of his sayings possibilities of development along lines more suited to the mentality of the masses. It was not difficult to transfigure an indescribable and inexplicable peace into a heaven blazing with gold and jewels, where birds of miracle sang the praises of the Law, in trees flowering in unearthly beauty, and where redeemed souls, their sins forgiven, might sit immortal in the purity of unfolded lotos-blossoms, to laud the divine Buddhas who had rescued them from all evil. We know that process in the West also.

It was a philosophy still—in the sense that the Nicene and Athanasian creeds are philosophies—but one which fused hopes human and divine. In place of a remote and questionable heaven and wilderness of dubious spirits, China was to be given, for those who could take it, a philosophy of the soul more reasoned than any her own philosophers had offered, and, for those who could not, a God loving and compassionate—who having lived on earth could hear, help, and forgive sin, and at the end of the disappointments of life receive those who believed in Him into the Boat of Souls, which would transfer them to the Western Paradise, there to dwell in immortal peace. And China was to give both of these new aspects to Korea and Japan, where each would be accepted according to the capacity of the recipients.

It would have been easy to prophesy which would eventually possess and leaven China—the more so as the teaching of paradise and propitiation blended well with Confucianism, filling the dry cracks and crevices with living water, in which the lotus of purity could blossom. The greater Buddhist saints would act as mediators and guides, and the teachings of Lao Tsŭ and Chuang Tsŭ could also be revised and pressed into the service of the new hope, with a meaning they had lacked for many.

Was it wonderful that such Chinese pilgrims as Fa Hien and Hiuen T'sang, preceded and followed oy many other seekers less famous, should have set out along the frightful wastes of the Gobi Desert and over the terrible Himalayan snow-peaks to find their way to India, the Land of the Holy Grail, and to return laden with glorious manuscripts, statues of strange and shining beauty, and other spiritual riches, to confirm China in the Buddhist faith, which had opened a new heaven and a new earth?

For those who desire romance there are few such noble romances as the journeys of Fa Hien, I-tsing, Hiuen T'sang, and their like. All who care for the fairylands of religion will read them with delight.

So when Buddhism came to China in power, it was in the form of the popular Buddhism, and on that head I need say little. Both in China and Japan, as in the wide world, worship will be given to a God easily accessible, swift to hear prayer, to reward virtue, and to pardon sin. It brought exultation with it, a secular triumph of faith; and because of this it brought also a great wave of art in China.

Buddhism, which taught with more than Wordsworthian force an indwelling and divine presence in plant and tree, bird and animal, as in man, unlocked the doors dividing life into separate compartments. Making all one it brought a passion of understanding, and desire to represent that understanding in the highest forms of art. So, in the sixth century *A.D.*, partly under the influence of the cognate teachings of Taoism as well as in the new inrush of Buddhist thought, there were formulated in China the six great canons of art to which it has conformed ever since. These are in themselves a high form of the philosophy of art to which life itself must conform. Of these the first only is necessary here: Rhythmic Vitality or Spiritual Vitality—or, as a gifted Japanese has rendered it, "The Life Movement of the Spirit through the Rhythm of things." Without this no great art is possible.

Rhythm is the vital point, and it had been so recognized by Lao Tsŭ and Chuang Tsŭ centuries before. It connotes acting in harmony with the swing of the universe—whether spiritually, intellectually, or in the least movement of the body—from the physical movements of the dance of happy youth to the dance of the planets about the sun and the systems about the Infinite. In each and all, they beheld this rhythm and harmony in the highest art—so that religion itself, working upon human stuff, is the Great Artist, sculpturing it into what Confucius recognized as the princely man and Lao Tsŭ as the perfection he saw but could find no words to define.

In the actions and being of all great men, whether rightly or wrongly directed according to our human notions, this rhythm can be perceived. They march to an unstruck music, terrible or beautiful as the case may be. With the preparation which had already been theirs, the Chinese realized when Buddhism came with its doctrine of the Indwelling Spirit that here was the whole secret of the philosophy of art. This Buddhism taught that "to the eye of flesh plants and trees appear to be gross matter. But to the eye of the Buddha they are composed of minute spiritual particles," and that "grass, trees, countries, the earth itself, all these shall wholly enter into Enlightenment."

Thus all was spirit, and the office of art was to make that spirit, that wonderful efflux of life and vibration visible to all! Art could never be an imitative thing; it must be like religion itself the thought of man's heart, the work of his hand: the two were in the deepest sense one. The point was not so to represent fruit that man would stretch out his hand to pluck it, but to suggest the silent indwelling life that gives first the seed, the bud, the blossom, and lastly the fruit, with all the unity of the process with the life of man. Therefore, in the Chinese philosophy of art there is something God-possessed—the whirling on an orbit not to be calculated, but touching the outer spaces of vision and immortality. There are those who hold the belief that at a certain period of their art these people stand unrivaled in portraiture and landscape. The descriptions already given of their philosophies may, if analyzed, yield the secret why with the fusion of Buddhism to complete them this result followed ; but the fact remains that so it was.

They had learned the secret that art consists in the approach from the *subjective* side of the artist to the *subjective* side of whatever is painted, from a blade of grass to the face of a man; and having mastered the essential rhythm of life they themselves became masters.

But it was not by the road leading to singing paradises that the deepest secrets of unity and realization, whether in art or elsewhere, were to be approached in China and Japan. There was an austerer way for those selected minds who could scale the heights—the Way of Concentration, contemplation, and realization. Yoga of the sternest type—such as is called in India *Jnana,* in China *Ch'an,* and in Japan *Zen*—was to make an indelible mark upon the Far East. It cannot be called exclusively Buddhist, for its foundations were laid earlier than the Vedanta ; but to China it came in a Buddhist guise about the year 520 *A.D.,* by the means of a most singular man, who can have little understood what the influence of his teaching would be in China and Japan.

His name in religion was Bodhidharma—or the Law of Enlightenment—and what he taught was the Yoga of the earlier Upanishads in its most ascetic and unconcilia- tory form.

One sees him, a man of huge stature and haughty gesture, with the temperament of the militant monk which is common to all the faiths. He was ushered into the presence of the Chinese emperor, a devout and generous Buddhist, who said with reverence:

"Many monasteries have I built, many scriptures have I distributed. Many alms have I given, and I have upheld the Faith. Have I acquired merit?"

"None whatever," answered Bodhidharma.

"In what then does true merit consist?"

"In the obliteration of matter by absolute knowledge and not by external acts."

This is the great truth acquired in the flash of cosmic consciousness, but very useless to present to a soul slowly developing along the path of evolution, which must eventually lead it to Absolute truth. The emperor ventured again:

"Which is the divine and primal aspect of reality?"

One may suspect him of trying to suggest that after all he was not quite a beginner in these high subjects, and Bodhidharma of determination to stamp out any nascent sparks of imperial vanity.

"Reality has no aspect that is divine," was his answer.

"What are you, who have come before my throne?"

"I do not know."

Nor as a matter of fact does anyone else by experience, excepting the enlightened few who have reached the goal of *samadhi* or ecstatic contemplation. But Bodhidharma

was mistaken in thinking he had brought a new gospel to China. He had brought systematized extension of the teachings of Lao Tsŭ and Chuang Tsŭ; and for that reason his mission was certain to have results beyond what he could guess and quite independently of his own efforts.

His philosophy may be summed up as follows:

"There is no such person as the Buddha." A rude shock until it is realized that there is no true individuality or personality in the Universe. There is only the One of whom each and all are manifests or phenomena—if even that statement does not go too far.

"The Absolute is immanent in every man's heart, and this Treasure of the heart is the only Buddha that exists." With this statement all who have truly understood the Upanishads would agree.

"Prayer, scripture-reading, fasting, the observance of monastic rules; all are useless." This statement is more open to question, and appears more like the petulance of a man who having found one way denies the existence of all others. There are different levels of road for souls in every stage of evolution, and none is to be despised.

"Those who seek the Buddha do not find him." This may be qualified into the statement that those who seek the Truth will find the Buddha and finding, comprehend, not the Buddha, but the cause which underlay the phenomenon of his life and teaching.

"One thing alone is necessary. To discover the unreality of the world by contemplation of the Absolute, which is at the root of each man's nature." This is of course absolutely true.

Being asked to explain the word "Zen" he replied: "This word 'Zen' cannot be understood even of the wise. Zen means that a man should behold his fundamental nature. I have come from India only to teach that Buddhism is thought. As to so-called miracles—all such practices are heretical. They belong to the world of Being." In other words to the world of Appearances.

Such was the philosophy of Bodhidharma. It was. driven home with austerities of thought, speech, and practice, calculated to repel the many, yet it invited chosen minds by giving the detailed instructions of India for attainment in Yoga and the practice of contemplation by concentration. Lacking Buddhistic tradition—though it was rich in that of Yedanta—it fell back upon a legendary and beautiful scripture in which the Buddha passes on in utter silence the mystic meaning of the Nirvana to his great disciple Mahakasyapa, who receives it in its fulness with a smile and no word. So it should still need no words. It should be vision only.

Zen became a power in China, and had its own patriarchate, dividing into the northern and southern schools. Its very austerities recommended it as a refreshing exercise to the rich and great. There is a very beautiful mystic poem relating to it, known as the Taming of the Bull, which should be given here were there space. It has been illustrated often both in Japan and China, and represents in wonderful symbols the attainment of realization or the highest consciousness by the soul of man, at first undisciplined, afterwards trained into perfect subjugation and finally into union.

The influence of Zen on art in both China and Japan has been amazing for two reasons: first, the influence of contemplation upon the little understood psychology of the artist, and second, its reaction in the form of a better understanding of how to manipulate (if such an expression may be used) the strange weapon of creative power. It is not too much to say that if artists (speaking of course generally of art) studied the science of contemplation as taught in Zen, unknown sources of power would be opened and the world be the richer. That it often has been done unconsciously and temperamentally there can be no doubt, but seldom with knowledge.

China at all events received it as the language of art. They realized that as a shadow is to the object which casts it so is the object itself to its Eternal Idea as perceived by a man possessing the higher consciousness. To this Zen taught the way, and the more so, because in teaching the doctrine of the Universal it corresponded with the teaching of Unity with the Eternal, not only in man but in stone and plant and bird and beast.

"Cleave the stone and there am I," says Christ in one of the lately recovered logia. And China echoed the phrase as a new law. Yet in China its influence has almost died. Would art revive there if the spirit of Zen lived once more? Some allude to Zen, with a certain want of comprehension, as a system of self-hypnosis. That is an assumption that no mystic would for a moment admit. Some find an analogy in Quakerism. That there is a superficial likeness in the serenity and repose of Zen cannot be denied; but on that ground Zen may be likened to any belief which recognizes the indwelling Divine. It is in truth that and much more and when the suggestion is made that it may assuage the growing desire of Europe for the spiritual wine which alone quenches the thirst of the nations I am inclined to agree, though Zen will always be for the highly evolved souls, and the more simple forms of Vedantic and Buddhistic philosophy for the many. Neither has anything to fear from science, for neither is inseparable from historic dogma, and each is based on personal experience. Meditate and do, and you shall know. Knowledge and deed are then one.

Zen was transplanted to Japan with extraordinary effect. There too it became a mighty influence for art and still more, or perhaps concordantly, for the molding of character. It cannot be doubted that it strengthened the natural bent of the Japanese toward the sympathetic and passionate contemplation of the beauty of nature, for to Zen the vibration of nature is in accord with the inmost rhythm and vibration of man. Lao Tsŭ and Chuang Tsŭ had known this, but had not systematized the knowledge or experience as did the yoga-discipline of Zen. They knew that belief in the false individuality of man must be expelled by contact with the influences of nature, and that on entering this experience he would recover the lost unity which makes him a participator in all the forces of the universe.

This is a secret which the western world has forgotten in its urbanization. It must relearn it at great cost—or lose it at greater. Our poets and the greatest of our artists have known this for themselves if not for others. Hear Keats, almost in the words of Chuang Tsŭ:

"The only way to strengthen one's intellect is to make up one's mind about nothing. ... Be passive and receptive. . . . The poetic nature has no self. It is everything and nothing. ... A poet has no identity ... he is continually in and filling some other body."

I myself should say that the nature of those who *know* is impersonal as a sunbeam. It flits here and there, resting alike on the fetid swamp and the purity of the flashing waterfall. It dreams in the green gloom of the forest, is radiant on the sparkling snow-peaks—the inhabitant, the spirit of the universe, everywhere glad and at home.

In Japan Zen became a great philosophy for men of high intellect and percipience, blending naturally with the knightly austerity of the Japanese character. There are many sects or, as I prefer to call them, angles of Buddhist thought in Japan; the ethical *Tendai,* the mystic *Shingon, Jodo,* and the other paradisiacal angles so attractive to the masses; but Zen is, and probably will remain, an influence upon the educated and intellectual classes. It has a noble hardness, which appeals to the luminous mind. The sentimentality that tends to sweeten the developments of Buddhism otherwise and to crown them with compassionate saints as intercessors is absent there, for what is called "the Buddha consciousness" of Zen is the same as the perception of the Formless world taught by early Buddhist saints. It corresponds with the higher states of consciousness now felt after by modern science. The teachers of Zen in Europe will probably be enlightened Japanese and those few men and women of the West who—very far removed from the charlatans and frauds that come from the mysterious Orient—have themselves experienced something of its effects on the intellect and the spirit.

It is not necessary to speak much individually of the philosophy of Japan. What is ancient in her thought besides her own *Shinto* is derived from India, the great original mother of Asiatic philosophy. Of her acceptation of western philosophies little need here be said. On Shinto some words are necessary.

There is a singularity in Shinto, the state religion of Japan, which renders it alien to the western mind. Despite certain aspects of beauty and a Spartan element, which did much to foster the knightly code of the samurai, it is difficult for a European to connect it with any ideas of a philosophy to be ranked beside the Vedant ist or Buddhist, the Confucian, Taoist, or any western system. And yet it is impossible to leave it wholly out of account. It is based on myth and nature-worship; and it has resulted in a belief in myriads of spirits, male and female, who inhabit not only natural objects but many others. The name "Shinto" is Chinese and signifies "The Way of the Spirits." Its Japanese equivalent is *"Kami no Michi"* and these *Kami* are the indwelling spirits.

So far one might take it as a parable of natural forces, as indeed it probably partly is; but its origin is lost in obscurity for the reason that until the fifth century of our era the Japanese had no writing, and all was handed down by tradition and memory. At that time Japan received the Chinese learning through Korea, and a book dating from 712 *A.D.* is the earliest written informant on these beliefs. It is said to have been taken down from the lips of an old man, a famous reciter of the myths and traditions. This, the *Kojiki*, is a storehouse of them. The *Nihongi* which purports to be a fuller account, dates from 720 *A.D.* And the greatest authority on the deeply interesting ritual of Shinto is the *Yengishiki,* which gives minute directions for it—a ritual still faithfully carried out, though it cannot be denied that Buddhist influence has crept into Shinto thought. This was unavoidable, and many Japanese do not regret it. More than one highly educated Japanese has told me that he is Confucian, Buddhist, and Shintoist, and that the ideals do not clash.

The fact that the emperor's family traces back to the sun goddess—formerly known as *Amaterasu-Omi-Kami* "the great god who illumines heaven," known chiefly now by the Chinese form of *Tenshod*—and that many of the nobler families are said to spring from the lesser gods, is sufficient to account for the retention of Shinto as a state religion, even if its antiquity and its purely Japanese origin did not insure its position for patriotic reasons. The Shinto temples have also a peculiar beauty, which exercises influence both on art and character. An exquisiteness of extreme simplicity and delicacy of purity and cleanliness cannot but have a reflex action upon the souls of those who worship.

The gods have mystic souls or "jewels," dwelling invisibly in the temples, and through them earth may have audience of Heaven. These are known as, and

in each great shrine the *mitama* is represented by a material object known as the *shintai* or spirit-body. Sometimes it is a mirror or a sword, such as are used at the "coronation," more exactly, the investiture, of the emperor at Kyoto. Sometimes it may be a round stone. But be the *shintai* what it may, it is only an earthly symbol of the mysterious *mitama,* and the two must not be confounded.

The chief points of the Shinto faith are patriotism and loyalty. There is little individual prayer, and the emperor and his delegates are spokesmen (as in China) for national needs. There is much propitiation, much deprecation of the anger of the easily offended deities. The dance is a part of the ritual, especially the pantomimic dance with masks and music. There is much pilgrimage to famous shrines.

As an ethic or philosophy what shall be said of it? There is an ethic but it is based not so much on the spiritual results to the offender as on the offense, physical or spiritual, of impurity in the sight of the gods. With death the Shinto gods have no concern. It is impure and therefore outside their province. As in the Greek play of Hippolytus the divine Artemis cannot approach her devoted worshiper in his unjustly caused death agonies, but "hangs a span's length from the ground pollute," so with the Shinto *Kami*. Shinto funerals in Japan date only from 1868. They did not concern the *Kami*.

Here is a specimen of an old Shinto prayer, slightly shortened:

If the high gods will bestow the latter harvest in rice-ears many a hand's breadth long and abundant, produced by the labor of men from whose arms the sweat drops down and on whose opposing thighs the mud has gathered, I will fulfil their praises by humbly offering a thousand first-fruits of ears, setting up the jars of sake and setting in rows the bellies of the sake-jars.

And I will present them plain sweet herbs and bitter herbs of plants growing in the great moors; and of dwellers in the blue sea-plain I will give edible seaweed from the offing and seaweed from the shore. Also blight stuffs and shining stuffs and coarse stuffs. And with these I will fulfil your praise.

Japanese who should know claim that the influence of Shinto upon the national character has been wholly good and that the *kannushi* (the Shinto priest) has played his part satisfactorily in national life. They are not, however, priests in any sense of the word recognized in the West. They are appointed by the civil authorities. They have no care of the people and, clad in nothing priestly or symbolic but in an ancient court-habit, they have only ritual as their duties. In Japan, as in China, deep and reverent honor is paid to the spirits of dead ancestors and relatives. In Japan this has been found a great and noble binding influence in family life and therefore in the national life spiritual and material.

But on the whole the cold austerity of Shinto produced an atmosphere in Japan that required the Buddhist fire to warm it, the Confucian ethic to animate it and make it emotional. To Buddhism it owes its magnificent *Noh* plays and the higher forms of art, and uncountable debts besides. Japan would not be Japan without it. She accepted all with avid hands. What the future of Shinto may be who dares to prophesy? There have been many Japanese philosophers, men whose writings breathe serenity, tranquil wisdom, and a joy in nature and beauty intellectual and spiritual. These will repay western readers fully for any search they make; such writers as Kaibara Ekken in his "Way of Contentment" and many others. But this book concerns itself with sources, and Japanese philosophy is so largely derivative that it requires treatment from quite another point of view than mine.

It should, I think, be accepted more as literature and literature of a very high order. It is deeply indebted to Shinto also, but Shinto so interwoven with Buddhism and Confucianism that the effect upon the mind is that of a cord of three strands, each strand a different color yet blending into a whole that forms a new and beautiful revelation of color in itself.

It would never be surprising if the acute Japanese mind brooding on the philosophies of East and West should evolve new and startling applications and combinations of all three, for the understanding of the world of causes and that of appearances. Among nations Japan is the great transmuter, and it may be well indeed for the West that their circle has been opened for an oriental sister bringing aptitudes new to us to bear upon the problems of life and death.

I conclude this survey of Asiatic thought and thinkers with the words of a distinguished Asiatic, Ananda Coomaraswamy, for they sum up all philosophic aspiration :

"The chosen people of the future can be no nation, no race, but an aristocracy of the whole world in whom the vigor of European action will be united to the serenity of Asiatic thought."

That is the only hope I know of for the future of East and West.

CHAPTER 30

PROPHECY

The main streams of thought flowed from the heights. as the rivers Indus, Ganges, Brahmaputra, and Jumna rise in the great northern mountains and, flowing through, irrigate and fertilize the harvests of widely differing countries. Will it be so with the thoughts I have outlined in this book or will they remain only the sustenance of Asia?

That, I think, cannot be. Europe, in which I include America, has gone her own way, protesting that the religion she derived from the nearer East was good enough for her, and that she needed no light from outer Asia. She little knew what was hidden by the ramparts of the Himalayas and the boundaries of the great passes. But she can scarcely have been said to have found her own soul in the teachings of the Semitic peoples. Will she return to what was in its undeveloped stage the teaching of men of the same blood and spirit as her own?

I cannot think that Europe will ever profess one of the great Asiatic faiths in the sense of calling itself Ve- dantic or Buddhist. Perhaps even in Asia such labels will tend to disappear, because as time goes on the mind of man will become more and more eclectic, assimilating the best from all. But since the great faiths are bridges, not barriers, I believe they will encourage the passage of the thought of mankind across all the frontiers of faith.

In all such matters India must lead the world, for she made spiritual exploration her chief preoccupation and, knowing where others guessed, charted the ways. Now that the narrow theology of the Jews is passing away, and a new aspect of Christianity developing in the West, I believe it will tend more and more to identify itself with the great Vedantic teachings, and the utilitarian philosophies of Europe will plume themselves with the wings of the Himalayan eagles.

Spinoza, Blake, Nietzsche, and many more envisaged the possibility of a race of supermen who should guide the earth when the will-o'-the-wisps of democracy have led the destinies of mankind into quagmires from which they will be long in escaping. India has shown the very different road by which these supermen may assume their birthright, and I believe the West will realize steadily if slowly that for philosophy, science, and social evolution—all that concerns the daily life of man—there is only one unshakable basis, and that divine—as the East has taught, but scarcely practiced in its fulness.

This is prophecy, and those entrenched in their own beliefs will laugh at the possibility. Even they, however, may see in the outlines I have traced something grand, shadowy, and immutable, like the peaks of mountains seen in mist where the gods dwell above the thunder.

I write in Ceylon with all the thought of Asia surging round me, and meeting the science and commerce of the West like contending breakers. If either conquers it will be a calamity for the world, for it is the hope of the future that East and West may meet and mingle in the brotherhood of the spirit, beside which outer forms are as nothing. Each has much to conquer before that day dawns. That its rising sun may not long be below the horizon is the aspiration of all who know and love both.